Judicial Reflections of Justice Bhagwati

Kolkata

Eastern Law House Private Ltd.
54 Ganesh Chunder Avenue
Kolkata (Calcutta) 700 013

New Delhi

Eastern Law House Private Ltd.
36 Netaji Subhash Marg, Daryaganj
New Delhi 110 002

Judicial Reflections of Justice Bhagwati

Ram Kishore Choudhury
Tapash Gan Choudhury

FOREWORD

The Rt. Hon. The Lord Woolf
Former Chief Justice of England and Wales

INTRODUCTION

The Hon. Justice Michael Kirby
AC CMG High Court of Australia

Kolkata New Delhi
EASTERN LAW HOUSE
2008

Produced and distributed by
EASTERN LAW HOUSE PRIVATE LTD.
54 Ganesh Chunder Avenue
Kolkata (Calcutta) 700 013
Tel: (033) 2215-1989/2301 Fax: (033) 2215-0491
E-mail: elh@cal.vsnl.net.in
www.easternlawhouse.com

Published by
Academic Foundation & Publication Pvt. Ltd.
306 Central Plaza, 2/6 Sarat Bose Road
Kolkata 700 020

ISBN 978-81-7177-211-7

Printed at
Swapna Printing Works Private Ltd.
Kolkata

Dedicated to the
common cause of the people

*As told to his American disciples on Wednesday 26th June 1895 and recorded in the book Inspired Talks by Swami Vivekananda published by Sri Ramkrishna Math Madras

Justice P.N. Bhagwati

Foreword

by

The Rt. Hon. The Lord Woolf
Former Chief Justice of England and Wales

Thanks to the imaginative inspiration of the late Dr. L.M. Singhvi when he was High Commissioner in London, many initiatives took place designed to bring India and the United Kingdom closer together. One area in which Dr. Singhvi had an influence was in the relationship between our two legal systems. He was responsible for initiating judicial exchanges between senior judges from both countries. The leader of the British Delegation on the first exchange was the former Law Lord, Lord Templeman, who as a result developed a great number of friendships with his Indian colleagues.

I was fortunate enough to be on the first exchange and subsequently, to follow Lord Templeman as the head of the British Team on a number of occasions. Happily the exchanges are continuing to occur. The reason for this success is because members of the British team found we had to much to learn from our Indian colleagues.

The exchanges were always stimulating and we were astonished that the Indian Judiciary were so familiar with what was happening in the courts of my country. Among the Indian Judiciary who I met as a result of the exchanges was the form Chief Justice of India, Justice Bhagwati. His contribution and knowledge of the Indian legal system is unique. He helped the developments which have made the Indian legal system one of the most, if not the most, creative in the common law world.

I was particularly interested in his contribution to public interest litigation, his liberalization of the concept of starre decisis and his approach to human rights. He had a deep understanding of the Indian Constitution. His contributions to the interpretation of that Constitution will influence the development of Indian law in relation to civil rights for generations to come.

In addition to his great learning, Justice Bhagwati was also an outstanding judicial administrator. The scale of his responsibilities as Chief Justice for the workings of the courts throughout India gave him great insight as to the most satisfactory way in which a country the size of India should provide access to justice. His work in this regard no doubt explains why he and I were both co-opted by the World Bank to sit on the Bank's Advisory Committee on Providing Justice in the Undeveloped World.

I have read a number of Justice Bhagwati's judgments and speeches. Based on my knowledge of his writing and our many discussions, I have no doubt that this book will be of the greatest importance to those interested in Justice in India. Everybody will benefit from doing so, but it is those who are concerned with the values that Justice Bhagwati holds dear who will benefit the most. His great experience means that what he writes deservedly has great authority; to be able to read what he has to say on so many important subjects is a wonderful opportunity not to be missed.

I extend Justice Bhagwati my earnest hope that he will continue to enjoy what is apparently eternal youth and that he in due course will provide the material for a second volume of his writings.

THE RT HON THE LORD WOOLF
Former Chief Justice of England and Wales
3 April 2008

Introduction

by

The Hon'ble Justice Michael Kirby
AC CMG High Court of Australia

With judges, lawyers and many others around the world, I honour the life and achievements of Justice P.N. Bhagwati. For me he has been a guide, a mentor and an inspiration.

Guide I first met Justice Bhagwati in late 1984 when he was visiting Australia. I had then recently assumed office as President of the New South Wales Court of Appeal. A case had recently been argued concerning the right to demand from an official, acting under statutory power, reasons for a decision made in the exercise of that power, adverse to the applicant. In Australia, it was already clear law that a judicial officer was obliged to give such reasons.[1] However, save for instances where an Act of Parliament had so provided, the obligation at common law in respect of administrative officials was still in doubt.

In discussing this problem with me, in the way judges frequently do, Justice Bhagwati mentioned two of his own decisions in the Supreme Court of India. They were *Siemens Engineering and Manufacturing Co of India Ltd* v *Union of India*[2] and *Maneka Gandhi* v *Union of India*.[3] Encouraged by our conversation, I read the decisions. They provided guidance for me on the direction that the common law was taking. I cited them in my reasons in the case in hand.[4] One of my colleagues in

1 *Pettitt* v *Dunkely* [1971]1 NSWLR 376 at 388.
2 AIR 1976 SC 1785.
3 AIR 1978 SC 597.
4 *Osmond* v *Public Service Board of NSW* [1984]3 NSWLR 447 (CA).

the Court of Appeal supported my approach; but the other dissented. The case was taken on appeal to the High Court of Australia. This was a decade before my appointment to that Court in 1996.

In *Public Service Board of NSW* v *Osmond*,[5] the High Court of Australia reversed my ruling. The Court distinguished the Indian cases for perceived reasons of constitutional consideration. The common law of Australia reverted to its traditional state: no right to reasons. But to me, as for Justice Bhagwati, it was contrary to basic legal principle that a donee of statutory power, entrusted by Parliament with making decisions affecting individuals in society, should act like a tyrant or despot without giving, or necessarily having, good reasons for the action.

My encounter with Justice Bhagwati taught me that, in the judicial world, there are great judges of other lands who look deeply into the fundamental principles and purposes of the law. They adjust old rules so as to adapt them to new, contemporary times and values. Thereafter, I commonly looked to the case law of the Supreme Court of India – apex court of the largest democracy in the Commonwealth of Nations, indeed the world. In the judicial writings of Justice Bhagwati and of other judges I frequently found guidance in expressing the basic principles of law in my own country which shares much in common with the law of India.[6]

Mentor Four years later, in 1988, I took part in a meeting in Bangalore which was chaired by Justice Bhagwati. The meeting was to prove highly influential. It resulted in the formulation of the Bangalore Principles on the Domestic Application of International Human Rights Norms.[7] The only non-Commonwealth judge at the meeting was Ruth Bader Ginsburg, then a Judge of the District of Columbia Circuit of the Federal Court of Appeals in the United States of America. Like me, she was later elevated to the highest court in her country. As in my own case, I believe that the experience in Bangalore proved an epiphany.[8]

5 (1986)159 CLR 656.

6 M D Kirby: *"Constitutional Law: Indian and Australian Analogues"* in V. Iyer (ed.) Constitutional Perspectives (Essays in Honour and Memory of H M Seervai), Universal, 2001, 166; M.D. Kirby: *"Centenary of H M Seervai – Doyen of Indian constitutional law – an Australian appreciation"*, (2007)27 Legal Studies 361.

7 "The Bangalore Principles on the Domestic Application of International Human Rights Norms" (1988) 14 Commonwealth Law Bulletin 1196.

8 See eg. Michael Kirby: *"International Law – The Impact on National Constitutions"* (7th Grotius Lecture, 2005) 21 American University International Law Review 327 (2006).

The fundamental principle espoused under Justice Bhagwati's leadership in Bangalore was simple. If the language of the Constitution was unclear; if the words of a statute were ambiguous; or if the common law was obscure and in need of development, resort might be had by a judge faced with these dilemmas to any relevant principles of international human rights law. In this way, by a gradual process, those basic principles of humanity would be given effect by municipal judges. In effect, those judges would exercise international jurisdiction and render their decisions (so far as appropriate) conformable to the basic principles of the international law of human rights.

When I returned to Australia and expressed these views, they were at first regarded by some as heretical.[9] For some judges (especially in constitutional decision-making) they are still so.[10] However, gradually in Australia, recourse to universal human rights norms has become more common both in the general law[11] and, as a contextual factor, in constitutional elaboration.[12]

Justice Bhagwati's influence in this respect has spread throughout the Commonwealth of Nations, indeed the wider world. It demonstrates the power of an individual human mind, by persuasion and example, to influence the course of legal history in countries far from one's own.

Inspiration Upon laying down the judicial robe, it might have been expected that Justice Bhagwati would perform occasional honorific services in India and exchange New Year greetings with his friends overseas. Such was not, however, to be the case. In judicial retirement, he assumed, with unflagging energy, a wide range of activities in national and international bodies. These and his engaging personality have made him an inspiration to judges and lawyers throughout the world, including myself.

On four occasions Justice Bhagwati has been elected to membership of the United Nations Human Rights Committee. His most recent re-election was in September 2006. He has served as Chairman and Vice-Chairman of the Committee which considers communications from

9 See eg. *Young* v *Registrar, Court of Appeal* [No 3] (1993) 32 NSWLR 262 (CA) at 290-3 per Rowell JA.

10 *Al-Kateb* v *Godwin* (2004)219 CLR 562 at 589 [62] per McHugh J; of at 617 [152]. *Contrast Roach* v *Australian Electoral Commission* (2007) 81 ALJR 1830 at 1864-1865 [181] per Heydon J; see also 1836-1837 [16] per Gleeson CJ, 1852 [100]-[101] per Gummow, Kirby and Crennan JJ.

11 *Mabo* v *Queensland* [No 2] (1992) 175 CLR 1 at 42.

12 *Roach* (2007) 81 ALJR 1830 at 1852 [100]-[101].

persons alleging that states parties to the International Covenant on Civil and Political Rights have not complied with their obligations under that Covenant. A state party found in default is expected to bring its law and practice into compliance with the views expressed by the Committee.

In addition to this important post, Justice Bhagwati has served for twenty-seven years on the Committee of Experts of the International Labor Organisation; as Regional Advisor for the Asia-Pacific Region to the United Nations High Commissioner for Human Rights; as a participant in countless international missions concerned with peace and human rights in troubled countries. This volume will indicate the variety, importance and depth of the activities in which he has been engaged.

In discharging these obligations, Justice Bhagwati has been an inspiration because he has taught a vital lesson to lawyers and judges of the present age. It is that, however important our national and sub-national jurisdictions may be, they must now be viewed in the context of international law—specifically the international law of human rights. His energy is legendary. But so is his idealism and full-heartedness.

How did it happen that a boy, born in December 1921 at the height of the British Raj in India, should grow to maturity in a somewhat conservative profession of law yet never lose his empathy for the disadvantaged, the vulnerable, the down-trodden? Why, when so many other lawyers were content with the status quo or desiring personal wealth, was P N Bhagwati engaged constantly with the cause of law and justice for those in need? How was it that this child of legal India became a strategist for public interest litigation to make law truly meaningful to the poor and disadvantaged? What gifts were given to him by his parents, his community, his family, his times and life's experience that made him empathise with the disadvantages in law of women, of indigenous peoples, of children in bonded labour, of refugees, of homosexuals, prisoners, of people of different races and religions, the illiterate and not just in India but far beyond?

Fundamentally, P N Bhagwati could empathise with these and others who are disadvantaged because he shared with them their humanity. He felt empathy for their fate and confident in their fundamental goodness. He lives out the ideas of those who struggled for freedom, independence and human dignity in India and other lands.

If ever there was living symbol of the principle "equal justice under law", it can be found in the life of P.N. Bhagwati. Being human, he has no doubt erred from time to time, as we all have. Being a lawyer, he has no doubt sometimes felt obliged to give effect to laws with which he fundamentally disagreed. That is inherent in the rule of law. But being the guide, mentor and inspiration that he is, he has brought hope to many and a special example to judges and lawyers everywhere. As a Justice of the High Court of Australia and as a judicial brother, I am proud to be associated with this volume on his life and work.

High Court of Australia
Canberra
18 March 2008

THE HON JUSTICE MICHAEL KIRBY
AC CMG

Gratitude to Authors

by

The Hon'ble Justice P.N. Bhagwati
Former Chief Justice of India
Member–U.N. Human Rights Committee

I must thank Mr. Ram Kishore Choudhury and Mr. Tapash Gan Choudhury for having undertaken the analysis of the judgments delivered by me during my career first as a Judge of the Gujarat High Court and then as Judge and later as Chief Justice of the Supreme Court of India. It was a stupendous task having regard to the large number of judgments delivered by me on various subjects of constitutional, legal and social importance, but I must say that they have carried out the task most efficiently. They have analysed my judgments, examined them critically and explored their true meaning and significance. They have also made a comparative study of my judgments with reference to the judgments of courts of various other countries, particularly those of England and USA. The book produced by them also presents a comparative study of human rights jurisprudence of different countries against the background of Indian decisions with particular reference to my decisions covering a wide area of jurisprudential thinking. The book covers a wide range of topics dealt with in my judgments as would be apparent from the index to the book.

I would like to pay my tribute to Mr. Ram Kishore Choudhury, an eminent Advocate practising in the Calcutta High Court, who has undertaken the task of preparing this book. He has spared no pains in making the necessary resources available for the preparation of this book and but for his sincerity of purpose, his unstinted support, this book would not have seen light of the day. His services and help were available at every stage of the preparation of this book.

But more than any one else, I must pay my tribute to Mr. Tapash Gan Choudhury for preparing this book making analysis of my judgments. He was a distinguished Professor of Law and has been a practicing Advocate of High Court of Calcutta for more than 32 years. He is a lawyer with considerable experience in constitutional and taxation matters and has brought his profound knowledge of law in the preparation of this book. He has carefully and intensively studied not only my judgments but also judgments of United States and English Courts for the purpose of arriving at comparative assessment of various decisions of these courts in reference to my decisions.

Every chapter in this book deals with a particular aspect of my judgments in a critical and exhaustive manner with references to comparative jurisprudence and is a self-contained analysis of the subject dealt with in that chapter. I must particularly mention the chapter on "Death Penalty" which is a thesis by itself. I can well imagine how much time the authors must have spent in reading my judgments as well as the judgments of USA and UK Courts and the entire comparative jurisprudence in order to produce this book. I am struck with awe and wonder at the immense work and industry which have gone into the preparation of this book.

I may end by saying that after reading these eloquent pages I have discovered my true achievement as a judge.

P N Bhagwati

New Delhi
29th July 2008

P.N. BHAGWATI

Preface

Justice Bhagwati is one of India's, and indeed one of the world's, most outstanding jurists, a great thinker, philosopher and visionary. His judgments delivered first as a Judge of the Gujarat High Court and then as a Judge and the Chief Justice of the Supreme Court of India have laid great stress and emphasis on the social upliftment of the poor and the downtrodden.

In many of his judgments Justice Bhagwati said that law has to respond to the unsatisfied urges and demands of the people and bring about a socio-economic revolution. If justice is to be done, he said often, then law must not become stagnant or archaic while society moves forward. It must be accessible, intelligible and must change with the time, responding to the realities of modern life. By his skill, he was able to develop the law and adopt it to the needs of his own time.

Justice Bhagwati is an illustrious example of a judicial activist. He used to believe that his job was to do justice in accordance with law and although, as we all know, this is a necessary ingredient of judicial activism, it is only one aspect. There are many judges who can in no way be described as judicial activists who do just that. One of the distinguished judges of the seventeenth century Sir Matthew Hale strove mightily to do justice in accordance with law, but he would not stretch the law to any degree to do or obtain justice. He was very meticulous in keeping strictly to the letter of the law. Justice Bhagwati crossed that barrier. He holds the view that it is the judge's duty to mould the law and interpret statutes to meet the justice of the case and the needs of the time and this found reflection in many of his judgments.

Justice Bhagwati strongly believes that personal liberty is one of the most precious rights of human being and it cannot be allowed to be smothered by bureaucratic or judicial inadequacy or inefficiency. This view of his found strong reflection in *Veeni Sethi* v. *State of Bihar* [(1982) 2 SCC 583].

The sweep of the right to life conferred by Article 21 of the Constitution of India is now wide and far reaching after the interpretation given by Justice Bhagwati in *Francis Coralic Mullin* v *Union Territory of Delhi* [AIR 1981 SC 746]. It is known to all that Article 21 of the Constitution dealing with life and personal liberty received creative interpretation and connotation in Justice Bhagwati's hands in *Maneka Gandhi* v *Union of India* [AIR 1978 SC 597].

It was for the first time in *Maneka Gandhi's* case that the Supreme Court acting through Justice Bhagwati laid down that under Article 21 a procedure prescribed by law for depriving a person of his life or personal liberty should be 'reasonable, fair and just' and if a law depriving any person of his life or personal liberty prescribes a procedure which is unreasonable, unfair or unjust, the law would be void.

Judicial activism in India through the process of judicial review got its steam in Public interest Litigation which has gained momentum day by day, taken its root firmly in the Indian judiciary and fully blossomed with fragrance in *S.P. Gupta* v *Union of India* [AIR 1982 SC 149]. Justice Bhagwati was instrumental in developing the concept of participatory justice promoted through mass based organization by widening the rules of *locus standi*. In *S.P. Gupta's* case, the learned Judge observed that where a legal wrong or legal injury is caused to a person or to a determinate class of persons by reason of violation of any constitutional or legal provision or without authority of law or any such legal wrong or legal injury or legal burden is threatened and such person or determinate class of persons is by reasons of poverty, helplessness or disability or socially or economically disadvantaged position, unable to approach the Court for any relief, any member of the public can maintain an application for an appropriate direction or order or writ in the High Court under Article 226 and in case of breach of any fundamental right of such person or class of persons in Supreme Court under Article 32 seeking judicial redress for the legal wrong or injury caused to such person or determinate class of persons. In such cases, the Court will allow any member of the public acting in a *bona fide* manner to espouse the cause of such person or class of persons. It is because of the lead taken by Justice Bhagwati that the Court's concern is now focused on different occasions on the rights of detenues and under-trials, police excesses, custodial violence, conditions in prisons and other custodial institutions based upon postcards, letters, articles in newspapers, press reports and petitions from a cross section of citizens.

Justice Bhagwati's concern for the welfare of children and labourers hardly needs any mentioning. His dissenting opinion in favour of abolition of death penalty in *Bachan Singh* v *State of Punjab* [(1982)3 SCC 24] is a thought provoking one and needs serious consideration in view of the worldwide wave in favour of abolition of death penalty.

The book covers a wide range of subjects of constitutional, legal and social importance dealt with in the judgments delivered by Justice Bhagwati during his long judicial career analysing and examining them critically with reference to the judgments of courts of various other countries, particularly those of USA and England and exploring their true meaning and significance. A comparative study of human rights jurisprudence of different countries against the backdrop of Indian decisions with particular reference to Justice Bhagwati's decisions covering a wide area of jurisprudential thinking is a special feature of the book.

At the outset have been appended table of cases, table of statutes and bibliography. Appropriate sub-headings under each topic and index in the end have been provided to assist the reader to find out what he is looking for at the right place.

Efforts will be fruitful if this humble work is found worthwhile by those for whom this endeavour is made. Any suggestion given to improve the book further in its quality will be gratefully acknowledged.

Kolkata
15th August 2008

RAM KISHORE CHOUDHURY
TAPASH GAN CHOUDHURY

in newspapers, press reports and petitions from a cross section of [illegible]

[illegible]

[illegible]

Acknowledgment

We are indebted to Justice P.N. Bhagwati for his untiring efforts in approving the chapterwise manuscript of the book. Inspite of his busy schedule within and outside India, Justice Bhagwati devoted considerable time in advising improvement of the manuscript with valuable suggestions.

Indebted we are also Mrs. Prabavati P. Bhagwati who at all times assisted the authors and co-operated in many ways.

We are grateful to the Rt Hon the Lord Woolf, former Chief Justice of England and Wales, for contributing the Foreword and to the Hon Justice Michael Kirby AC CMG of Australia for contributing Introduction to the book.

We gratefully acknowledge the contribution of Mrs. Kusum Agarwal, Mr. Krishna Bhubna and Mr. Subhasish Ghosh, Advocates in checking up cross reference of case laws; express our gratitude to Mr. Deepak Choudhury, Managing Director of Academic Foundation and Publication Pvt. Ltd. for taking the responsibility of publication of this book and Mr. Asok De, Director of Eastern Law House Private Ltd., Kolkata, for taking inter alia the responsibility of worldwide distribution of the book notwithstanding the time constraints in hand.

We shall be failing in our commitment if proper acknowledgement is not made of the services rendered by late S.S. Srivastava, former personal secretary of Justice P.N. Bhagwati, who had helped in collecting and correlating the diverse speeches delivered by Justice Bhagwati worldwide and making copies thereof available to the authors.

Kolkata
15th August 2008

RAM KISHORE CHOUDHURY
TAPASH GAN CHOUDHURY

Contents

Table of Cases

Table of Statutes

Bibliography

35th Report of the Law Commission of India on Capital Punishment ... 362

46th Report of the Law Commission of India on Constitution (Twenty-fifth Amendment) Bill 1971 ... 217

78th Report of the Law Commission of India on 'Congestion of Under-trial Prisoners in Jails' (February, 1979) ... 306

A.N. Mulla Committee on Jail Reforms ...315

An Autobiography by Jawaharlal Nehru ... 318, 320

Bimal Jalan: *India's Politics–A View from the Backbench*, Penguin/Viking ... 229, 230

Black's Law Dictionary, 6th & 7th Eds. ... 246

Black's Law Dictionary, 8th Ed. ... 174, 246

Convention No. 59 of the International Labour Organisation, 193

Craig R. Ducat and Harld W. Chase: *Constitutional Interpretation*, 5th Ed. ... 255

Debating the Death Penalty edited by Hugo Bedau and Paul Cassell (Oxford University Press) ... 328

Declaration of the Rights of the Child, 1959 ... 19, 45- 46

Discussion Paper No. 4–Access to the Court-1 Standing: Public Interest Suits (Australian Law Commission) ... 181

Draft Principles of Freedom from Arbitrary Arrest and Detention (UN) ... 312

Draft Principles on Equality in the Administration of Justice (UN) ... 312, 314

Dyson Heydon, J.: *Judicial Activism and the Death of the Rule of Law* (2004) 10 Otago LR 493 ... 274

European Convention for the Protection of Human Rights and Fundamental Freedoms 1950 ... 142-143

European Convention on Human Rights ... 347

Freedom of Expression and Freedom of Information–Essays in Honour of Sir David Williams, Edited by Jack Beatson and Yvonne Cripps, Oxford University Press ... 140

Government of India Resolution on Industrial Policy, 6th April 1948 ... 130

Holmes: *The Path of Law* (1920) ... 277

Indian Bar Review, vol. 10(4), 1983–Human Rights and Democratisation of Remedies, 16, 17

International Commission of Jurists... 292

International Covenant on Civil and Political Rights, 1966 ... 19, 288, 289, 311, 314, 315, 330

International Covenant on Economic, Social and Cultural Rights, 1966 ... 81, 287

International Human Rights Conference (Tehran), 1968 ... 292

International Labour Organisation, Convention No. 59 ... 20

Justice Bhagwati: *Domestic Application of Human Rights Norms* (Abuja, 1991).

Justice Brennan: *New Growth of the Law–The Judicial Contribution*, 6 Monash ULR 8 (1978) ... 252

Lon L. Fuller: *The Morality of Law*, rev. ed., (New Haven, Conn., 1969) ... 139

Lord Reid: *The Judge as Law Maker*, 252

Michael Kirby, J.: *Attacks on Judges–A Universal Phenomenon*, 72 ALJ (1998) ... 274

Minds Behind Bars published in Listner, December 1977 ... 360

'Now' (May, 1985), 3

Oxford English Dictionary, 2nd Ed., vol. XII ... 174

Practice Statement [1966]1 WLR 1234 ... 259

Professors Bernerd Schwartz and H.W.R. Wade: *Legal Control of Government*, (1972)

Prof. H.P. Lee: *Subverting Judicial Independence*, 1 CPLR (3) 1998 ... 272

Prof. K.E. Scott: *Standing in the Supreme Court: A Functional Analysis* (1973) ... 181

Report of Public Interest Law, USA, 1976 by The Council for Public Interest Law (set up by Ford Foundation) ... 175

Report of the Expert Committee on Legal Aid: Processual Justice to the People, May 1973 ... 177

Report on National Judicare: Equal Justice–Social Justice, August 1977 ... 177

Richard A. Posner: *The Federal Courts: Crisis and Reform* (1985) ... 252

Swami Vivekananda: *Inspired Talks* ... 4

T. Scanlon: *A Theory of Freedom of Expression*, in R.M. Dworkin (Ed), the Philosophy of Law (Oxford, 1977) ... 141

U.N. General Assembly Resolution A/32/130 dated 16th December 1977 ... 292

Universal Declaration of Human Rights, 1948 ... 81, 85, 143, 147, 287, 330, 331

V.R. Krishna Iyer: *Death Penalty: An Unmitigated Evil?*–an essay published in perspectives in Criminology Law and Social Change ... 322

"Look upon every man, woman and every one as God. You cannot help anyone, you can only serve: serve the children of the Lord, serve the Lord Himself ...."

— SWAMI VIVEKANANDA

1

A Judge is Born

SYNOPSIS

1 Family background
2 Childhood reminiscence
3 Educational platforms
4 Professional career
5 Judicial career
6 Role as a seeker of justice
7 Role in lawmaking and liberal interpretation of Constitution
8 Role in mitigating administrative wrongdoing
9 Role in developing social action litigation
10 Role in developing Legal Aid Schemes
11 Role in welfare of children
12 Role in welfare of labour and employees
13 Role in protection of environmental pollution
14 Social achievements
15 Laurels in cap
16 Conclusion

1 Family background Prafulla Chandra Natwarlal Bhagwati, popularly known as P.N. Bhagwati, was born on 21st December 1921 in a lower middle class family out of the wedlock of late Mrs. Saraswati Bhagwati and late Natwarlal Harilal Bhagwati. He is the first child born of his parents in a family of seven brothers. "All the seven brothers have excelled in whichever field they chose to be in", says former Chief Justice of Gujarat High Court B.J. Diwan, a close family friend. They are Gujarat's magnificent seven. Leading the judiciary, crusading for human rights, brilliant in the field of engineering, knocking on the Nobel's door, heading world body on child neuro-surgery, they have done it all.

Born on 11th November 1900, Justice Bhagwati's mother Saraswati Bhagwati who was a housewife breathed her last in 1976. Though read upto the eighth standard, she, in the words of Justice Bhagwati, "was more intelligent in practical life than my father ... She had tremendous common sense and was very dynamic in her approach to life. Her reading of any person was far deeper than most so-called intelligent people. Most of the practical education we gathered was from our mother, as my father was busy practicing law."

Born on 25th July 1896 at Mehsana in Baroda State, Justice Bhagwati's father Natwarlal Harilal Bhagwati became a graduate with law degree in 1921, started his practice in Bombay High Court and was also a part-time lecturer in a law college at Bombay (now christened Mumbai). N.H. Bhagwati began his career from a Chawal in Bombay and had to borrow money for obtaining Sanad for practicing law. A scholar in Sanskrit, he was elevated to the Bench of Bombay High Court in July 1944, to the Bench of the Supreme Court in 1948. He retired from the apex court in 1960. After retirement from the apex court, N.H. Bhagwati became the Vice-Chancellor of the Benaras Hindu University wherefrom he retired in 1965. N.H. Bhagwati breathed his last in 1970 at Ahmedabad at P.N. Bhagwati's residence after hearing the Ramayana recited by Krishnashankar Shastri. In his success, N.H. Bhagwati got inspiration from his wife Mrs. Saraswati Bhagwati. This is what Justice Bhagwati says about this inspiration: "Having no support or a godfather he (N.H. Bhagwati) fought through life and made it a success with the full support from my mother. My mother proved that intelligence is not the privilege of the rich".

2 Childhood reminiscence Bhagwati grew up in a family having deep religious bondage and the belief that infinite strength lies in religion and God. Surrounding him was a strong scholastic environment in his family. As a student in the age group of 17 and 18 he deeply studied a number of religious scriptures, classic literatures and biographies, notable among which are Bhagavad Gita, Shivaparvati, Meghdoot, Kalidas, Kaveriparamjeevani of Kashmir.

When he was merely a kid, a family friend of Sri Aurobindo Ashram, Pondichery, saw him playing with marbles and said: "Let him play with marble made of gold so that he will realize that gold is just something to be thrown away like marble." How true the utterances were could be found from his later life actions in each area of which he literally threw marbles made of gold. Spectacular incidents studded his career.

3 Educational platforms Bhagwati's schooling started in a municipal school where no fees were required to be paid. Completing elementary schooling, he joined Tutorial High School in Bombay. After a couple of years in that school, he joined the Elphinstone School. He did his school leaving certificate examination extremely well and was a topper standing second in the entire State of Bombay. Bhagwati completed the first two years of college education at Elphinstone College in Bombay ranking first class throughout. He graduated with first class honours and joined the post graduate course in Mathematics, his favourite subject. He was awarded the honorary fellowship in Mathematics during his post graduate studies. His youthful days saw the country struggling and fighting for its independence, the ramification of which fell on him too. Gandhiji's speeches during the freedom struggle had tremendous impact on him and his life. "On 14th August 1942", so said Justice Bhagwati,[1] "I broke off my studies and was arrested from my college and was in jail for a month for boycotting college, preventing other students from attending classes, distributing leaflets." Thereafter, he did his law joining the Government Law College in June 1943 and passed both the first and the second law degree examinations with high merit.

4 **Professional career** Bhagwati started his practice in law in February 1948 as an Advocate in the Original Side of the Bombay High Court. During a little over 12 years of professional career, he conducted a number of important cases in the constitutional and company matters in Bombay and other High Courts as also in the Supreme Court and became one of the leading lawyers in the country.

5 **Judicial career** Bhagwati was elevated to the Bench of the Gujarat High Court on 21st July 1960 when he was just 38 years old and became the youngest Chief Justice of the same High Court on 15th September 1967. This was the beginning of Justice Bhagwati's long and illustrious career.

On 17th July 1973 Justice Bhagwati was elevated to the Bench of the Supreme Court and became the Chief Justice of the apex court on 12th July 1985 and retired therefrom after 18 months' stint at the end of 1986 and more specifically on 21st December 1986 on reaching the statutory age limit of retirement of 65.

As a judge, Justice Bhagwati possessed bewitching personality and the rare gift of explaining the most abstruse subjects in a most perspicuous manner. A study of his judgments would reveal that his reasonings in every judgment were logical, convincing and never in any judgment he lost sight of the main issue—the truth he wished to drive home. In his judgments, he fearlessly attacked conservatism in any

1 Excerpts from interview given to magazine 'Now' in May, 1985 issue.

form. Through his judgments, Justice Bhagwati tried to diffuse the balmy rays of his inner light and through these tried to take the suffering magnitudes beyond the ocean of ignorance and misery. He believed in what Woodrow Wilson said in one of his speeches in 1916 "One cool judgment is worth a thousand hasty councils. The thing to do is to supply light and not heat".

Justice Bhagwati's determination to frame and resolve the great legal issues of the day as he saw them against the background of international and comparative and by reference to underlying purpose, justice and comparative need prompted him to be in dissent on many occasions. One acknowledges his propensity to dissent as a measure of his deep commitment to the values and attributes we expect of all our judges: transparent reasoning, fearless independence, and unremitting courage. "The only way", says Justice Bhagwati quoting Sydney Smith, "to make the mass of mankind see the beauty of justice, is by showing them, in pretty plain terms, the consequence of injustice".

As a judge, he harboured no grievance against any one. Did any one criticise him, he would look thoughtful and say gently: 'It is only the voice of the Beloved.' When some one criticised his judicial action on any particular issue, though such occasions arose rarely, he never reacted adversely for he felt that to be breach of judicial etiquette, propriety and discipline and a breach of the oath he took as a judge. A story seems to have given him the inner strength to bear with such criticisms and the story runs like this: "A mosquito sat long on the horn of a certain bull; then his conscience troubled him and he said: 'Mr. Bull, I have been sitting here a long time, perhaps I annoy you. I am sorry, I will go away.' But the Bull replied: 'Oh no, not at all! Bring your whole family and live on my horn; what can you do to me?[2]

6 Role as a seeker of justice Sparkling originality, force of intellect, high confidence in himself dominated the judicial career of Justice Bhagwati spanning a little over 26 years. The mark of a timorous judge following the rule of precedent was apparent in him early in his judicial career which started diluting with the passage of time and his gradual understanding of the social conditions of the people and their expectations. Justice Bhagwati by his actions established that he did not belong to those timorous soul who were fearful of allowing a new

2 As told by the famous Hindu monk Swami Vivekananda to his American disciples on Tuesday, 25th June 1985 and recorded in 'Inspired Talks' by Swami Vivekananda, published by Sri Ramakrishna Math, Madras.

cause of action; on the other hand, he belonged to those spirits who were ready to allow it if justice so required. Between two points of view, certainty on the one hand and justice on the other, Justice Bhagwati's preference was always for justice. Quoting Dainiel Webster, Justice Bhagwati says: "Justice is the great interest of man on earth. It is the ligament which holds civilised beings and civilised nature together. Wherever her temple stands, and so long as it is duly honored, there is a foundation for social security, general happiness, and the improvement and progress of our race". When confronted with a difficult case, he would always find for justice some new approach, new concept which could enable him to get away from precedents if he wanted to. In many cases, judgments of the lower courts delivered in accordance with precedents were overturned for some notion of justice as it appealed to him. In this respect it can be called that in the road to justice, he is a specimen tree, you must not have a whole avenue with such a tree. Justice Bhagwati did not subscribe to the view that the law is replete with valuable principles which can be a guide or can provide an analogy even in cases to which they do not strictly apply or which cannot be changed even when circumstances called for its change and that a judge is never completely free to give effect to his own value judgments. His view was that the principles we talk about were made by judges in the 18th or the 19th or the early part of the 20th century. They made principles because they thought those were the principles which were best suited to their society. Now society has changed. Because of the experience and passage of time it is our duty to reshape those principles and to adapt them to the need of our own society. This duty of reforming the principles, according to Justice Bhagwati, does not clash with the strong traditions of maintaining consistency, coherence and continuity. He was very mindful of the expectation of the community that the law should be ascertainable and predictable.

Commenting on Justice Bhagwati's contribution and knowledge of the Indian legal system, the Rt. Hon. the Lord Woolf, former Chief Justice of England and Wales, said: "His contribution and knowledge of the Indian legal system is unique. He helped the developments which have made the Indian legal system one of the most, if not the most, creative in the common law world".

Justice Bhagwati's search for justice has not waned even after retirement. From morning till night, it is ever the same every day—he lives in a constant atmosphere of intense search for justice. He is never for a moment far from the dominating note of his mind.

7 Role in law making and liberal interpretation of Constitution The democratic theory having overtaken the role of judges as traditional lawmakers and the same having been supplanted by Parliament, judges lay great stress on the law making role of Parliament. The ideology now is one of democratic legitimacy; laws are legitimate because they are enacted by an elected Parliament which represent the people. Parliament is now recognised as a legitimate law maker and the ideology of parliamentary sovereignty has now invaded the judiciary. The growth of democratic theory though made it crystal clear that making law is the primary responsibility of the elected representatives and not for the judges who merely applied the existing laws, this could not end the debate as to who is more important—Parliament or the Judiciary. Sometimes the debate developed into a lively dispute. During his tenure as the Chief Justice of the apex court of the country, Justice Bhagwati shifted the ground around it. He did not subscribe the view that judges should not make law; that's for the legislators. He took the opposite view and thought that judges should, from time to time, make law. Justice Bhagwati firmly believes that in today's democratic system Parliament makes grand law covering the whole social life. Judges only legislate in a very limited way to fill in the gaps overlooked by Parliament in the fulfillment of its grand vision keeping eyes broadly open to ensure social justice to the people. In this context, the famous assertion of the great American Judge Oliver Wendell Holmes is appreciated keenly: "I recognise without hesitation that judges must and do legislate but they do so only interstitially; they are confined from molar to molecular motions". Justice Bhagwati's view on the role of a judge in making law may be called to be akin to that of late Justice Lionel Murphy, a judge of the Australian High Court for 11 years before he died of cancer in 1986, who at an address to the National Press Club (Australia) in 1980 told them: "One part of the role of a judge, especially in the higher courts, is that he not only applies the law, he often makes or helps to make it ... Now it is the function of the judges, I believe to bring [*the*] laws up to date with the expectations and needs of our changing society. [*They*] should produce laws which are rational, humane, just and simple. Regrettably the courts and this is why they are described as conservative, tend to stick to the precedents of many, many years ago .... I regard that is not fulfilling the function of the judiciary."

The real opportunity to use law as an instrument of socio-economic justice and as a powerful weapon for ensuring protection and preservation of human rights came before Justice Bhagwati when he was elevated to the Bench of the Supreme Court of India. He realised that in the apex court he could lay down the law without interference of any superior court, following the dictum of Justice Jackson that he was right because he was final and not that he was final because he was right. He accordingly started moulding and developing the law through creative interpretation of the Constitution and the laws.

Justice Bhagwati viewed that the Constitution must be read as the charter of a democratic society and strongly believed that on constitutional questions there is nothing to limit the power of the Supreme Court and the High Courts except the sense of restraint of each member of the court.

On the role of a constitutional authority in discharge of his functions, Justice Bhagwati said:[3] "It is settled law that a constitutional authority cannot do indirectly what it is not permitted to do directly. If there is a constitutional provision inhibiting the constitutional authority from doing an act, such provision cannot be allowed to be defeated by adoption of any subterfuge."

On interpretation of the provisions of the Constitution conferring fundamental rights, Justice Bhagwati reflected his views to the effect that the attempt of the court should be to expand the reach and ambit of the fundamental rights rather than attenuate their meaning and content by a process of judicial construction.[4] Based on this conviction, he expanded the concept of Article 14 of the Constitution of India which embodied the equality clause in the same terms as the US Constitution and read it not in a traditional sense but in a wide angle so as to include the guarantee against arbitrary action. According to Justice Bhagwati, the rule of law constitutes the core of our Constitution and it is the essence of the rule of law that the exercise of the power by the State whether it be the legislature or the executive or any other authority should be within the constitutional limitations and if any practice is adopted by the executive which is in flagrant and systematic violation of its constitutional limitations, a member of the public would have sufficient interest to challenge such practice by filing a writ petition and it would be the constitutional duty of the Supreme Court to entertain the writ petition and adjudicate upon the validity of such practice.[5]

3 *Dr. D.C. Wadha* v *State of Bihar* AIR 1987 SC 579: (1987)1 SCC 378.
4 *Maneka Gandhi* v *Union of India* AIR 1978 SC 597: (1978)1 SCC 248.
5 *Dr. D.C. Wadha* v *State of Bihar* AIR 1987 SC 579: (1987)1 SCC 378.

Known all over the world as a powerful exponent of human rights, Justice Bhagwati held that the guarantee of human rights conferred by the Constitution is directed not only against the State *stricto sensu* but also against all individuals and corporations acting under the authority of the State and all public sector corporations which though having their own corporate existence are instruments of the State for the purpose of performing legitimate State function. An instrumentality of the State, in the words of Justice Bhagwati, is to regulate its activities not only in accordance with the statutory requirements but also act in a manner satisfying the requirements of the constitutional provisions contained in Articles 21 and 24 as also the Directive Principles of State Policy.[6]

Justice Bhagwati was instrumental in expanding the scope and ambit of Article 21 of the Constitution of India which ensures: "No person shall be deprived of his life or personal liberty except according to procedure established by law." The view held by the apex court of the country for a long time was that the guarantee embodied in Article 21 was a limited one. That article was understated to embody only that aspect of the rule of law, which requires that no one shall be deprived of his life or personal liberty without the authority of law. It was construed only as a guarantee against executive action unsupported by law. So long as there was some law, which prescribed a procedure authorising deprivation of life or personal liberty, it was supposed to meet the requirements of Article 21. Justice Bhagwati found this prevailing view to be too narrow and not affording sufficient protection to the right to life and personal liberty. Broadening the view, he in a decision[7] held that Article 21 is not only a guarantee against executive action unsupported by law, but is also a restriction on law making. It is not enough to secure compliance with the prescription of Article 21 that there should be a law prescribing some semblance of a procedure for depriving a person of his life or personal liberty, but the procedure prescribed by the law must be reasonable, fair and just and cannot be arbitrary, unfair or unreasonable and if it is not so, the law would be void as violating the guarantee of Article 21. The concept of reasonableness, Justice Bhagwati viewed, must be projected in the procedure contemplated by Article 21 having regard to the impact of Article 14 on Article 21. Justice Bhagwati thus introduced by a process of judicial interpretation the due process clause of the American

6 *Sheela Barse* v *Secretary, Children's Aid Society* (1987)3 SCC 50.
7 *Maneka Gandhi* v *Union of India* AIR 1978 SC 597: (1978)1 SCC 248.

Constitution which it was originally not the intention of the constitution makers of India to enact and laid the foundation for a remarkable development of constitutional law in India by making State action subject to the requirement of due process procedure. He introduced two new doctrines in the area of constitutional law, namely, the requirement of non-arbitrariness in State action and the necessity of compliance by the State with the requirement of due process procedure so that the State action must be reasonable, fair and just.

Similarly, he also expanded the meaning of the expression "right to life" as included in Article 21 of the Constitution. In a landmark decision,[8] Justice Bhagwati observed that the right to life guaranteed under Article 21 is not confined merely to physical existence or to the use of any faculty or limbs through which life is enjoyed or the soul communicates with outside world but it also includes within its scope and ambit the right to live with human dignity and all that goes along with it, namely, the bare necessaries of life such as adequate nutrition, clothing and shelter and facilities for reading, writing and expressing oneself in diverse forms, freely moving about and mixing and commingling with fellow human beings.

The concept of human rights embodied in Part III of the Constitution (which deals with enforceable human rights) were given an expanded meaning by Justice Bhagwati by invoking the aid of Directive Principles of State Policy in Part IV of the Constitution (which are declared to be unenforceable). He made a determined effort to make certain Directive Principles of State Policy enforceable by courts by reading them as included in Article 21 of the Constitution. Justice Bhagwati held that the right to health and the right to education though placed in the Directive Principles of State Policy are part of the right to life because without health and education, life, its fullness is not possible and hence the right to health and the right to education are protected by Article 21 of the Constitution and are therefore enforceable.

8 Role in mitigating administrative wrongdoing When Justice Bhagwati was elevated to the Bench of the Gujarat High Court in 1960, the prevailing view emphasised the need for executive discretion and power. Administration was to be left free to get on with its job. Courts should be 'the handmaidens of the administration rather than its governor' and 'have a duty to facilitate the objectives of administrative action as

8 *Francis Coralie Mullin* v *Administrator, Union Territory of Delhi* (1981)1 SCC 608: (1981)2 SCR 516: 1981 Cr LJ 306: AIR 1981 SC 746.

approved and authorized by Parliament.' But the era of Justice Bhagwati in the Supreme Court coincided with a change in this judicial approach. Justice Bhagwati along with his colleagues having the same wave length started intervening in executive action every now and then whenever the ends of justice so required. There was a realisation that India, unlike most countries in Europe and elsewhere in the world, did not have a coherent body of law which tried to determine the proper limits of executive power. Through a process of judicial decision making, the apex court, with Justice Bhagwati and his colleagues taking the lead, developed a striking down jurisdiction to reign in and correct miscarriages of justice resulting from misuse or abuse of governmental discretion and refused to follow strict legalism in deciding cases and adopted an approach which curved and controlled the executive discretion in order to protect and safeguard the rights of the citizens guaranteed by the Constitution. Justice Bhagwati and his colleagues on the Bench took a consistent stand that if Government ministers or administrators purported to exercise powers they did not hold, had taken into account wrong principles of law in arriving at decisions, or had behaved unfairly and unreasonably, the courts would intervene to strike down their decision or directive. In favour of this approval, the judges affirmed the principle that the executive Government is under no man save God and the law. The mood was that we have judicial review now. We would strike aside decisions of ministers or administrators when they are wrong in law, when they are utterly unreasonable, in fact when they go beyond their powers.

The action of the activist judges, as they were so called, intruding more and more into the administrative arena was not taken well by many administrators and parliamentarians and even by persons in legal profession. They initially started raising a hue and cry and called for curving this power of the judges. Otherwise, they thought, this process which is a heady process and very attractive to judges might get out of control. But the judges did not relent and went on following the doctrine of the rule of law which required that the executives conform to and obey the legal principles enunciated by the courts.

Rule of law, views Justice Bhagwati, is a basic and essential feature of the Constitution. It is a basic principle of the rule of law that the exercise of the power by the executive or any other authority must not only be conditioned by the Constitution but must also be in accordance with law and the power of judicial review is conferred by the Constitution with a view to ensuring that the law is observed and there is compliance with the requirement of law on the part of the executive and other authorities.[9]

Where the court finds that the executive is remiss in discharging its obligations under the Constitution or the law, so that the poor, and the underprivileged continue to be subjected to exploitation and injustice or are deprived of their social and economic entitlements or that social legislation enacted for their benefit is not being implemented thus depriving them of the rights and benefits conferred upon them, Justice Bhagwati observed,[10] the court certainly can and must intervene and compel the executive to carry out its constitutional and legal obligations and ensure that the deprived and the vulnerable sections of the community are no longer subjected to exploitation or injustice and they are able to realise their social and economic rights.

When power is vested in a high authority, abuse of power, according to Justice Bhagwati, cannot be lightly assumed. If there is abuse of power, the arms of the court are long enough to reach it and strike it down.[11] Every order made under a statutory provision, asserts Justice Bhagwati, must not only be within the authority conferred by the statutory provision but must also stand the test of fundamental rights. Parliament cannot be presumed to have intended to confer power on an authority to act in contravention of fundamental rights. It is a basic constitutional assumption underlying every statutory grant of power that the authority on which the power is conferred should act constitutionally and not in violation of any fundamental rights. This would seem to be elementary and no authority is necessary to support it.[11]

The law, Justice Bhagwati further says, is well settled that when a statute vests unguided and unrestricted power to an authority to affect the rights of a person without laying down any policy or principle which is to guide the authority in exercise of this power, it would be affected by the vice of discrimination since it would leave it open to the authority to discriminate between persons and things similarly situated.[11]

Justice Bhagwati always insists on giving reasons while passing an administrative or quasi-judicial order and explains that the necessity of furnishing reasons while passing an order may act as a healthy check against abuse or misabuse of power. If the reasons given are not relevant and there is no nexus between the reasons and the ground on

9 *P. Sambamurthy* v *Union of India* (1987)1 SCC 124, per Bhagwati, CJ.
10 *State of HP* v *A. Parent of a Student of Medical College, Simla* (1985)3 SCC 169.
11 *Maneka Gandhi* v *Union of India* AIR 1978 SC 597: (1978)1 SCC 248.

which action has been taken, it would be open to the aggrieved person to challenge the action in a court of law and if the court is satisfied that the reasons are extraneous or irrelevant, the court would strike down the order. This liability to be exposed to judicial scrutiny would by itself act as a safeguard against improper and *mala fide* exercise of power.

Though a strong supporter of judicial reform, it is not to say that Justice Bhagwati wanted any outbreak of trench warfare between the executives and the courts. In fact, he scrupulously avoided the same. He believes that the courts should be very wary about interfering too much and only interfere in the extreme cases, that is, in cases when the courts were sure the executives have gone wrong in law or they have been utterly unreasonable or unfair.

9 Role in developing social action litigation Social action litigation, otherwise also called public interest litigation (PIL), was almost non-existent in Indian law till before the withdrawal of emergency proclaimed in 1975. Then suddenly it did. During emergency, the citizens' fundamental rights were trampled and the executive tyranny ruled the everyday life of the people. With the withdrawal of emergency, sensitive citizens of the country came forward to build a net around the Constitution so that it could not be made so fragile as it was found to be during emergency. The result was the emergency of a number of social action groups. After the emergency, with the initiatives of those social action groups certain kinds of cases came before the courts which offered an opportunity to the judges to adopt a very radical approach. The courts of the country with Justice Bhagwati at the forefront seized this opportunity and started developing the law that can meet the growing social need.

The doctrine as we inherited from Anglo-Saxon jurisprudence required that only a person to whom a legal wrong was done could approach the court for justice. But Justice Bhagwati and a few of his brother judges on the Bench of the apex court felt that this would bar the doors of the court to large sections of people who are too poor to go to court, who lack awareness of their rights and its assertiveness. They thought that the court cannot allow judicial thinking to get constructed by reference to the law as it prevails in England or in any other foreign country. The court has to build up its own jurisprudence according to the need of the people and has to evolve new principles and lay down new norms which would adequately deal with their problems. They, therefore, decided to jettison the traditional rule of standing which confined access to the judicial process only to those to whom legal injury is caused or legal wrong is done and break the narrow confines within which the rule of standing was imprisoned for long years as a result of inheritance of the Anglo-Saxon system of jurisprudence. They gave new dimension to the doctrine of *locus standi* which has revolutionarised the whole concept of access to justice in a way not known before to the western system of jurisprudence.

In a trend-setting decision,[12] Justice Bhagwati observed that where a legal wrong or a legal injury is caused to a person or to a determinate class of persons by reason of violation of any constitutional or legal right or any burden is imposed in contravention of any constitutional or legal provision or without authority of law or any such legal wrong or legal injury or illegal burden is threatened and such person or determinate class of persons is by reason of poverty, helplessness or disability or socially or economically disadvantaged position, unable to approach the court for relief, any member of the public can maintain an application for an appropriate direction, order or writ in the High Court under Article 226 and in case of breach of any fundamental right of such person or determinate class of persons in the Supreme Court under Article 32 seeking judicial redress for the legal wrong or injury caused to such person or determinate class of persons.

Keeping in mind the fact that the cause of justice can never be thawarted by any procedural technicalities, Justice Bhagwati further observed[12] that where the weaker sections of the community are concerned who are living in poverty and destitution, who are barely eking out a miserable existence with their sweat and toil, who are helpless victims of an exploitative society and who do not have easy access to justice, the court is not to insist on a regular writ petition to be filed by the public spirited individual espousing their cause and seeking relief for them and would readily respond even to a letter addressed by such individual acting *pro bono publico*. The apex court thus allowed citizens of the country to activate the jurisdiction of the court simply by writing a letter.[13] This opened the court's door to the

12 *S.P. Gupta* v *Union of India* AIR 1982 SC 149 at p. 188.

13 AUTHORS' NOTE: It is now settled law that the Supreme Court under Article 32 of the Constitution and the High Courts under Article 226 of the Constitution can treat a letter as a writ petition and take action upon it. It is not, however, every letter which may be treated as a writ petition by the Supreme Court or the High Court. It is only where a letter is addressed by all aggrieved persons or by a public spirited individual or a social action group for enforcement of the constitutional or legal rights of a person in custody or of a class or group of persons who by reason of poverty, disability or socially or economically disadvantaged position find it difficult to approach the court for redress that the Supreme Court or the High Court would be justified, nay bound, to treat the

poor. Social activists, social action groups and public spirited individuals started coming to the court with problems which the court never confronted so directly. In doing so, they started seeking extra-ordinary remedies. An office was set up by Justice Bhagwati in the apex court, the job of which was to sort out two to three hundred letters he received everyday. Evidentiary problems were massive in those cases because the state, in affidavits, frequently denied everything and the Supreme Court not being trier of facts could not look into it. To avoid such problems, the court established fact finding commissions of enquiry to verify allegations. According to this device, the court used to appoint a panel which included a social scientist, a journalist, a social worker, a legal aid activist who used to act as officers of the court. They used to go to the location to verify and comment on the common facts and allegations. As social action legislation grew, this was taken further and the panels were asked to suggest alternations.

Simultaneously with the growth of the social action litigation grew up also investigative journalism. The press lent its hand to the social action group. Justice Bhagwati started giving due importance to investigative journalism which exposed government lawlessness, administrative deviance and exploitation of the poor and disadvantaged. A letter to the Editor of the Indian Express protested about the sub-human conditions, involving torture and disease including psychiatric disease of more than one hundred women in a remand home in Agra, UP. The women with children were herded together in two rooms in the basement and that there was no proper ventilation or sanitation. The women were suffering from epilepsy, T.B., sexually transmitted diseases. A social action litigation was initiated by Dr. Upendra Baxi and Mrs. Lotika Sarkar, two law professors, who clipped the letter to the Editor and wrote to Justice Bhagwati seeing the worst violation of fundamental rights and suggested that their letter be treated as a writ petition on behalf of the women. The two law professors filed the petition as a "public interest litigation" with a view to ensuring to inmates of the home the right to live with human dignity enshrined in Article 21 of the Constitution. The Supreme Court treated the letter as

---

letter as a writ petition. There may also be cases where even a letter addressed for redressal of a wrong done to an individual may be treated as a writ petition where the Supreme Court or the High Court considers it expedient to do so in the interests of justice. *State of HP* v *A. Parent of a Student of Medical College, Simla* (1985)3 SCC 169, per Bhagwati, J.

a writ petition[14] and permitted the two law professors to maintain an action for an appropriate writ for the purpose of enforcing the constitutional right of the inmates of the protective home and providing judicial redress to them. The apex court led by Justice Bhagwati issued a notice to the State Government and asked the District Judge to visit the home to find out whether the allegations were true. The District Judge made a report to the court on which basis the women were sent by the order of the court to the hospital for complete check up and were provided with facilities. After this, a journalist filed a writ petition regarding bad treatment of prisoners in Madras jails; three journalists filed a writ petition demanding prohibition of a thribing market in which women were bought, sold and sought immediate relief for the victims through programmes of compensation and rehabilitation; a journalist of the Hindustan Times brought to the court a social activist's report on the forced importation of seventy five young children for homosexual relationship in Kanpur jail. In all these cases, the Supreme Court led by Justice Bhagwati adopted new jurisdiction through an imaginative extension of the law of *'locus standi'* to vindicate the individual and collective rights of those who were denied access to justice on account of poverty or socially or economically disadvantaged position.

"The transition", in the words of Justice Bhagwati, "from a traditional captive agency with a low social visibility into a liberal agency with a high socio-political visibility is a remarkable development in the career of our appellate judiciary. The courts are now through social action litigation forcing the pace of socio-economic change and compelling the Governments and the bureaucrats to perform their constitutional duty of protecting the poor against social and economic injustices and ensuring realisation of basic human rights".[15]

The judicial activism thus initiated by apex court led by Justice Bhagwati was not, however, taken well by some bureaucrats and politicians. Even resistance came from the Bar with the feeling that this kind of legislation was occupying time of the court which could perhaps have been devoted to disposing of the regular cases. But Justice Bhagwati overlooked those objections and resistance on two

14 *Dr. Upendra Baxi* v *State of UP* (1981)3 Scale 1137.

15 Excerpts from S.D. Gupta Memorial Lecture delivered in Bombay in July 1983 and published in Indian Bar Review, vol. 10(4), 1983 under the title: Human Rights and Democratisation of Remedies.

grounds: firstly, the social action litigation that was coming into the courts was only a fraction of the total litigation involving the courts. We have on an average forty thousand cases coming into the court every year out of which social action litigation does not consist of more than a hundred, or may be a little more. Therefore, it is a very infinitesimal fraction and it does not occupy very much of the time of the court. Secondly, no State and no lawyer has a right to tell the court that a large number of cases involving those who can afford it are pending and that, therefore, until those cases are disposed of, the court must tell the poor and disadvantaged that they must wait. Justice Bhagwati took these criticisms as inevitable, because whenever there is change, there is bound to be resistance and whenever there is forward movement, there is bound to be turbulence and expressed his reactions to such criticisms thus:[16] "The causes of the poor are bound to frighten the custodians of *status quo*. The entry of the masses into court premises with litigations which seek enforcement of human rights for large groups of communities, especially the weaker section, would inevitably scare the upper classes. The reason is that the non-poor have a vested interest in perpetuation of poverty because that is the only way they can not only corner for their benefit the scarce resources of the country but also exercise domination and power over the lines of large numbers of people by keeping them dependent and servile; once the problems of the poor start coming before the courts through social action litigation, this vested interest is certain to be affected. Till now laws for the welfare of the deprived people had no life and they only decorated the statute book with harmless socialistic or egalitarian pretences. But, if through process of democratisation of remedies, courts are pressed by the people to activise human rights and extinguish and wipe out exploitative injustice and executive arbitrariness, that is bound to provoke opposition from those interested in maintaining the *status quo*."

Tracing the source of the criticism, Justice Bhagwati says:[16] "Some part of the criticism comes from those who have been trained in the British tradition of justicing and they believe that the function of a judge is merely to administer the law as he finds it and it is not for him to make the law; the function is *jus dicere* and not *jus dare*; he must look upon the people's causes merely as issues argued arcanely by lawyers and decided in the mystery and mystic of the inherited Anglo-Saxon judicial

16 Excerpts from S.D. Gupta Memorial Lecture delivered in Bombay in July 1983 and published in Indian Bar Review, vol. 10(4), 1983 under the title: Human Rights and Democratisation of Remedies.

process. They think that in entertaining social action litigation and making orders for securing basic human rights to the poor and helpless, the judiciary is placing itself above the law and is transgressing its limitations. This criticism too is unfounded because law cannot remain static; it has to adopt itself to the needs of the people and to satisfy their hopes and aspirations ...... It is a dynamic instrument fashioned by society for the purpose of eliminating friction and conflict and unless it secures social justice to the people, it will fail of its purpose and some day people will cast it off."

Justice Bhagwati cautions[17] that "jurisprudential feudalism is bound to raise opposition to this basic change which is taking place in the legal and judicial process. As T.H. Huxley long ago warned, it is the customary fate of new truths to begin as heresies and George Barnard Shaw also said to the same effect that all great truths begin as blasphemies. But the illuminating light of people's jurisprudence cannot be allowed to be darkened by the forces of high brow resistance. Despite various and motivated criticism by persons who have arrogated to themselves the position of saviours of democracy and human rights but who are nothing more than sanctimonious humbugs far removed from the realities of Indian life and totally oblivious of the miseries and sufferings of millions of our people, the courts have been battling for people's rights and with the sword of justice in their hands, the courts will continue to do so undeterred by these critics, for the courts owe an obligation to the people of this country and under the Constitution they are created as sentinels on the *qui vive* for protection of the rights not only of a fortunate few but of the large masses of people steeped in poverty and ignorance."

There are all sorts of cases coming before the courts now presenting problems of the deprived and vulnerable sections of the community; there are cases of under-trial as well as convicted prisoners, women in protective custody, children in juvenile institutions, bonded and migrant workmen, organised labour, untouchables and scheduled tribes, landless agricultural labourers who fall prey to faulty mechanism, women who are bought and sold, pavement dwellers and victims of extra-judicial executions and many more. The courts are through judicial creativity evolving for the poor and the downtrodden new rights which are part of basic human rights but which are today inchoate and struggling to

17 Excerpts from S.D. Gupta Memorial Lecture delivered in Bombay in July 1983 and published in Indian Bar Review, vol. 10(4), 1983 under the title: Human Rights and Democratisation of Remedies.

be born and which before their births are sought to be stifled by the exploiting class. The judiciary has for the first time come out in the service of the weaker sections of Indian humanity. Some little has been done for the poor and destitute, but much still remains to be done. Social action litigation has become one of the most powerful instruments for protecting the poor and the weak against violation of their basic human rights.

10 Role in developing Legal Aid Schemes During the emergency in 1975, Prime Minister Mrs. Indira Gandhi made legal aid part of her 20 Point Programme she launched. Justice Bhagwati readily embraced the concept. When Mrs. Gandhi's Government came back to power in 1980, it set up a Committee under the Chairmanship of Justice Bhagwati for implementing Legal Aid Schemes. The programmes that Justice Bhagwati had set up had two different facets. Apart from the traditional court-oriented legal aid programme, there was also what Justice Bhagwati called the strategic legal aid programme. The first strategy was promotion of legal literacy and creation of legal awareness among the people. This was based on the fact that we have a lot of social welfare legislations in this country but the consumers, the beneficiaries of it, are not aware of the rights and benefits conferred upon them. Unless the people are aware, they will never be able to identify the wrong done to them and will never be able to know that a legal wrong is capable of legal redress. To give the programme necessary thrash, small booklets were produced, radio and television were used and documentary films were made. A second strategy was adopted to carry legal services to the doorstep of the people by organizing legal aid camp in selected rural areas. Thousands of people attended those camps. The legal problems of the people were used to be answered by a lawyer and the financial problems were answered by various revenue authorities who also attended such camps. People's courts were set up where retired judges, socially committed lawyers and social activists were involved and pending cases were mediated. This system has struck roots in national soil and has become very popular. The third strategy was organization of legal aid clinics in selected universities and law colleges. A course on law and poverty was introduced in the final year of law course. Legal aid clinics were opened in Universities where the students see clients and give them advice under the guidance of a teacher. Not only that, under the scheme students are sent to the rural areas for the purpose of carrying out social-legal surveys. The fourth strategy that was adopted was a little bit unconventional. This runs in the words of Justice Bhagwati thus: "We felt that if we really wanted to reach the people then we had to work through social action groups.

We have a large number of young men and women, full of idealism and enthusiasm, who have given up a life of comfort and luxury in order to go to the rural areas to work among the poor at the grassroot level. We found they were scattered, isolated and one group did not know what the other was doing. We started forming centers where social action groups operating within a geographical area would come together. My organization, the Committee for Implementing Legal Aid Schemes, would find them and provide them with a lawyer. They carry out social-legal surveys and we started holding camps for training social workers as paralegals." The strategy as adopted became highly fruitful.

11 Role in welfare of children Justice Bhagwati says: "Children are the citizens of the future era. On the proper bringing up of children and giving them the proper training to turn out to be good citizens depends the future of the country.[18] He further views "like a young plant a child takes routes in the environment where it is placed. Howsoever good the breed be if the sapling is placed in a wrong setting or an unwarranted place, there would not be the desired growth. Same is the situation with the human child."[18]

Improvement of the performance of the Children's Act 1948 suggested. The Declaration of the Rights of the Child was adopted by the General Assembly of the United Nations in 1959[19] and Article 24 of the International Covenant on Civil and Political Rights 1966[20] also contained the said Declaration. The importance of the child has been appropriately recognised there. India as a party to these International Charters having ratified the Declaration, Justice Bhagwati views, it is an obligation of the Government of India as also the State machinery to implement the same in the proper way. The Children's Act 1948 has made elaborate provisions to cover this and if these provisions are properly translated into action and the authorities created under the Act become cognisant of their role, duties and obligations in the performance of the statutory mechanism created under the Act and they are properly motivated to meet the situation that arises in handling the problems, Justice Bhagwati opined that the situation would certainly be very much eased. To make the provisions of the Act properly translated into action, Justice Bhagwati offered a number of suggestions: (*i*) The Child Welfare Officer (Probation) as also the Superintendent of

18 *Sheela Barse* v *The Secretary, Children's Aid Society* (1987)3 SCC 50.
19 Proclaimed by General Assembly Resolution 1386 (XIV) of 20th November 1959.
20 Adopted and opened for signature, ratification and accession by General Assembly Resolution 2200A (XXI) of 16th December 1966.

the Observation Home must be duly motivated. They must have a working knowledge in psychology and have a keen sense of observation and on their good functioning would depend the efficacy of the scheme; (*ii*) Children in Observation Homes should not be made to stay long and as long as they are there, they should be kept occupied and the occupation should be congenial and intended to bring about adaptability in life aimed at bringing about a self-confidence and picking of human virtues; (*iii*) Dedicated workers have to be found out, proper training to them has to be imparted and such people alone should be introduced into the Children's Home; (*iv*) The Juvenile Court has to be manned by a Judicial Officer with some special training. Creation of a court with usual Judicial Officer and labelling it as a Juvenile Court does not serve the requirement of the statute. If that were so, the statute would have no necessity of providing a Juvenile Court. The statutory scheme contemplates a Judicial Officer of a different type with a more sensitive approach-oriented outlook. Without these any Judicial Officer would, indeed, not be competent to handle the special problems of children.[21]

Children's employment in hazardous occupation decried Justice Bhagwati strongly opposed the employment of children in a hazardous occupation. Construction work being a hazardous occupation, Justice Bhagwati called for prohibition of employment of children under the age of 14 years in every type of construction work and called for amendment of the Schedule of the Employment of Children Act 1938 by including construction industry in it.[22] In support of his call, Justice Bhagwati referred to Convention No. 59 adopted by the International Labour Organisation and ratified by India. But apart altogether from the requirement of Convention No. 59, Justice Bhagwati also referred to Article 24 of the Constitution which provides that no child below the age of 14 years shall be employed to work in any factory or mine or engaged in any other hazardous employment. This is a Constitutional prohibition which, according to the learned Judge, even if not followed up by appropriate legislation, must operate *proprio vigore* and construction work being plainly and indubitably a hazardous employment, it is clear that by reason of this Constitutional prohibition, no child below the age of 14 years can be allowed to be engaged in a construction work. Justice Bhagwati, therefore, observed that notwithstanding the absence of specification of construction industry in the Schedule to the Employment of Children's Act 1938, no child

21 *Sheela Barse* v *The Secretary, Children's Aid Society* (1987)3 SCC 50.
22 *People's Union For Democratic Right* v *Union of India* AIR 1982 SC 1473: 1982 Lab IC 1646: (1982)3 SCC 235: 1982 SCC (L&S) 275.

below the age of 14 years can be employed in construction work and urged the Government to ensure that this Constitutional mandate is not violated in any part of the country.[1]

Inter-country adoption norms laid down In his anxiety to reduce the chances of abuse to which inter-country adoptions may be subjected to if allowed to continue without any safeguards and to protect the welfare of the child and to enable a child to find a new home where it can grow in an atmosphere of warmth and affection of family life with full opportunities for physical, intellectual and spiritual development, Justice Bhagwati in a leading case[2] laid down the elaborate principles and norms which must be observed and the procedure which must be followed in giving a child in adoption to foreign parents.

Justice Bhagwati warned that the problems of the children are of such enormous magnitude that all that has been done till now is not sufficient. If there be no proper growth of the children of today, the future of the country will be dark. It is the obligation of every generation to bring up children who will be citizens of tomorrow in a proper way. Today's children will be the leaders of tomorrow who will hold the country's banner high and maintain the prestige of the nation. If a child goes wrong for want of proper attention, training and guidance, it will indeed be a deficiency of the society and of the Government of the day. A problem child is indeed a negative factor. Every society must, therefore, devote full attention to ensure that children are properly cared for and brought up in a proper atmosphere where they could receive adequate training, education and guidance in order that they may be able to have their rightful place in the society when they grow up.[3]

12 Role in welfare of labour and employees

Need for special attention emphasised in respect of employees working in stone quarries and stone crushers Poverty and helplessness of the workmen employed in stone quarries and stone crushers touched Justice Bhagwati

1 AUTHORS' NOTE: Pursuant to the decision in *People's Union for Democratic Right* v *Union of India*, ibid, fn. 22, the Schedule to s. 3(3) of the Employment of Children Act 1938 was amended by adding to the schedule 'Building and Construction Industry' as an area where employment of children below 14 is prohibited. (*Vide* Notification No. S.O. 594(E), dated 12.8.1983). Part B of the Schedule to s. 3 of the Child Labour (Prohibition and Regulation) Act 1986 also includes 'Building and Construction Industry' as an area where employment of children is prohibited.

2 *Lakshmi Kant Pandey* v *Union of India* (1984)2 SCC 244: 1985 (Supp) SCC 701. AUTHORS' NOTE: For detailed discussion on the subject, vide chapter 3.

3 *Sheela Barse* v *The Secretary, Children's Aid Society* (1987)3 SCC 50.

so much so that he urged[4] to educate the workmen employed there so that they become aware as to what are the rights and benefits to which they are entitled under the various social welfare laws. The knowledge of their rights and entitlements, Justice Bhagwati opined[4] will give them the strength to fight against their employers for securing their legitimate dues and it will go a long way towards reducing, if not eliminating, their exploitation.

Justice Bhagwati had equal concern for the health of the workers. Finding that the entire air in the area where stone crushers are being operated is heavily laden with dust and it is this air which the workmen breathe day in and day out and many workmen contact tuberculosis by inhaling such air, Justice Bhagwati directed[5] the Central Government and the State of Haryana to immediately take steps for the purpose of ensuring that the stone crusher owners do not continue to foul the air and they adopt either of two devices, namely, keeping a drum of water above the stone crushing machine with arrangement for continuous spraying of water upon it or installation of dust sucking machine.

The delay in getting compensation under the Workmen's Compensation Act 1923 whenever any workman suffers any injury or contacts any disease in the course of employment did not escape the attention of Justice Bhagwati. He understood that this happened more in case of workmen employed in stone quarries and stone crushers. Justice Bhagwati, therefore, directed[5] that as soon as any workman employed in a stone quarry or stone crushers receives injury or contacts disease in the course of his employment, the concerned mine lessee or stone crusher owner shall immediately report this fact to the Chief Inspector or Inspecting Officers of the Central Government and/or the State Government and such inspecting officers shall immediately provide legal assistance to the workman with a view to enabling him to file a claim for compensation before the appropriate court or authority and they shall also ensure that such claim is pursued vigorously and the amount of compensation awarded to the workman is secured to him. The court or authority before which a claim for compensation is filed by or on behalf of the workman is to dispose of such claim without any undue delay, says Justice Bhagwati, since delay in the awarding of compensation to the workman would only add to his misery and helplessness and would be nothing short of gross denial of justice to him.

4 *Bandhua Mukti Morcha* v *Union of India* (1984)3 SCC 161.
5 *Bandhua Mukti Morcha* v *Union of India* (1984)3 SCC 161.

Payment of minimum wage mandated a must Justice Bhagwati played an important role in the welfare of labour force of the country. In a landmark decision,[6] the learned Judge observed that every person who provides labour or services to another is entitled at the least to the minimum wage under the Minimum Wages Act 1948 and if anything less than the minimum wage is paid to him, he can complain of violation of his fundamental right under Article 23 of the Constitution and ask the court to direct payment of the minimum wage to him so that the breach of Article 23 may be abated. Article 23 mandates that no person shall be required or permitted to provide labour or service to another on payment of anything less than the minimum wage.

Justice Bhagwati warned that the State cannot be permitted to take advantage of the helpless condition of the affected persons and extract labour or service from them on payment of less than the minimum wage. No work of utility and value can be allowed to be constructed on the blood and sweat of persons who are reduced to a state of helplessness on account of scarcity condition. The State cannot under the guise of helping these affected persons extract work of utility and value from them without paying them the minimum wage. Whenever any labour or service is taken by the State from any person, whether he be affected by scarcity condition or not, the State must pay minimum wage to such person on pain of violation of Article 23. Justice Bhagwati said the employer may fix any norm he thinks fit specifying the quantity of work which must be turned out by the workman during the day but if the workman does not turn out work in conformity with such norm, the employer cannot pay him anything less than the minimum wage. If the norm fixed by the employer is reasonable and the workman does not turn out work according to such norm, disciplinary action may be taken against the workman and in a given case, he may even be liable to be thrown out of employment but he cannot be paid less than the minimum wage.

Gratuity recognised a matter of right On the issue of gratuity payable to an employee, Justice Bhagwati viewed in a case[7] that gratuity is no longer a bounty but it is a matter of right of the employee. It can no longer be regarded as a provision in the discretion of the President as provided in the Pension Regulations. In the absence of any legal provision

6 *Sanjit Roy* v *State of Rajasthan* (1983)1 SCC 525.

7 *F.R. Jesuratnam* v *Union of India* 1990 (Supp) SCC 640 decided on 30th September 1986.

empowering the authorities to forfeit the gratuity payable to an employee, the same cannot be forfeited.

Guidelines for promotion of Government employees in case of quota rule provided

In the matter of promotion of Government employees, Justice Bhagwati observed that where the quota rule is a statutory rule which had to be scrupulously observed in the matter of promotion, a vacancy which according to the quota rule is allocable to promotees from one source cannot be filled by a promotee from another source and if, notwithstanding a quota rule, the vacancy is filled by a promotee from that other source, such promotion would be irregular and the vacancy would continue to remain a vacancy liable to be filled in by a promotee from the first mentioned source.[8]

Justice Bhagwati further observed that even where there is a quota rule governing recruitment to a cadre from different source, it is not necessary that there should be any particular rule of seniority. The Government may in its wisdom adopt an appropriate rule of seniority which should be based on length of continuous officiation or may follow a roster arranged in conformity with the quota rule so that seniority may be determined according to the rotation of vacancy under the quota rule. There may also be any other appropriate rule for determining seniority in a cadre. Myriad ways can be conceived for determining seniority of officers on entry into a cadre but whatever may be the rule of seniority adopted by the Government, it is well settled that it must satisfy the test of equality enshrined in Articles 14 and 16 of the Constitution.

Industrial peace through direct negotiation or collective bargaining stressed upon

As the best guarantee for industrial peace, Justice Bhagwati favoured settlement of labour disputes by direct negotiation or settlement through collective bargaining. In a judgment concurred by Justice Bhagwati[9] it was observed that in order to bring about such a settlement more easily and to make it more workable and effective, it is no longer necessary, under the law, that the settlement should be confined to that arrived at in the course of a conciliation proceeding, but now includes, by virtue of the definition of s. 2(*p*) of the Industrial Disputes Act 1947, a written agreement between the employer and the workmen arrived at otherwise than in course of a conciliation proceeding where such agreement has

8 *P.S. Mahal* v *Union of India* (1984)4 SCC 545: AIR 1984 SC 1291.

9 *New Standard Engineering Company Limited* v *N.L. Abhyankar* (1978)2 SCC 133.

been signed by the parties in the prescribed manner and a copy thereof has been sent to the authorised officer.

Punishment for violation of labour laws favoured Justice Bhagwati was always in favour of strict compliance of labour laws enacted for improving conditions of workers. In a decision[10] he observed that violation of labour laws must be viewed with strictness and whenever violation of labour laws are established, adequate punishment should be imposed on the errant employers. If violation of labour laws, Justice Bhagwati asserts, are going to be punished only by measure of fines, it would be impossible to ensure observance of labour laws and the labour laws would be reduced to a nullity, would remain merely paper tigers without any teeth or claws.

13 Role in protection of environmental pollution

Evolving a national policy for location of hazardous industries stressed Justice Bhagwati views that when science and technology are increasingly employed in producing goods and services calculated to improve the quality of life, there is a certain element of hazard or risk inherent in the very use of science and technology and it is not possible to eliminate such hazard or risk altogether. The learned Judge points out that we cannot possibly adopt a policy of not having any chemical or other hazardous industries merely because they pose hazard or risk to the community. If such a policy were adopted, he apprehends, it would mean the end of all progress and development. Such industries, even if hazardous, he views, have to be set up since they are essential for economic development and advancement of well-being of the people. He, therefore, suggested reduction of the element of hazard or risk to the community by taking all necessary steps for locating such industries in a manner which would pose least risk of danger to the community and maximising safety requirements in such industries. So, he urged[11] upon the Central Government to evolve a national policy for location of chemical and other hazardous industries in areas where population is scarce and there is little hazard or risk to the community, and when hazardous industries are located in such areas, he favoured[12] taking every care to see that large human habitation does not grow around them. There should, he suggested,[12] preferably be a green belt of 1 to 5 kms width around such hazardous industries.

10 *People's Union For Democratic Right* v *Union of India* AIR 1982 SC 1473: 1982 Lab IC 1646: (1982)3 SCC 235: 1982 SCC (L&S) 275.

11 *M.C. Mehta* v *Union of India* (1986)2 SCC 176.

12 *New Standard Engineering Company Limited* v *N.L. Abhyankar* (1978)2 SCC 133.

Neutral scientific expertise stressed as an essential input in judicial decision making In respect of cases based on environmental pollution and ecological destruction, Justice Bhagwati seriously felt the need for neutral scientific expertise as an essential input to inform judicial decision making, since these cases require expertise at a high level of scientific and technical sophistication. Justice Bhagwati, therefore, suggested[13] that there should be an independent centre with professionally competent and public spirited experts to provide the needed scientific and technical input and urged upon the Government of India to set up an Ecological Sciences Research Group consisting of independent, professionally competent experts in different branches of science and technology, who would act as an information bank for the court and the Government departments and generate new information according to the particular requirements of the court or the concerned Government department.

Setting up of environment courts stressed upon Justice Bhagwati further suggested to the Government of India that since cases involving issues of environmental pollution, ecological destruction and conflicts over natural resources are increasingly coming up for adjudication and these cases involve assessment and evolution of scientific and technical data, it might be desirable to set up Environment Courts on the regional basis with one professional judge and two experts drawn from the Ecological Sciences Research Group keeping in view the nature of the case and the expertise required for its adjudication. There would of course be a right of appeal to the court from the decision of the Environment Court. It is pertinent to note that pursuant to the suggestion as made by Justice Bhagwati, environment courts have been set up in different regions of the country under the Environment (Protection) Act 1986 and Rules made thereunder. Apart from that, Green Bench has been formed in different High Courts including Calcutta High Court where matters relating to environmental hazards are taken up for consideration and disposed of with necessary guidelines on regular basis.

14 Social achievements Justice Bhagwati was not a judge to live in a glass house. He was a judge who loved to know the people, their expectations and tried to address it within his capable limit. That made him the judge of the common people. The trend continues even after his retirement from the apex court.

13 *M.C. Mehta* v *Union of India* (1986)2 SCC 176.

A crusader in legal aid movement Justice Bhagwati is known as a crusader in legal aid movement in India. As Chairman of the Legal Aid Committee appointed by the Government of Gujarat he brought out a comprehensive report for providing free legal aid to the poor and weaker sections of the community. The report was hailed by every one not only as a legal document but also as a sociological document of high distinction. On the basis of the said report, the Government of Gujarat set up a Legal Aid Committee and Justice Bhagwati was appointed as its Chairman for running a Pilot Project in several parts of the State of Gujarat and in such capacity he supervised the arrangement for giving free legal aid and advice to the needy. The Government of Gujarat also appointed him as Chairman of the Judicial Reforms Committee where he made recommendations for reforms in the legal system in the State.

Finding his deep concern for the poor and the downtrodden, the Government of India appointed him Chairman of the Committee on Juridicare in 1976 with a view to preparing a comprehensive and activist legal service programme throughout the country on a uniform basis and the report submitted by him resulted in the Government of India setting up a Committee for Implementing Legal Aid Schemes popularly known today as CILAS under his chairmanship for organizing, supervising and monitoring the legal aid programme in the country. He was invited at various international conferences and seminars to speak on legal aid. Justice Bhagwati addressed the conference of Appellate Court Judges from all over the world on "Access to Justice and Mode of Delivery of Legal Services". He also addressed the conference of the International Bar Association on "Legal Aid and Human Rights" and was invited by the Columbia University to speak on "Judicial Activism and Public Interest Litigation".

Justice Bhagwati strongly views that the social action groups engaged in the betterment of the social and economic conditions of the poor and the disadvantaged can play an important role and with this end in mind he organized and addressed several social action groups in different parts of the country. He was instrumental in bringing together the social action groups working in South India and addressed them at a conference in Bangalore. Action for Welfare and Awakening in Rural Environment, popularly known as AWARE, Society for Community Organisation Trust, known as SOCO and Banwasi Seva Ashram under Prembhai, a great social activist, among several other social action groups made great efforts under his guidance to reach human rights and social justice to the needy poor and down-trodden. He is also associated with Partnership in Action, popularly known as PARINAC, consisting of NGOs from different parts of the world and closely associated with EL TALLER, an international organization engaged in working and guiding the social action groups from various countries.

A champion of the cause of workers Justice Bhagwati's name is remembered as a champion of the cause of workers and labourers. His thought provoking judgements on bonded and unorganised labour and child labour have resulted in various legislations and Government schemes in improving their social and economic conditions. He is a member of the Committee of Expert on the Application of Conventions & Recommendations of the International Labour Organisation (ILO) and led a Technical Assistant Mission of the ILO to Jakarta, Indonesia.

A great humanist looking environmental problem as a human right problem Justice Bhagwati looks environmental problem as a human right problem in India and abroad. The Australian National Law Environmental Association invited him to the Second International Conference on Environmental Law in August 1991. He was commissioned by the United Nations to prepare a study on Avoidance and Settlement of Environmental Disputes for the conference in Rio and invited to a conference on Trade & Environment organised by the Rockfeller Brothers Fund in New York in March 1994.

An acknowledged human rights activist Justice Bhagwati felt that the interest he awakened as a judge in developing the human rights movement in India was not enough. So, he wanted to be deeply involved in human right activities beyond the horizon of the country of his origin after his retirement from the apex court of the country.

As an acknowledged human rights activist many countries have drawn upon him for including human rights components in framing their constitutions and they include, amongst others, South Africa, Mongolia, Nepal, Ethiopia and Cambodia. His services in the cause of human rights have been recognized by different world bodies. He was associated with the United Nations High Commission for Refugees, Nepal Branch, to discuss the need for improved collaboration between Governments, United Nations agencies and NGOs in undertaking humanitarian action worldwide, particularly in the context of refugees' problems. He presided over the Global Tribunal which was organized by the Centre for Women's Global Leadership as part of the Vienna World Congress on Human Rights to look into the violations of women's human rights. He also presided over the Asia-Pacific Peoples' Tribunal on the issues of Burma, East Timor and Thailand set up by concerned citizens committed to human rights and social justice under the People's Plan for the 21st Century (PP21) in Bangkok in December 1992. He also participated in a mission organized by International Commission of Jurists and Centre for Independence of Judges and Lawyers to the occupied territories in West Bank and Gaza in December 1993 to study the judicial structure and functions and human rights components in the occupied territories. He participated in a seminar organized by the United Nations Transitional Authority in Cambodia (UNTAC) on the constitutional machinery for implementation of the Bill of Rights in the new Cambodian constitution in March-April 1993. Justice Bhagwati was invited to deliver the keynote addresses at various conferences on human rights around the world. To mention a few of them, he addressed the African Chief Justices Conference in 1986 and 1988. In 1987 he addressed the International Appellate Judges Conference in Malaysia and in the same year he addressed the Australian Legal Convention in Perth, Australia. The Commonwealth Secretariat has also drawn on him as a resource person at Judicial Colloquia on the Domestic Application of International Human Rights Norms organized by it alongwith INTERRIGHTS. The first colloquium was organized by Justice Bhagwati in Bangalore in India for South Asian and South East Asian Chief Justices in 1988 and it was at the Bangalore Colloquium that the principles were enunciated which have come to be popularly known as Bangalore Principles. Subsequently, these colloquia were organized in Zimbabawe, Gambia, Nigeria, Oxford and South Africa. These colloquia have drawn considerable attention of judges around the world. His sincere work for the cause of realization of human rights was recognized with his election as a member of the Human Rights Committee of the United Nations on 8th September 1994 where at its first meeting he was elected as its Vice-Chairman.

A guide to many national and international bodies It would take most of the evening to list all of the national and international positions Justice Bhagwati has held over the years. Although he kept himself very busy in court and other social engagements, he found time to guide many national and international bodies, either as president, chairman, member or patron, to name a few, the Indian Chapter of the International Law Association, the Law Association for Asian and the Pacific (LAWASIA), the International Jury for the Award for Templeton Prize for progress in religion, the Commonwealth Legal Education Association, London, the World Congress on Human Rights, the Indian Chapter of SAARCLAW which is the association of lawyers, judges and jurists of the countries in the South Asian region, the International Society for Labour Law & Social Security, the Centre for the Independence of Judges and Lawyers (CIJL) formed by the International Commission of Jurists, Geneva, the Expert Group set up by the Secretary General of the Commonwealth Secretariat for reviewing and revitalizing the Commonwealth Plan of Action on Women and Development, the Asian Legal Resource Centre, Hong Kong, the Federation of Indian Chamber of Commerce and Industry (FICCI) for Selection of Individual Enterpreneur for FICCI Award, Shri Birla Samarak Kosh Award for outstanding research in the field of medical and allied sciences, the Indian Council for Enviro-Legal Action (ICELA), the Law Reports of the Commonwealth, the International Association of Lawyers Against Nuclear Arms (IALANA), the South Asian Task Force on Judiciary, the El Taller, an international organisation of NGOs, International Citizens Forum (formerly International Forum of Tax-Payers Trust) and Indian National Forum of Art and Culture. He was also a member of the Board of Studies in Law of the M.S. University at Baroda and Bombay University.

15 Laurels in cap Justice Bhagwati has been honoured by many national, international and governmental bodies. The International Bar Association gave him the International Award for his contribution to the cause of the underprivileged and to the legal aid movement in India. The Bar Council of India has honoured him with a plaque of honour for his contributions in the field of human rights. The Andhra University conferred on him the LL.D. degree (Honoris Causa). He was admitted as a Samuel Rubin Fellow of the Columbia University for the year 1984 for his work on Judicial Activism and Public Interest Litigation. The Xavier Labour Institute awarded him Sir Jehangir Ghandy Medal for his work on bonded labour and labour engaged in stone quarries. He has been made an Honorary Fellow of India Association for Environment Management for outstanding contribution to the cause of environmental protection; awarded Rajiv Gandhi Excellence Award by Shiromani Institute for Excellence in Judiciary and Human Rights. The Indian Society of Criminology awarded him the Kumarrappa-Reckless Award. The Rotary International, New Delhi, awarded him Human Rights Par Excellence Award. At the Convention of social activists of India, Justice Bhagwati was awarded in 1988 the honorary award of PRIDE OF INDIA. He is a member of the International Advisory Council of the World Bank for Legal and Judicial Reforms and is the first Asian who has been conferred with the honorary membership of the Association of the Bar of the City of New York which is the strongest Bar Association in USA. Justice Bhagwati was also the Chancellor of Hyderabad University. He is the present Chancellor of Shri Lal Bahadur Shastri Rashtriya Sanskrit Vidyapeeth. The year 2007 also witnessed the University of Malaya conferring him with the Degree of Doctorate of Law.

For his contribution in the legal field, the President of India, though belated, honoured him with Padma Vibhushan in 2007.

16 Conclusion In paying his tribute to Justice Bhagwati, Justice V.R. Krishna Iyer in a recent communication said:

> "Mr. Justice P.N. Bhagwati is a great jurist, a highly humanitarian judge, a progressive humanist, a person of versatile talents whose long career in public life has been a blessing for vast masses of Indian people in several planes of well-being. He has been a defender of labour, arguing for the rights and welfare of the working class. He has been through his judgments from the highest court of India, a champion of gender justice and environmental preservation. He has advocated free legal aid to the poor and judicare in the larger sense of that expression. Poverty jurisprudence has been a major concern of his so as to enable the weaker sections of society to secure social justice. He has authored many reports in this behalf and has been regarded as an institution in action rather than a respected 'robed brother' on the High Bench. He has campaigned for public causes, especially those which facilitate availability of economic egalite and equity for those in want. He is a creative constitutional lawyer who has interpreted statutory measures liberally and compassionately. He can rightly be described as among the rarest of the rare crusaders for the work, wealth and happiness of people everywhere. In my perspective, he has used his large capabilities for a revolutionary transformation of a feudal society with the determined objective of inaugurating a democratic world order. This human rights activist has adorned the Supreme Court of India with phenomenal success and his judgments have made a rich addition to the treasury of welfare jurisprudence. The supremacy of human rights, the importance of environmental law and the need for a fair deal to labour if development is to be a reality of society, has been the mission of Justice Bhagwati as Chief Justice of India. We have been colleagues for a number of years on the high bench and have shared progressive principles of criminal justice. In short, social injustice has been his anathema and economic exploitation his bete noire."

"[Law] is an institution of social engineering, a mighty weapon in the armoury of democracy by which socio-economic objectives set out in the Constitution can be achieved".

— P.N. BHAGWATI*

2

Law as an Instrument of Social Justice

SYNOPSIS

1 **Introduction**
2 **Law as old as the society itself**
3 **Natural law and positive law, influence on society**
4 **Sociological function of law**
5 **Common law as an instrument of social justice in India**
6 **Law and social change**
7 **Law as an instrument of social justice**
8 **Judiciary's role in the task for delivery of social justice**

1 Introduction In his early judicial career the 'timorous judge' mark keen to follow the rule of precedent was apparent in Justice Bhagwati. His gradual understanding of the social conditions of the people of rural India in particular and their expectations helped in lifting that timorous vail from him. This is how Justice Bhagwati recalls his transformation: "When I was a judge in the Gujarat High Court, I was trained in the British tradition. Dispensing justice mechanically, unconcerned with the repurcussions and consequences—concerned only with the mechanical interpretation of the laws. Thereafter, I happened to go to the rural areas. There I saw real India. I saw stark, naked poverty. I saw people who had hardly any clothes to hide their shame. Poverty has broken their back and corroded their soul. And I realised that justice that I was administering in my court had no meaning for them. That justice did not reach their hearth and home. They looked upon me with awe and wonder. They could see the majesty of the law without feeling its justice. It was then that I realised that law had an important

* Excerpts from the inaugoral address of Justice Bhagwati delivered at Second District Judges Conference in Ahmedabad in 1970.

function towards society. Law had to be an instrument of socio-economic change. I began to realise that I must now use law for the purpose of giving social justice to the vast million of my countrymen who are half clad, half hungry." Justice Bhagwati is recognised as masiha of the poor and disadvantaged for bending law to reach social justice to the people.

2 Law as old as the society itself Law must lead to justice. There is nothing more exhilarating in life than the feeling of achieving justice through law. It seeks to prevent wrongful conduct which harms any other person. The people respect law for it affords protection to them from social vagaries and promises stability and progress. Law holds the society together and sustains different views conducive to the stability of the social structure, maintenance of social order and welfare of humanity. A society sans the existence of law can hardly be imagined. Law is what the society has given to itself but with the passage of time law is absorbed in the society itself and becomes an integral part of it. When it fails to be so absorbed, chaos and conflicts rule the society. That is why we say that the history of law is as old as the society itself. Where law accords with human values, the society is bound to be more developed and disciplined.

3 Natural law and positive law, influence on society Justice Bhagwati looks on law either as natural law or positive law. Natural law or the law of nature, according to him, means not only laws of the physical universe which operate with an amazing smoothness of regularity, and therefore, as a result of it there is complete order and harmony in the nature, but it also includes laws which govern human thought and behaviour. Justice Bhagwati summarises his view thus: "There is bound to be complete balance and harmony in personal and social life where action is according to the law of nature, where every thought, every activity, every relationship is guided by the knowledge of oneness or identity between the individual self and the other world. Once the man lives and acts in a higher state of consciousness, his action will be in accordance with law of nature and will be conducive to the good of the society. His internal self-regulation by natural laws is the only safeguard for individual and societal peace and harmony."

Positive law, on the other hand, consists of rules of human conduct with authority to punish the defaulters. In the view of Justice Bhagwati State made positive laws for regulating human conduct and it must, therefore, approximate as closely as possible with the natural laws which govern human thought and behaviour. "The measure of excellence of a society is to be found in the extent to which its positive laws approximate with natural laws", so says Justice Bhagwati.

It is said that Romans were the first to make a systematic study of law and legal system. While Homer, Socrates, Plato and Aristotle concerned themselves with natural law, it is believed that sociological theory of law was formulated or discovered for the first time by Dean Roscoe Pound.

4 Sociological function of law In the beginning law was considered as a logically consistent body of precepts, having no insight into its objectives. This approach to law did not take into account the sociological function of law which on its part takes into account human and social relations which are based on the infinitely varied and constantly varying facts of social life. Justice Bhagwati views that law should have a social purpose too. It is as important as organising and integrating a body of rules and precepts in logical order. At an interaction Justice Bhagwati said: "The law deals with human and social relations and these relations which are based on the infinitely varied and consistently varying facts of social life cannot be pressed into a strait jacket of logical and consistent propositions. If we postulate that problems can be solved purely by logical deductions from the actual rules in force, we would deprive the law of all power of development and the dead hand of the past will crush its growth". If logic in itself becomes the end of law, the law would thwart the realization of justice. The purpose of law is to bring harmony in human behaviour, but harmony is possible if law is accepted by people. "Law is something that the people give to themselves under their own social development. Law is rather like an old yet vigorous tree having its roots in history, but still taking new grafts, putting out new sprouts and occasionally dropping dead woods. It is a human institution created by human agents to serve needs and to secure social interests to the maximum extent possible by eliminating conflicts and friction. It is for this reason that law cannot be either formal logic or an embodiment of inexorable scientific laws. It is an institution of social engineering, a mighty weapon in the armoury of democracy by which socio-economic objectives set out in the Constitution can be achieved".[1] It is a social institution, in Justice Bhagwati's perception, democratically evolved for achieving the object of making social adjustments to meet the challenge which increasingly flows from unsatisfied legitimate human desires and ambitions.

5 Common law as an instrument of social justice in India Our system of law is primarily based on common law. We find that common law is

1 Excerpts from the inaugoral address of Justice Bhagwati delivered at Second District Judges Conference in Ahmedabad in 1970.

prevalent wherever the Englishmen went. Today common law, which forms a very strong relationship between the various countries of the Commonwealth, has been adopted in the Commonwealth countries not because it was imposed by the British rulers, but because it was accepted by the people. It also provided a legal system which effectively deliver justice which the people expects from it and this expectation of justice is inherent in every human being. If a foreign legal system meets the cultural values of the society, the society will accept such a legal system. Justice Bhagwati views that no legal system can be transplanted wholly and in all its features in a foreign soil. The transplant cannot foliate and flower unless the legal system, which is transplanted, accords with the cultural values and social inheritance of the society in which it is transplanted.

Two basic reasons justify the acceptance of common law by the Indian society. One is the rule of law under which no State organ can act outside the scope or beyond the limits of its powers and no one can interfere with the liberty or property of a person except under the authority of law, and the other is that it is solely and exclusively for an impartial and independent judiciary to decide the limits of the powers conferred on each organ of the State. These two reasons constitute the greatest safeguard of the citizen against abuse or misuse of power. Justice Bhagwati once said: "The Judges in the Commonwealth countries are all united by the bond of common law. The judges administering the common law have a considerable margin of choice in the decisions which they have to make and that explains how the common law has developed and grown over the years by responding to the changing needs and requirements of the society. We have all inherited the common law traditions and we are trying to build our own national jurisprudence on the solid foundations of the common law traditions".[2]

6 Law and social change Law and social change is a very fascinating subject as law is not a body of rules and precepts only, which can be interpreted by legal sophistry or verbal jugglery regardless of the needs of the social conditions. The society is not static. It changes with the changing time. In *National Textile Workers' Union* v *P.R. Ramakrishnan*,[3] Justice Bhagwati observed: "Law cannot stand still; it must change with the changing social concepts and values. If the bark

2 Excerpts from the speech of Justice Bhagwati delivered at the Democratic Application of Human Rights Norms at the Judicial Colloquia at Abuja in 1991.

3 (1983)1 SCC 228, per Bhagwati, J.

that protects the tree fails to grow and expand along with the tree, it will either choke the tree or if it is a living tree, it will shed that bark and grow a new living bark for itself. Similarly, if the law fails to respond to the needs of changing society, then either it will stifle the growth of the society and choke its progress or if the society is vigorous enough, it will cast away the law which stands in the way of its growth. Law must, therefore, constantly be on the move adapting itself to the fast changing society and not lag behind. It must shake off the inhibiting legacy of its colonial past and assume a dynamic role in the process of social transformation". It does not operate in vacuum. Justice Bhagwati says: "It is not an antique to be taken down, dusted, admired and put back on the shelf. It is a dynamic instrument fashioned by society for the purpose of achieving harmonious adjustment of human relations by eliminating social tension and conflicts. It must change with the changing socio-economic conditions".

A study of the Indian concept of law which is supposed to be 5000 years old would show that law in ancient India was never static and always kept pace with the changing social values. The word 'dharma' is employed in our ancient texts to describe the concept of law in the abstract. "'Dharma' is that which bears, maintains and sustains the stability of the social structure".[4] If we trace the history of development of dharma, i.e., law, we would find that in the course of its progress and growth over the centuries, it showed extreme resilience and dynamism in responding to the challenge of changing customs and beliefs, says Justice Bhagwati.

In today's world, with the progress made in the fields of science and technology, on the one hand, and in industry and commerce, on the other, a change has taken place in the values giving new hopes to the people and they are now clamouring for a new social order. Law can hardy ignore these developments. It has to respond to the aspirations of the people to bring about a socio-economic revolution and play a dynamic role in building a new social order and new social structure. Law, views Justice Bhagwati, has to play a definite and positive role in order to achieve the new socio-economic structure where everybody can enjoy the fruits of freedom and liberty, where there will be enough for everyone according to his needs, where the downtrodden, povertystricken and illiterate people are made aware of their rights and duties. If

4 This is the broad content of the word 'dharma' which is emphasised in Shloka 59, Addhyaya 69 of 'Kama Parva' of the Mahabharata.

democracy is to become a living reality, asserts Justice Bhagwati, law has to become an instrument of socio-economic change so as to bring about a human order rooted in the past but ready to meet the demands of the present and the challenges of the future. Law has, therefore, to adopt a dynamic approach, it has to acquire a new meaning and propose: it has to be people oriented and above all it has to become an instrument for delivery of justice. Law can do it in two ways. The first way it can be done is by bringing into existence various socio-economic enactments. In a democracy, this is the responsibility that the State is to discharge through legislature. The legislature is to bring laws keeping in mind the social change in order to make harmonious social adjustments amongst its people and to bring laws which could be used, bent and interpreted in favour of the people suffering from poverty and illiteracy. The second way law can play its role is through judiciary. Legislature makes grand laws covering the whole of social life. Judges only legislate in a very limited way, to fill in the gaps overlooked by the legislature in the fulfilment of its grand vision. Justice Lionel Murphy, a judge of the Australian High Court, at an address said: "One part of the role of a judge, especially in the higher courts, is that he not only applies the law, he often makes or helps to make it ...... Now it is the function of the judges .... to bring [the] laws up to date with the expectations and needs of our changing society. [They] should produce laws which are rational, humane, just and simple ...."[5] Justice Bhagwati fully agrees with the view of Justice Lionel Murphy and says that in a new social structure, legislature and the judiciary must work shoulder to shoulder. At the 36th anniversary of the Adoption of the Constitution of India, Justice Bhagwati said: "We must resolve to make effort to create confidence in the poor and disadvantaged sections of the society that they can fight through law and seek assistance of the judicial process to win their rights and entitlements. We must review the state of the law and the judiciary and devise ways and means to improve our legal and judicial system ...... to reinforce and augment the confidence of the public and particularly of the weaker sections in the legal and judicial process."[6]

7 Law as an instrument of social justice Law, to Justice Bhagwati, is not a set of mechanical rules to be administered in a lifeless manner without regard to social consequences. Law is a reflex of the social

5 Excerpts from the address to the National Press Club (Australia) in 1980 of Justice Lionel Murphy, a judge of the Australian High Court for 11 years before he died of cancer in 1986.

6 Excerpts from the speech of Justice Bhagwati delivered on the 'State of Judicial System' at the 36th anniversary of the Adoption of the Constitution of India.

conscience, expression of the social will of the people and it should, therefore, be a major promise of the legal process to give effect to the social conscience, the social habits, the social norms and social mores. In short, the hopes and aspirations of the people are expressed through the words spoken by the legislature.

"Justice", in the words of Justice Bhagwati, "is not an absolute concept. It is relative and it changes with the changing social concepts and values". What may be regarded as fair and just in one society may not be regarded so in another; and even within the same society, what is fair and just at one time may not be so at another. It is not a constant which has a fixed definite content. But whatever may be the prevailing concept of justice, it is a subject which is charged with tremendous power and emotion sufficient to move millions into action. Justice, says Justice Bhagwati, "means not mere cumulative justice, but distributive justice, human justice, socio-economic justice, justice which takes within its compass not only a few privileged persons, but large masses of underprivileged segments of the society—justice which not only penetrates and destroys the inequalities of race, sex or wealth but also heavily weighted in favour of the weaker sections of the community".

And social justice, according to Justice Bhagwati, means social and economic justice. Social justice is that justice which is not confined to the rich and the powerful but takes within its purview the ailing sections of humanity. It is justice which seeks to bring about equitable distribution of social, material, economic and political resources of the community.

There is a close relationship between law and justice, in that the law should be such that it must ultimately lead to justice. Judges must dispense justice according to the prevailing law passed by the legislature interpreting the same boldly and creatively keeping in mind the interest of the large masses of the people. The legislatures must on their part ensure that the Acts they are enacting have vision of socio-economic justice.

Our Constitution is charged with economic mission. The Preamble of the Constitution sets out the socio-economic goals by laying down objectives of justice, social, economic and political. Fundamental rights provide for liberty of thought, expression, belief, faith and worship, equality of status and opportunity and to promote fraternity among the people, assuring dignity of the individual and the unity and integrity of the nation. The Constitution of India provides for the right to the adequate means of livelihood to every citizen; ownership of material resources of the community and their distribution for the commongood of the people, equal pay for equal work, both for men and women; prohibits abuse of workers, including women and children, and provides for equal justice and free legal aid. The Constitution also says that the State shall strive to promote the welfare of the people by securing and protecting, as effectively as it may, a social order in which justice, social, economic and political, shall inform all the institutions of the national life. Though our Constitution is an instrument which completely protects and advances the interests of the weaker sections of our people, yet very often it becomes impossible for the weaker sections of the community to get justice on account of their poverty and ignorance of their constitutional and legal rights which provide for new socio-economic order based on social justice.

It is an irony of fate, laments Justice Bhagwati, that justice in India is not only costly, time consuming, tormented by appeals and revisions and lacking sufficient support from the legal profession, but it also has dream-shattering effect on the psyche of the common man at the grass root level. Although the greatest service to man would be to dispense justice to him, yet justice is not so easily accessible to him. In the words of Justice Bhagwati "today, unfortunately, the poor and the disadvantaged are 'priced out' of the legal system. They have lost faith in the capacity of the legal system to bring about any change in their life conditions. They have seen only the oppressive side of the law and never experienced its beneficent aspect. Justice has ceased to have any meaning for them. Today there is a growing feeling amongst them that legal process has no role in social change and law is simply a tool of the establishment. This is a dangerous feeling in a democracy." If it is to be stopped, Justice Bhagwati views, the existing distrust in the legal process as an instrument of social and economic change must be removed and the poor and the disadvantaged must be made to feel that they can effectively fight through law and successfully transform society through the legal process. The poor and helpless masses are today raising their heads with new hope and expectation demanding freedom from poverty and destitution and the law has to satisfy the demand and urges of these people. Law, therefore, has to reach the socio-economic justice to the millions of the people suffering from want and destitution. Law has to see that the people have easy access to justice and they are made aware of their rights, constitutional and legal. People of the country now want freedom from want and dependence, freedom from poverty and destitution, freedom from ignorance and illiteracy so that every one, irrespective of accident of birth, possession of wealth or cast, creed or community must have equal opportunity for advancement and gain. It is, therefore, necessary to uplift the conditions of have-nots and the deprived segments of the society by providing them with social justice.

Law of the twenty-first century welfare state has a great role to play in fulfilling the growing aspirations of the people. Its guiding principle is no longer maintenance of peace which was the rule of the old order but justice, not formal but substantive, and that too in all spheres of society. The growing use of law as a device of organised social action directed towards achieving social change is one of the main characteristics of modern society.

Law and justice cannot afford to remain distant neighbours. There must be harmony between law and justice. We must, asserts Justice Bhagwati, in all seriousness ask ourselves the question as to how far we have been able to fulfil the mission of law to deliver justice and to what extent we have succeeded in using law as a vehicle for ensuring social justice to the large masses of people in the country.

In a democratic country like India, any social change is possible only through the process of law, and therefore, in order to bring about change in the life conditions of the poverty stricken people, the legal process has to be utilized. It is through the process of law that social benefits emanating from social welfare legislations, which were denied to the poor and disadvantaged for centuries, can reach them, exploitation can be brought to light, administration can be made devoid of corruption, oppressive and lawless forces, and abuse and misuse of power by those entrusted with the enforcement of law can be eliminated.

The Supreme Court through Justice Bhagwati by use of the legal process took upon itself the onerous task of bringing about change in the life conditions of the downtrodden and poverty stricken people of the country. A number of decisions set tone for such action.

In *R.D. Shetty* v *International Airport Authority*,[7] the Supreme Court through Justice Bhagwati observed: "Today with tremendous expansion of welfare and social service functions, increasing control of material and economic resources and large scale assumption of industrial and commercial activities by the State, the power of the executive Government to affect the lives of the people is steadily growing. The attainment of socio-economic justice being a conscious end of State policy, there is a vast and inevitable increase in the frequency with

7 (1979)3 SCC 489.

which ordinary citizens come into relationship of direct encounter with State power-holders. This renders it necessary to structure and restrict the power of the executive Government so as to prevent its arbitrary application or exercise". So the court observed that "Government cannot be permitted to say that it will give jobs or enter into contracts or issue quotas or licences only in favour of those having grey hair or belonging to a particular political party or profession or a particular religious faith. The Government is still the Government when it acts in the matter of granting largesse and it cannot act arbitrarily" [Per Bhagwati, J.].

In *S.P. Gupta* v *Union of India*,[8] the apex court through Justice Bhagwati observed; "Today a vast revolution is taking place in the judicial process; the theatre of the law is fast changing and the problems of the poor are coming to the forefront. The court has to innovate new methods and devise, new strategies for the purpose of providing access to justice to large masses of people who are denied their basic human rights and to whom freedom and liberty have no meaning." To enable such access to justice, the Supreme Court enlarged the scope of the traditional rule in regard to *locus standi* which restricted availability of judicial redress only to a person who has suffered a legal injury by reason of violation of legal or constitutional right by the action of the State or public authority. This was a rule of 'ancient vintage' based on 'right-duty pattern'. The Court in so enlarging the scope of *locus standi* observed:[8] "Where a legal wrong or a legal injury is caused to a person or to a determinate class of persons by reason of violation of any constitutional or legal right or any burden is imposed in contravention of any constitutional or legal provision or without authority of law or any such legal wrong or legal injury or illegal burden is threatened and such person or determinate class of persons is by reason of poverty, helplessness or disability on socially or economically disadvantaged position, unable to approach the Court for relief, any member of the public or social action group can maintain an application for an appropriate direction, order or writ in the High Court under Art. 226 and in case of breach of any fundamental right of such person or class of persons, in this court (Supreme Court) under Art. 32 seeking judicial redress for the legal wrong or injury caused to such person or determinate class of persons" [Per Bhagwati, J. as he then was].

In *People's Union for Democratic Rights* v *Union of India*,[9] the Supreme Court observed that the Government of India, which entrusted

8 1981 (Supp) SCC 87: AIR 1982 SC 149.
9 (1982)3 SCC 235: AIR 1982 SC 1473: 1982 Lab IC 1646.

the work to the contractors, cannot escape their obligation of providing statutory benefits and amenities as provided under the labour laws. Justice Bhagwati in this case observed: "When a person provides labour or service to another against receipt of remuneration which is less than the minimum wage, he is acting under the force of some compulsion which drives him to work though he is paid less than what he is entitled under law to receive .... It is not un-often that in a capitalist society economic circumstances exert much greater pressure on an individual in driving him to a particular course of action than physical compulsion or force of legislative provision. The word 'force' must therefore be construed to include not only physical or legal force but also force arising from the compulsion of economic circumstances which leaves no choice of alternatives to a person in want and compels him to provide labour or services even though the remuneration received for it is less than the minimum wages."

In *State of Himachal Pradesh* v *Parent of a Student,*[10] Justice Bhagwati pointed out about his vision of economic justice thus: "Where the court finds that the executive is remiss in discharging its obligations under the Constitution or the law, so that the poor and the under privileged continue to be subjected to exploitation and injustice or are deprived of their social and economic entitlements or that social legislation enacted for their benefit is not being implemented, thus depriving them of the rights and benefits conferred upon them, the Court certainly can and must intervene and compel the executive to carry out its constitutional and legal obligations and ensure that the deprived and vulnerable sections of the community are no longer subjected to exploitation or injustice and they are able to realize their social and economic rights."

8 Judiciary's role in the task for delivery of social justice Justice Bhagwati strongly advocates the view that the judiciary has a vital role to play in the task for delivery of social justice to the large masses of people. If the judiciary wants effectively to meet the challenge of social justice, it must give up its old antiquated approach which believes in the policy of restraint and passive interpretation. It is this mechanical and antiquated approach which at occasions has made the judiciary an upholder of the *status quo*. The Goddess of justice is traditionally shown as blind with an opaque bandage on her eyes and under the self-induced hypnosis of holding the scales even. The judiciary has in many

10 (1985)3 SCC 169 (175).

countries ignored the stark realities of life in dispensing justice. It is, therefore, necessary, says Justice Bhagwati, to re-evaluate the function of the judiciary and to bring about a qualitative change in the justice delivery system so as to bring it in tune with the hopes and aspirations of the people which have on occasions been thwarted to blind adherence to obsolete judicial methodology and antiquated obsolete legal doctrines which are calculated to protect the vested interest. The judiciary has to devise new methods, forge new tools and innovate new strategies for the purpose of reaching social justice to the common man. It must abjure reactive approach and adopt a pro-active role. It must respond to the demands and urges of the large masses of people for social justice, and by adopting a creative and activist approach, it must mould and develop the law and bring it closer to the people so that the rule of law becomes meaningful and social justice a reality for them.

"Child shows the man as morning shows the day"

—MILTON

3

Child Welfare and Inter-country Adoptions

Principles, Norms and Procedures

SYNOPSIS

1 Introduction In a civilized society the importance of child welfare cannot be overemphasized, because the welfare of the entire community, its growth and development, depend on the health and well-being of its children. Children, according to Justice Bhagwati, are a "supremely important national asset" and the future well-being of the nation depends on how its children grow and develop. The child is a soul with a being and a nature and capacities of its own, who must be helped to find them, to grow into their maturity, into fulness of physical and vital energy and the utmost breath, depth and height of its emotional, intellectual and spiritual being; otherwise there cannot be a healthy growth of the nation, so says Justice Bhagwati.

2 Global awareness of child welfare

U.N. Declaration of the rights of the child There is a growing realisation, says Justice Bhagwati, in every part of the globe that children must be brought up in an atmosphere of love and affection and under the tender care and attention of parents so that they may be able to attain full emotional, intellectual and spiritual stability and maturity and acquire self-confidence and self-respect and a balanced view of life with full appreciation and realisation of the role which they have to play in the nation building process without which the nation cannot develop and attain real prosperity because a large segment of the society would then be left out of the development process. The concern for the welfare of the children at the international level culminated in the Declaration of the Rights of the Child adopted by the General Assembly of the United Nations on 20th November 1959. The Declaration in its Preamble points out that "the child, by reason of his physical and mental immaturity, needs special safeguards and care, including appropriate legal protection, before as well as after birth", and that "mankind owes to the child the best it has to give" and proceeds to formulate several principles of which the following are material for our present purpose:

* * *

"PRINCIPLE 2. The child shall enjoy special protection, and shall be given opportunities and facilities, by law and by other means, to enable him to develop physically, mentally, morally, spiritually and socially in a healthy and normal manner and in conditions of freedom and dignity. In the enactment of laws for this purpose, the best interests of the child shall be the paramount consideration.

PRINCIPLE 3. The child shall be entitled from his birth to a name and a nationality.

* * *

PRINCIPLE 6. The child, for the full and harmonious development of his personality, needs love and understanding. He shall, wherever possible, grow up in the care and under the responsibility of his parents, and, in any case, in an atmosphere of affection and of moral and material security; a child of tender years shall not, save in exceptional circumstances, be separated from his mother. Society and the public authorities shall have the duty to extend particular care to children without a family and to those without adequate means of support. Payment of State and other assistance towards the maintenance of children of large families is desirable.

* * *

PRINCIPLE 9. The child shall be protected against all forms of neglect, cruelty and exploitation. He shall not be the subject of traffic, in any form.

PRINCIPLE 10. The child shall be protected from practices which may foster racial, religious and any other form of discrimination. He shall be brought up in a spirit of understanding, tolerance, friendship among peoples, peace and universal brotherhood, and in full consciousness that his energy and talents should be devoted to the service of his fellow men.

* * * ”

3 Indian awareness regarding child welfare

Constitutional provisions Indian awareness about the welfare of the children is well reflected in various provisions enacted in the Constitution. Clause (3) of Article 15 enables the State to make special provisions *inter alia* for children. Article 21A* casts a duty on the State to provide free and compulsory education to all children of the age of six to fourteen years in such manner as the State may, by law, determine. Article 24 provides that no child below the age of 14 years shall be employed to work in any factory or mine or engaged in any other hazardous employment. Clauses (*e*) and (*f*) of Article 39 provide that the State shall direct its policy towards securing *inter alia* that the tender age of children is not abused, that citizens are not forced by economic necessity to enter avocations unsuited to their age and strength and that children are given facility to develop in a healthy manner and in conditions of freedom and dignity and that children and youth are protected against exploitation and against moral and material abandonment. These constitutional provisions, says Justice Bhagwati, reflect the great anxiety of the constitution makers to protect and safeguard the interest and welfare of children in the country.

National policy for the welfare of children Government of India has also in pursuance of these constitutional provisions evolved a National Policy for the Welfare of Children. This Policy, says Justice Bhagwati, starts with a goal-oriented preambulatory introduction: “The nation's children are a supremely important asset. Their nurture and solicitude are our responsibility. Children's programme should find a prominent part in our national plans for the development of human resources, so that our children grow up to become robust citizens, physically fit, mentally alert and morally healthy, endowed with the skills and motivations needed by society. Equal opportunities for development to all children during the period of growth should be our aim, for this would serve our larger purpose of reducing inequality and ensuring social justice.”

The National Policy sets out the measures which the Government of India proposes to adopt towards attainment of the objectives laid down in the preambulatory introduction and they include measures designed

* *Inserted* by the Constitution (Ninety-third Amendment) Bill 2001 which is called the Constitution (Eighty-sixth Amendment) Act 2001.

to protect children against neglect, cruelty and exploitation and to strengthen family ties "so that full potentialities of growth of children are realised within the normal family neighbourhood and community environment". The National Policy also lays down priority in programme formation and it gives fairly high priority to maintenance, education and training of orphan and destitute children. There is also provision in the National Policy for constitution of a National Children's Board and pursuant to this provision, the Government of India has constituted the National Children's Board with the Prime Minister as the chairperson. It is the function of the National Children's Board to provide a focus for planning and review and proper coordination of the multiplicity of services striving to meet the needs of children and to ensure at different levels continuous planning, review and coordination of all the essential services. The National Policy also stresses the vital role which the voluntary organisations have to play in the field of education, health, recreation and social welfare services for children and declares that it shall be the endeavour of State to encourage and strengthen such voluntary organisations.

Critical appraisal of the present day scenario According to Delhi police sources, nearly 46 million children are estimated to be missing in the country. When they eventually surface far away from where they were born, they can be seen as either beggars or bonded labourers, delinquents. No central agency exists to look into this vanishing act.

According to a government estimate, about 12 million children roam the Indian streets doing things they should not be doing to make both ends meet. According to the Human Rights Watch Report, the number of street children is 115 million. If the truth is somewhere in between, it is still a number large enough to cover the population of several European countries.

New government data has revealed in September 2007 that only three out of 100 child labourers have made it to school twenty years after India launched its ambitious programme to put every child in a classroom. Faced with the weight of its own statistics, the Centre appears to have accepted the failure of the National Child Labour Policy started by Rajiv Gandhi's government in 1988. A Planning Commission working group on child labour has recommended detailed changes to the Policy ahead of the 11th five-year plan and the recommendations have been accepted by the Ministry of Labour which is in charge of fighting against child labour. It bears mentioning that the number of child workers in India rose from 11.3 million in 1991 to 12.7 million in 2001. Statistics collated from a state-wise evaluation of the Policy at the end of 2006 have revealed that only 3,74,255 children have been successfully taken out of work and put in school since it was launched. If the 2001 census figure is taken as the total number of child labourers in India since the Policy was launched, less than 3 per cent have received the education promised.

On 10th October 2006, the Union Government banned children below the age of 14 from working in residences, hospitality industry and hazardous jobs. Despite this gesture being a laudable one, there has been no follow-up. It is not clear as yet how boys and girls freed from labour are to support themselves in the utter absence of an income. The question of rehabilitation of nearly 20 million children "rescued" from hostile environments remains to be settled. The ban imposed in 2006 is an extension of India's Child Labour (Prohibition and Regulation) Act of 1986 which banned children under the age of 14 from working in hazardous industries like fireworks and matchstick-making. It remains to be seen how far the Act has been implemented.

In line with the National Commission, the Delhi Cabinet in October 2007, decided to set up a Delhi Commission for Protection of Child Rights following international brand GAP's decision to withdraw stock of garments from 3000 stores worldwide after allegations of child labour in one of its factories in India. The State panel, to be formed along the lines of the National Commission, shall have a chairperson and six members with powers to examine and review safeguards provided under the law for protection of child rights and recommend measures for their effective implementation. It will also be authorised to inquire into any violations of child rights and recommend measures for their effective implementation.

4 Role of biological parents and adoptive parents in rearing up a child

Every child has a right to love and be loved and to grow up in an atmosphere of love and affection and of moral and material security and this is possible only if the child is brought up in a family, says Justice Bhagwati. The most congenial environment would, of course, be that of the family of his biological parents. But if for any reason it is not possible for the biological parents or other near relative to look after the child or the child is abandoned and it is either not possible to trace the parents or the parents are not willing to take care of the child, the next best alternative, Justice Bhagwati views, would be to find adoptive parents for the child so that the child can grow up under the loving care and attention of the adoptive parents. The adoptive parents would be the next best substitute for the biological parents.

5 Principles, norms and procedures to be followed in inter-country adoptions

In a leading judgment,[1] Justice Bhagwati, after a careful study and serious research work, laid down the following broad principles and norms which should be followed in determining whether a child should be allowed to be adopted by foreign parents, and if so, the procedure to be followed for that purpose, with the object of ensuring the welfare of the child.

A. ***Adoptive parents within the country to be first preference*** Justice Bhagwati observed that when the parents of a child want to give it away in adoption or the child is abandoned and it is considered necessary in the interest of the child to give it in adoption, every effort must be made first to find adoptive parents for it within the country, because such adoption would steer clear of any problems of assimilation of the child in the family of the adoptive parents which might arise on account of cultural, racial or linguistic differences in case of adoption of the child by foreign parents.

If it is not possible to find suitable adoptive parents within the country, it may become necessary to give the child in adoption to foreign parents rather than allow the child to grow up in an orphanage or an institution where it will have no family life and no love and affection of parents and quite often, in the socio-economic conditions prevailing in the country, it might have to lead the life of a destitute, half-clad, half-hungry and suffering from malnutrition and illness.

B. ***Normative and procedural safeguards to be followed in case of adoption of destitute or abandoned children and children living in social or child welfare centres***

(I) APPLICATION FROM A FOREIGNER TO BE SPONSORED BY A RECOGNISED OR LICENSED SOCIAL OR CHILD WELFARE AGENCY OF THE FOREIGNER'S COUNTRY. Every application from a foreigner desiring to adopt a child must be sponsored by a social or child welfare agency recognised or licensed by the Government of the country in which the foreigner is resident. No application by a foreigner for taking a child in adoption should be entertained directly by any social or welfare agency in India working in the area of inter-country adoption or by any institution or centre or home to which children are committed by the juvenile court. This is essential primarily for three reasons. First, it will help to reduce, if not eliminate altogether, the possibility of profiteering in children, because

1 *Lakshmi Kant Pandey* v *Union of India* (1984)2 SCC 244.
AUTHORS' NOTE: Judgment of the court was delivered by Bhagwati, J. on behalf of himself, R.S. Pathak and Amarendra Nath Sen, JJ.

if a foreigner is allowed to contact directly agencies or individuals in India for the purpose of obtaining a child in adoption, he may, in his anxiety to secure a child for adoption, be induced or persuaded to pay any unconscionable or unreasonable amount which might be demanded by the agency or individual procuring the child. Secondly, it would be almost impossible for the court to satisfy itself that the foreigner who wishes to take the child in adoption would be suitable as a parent for the child and whether he would be able to provide a stable and secure family life to the child and would be able to handle trans-racial, trans-cultural and trans-national problems likely to arise from such adoption, because, where the application for adopting a child has not been sponsored by a social or child welfare agency in the country of the foreigner, there would be no proper and satisfactory home study report on which the court can rely. Thirdly, in such a case, where the application of a foreigner for taking a child in adoption is made directly without the intervention of a social or child welfare agency, there would be no authority or agency in the country of the foreigner who could be made responsible for supervising the progress of the child and ensuring that the child is adopted at the earliest in accordance with law and grows up in an atmosphere of warmth and affection with moral and material security assured to it.

The court should not make an order for appointment of a foreigner as guardian unless it is satisfied that the application of the foreigner for adopting a child has been sponsored by such social or child welfare agency.

(II) SPONSORING AGENCY TO GET A HOME STUDY REPORT PREPARED BY A PROFESSIONAL WORKER. The social and child welfare agency which sponsors the application for taking a child in adoption must get a home study report prepared by a professional (social) worker indicating the basis on which the application of the foreigner for adopting a child has been sponsored by it.

The home study report is intended to provide social and legal facts in regard to the foreign parent with a view to assisting the court in arriving at a proper determination of the question whether it will be in the interest of the child to be given in adoption to such foreign parent and should broadly include information in regard to various matters, namely, referral source; personality of husband and wife; health details such as clinical tests, heart conditions, past illness etc.; social status and family background; nature and adjustment with occupation; relationship with community; description of home; accommodation for the child; schooling facilities; amenities in the home; standard of living as it appears in the home; type of neighbourhood; current relationship between husband and wife; current relationship between parents and children, if any; development of already adopted children, if any, and their acceptance of the child to be adopted; current relationship between the couple and the members of each other's families; if the wife is working, whether she will be able to give up the job; if she cannot leave the job, the arrangements she will make to look after the child; whether adoption is considered because of sterility of one of the martial partners; if not, whether they can eventually have children of their own; if a child is born to them, the way they would treat the adopted child; reasons for wanting to adopt an Indian child; attitude of grandparents and relatives, community and neighbourhood towards the adoption; anticipated plans for the adopted child; whether the child can be adopted according to the adoption law in the adoptive parent's country; whether permission has been obtained to adopt; whether the couple did apply for a child from any other source; if yes, the name of the source; the type of child the couple is interested in (sex, age and the reasons); name and address of the agency conducting the home study with name and qualification of social worker; name of agency responsible for post-placement, supervision and follow-up. The home study report should also contain an assessment by the social or child welfare agency as to whether the foreigner wishing to take a child in adoption is fit and suitable and has the capacity to parent a child coming from a different racial and cultural milieu and whether the child will be able to fit into the environment of the adoptive family and the community in which it lives.

(III) APPLICATION OF A FOREIGNER TO BE ACCOMPANIED BY HOME STUDY REPORT, AMONGST OTHERS. Every application of a foreigner for taking a child in adoption must be accompanied by a home study report and the social or child welfare agency sponsoring such application should also send along with it a recent photograph of the family, a marriage certificate of the foreigner and his or her spouse as also a declaration concerning their health together with a certificate regarding their medical fitness duly certified by a medical doctor, a declaration regarding their financial status along with supporting documents including employer's certificate where applicable, income-tax assessment orders, bank references and particulars concerning the properties owned by them, and also a declaration stating that they are willing to be appointed guardian of the child and undertaking that they would adopt the child according to the law of their country within a period of not more than two years from the time of arrival of the child in their country and give intimation of such adoption to the court appointing them as guardian as also to the social or child welfare agency in India processing their case, they would maintain the child and provide the child necessary education and upbringing according to their status and they would also send to the court as also to the social or child welfare agency in India reports relating to the progress of the child along with the child's recent photograph. The frequency of such progress reports should be quarterly during the first two years and half yearly for the next three years.

(IV) APPLICATION OF A FOREIGNER TO BE ACCOMPANIED BY A POWER OF ATTORNEY. The application of the foreigner must also be accompanied by a power of attorney in favour of an officer of the social or child welfare agency in India which is requested to process the case and such power of attorney should authorise the attorney to handle the case on behalf of the foreigner in case the foreigner is not in a position to come to India.

(V) SPONSORING AGENCY TO CERTIFY LEGAL FITNESS. The social or child welfare agency sponsoring the application of the foreigner must also certify that the foreigner seeking to adopt a child is permitted to do so according to the law of his country.

(VI) CERTIFICATES, DECLARATIONS AND DOCUMENTS ACCOMPANYING THE FOREIGNER'S APPLICATION FORM TO BE DULY NOTARISED. The certificates, declarations and documents which must accompany the application of the foreigner for taking a child in adoption, should be duly notarised by a Notary Public whose signature should be duly attested either by an officer of the Ministry of External Affairs or Ministry of Justice or Ministry of Social Welfare of the country of the foreigner or by an officer of the Indian Embassy or High Commission or Consulate in that country.

(VII) SPONSORING AGENCY TO UNDERTAKE ENSURING ADOPTION BY THE FOREIGNER ACCORDING TO THE LAW OF HIS COUNTRY AND SEND CERTIFIED COPIES OF THE ADOPTION ORDER. The social or child welfare agency sponsoring the application of the foreigner must also undertake, while forwarding the application to the social or child welfare agency in India, that it will ensure adoption of the child by the foreigner according to the law of his country within a period not exceeding two years and as soon as the adoption is effected, it will send two certified copies of the adoption order to the social or child welfare agency in India through which the application for guardianship is processed, so that one copy can be filed in court and the other can remain with the social or child welfare agency in India.

(VIII) SPONSORING AGENCY TO AGREE TO SEND PROGRESS REPORTS IN REGARD TO THE CHILD. The social or child welfare agency sponsoring the application must also agree to send to the concerned social or child welfare agency in India progress reports in regard to the child, quarterly during the first year and half yearly for the subsequent years or years until the adoption is effected.

(IX) SPONSORING AGENCY TO UNDERTAKE TO TAKE CARE OF THE CHILD IN CASE OF DISRUPTION OF THE FOREIGNER'S FAMILY BEFORE EFFECTING ADOPTION. The sponsoring agency must also undertake that in case of disruption of the family of the foreigner before adoption can be effected, it will take care of the child and find a suitable alternative placement for it with the approval of the concerned social or child welfare agency in India, and report such alternative placement to the court handling the guardianship proceedings and such information shall be passed on both by the court as also by the concerned social or child welfare agency in India to the Secretary, Ministry of Social Welfare, Government of India.

(X) GOVERNMENT OF INDIA TO PREPARE A LIST OF AGENCIES RECOGNISED FOR INTER-COUNTRY ADOPTION BY THE FOREIGN GOVERNMENTS. The Government of India shall prepare a list of social or child welfare agencies licensed or recognised for inter-country adoption by the Government of each foreign country where children from India are taken in adoption after getting necessary information from the Government of each such foreign country and the Indian Diplomatic Mission in that foreign country and make available copies of such list to the various High Courts in India as also to the social or child welfare agencies operating in India in the area of inter-country adoption under licence or recognition from the Government of India.

C. *Safeguards to be followed in case of biological parents of the child proposed to be taken in adoption*

(I) BIOLOGICAL PARENTS TO BE PROPERLY ASSISTED IN MAKING A DECISION ABOUT ADOPTION. If the biological parents are known, they should be properly assisted in making a decision about relinquishing the child for adoption by the institution or centre or home for child care or social or child welfare agency to which the child is being surrendered, be helped to understand all the implications of adoption including the possibility of adoption by a foreigner and they should be told specifically that in case the child is adopted, it would not be possible for them to have any further contact with the child.

(II) BIOLOGICAL PARENTS NOT TO BE SUBJECTED TO DURESS. The biological parents should not be subjected to any duress in making a decision about relinquishment and even after they have taken a decision to relinquish the child for giving in adoption, a further period of about three months should be allowed to them to reconsider their decision.

(III) NON-RECONSIDERATION OF DECISION BY BIOLOGICAL PARENTS TO RELINQUISH THE CHILD WITHIN THE TIME LIMIT TO MAKE SUCH DECISION IRREVOCABLE. Once the decision is taken by the biological parents to relinquish the child and such decision is not reconsidered within further period of three months, it must be regarded as irrevocable and the procedure for giving the child in adoption to a foreigner can then be initiated without any further reference to the biological parents by filing an application for appointment of the foreigner as guardian of the child. Thereafter there can be no question of once again consulting the biological parents whether they wish to give the child in adoption or they want to take it back. It would be most unfair, so observed Justice Bhagwati, if after a child is approved by a foreigner and expenses are incurred by him for the purpose of maintenance of the child and sometimes on medical assistance and even hospitalisation for the child, the biological parents were once again to be consulted for giving them a *locus penitentia* to reconsider their decision.

(IV) CHILD SURRENDERED AGENCY TO TAKE FROM BIOLOGICAL PARENTS A DOCUMENT OF SURRENDER. In order to eliminate any possibility of mischief and to make sure that the child has in fact been surrendered by its biological parents, it is necessary that the institution or centre or home for child care or social or child welfare agency to which the child is surrendered by the biological parents, should take from the biological parents a document of surrender duly signed by the biological parents and attested by at least two responsible persons and such document of surrender should not only contain the names of the biological parents and their address but also information in regard to the birth of the child and its background, health and development.

(V) BIOLOGICAL PARENTS' PREFERENCE FOR RELIGIOUS UPBRINGING OF THE CHILD TO BE RESPECTED. If the biological parents state a preference for the religious upbringing of the child, their wish should as far as possible be respected, but ultimately the interest of the child alone should be the sole guiding factor and the biological parents should be informed that the child may be given in adoption even to a foreigner who professes a religion different from that of the biological parents.

(VI) BIOLOGICAL PARENTS NOT TO TAKE DECISION ABOUT GIVING OF A CHILD IN ADOPTION BEFORE ITS BIRTH OR WITHIN A PERIOD OF THREE MONTHS THEREAFTER. The biological parents should not be induced or encouraged or even be permitted to take a decision in regard to giving of a child in adoption before the birth of the child or within a period of three months from the date of birth. This precaution is necessary because the biological parents must have reasonable time after the birth of the child to take a decision whether to rear up the child themselves or to relinquish it for adoption and moreover it may be necessary to allow some time to the child to overcome any health problems experienced after birth.

D. *Safeguards to be observed in so far as the child proposed to be taken in adoption is concerned*

(I) GOVERNMENT TO RECOGNISE ONLY AGENCIES ENJOYING GOOD REPUTATION AND WORKING IN THE FIELD OF CHILD CARE AND WELFARE FOR INTER-COUNTRY ADOPTIONS. Every application of a foreigner for taking a child in adoption shall be routed only through a recognised social or child welfare agency and an application for appointment of the foreigner as guardian of the child shall be made to the court only through such recognised social or child welfare agency. Accordingly, the Government of India or the Government of a State can *suo motu* or on an application made to it recognise any social or child welfare agency for the purpose of inter-country adoptions, provided such social or child welfare agency enjoys good reputation and is known for its work in the field of child care and welfare.

Before taking a decision to recognise any particular social or child welfare agency for the purpose of inter-country adoptions, the Government should do well to examine whether the social or child welfare agency has proper staff with professional social work experience, because otherwise it may not be possible for the social or child welfare agency to carry out satisfactorily the highly responsible task of ensuring proper placement of a child with a foreign adoptive family.

(II) GOVERNMENT NOT TO RECOGNISE ANY AGENCY SET UP ONLY FOR THE PURPOSE OF PLACING CHILDREN IN ADOPTION. The Government should not recognise an organisation or agency which has been set up only for the purpose of placing children in adoption. It is only an organisation or agency which is engaged in the work of child care and welfare which should be regarded as eligible for recognition, since inter-country adoption must be looked upon not as an independent activity by itself, but as part of child welfare programme so that it may not tend to degenerate into trading.

(III) MAINTENANCE OF ACCOUNTS AND AUDITING THEREOF BY AN AGENCY—A CONDITION OF RECOGNITION. The Government for recognising any social or child welfare agency for inter-country adoption must insist as condition of recognition that the social or child welfare agency shall maintain proper accounts which shall be audited by a chartered accountant at the end of every year.

(IV) ACCREDITED AGENCY NOT TO CHARGE FROM ANY FOREIGNER ANY AMOUNT IN EXCESS OF THAT ACTUALLY INCURRED. Any recognised social or child welfare agency shall not charge from the foreigner wishing to adopt a child any amount in excess of that actually incurred by way of legal or other expenses in connection with the application for appointment of guardian including such reasonable remuneration or honorarium for the work done and trouble taken in processing, filing and pursuing the application as may be fixed by the court.

(V) AN UNRECOGNISED AGENCY TO APPROACH A RECOGNISED AGENCY FOR PLACEMENT OF A CHILD IN INTER-COUNTRY ADOPTION. Since an application for appointment as guardian can, according to the principles and norms laid down, be processed only by a recognised social or child welfare agency and none else, any unrecognised institution, centre or agency which has a child under its care would have to approach a recognised social or child welfare agency if it desires such child to be given in inter-country adoption, and in that event it must send without any undue delay the name and particulars of such child to the recognised social or child welfare agency through which such child is proposed to be given in inter-country adoption.

(VI) EVERY RECOGNISED AGENCY TO MAINTAIN A REGISTER. Every recognised social or child welfare agency must maintain a register in which the names and particulars of all children proposed to be given in inter-country adoption through it must be entered.

(VII) EVERY RECOGNISED AGENCY TO PREPARE A CHILD STUDY REPORT IN RESPECT OF CHILDREN PROPOSED TO BE GIVEN IN INTER-COUNTRY ADOPTION. In regard to each child proposed to be given in inter-country adoption a recognised social or child welfare agency must prepare a child study report through a professional social worker giving all relevant information in regard to the child so as to help the foreigner to come to a decision whether or not to adopt the child and to understand the child, if he decides to adopt it as also to assist the court in coming to a decision whether it will be for the welfare of the child to be given in adoption to the foreigner wishing to adopt it. The child study report should contain as far as possible information in regard to the following matters: (*a*) identifying information, supported where possible by documents; (*b*) information about original parents, including their health and details of the mother's pregnancy and birth; (*c*) physical, intellectual and emotional development; (*d*) health report prepared by a registered medical practitioner preferably by a pediatrician; (*e*) recent photograph; (*f*) present environment—category of care (own home, foster home, institution etc.), relationships, routines and habits; (*g*) social worker's assessment and reasons for suggesting inter-country adoption.

(VIII) GOVERNMENT TO PREPARE A LIST OF RECOGNISED AGENCIES AND FURNISH SUCH LIST TO EACH FOREIGN COUNTRY AND EACH HIGH COURT IN THE COUNTRY. The Government of India should, with the assistance of the Governments of the States, prepare a list of recognised social or child welfare agencies with their names, addresses and other particulars and send such list to the appropriate department of the Government of each foreign country where Indian children are ordinarily taken in adoption so that the social or child welfare agencies licensed or recognised by the Government of such foreign country for inter-country adoptions would know which social or child welfare agency in India they should approach for processing an application of its national for taking an Indian child in adoption.

Such list shall also be sent by the Government of India to each High Court with a request to forward it to the district courts within its jurisdiction so that the High Courts and the district courts in the country would know which are the recognised social or child welfare agencies entitled to process an application for appointment of a foreigner as guardian.

Justice Bhagwati, however, favoured the setting up of a Central Adoption Resource Agency by the Government of India with regional branches at a few centres which are active in inter-country adoptions. Such Central Adoption Resource Agency can act as a clearing house of information in regard to children available for inter-country adoption and all applications by foreigners for taking Indian children in adoption can then be forwarded by the social or child welfare agency in the foreign country to such Central Adoption Resource Agency and the latter can in its turn forward them to one or the other of the recognised social or child welfare agencies in the country. Every social or child welfare agency taking children under its care can then be required to send to such Central Adoption Resource Agency the names and particulars of children under its care who are available for adoption and the names and particulars of such children can be entered in a register to be maintained by such Central Adoption Resource Agency. But until such Central Adoption Resource Agency is set up, an application of a foreigner for taking an Indian child in adoption must be routed through a recognised social or child welfare agency.

(IX) A RECOGNISED AGENCY TO PROVIDE ALL FACILITIES TO AN INDIAN FAMILY APPROACHING FOR TAKING A CHILD IN ADOPTION. Before any application for adoption from a foreigner is considered, every effort must be made by the recognised social or child welfare agency to find placement for the child by adoption in an Indian family. Whenever any Indian family approaches a recognised social or child welfare agency for taking a child in adoption, all facilities must be provided by such social or child welfare agency to the Indian family to have a look at the children available with it for adoption and if the Indian family wants to see the child study report in respect of any particular child, such child study report must also be made available to the Indian family in order to enable the Indian family to decide whether they would take the child in adoption. It is only if no Indian family comes forward to take a child in adoption within a maximum period of two months that the child may be regarded as available for inter-country adoption, subject only to one exception, namely, that if the child is handicapped or is in bad state of health needing urgent medical attention, which is not possible for the social or child welfare agency looking after the child to provide, the recognised social or child welfare agency need not wait for a period of two months and it can and must take immediate steps for the purpose of giving such child in inter-country adoption.

(X) A RECOGNISED AGENCY TO FURNISH PARTICULARS OF A CHILD TO A FOREIGNER SEEKING ADOPTION AND INSIST UPON APPROVAL OF A SPECIFIC KNOWN CHILD. The recognised social or child welfare agency should, on receiving an application of a foreigner for adoption through a licensed or recognised social or child welfare agency in a foreign country, consider which child would be suitable for being given in adoption to the foreigner and would fit into the environment of his family and community and send the photograph and child study report of such child to the foreigner for the purpose of obtaining his approval to the adoption of such child. The practice of accepting a general approval of the foreigner to adopt any child should not be allowed, because it is possible that if the foreigner has not seen the photograph of the child and has not studied the child study report and a child is selected for him by the recognised social or child welfare agency in India on the basis of his general approval, he may on the arrival of the child in his country find that he does not like the child or that the child is not suitable in which event the interest of the child would be seriously prejudiced. The recognised social or child welfare agency must therefore insist upon approval of a specific known child and once that approval is obtained, that recognised social or child welfare agency should immediately without any undue delay proceed to make an application for appointment of the foreigner as guardian of the child. Such application would have to be made in the court within whose jurisdiction the child ordinarily resides and it must be accompanied by copies of the home study reports, the child study report and other certificates and documents forwarded by the social or child welfare agency sponsoring the application of the foreigner for taking the child in adoption.

(XI) AN AGENCY LOOKING AFTER THE CHILD SELECTED BY A PROSPECTIVE ADOPTIVE PARENT TO RECEIVE MAINTENANCE EXPENSES AT A RATE NOT EXCEEDING RS. 60 PER DAY. A social or child welfare agency which is looking after the child selected by a prospective adoptive parent, may legitimately receive from such prospective adoptive parent maintenance expenses at a rate not exceeding Rs. 60 per day (this outer limit being subject to revision by the Ministry of Social Welfare, Government of India, from time to time) from the date of selection of the child by him until the date the child leaves for going to its new home as also medical expenses including hospitalisation charges, if any, actually incurred by such social or child welfare agency for the child. But the claim for payment of such maintenance charges and medical expenses shall be submitted to the prospective adoptive parent through the recognised social or child welfare agency which has processed the application for guardianship and payment in respect of such claim shall not be received directly by the social or child welfare agency making the claim but shall be paid only through the recognised social or child welfare agency.

(XII) VOLUNTARY DONATION BY A FOREIGNER TO AN AGENCY NOT PROHIBITED. A foreigner is not prevented from making voluntary donation to any social or child welfare agency but no such donation from a prospective adoptive parent shall be received until after the child has reached the country of its prospective adoptive parent.

This provision was made, says Justice Bhagwati, in order to prevent receipt of money by way of consideration for giving the child in adoption.

(XIII) DUTIES TO BE PERFORMED AND DISCHARGED BY A RECOGNISED AGENCY IN INTER-STATE ADOPTION. The recognised social or child welfare agency through which an application of a foreigner for taking a child in adoption is routed must, before offering a child in adoption, make sure that the child is free to be adopted. Where the parents have relinquished the child for adoption and there is a document of surrender, the child must obviously be taken to be free for adoption. So also where a child is an orphan or destitute or abandoned child and it has not been possible by the concerned social or child welfare agency to trace its parents or where the child is committed by a juvenile court to an institution, centre or home for committed children and is declared to be a destitute by the juvenile court, it must be regarded as free for adoption.

The recognised social or child welfare agency must place sufficient material before the court to satisfy it that the child is legally available for adoption.

It is also necessary that the recognised social or child welfare agency must satisfy itself, first, that there is no impediment in the way of the child entering the country of the prospective adoptive parent; secondly, that the travel documents for the child can be obtained at the appropriate time and lastly, that the law of the country of the prospective adoptive parent permits legal adoption of the child and that on such legal adoption being concluded, the child would acquire the same legal status and rights of inheritance as a natural born child and would be granted citizenship in the country of adoption and it should file along with the application for guardianship, a certificate reciting such satisfaction.

(XIV) INTER-COUNTRY ADOPTION DESIRABLE BEFORE THE CHILD COMPLETES THE AGE OF THREE YEARS. If a child is to be given in inter-country adoption, it would be desirable that it is given in such adoption as far as possible before it completes the age of three years. The reason is that if a child is adopted before it attains the age of understanding, it is always easier for it to get assimilated and integrated in the new environment in which it may find itself on being adopted by a foreign parent. Comparatively it may be somewhat difficult for a grown up child to get acclimatized to new surroundings in a different land and sometimes a problem may also arise whether foreign adoptive parents would be able to win the love and affection of such grown up child. This is, however, not to suggest for a moment, observed Justice Bhagwati, that children above the age of three years should not be given in inter-country adoption. There can be no hard and fast rule in this connection. Even children between the ages of three and seven years may be able to assimilate themselves in the new surroundings without any difficulty and there is no reason why they should be denied the benefit of family warmth and affection in the home of foreign parents, merely because they have past the age of three years. Even children above the age of seven years may be given in inter-country adoption but it was recommended that in such cases, their wishes may be ascertained if they are in a position to indicate any preference.

E. *Procedures to be followed by the court when an application for appointment of a foreigner as guardian of a child is made*

(I) ISSUING NOTICE UNDER SECTION 11 OF THE GUARDIANS AND WARDS ACT 1890 TO BIOLOGICAL PARENTS AND IN NEWSPAPER TO BE DISPENSED WITH. Section 11 of the Guardians and Wards Act 1890 provides for notice of the application to be issued to various persons including the parents of the child if they are residing in any State to which the Act extends. But, it was held[2] that no notice under this section should be issued to the biological parents of the child, since it would create considerable amount of embarrassment and hardship if the biological parents were then to come forward and oppose the application of the prospective adoptive parent for guardianship of the child. Moreover, the biological parents would then come to know who is the person taking the child in adoption and with this knowledge they would at any time be able to trace the whereabouts of the child and they may try to contact the child resulting in emotional and psychological disturbance for the child which might affect his future happiness. The possibility also cannot be ruled out that if the biological parents know who are the adoptive parents they may try to extort money from the adoptive parents. It is, therefore, absolutely essential that the biological parents should not have any opportunity of knowing who are the adoptive parents taking the child in adoption and, therefore, notice of the application for guardianship should not be given to the biological parents. For the same reasons, notice of the application for guardianship should also not be published in any newspaper.

2 *Lakshmi Kant Pandey* v *Union of India* (1984)2 SCC 244.
AUTHORS' NOTE: Judgment of the court was delivered by Bhagwati, J. on behalf of himself, R.S. Pathak and Amarendra Nath Sen, JJ.

(II) COURT TO PASS ORDER ON BEING SATISFIED ITSELF AS TO COMPLIANCE OF NORMS AND PROCEDURE PRESCRIBED FOR INTER-COUNTRY ADOPTION. It is the duty of the court to satisfy itself whether the principles and norms as also the procedure laid down in the judgment[2] delivered by Justice Bhagwati have been observed and followed; whether the foreigner will be a suitable adoptive parent for the child and the child will be able to integrate and assimilate itself in the family and community of the foreigner and will be able to get love and affection of family life as also moral and material stability and security; and, whether it will be in the interest of the child to be taken in adoption by the foreigner. If the court is satisfied then and then only it will make an order appointing the foreigner as guardian of the child permitting him to remove the child to his own country with a view to eventual adoption.

(III) COURT TO IMPOSE CERTAIN CONDITIONS IN THE ORDER. The court will introduce a condition in the order that the foreigner who is appointed guardian shall make proper provision by way of deposit or bond or otherwise to enable the child to be repatriated to India should it become necessary for any reason.

The order will also include a condition that the foreigner who is appointed guardian shall submit to the court as also to the social or child welfare agency processing the application for guardianship progress reports of the child along with a recent photograph quarterly during the first two years and half yearly for the next three years.

The court may also while making the order permit the social or child welfare agency which has taken care of the child pending its selection for adoption to receive such amount as the court thinks fit from the foreigner who is appointed guardian of such child. The order appointing the guardian shall carry and attach to the order a photograph of the child duly countersigned by an officer of the court.

(IV) COURT TO COMPLETE PROCEDURE WITHIN TWO MONTHS FROM THE DATE OF FILING OF THE APPLICATION. The entire procedure shall be completed by the court expeditiously and as far as possible within a period of two months from the date of filing of the application for guardianship of the child.

(V) PROCEEDINGS IN COURT BE IN CAMERA. The proceedings on the application for guardianship should be held by the court in camera and they should be regarded as confidential and as soon as an order is made on the application for guardianship, the entire proceedings including the papers and documents should be sealed.

(VI) INTIMATION OF THE ORDER BE GIVEN TO THE MINISTRY OF SOCIAL WELFARE, GOVERNMENT OF INDIA AND OF THE STATE. When an order appointing guardian of a child is made by the court, immediate intimation of the same shall be given to the Ministry of Social Welfare, Government of India, as also the Ministry of Social Welfare of the Government of the State in which the court is situate and copies of such order shall also be forwarded to the two respective ministries of social welfare.

(VII) MINISTRY OF SOCIAL WELFARE, GOVERNMENT OF INDIA TO MAINTAIN REGISTER. The Ministry of Social Welfare, Government of India, shall maintain a register containing names and other particulars of the children in respect of whom orders for appointment of guardian have been made as also names, addresses and other particulars of the prospective adoptive parents who have been appointed such guardians and who have been permitted to take away the children for the purpose of adoption.

(VIII) GOVERNMENT OF INDIA TO SEND TO ITS EMBASSY OR HIGH COMMISSION PARTICULARS OF ADOPTIVE PARENTS AND ADOPTED CHILDREN. The Government of India will also send to the Indian Embassy or High Commission in the country of the prospective adoptive parents from time to time the names, addresses and other particulars of such prospective adoptive parents together with particulars of the children taken by them and request the Embassy or High Commission to maintain an unobtrusive watch over the welfare and progress of such children in order to safeguard against any possible maltreatment, exploitation or use for ulterior purposes and to immediately report any instance of maltreatment, negligence or exploitation to the Government of India for suitable action.

6 Clarifications issued on problems faced in implementing the principles and norms as laid down Social and child welfare agencies engaged in placement of Indian children in inter-country adoption experienced various difficulties in implementing the principles and norms laid down by Justice Bhagwati and filed applications before the apex court seeking clarifications and alterations and those applications were disposed of with Justice Bhagwati issuing clarifications[3] as under:

3 *Laxmi Kant Pandey* v *Union of India* 1985 (Supp) SCC 701.
AUTHORS' NOTE: The judgment of the court was delivered by Bhagwati, CJ. on behalf of himself, R.S. Pathak and Amarendra Nath Sen, JJ.

(I) SCRUTINIZING AGENCY APPOINTED BY THE COURT NOT TO BE INVOLVED IN PLACEMENT OF CHILDREN IN ADOPTION. The scrutinizing agency appointed by the court for the purpose of assisting it in reaching the conclusion whether it would be in the interest of the child to be given in adoption to the foreign parents must not in any manner be involved in placement of children in adoption. The scrutinizing agency must be an expert body having experience in the area of child welfare and it should have nothing to do with placement of children in adoption for otherwise objective and impartial evaluation may not be possible. Where, therefore, there is an institution or agency which is engaged in the placement of children in adoption, it should not be appointed as scrutinizing agency by the court.

The two scrutinizing agencies usually commissioned by the courts are the Indian Council of Social Welfare and the Indian Council of Child Welfare. These two institutions or agencies have acquitted themselves very creditably so far and the courts may, therefore, continue to entrust scrutinizing work to them, but there may also be other scrutinizing agencies which can be employed for this purpose. They must, however, be basically child welfare agencies and must not be engaged in placing children in adoption.

(II) STEPS TO BE TAKEN IN CASE OF DISRUPTION IN THE FAMILY OF THE PETITIONER. To what was already laid down in this respect,[4] Justice Bhagwati suggested that additionally the social or child welfare agency sponsoring the application should also, in the event of disruption of the family of the foreigner before adoption can be effected, give intimation of this fact to the Indian Embassy or High Commission, as the case may be, and the Indian Embassy or High Commission shall also be kept informed about the whereabouts of the child so that they can take the necessary steps for ensuring that the child is properly taken care of and a suitable alternative placement for it is found. If a disruption in the family of the foreigner takes place after the child is adopted, nothing can be done by the social or child welfare agency sponsoring the application, because, on adoption, the child would acquire the nationality of its adoptive parents and would then be entitled to all the rights of a national in that country.

4 Vide under the head "Normative and procedural safeguards to be followed in case of adoption of destitute or abandoned children and children living in social or child welfare centres, sub-index 5B(IX) at p. 53.

(III) ROLE TO BE PLAYED BY A SCRUTINIZING AGENCY IN THE PROCEDURE RELATING TO INTER-COUNTRY ADOPTIONS. The scrutinizing agency should not be asked to make any inquiries before a child is offered in adoption to a foreigner or a petition for appointment of a foreigner as guardian is filed in court. The primary responsibility for ensuring that the child is legally free for adoption must be that of the social or child welfare agency processing the application of the foreigner for guardianship of the child. Whatever inquiries are necessary for the purpose of satisfying itself that the child has been voluntarily relinquished by its biological parents after understanding all the implications of adoption must be the responsibility of the social or child welfare agency processing the application for guardianship. But so far as the scrutinizing agency is concerned, it should not come into the picture at this stage. It has a vital role to play after a foreigner has approved of the child to be taken in adoption and a petition is filed in court for appointment of the foreigner as guardian of the child and it is at that stage that the scrutinizing agency is expected to assist the court in coming to the conclusion whether it would be in the interest of the child to be given in adoption to the foreigner.

The scrutinizing agency should not at that stage try to ascertain who are the biological parents of the child and whether they are willing to take back the child. That is primarily the responsibility of the social or child welfare agency processing the application. The court should, in order to make sure that the child is legally free for adoption, require the social or child welfare agency processing the application to place material before the court stating what efforts have been made to trace the biological parents and what are the circumstances in which the child came into the possession of such social or child welfare agency. Where the court feels some doubt as to how the child has been obtained and in what manner, the court may ask the scrutinizing agency to make inquiries with a view to finding out how the social or child welfare agency processing the application has got the child and if the child has been obtained by such social or child welfare agency from another institution or agency, how that institution or agency got the child and from what source and in what manner and the scrutinizing agency may then make discreet inquiries for this purpose without disclosing to anyone that the child is sought to be given in adoption. The court may also in an appropriate case where it has some doubt ask the scrutinizing agency to inquire whether the child has been voluntarily surrendered by the biological parents or whether such relinquishment has been obtained by fraudulent means. The scrutinizing agency should, while scrutinizing the application, adopt a sympathetic and sensitive approach with in-depth understanding of the dynamics of human behaviour.

(IV) SOCIAL OR CHILD WELFARE AGENCY ENGAGED IN PLACING CHILDREN IN ADOPTION NOT TO READILY ASSUME THAT CHILDREN FOUND ABANDONED ARE LEGALLY FREE FOR ADOPTION. The social or child welfare agency engaged in the work of placing children in adoption should not readily assume that children including cradle babies who are found abandoned are legally free for adoption. Such children must be produced before the juvenile court so that further inquires can be made and their parents or guardians can be traced. In States where there is no Children Act in force, such children should be referred to the Social Welfare Department for making further inquiries and tracing their parents or guardians. This procedure should be completed at the latest within three months and no children who are found abandoned should be deemed to be legally free for adoption until the juvenile court or the Social Welfare Department declares them as destitutes or abandoned. It should also be impressed upon the juvenile courts that when children are selected for adoption, release orders should be passed by them expeditiously and without delay and proper vigilance in this behalf must be exercised by the High Courts.

(V) ROLE THE COURT TO PLAY IN ENTERTAINING AN APPLICATION FOR INTER-COUNTRY ADOPTION. No court in a State will entertain an application for appointment of a foreigner as guardian of a child which has been brought from another State, if there is a social or child welfare agency in that other State which has been recognised by the Government of India for inter-country adoption. The social or child welfare agency processing the application for guardianship should then be directed to send the child to the recognised social or child welfare agency in the other State, so that whatever proceedings are necessary for giving the child in adoption may be instituted by that social or child welfare agency and in such an event, the complete details of the case history and background including the home study report, the child study report, if any, and all other information relating to the child should be made available to the latter social or child welfare agency. If there is no recognised social or child welfare agency in the State where the child is found or obtained, the child shall be transferred to a recognised social or child welfare agency at the nearest place in the immediate neighbouring State.

(VI) FOREIGN SPONSORING AGENCY TO SUBMIT PROGRESS REPORTS AS DIRECTED.[5] It is necessary that progress reports as directed must be submitted to the court and to the social or child welfare agency in India quarterly during the first two years and half yearly for the next three years by the social or child welfare agency sponsoring the application for adoption by a foreigner, but after adoption had taken place the courts may not insist on strict observance of this requirement. The order to be made by the court should also provide that progress reports shall be submitted by the social or child welfare agency sponsoring the application of the foreigner until adoption is effected. That would provide greater assurance because it may not be possible to take any action if the foreigner fails to provide progress reports, but if the social or child welfare agency sponsoring the application for guardianship fails to submit progress reports, the court can in future decline to entertain any application for guardianship where the foreigner seeking appointment as guardian is sponsored by such social or child welfare agency.

(VII) ROLE TO BE PLAYED BY REPRESENTATIVE OF FOREIGN AGENCIES IN INTER-COUNTRY ADOPTION. There can be no objection to a foreign social or child welfare agency having its representative in India. It would undoubtedly help to ensure proper and timely medical care for the child selected for adoption as also smooth carrying out of legal formalities in connection with guardianship proceedings and travel arrangements for the child to go to the country of its prospective foreign parents and also facilitate communication between the foreign parents and the sponsoring social or child welfare agency on the one hand and the social or child welfare agency processing the application for guardianship on the other. There is, therefore, no objection to a foreign social or child welfare agency having a representative in India, but it is necessary, Justice Bhagwati noted, to lay down certain parameters within which such representative can be allowed to operate. In the first place, the representative should be an Indian citizen with a degree or diploma in social work coupled with experience in child welfare. Secondly, the representative should be acting only for one foreign social or child welfare agency and not more nor should be working on a free lance basis. It would also be desirable to limit the sphere of operation of the representative to a particular geographical area so that he is able to

5 Vide under the head "Normative and Procedural safeguards to be followed in case of adoption of destitute or abandoned children and children living in social or child welfare centres sub-index 5B(*viii*) at p. 53.

attend to his functions and duties properly and diligently. The representative should have a general power of attorney to act in India on behalf of the foreign social or child welfare agency and he should also have the authority to operate banking accounts in the name of the foreign social or child welfare agency with the permission of the Reserve Bank of India. It is insisted that, in order to prevent taking of children from needy parents by offering them monetary inducement and to eliminate trafficking in children, the representative of the foreign social or child welfare agency should not be permitted to go scouting for children or to receive children directly from parents. He should be allowed to act as representative only if he is recognised as such by the Central Government and such recognition may be given by the Central Government subject to the condition that the various requirements set out above are complied with by such representative.

(VIII) A FOREIGNER TO ROUTE HIS APPLICATION FOR ADOPTION THROUGH AGENCY OWNED OR OPERATED BY THE GOVERNMENT WHEN THAT EXISTS. If there is a social or child welfare agency owned or operated by the Government in a foreign country, it would not be necessary for a foreigner to route his application through a recognised social or child welfare agency within his country and he can approach a recognised social or child welfare agency in India through such Government agency.

(IX) IN CASE OF A GOVERNMENT AGENCY ROUTING APPLICATIONS, PROGRESS REPORTS REGARDING THE CHILD TO BE SUBMITTED BY FOREIGN PARENTS. Where there is a Government agency in a foreign country through which applications for taking children in adoption are routed, as in Sweden, it may not be possible to insist that the progress reports in regard to the child should be submitted by the Government agency and in such a case it may be enough to provide in the order to be made by the court that the progress reports shall be submitted by the foreign parents through the Government agency.

(X) DIRECTION TO KEEP SECURITY DEPOSIT IN COURT MODIFIED.[6] It should be a matter to be decided by the court in the exercise of its judicial discretion. Of course, it may not ordinarily insist on making of the deposit by the foreigner but in an appropriate case, if it so thinks fit, it may pass such an order. The execution of a bond would ordinarily be sufficient. The bond should be by way of security for repatriation of the

6 Vide under the head "Procedure to be followed by the court when on application for appointment of a foreigner as a guardian of a child is made," sub-index 5E(III) at p. 62.

child to India in case it becomes necessary to do so as also for ensuring adoption of the child within the period of two years. The bond may be executed by the foreigner who is appointed guardian of the child, but there may be difficulty in enforcing such bond, unless the bond is executed in favour of the Indian Diplomatic Mission in the country of the foreigner. It might, therefore, be safer to take the bond from the representative of the foreign social or child welfare agency in India so that if the condition of the bond is violated, the court can proceed to enforce the bond against such representative who would be an Indian national. There is also another alternative which may be adopted by the court. The court may take the bond from the social or child welfare agency which may in its turn take a corresponding bond from the sponsoring social or child welfare agency in the foreign country. Ordinarily, the sponsoring social or child welfare agency would honour the bond in case the condition of the bond is broken, because if it fails to do so, no recognised social or child welfare agency in India would in future deal with it. But, though this alternative may, in a given case, be adopted by the court, where the recognised social or child welfare agency processing the application is ready to give the bond, the court should not insist upon execution of the bond by such foreign social or child welfare agency. It would be sufficient to take the bond from the representative of the foreign social or child welfare agency in India or to insist on the bond being executed by the foreigner in favour of the Indian Diplomatic Mission abroad.

(XI) IN CASE OF FAILURE TO COMPLETE THE ADOPTION PROCESS WITHIN THE SCHEDULE TIME, APPLICATION TO BE MADE FOR EXTENSION OF TIME. Where it is not possible for the foreigner to complete the adoption process within two years, an application should be made to the court for extension of time for making the adoption and the court may grant appropriate extension of time.

(XII) EXPENSES WHICH A RECOGNISED SOCIAL OR CHILD WELFARE AGENCY MAY RECOVER FROM ADOPTIVE PARENTS. Justice Bhagwati, on behalf of the Court, clarified that the sum of Rs. 60 per day as fixed earlier[7] represents the outer limit of the maintenance expenses which may be recovered from the prospective adoptive parents but it does not represent the rate at which maintenance expenses should be recoverable in every case. Justice Bhagwati further pointed out that when the court makes

7 Vide under the head "safeguards to be observed in so far as the child proposed to be taken in adoption is concerned", sub-index 5D(XI) at p. 59.

an order appointing a foreigner as guardian, the court should look into the question of recovery of maintenance expenses and sanction the amount to be paid by the foreigner to the social or child welfare agency by way of re-imbursement of maintenance expenses and only such amount as may be sanctioned by the court shall be recoverable.

So far as surgical or medical expenses incurred on the child are concerned, they should also be recoverable from the adoptive parents by the social or child welfare agency against production of bills and vouchers.

The recognised social or child welfare agency processing the application must also be entitled to recover from the foreigner who is sought to be appointed guardian of the child, costs incurred in preparing and filing the application and prosecuting it in court. Such expenses may include legal expenses, administrative expenses, preparation of child study report, preparation of medical and I.Q. reports, passport and visa expenses and conveyance expenses and they may be fixed by the court at such figure not exceeding Rs. 4,000 as may be thought fit by the court.

Justice Bhagwati is now of view that in the present day economic scenario the amount as suggested in the case seems insufficient and inadequate and the court may fix such amount as the maximum limit as may be deemed fit and proper taking into account the price index factor.

(XIII) PROCEEDINGS FOR APPOINTMENT OF GUARDIAN OF THE CHILD TO BE DISPOSED OF WITHIN SPECIFIC TIME LIMIT AS FIXED. Proceedings for appointment of guardian of the child with a view to its eventual adoption must be disposed of at the earliest and in any event not later than two months from the date of filing of the application. The High Courts shall call for returns from the district courts within their respective jurisdiction showing every two months as to how many applications for appointment of guardian are pending, when they were filed and if more than two months have passed since the date of their filing, why they have not been disposed of up to the date of the return. If any application for guardianship is not disposed of by the district courts within a period of two months and there is no satisfactory explanation, the High Courts must take a serious view of the matter.

(XIV) COURT NOT TO INSIST ON FOREIGN PARENTS' VISIT TO INDIA FOR APPROVING OF THE CHILD. The court dealing with an application for appointment of foreign parents as guardian need not insist on the foreign parents or even one of them coming down to India for the purpose of approving the child. Even in cases where the child is an older or handicapped child, it is not necessary to require the foreign parents to come down to India, because a complete dossier of the child consisting of photographs, detailed medical report, child study report and other relevant particulars is always forwarded to the sponsoring social or child welfare agency in the foreign country and it is after careful consideration of this dossier and a full and detailed discussion under the sponsoring social or child welfare agency that the foreign parents decide to accept the child to be taken in adoption and proceed further in the matter through the sponsoring social or child welfare agency.

(XV) INDIAN FAMILY TO GET PRIORITY IN ADOPTION. Where there is a voluntary co-ordinating agency or any other centralised agency which maintains a register of children available for adoption as also a register of Indian adoptive parents, it would be enough to wait for a period of three to four weeks to take a child in adoption. The voluntary co-ordinating or centralised agency can immediately contact the Indian family which is on its register as prospective adoptive parents and inform them that a particular child is available for inter-country adoption. But even where it is not possible to find an Indian family which is prepared to take a child in adoption and it is cleared for within the country adoption, the first priority for taking the child in adoption should be given to Indians residing abroad and if no such Indians are available, then to adoptive couples where at least one parent is of Indian origin; failing which the offer should go to foreign parents.

7 Conclusion The requirement of society is not static, says Justice Bhagwati. It is changing along with the economic and cultural changes. In ancient times, it was not contemplated that the foreign parents would adopt children from India under certain terms yet with the change in time it has happened. In the rural areas of India one can see crystal clear that poverty and lack of education of parents combined with little or no access to essential services of health, sanitation and education are preventing the realisation of full human potential of children making them more likely to grow up uneducated, unskilled and unproductive. Justice Bhagwati asserts that if it is not possible to provide to children decent family life where they can grow up under the loving care and attention of parents and enjoy the basic necessities of life such as nutritive food, heath care and education and lead a life of basic human dignity with stability and security, moral as well as material, there should not be objection of the children to be given in adoption to foreign parents. But the learned Judge issued a note of caution. While supporting inter-country adoption, "it is necessary to bear in mind that the primary object of giving the child in adoption being the welfare of the child, great care has to be exercised in permitting the child to be given in adoption to foreign parents, lest the child may be neglected or abandoned by the adoptive parents in the foreign country or the adoptive parents may not be able to provide to the child a life of moral or material security or the child may be subjected to moral or sexual abuse or forced labour or experimention for medical or other research and may be placed in a worse situation than that in his own country."[8]

In the context as above, the principles and the norms for observation and the procedure to be followed in giving a child in adoption to foreign parents laid down by Justice Bhagwati in *Lakshmi Kant Pandey's* case[8] and discussed above are of paramount importance inasmuch as there is no existing law in India governing adoption of a child from the biological parents to foreign adoptive parents. The said judgment of Justice Bhagwati is a landmark in the judicial history and the jurisprudence of adoption in particular.

AUTHORS' NOTE. The Central Government has prepared in 2007 new adoption rules to spare prospective foreign parents from harassment and delays of over a year in adopting Indian children. Foreigners will no longer need clearance from the State Governments adoption co-ordination agency. Under the new rules, the Government will be responsible for identifying the agency in India that can offer a child for adoption. Now, foreigners have to apply first to their Governments which have to find out and get in touch with the adoption agencies in India on their own.

8 *Lakshmi Kant Pandey* v *Union of India* (1984)2 SCC 244 at p. 253.

"India is one nation and we are all Indians first and Indians last"

— P.N. BHAGWATI[1]

4

India as a Nation– Evolution of the Concept

SYNOPSIS

1 History of evolution The history of India over the past centuries, says Justice Bhagwati,[1] bears witness to the fact that India was at no time a single political unit. Even during the reign of the Maurya dynasty, though a large part of the country was under the sovereignty of the Mauryan Kings, there were considerable portions of the territory which were under the rule of independent kingdoms. So also during the Moghul rule which extended over large parts of the territory of India, there were independent rulers who enjoyed political sovereignty over the territories of their respective kingdoms. It is an interesting fact of history that India was forged into a nation neither on account of a common language nor on account of the continued existence of a single political regime over its territories but on account of a common culture evolved over the centuries. It is cultural unity—something more fundamental and enduring than any other bond which may unite the people of a country together—which has welded this country into a

1 *Dr. Pradeep Jain* v *Union of India* (1984)3 SCC 654.
AUTHORS' NOTE: The Judgment of the Court was delivered by Bhagwati, J. for himself, A.N. Sen and Ranganath Misra, JJ.

nation. But, until the advent of the British rule, it was not constituted into a single political unit. There were throughout the period of history for which we have fairly authenticated account, various kingdoms and principalities which were occasionally engaged in conflict with one another. During the British rule, Justice Bhagwati says,[2] India became a compact political unit having one single political regime over its entire territories and this led to the evolution of the concept of a nation. This concept of one nation took firm roots in the minds and hearts of the people during the struggle for independence under the leadership of Mahatma Gandhi. He has rightly been called the Father of the Nation because it was he who awakened in the people of this country a sense of national consciousness and instilled in them a high sense of patriotism without which it is not possible to build a country into nationhood. By the time the Constitution of India came to be enacted, insurgent India, breaking a new path of non-violent revolution and fighting to free itself from the shackles of foreign domination, had emerged into nationhood and "the people of India" were inspired by a new enthusiasm, a high and noble spirit of sacrifice and above all, a strong sense of nationalism and in the Constitution which they framed, they set about the task of a strong nation based on certain cherished values for which they had fought.

The Preamble of the Constitution was, therefore, framed, continues Justice Bhagwati,[2] 'with the great care and deliberation so that it reflects the high purpose and noble objective of the Constitution makers. The Preamble declares in highly emotive words pregnant with meaning and significance:

WE, THE PEOPLE OF INDIA, having solemly resolved to constitute India into a SOVEREIGN SOCIALIST SECULAR DEMOCRATIC REPUBLIC and to secure to all its citizens:

JUSTICE, social, economic and political;

LIBERTY of thought, expression, belief, faith and worship;

EQUALITY of status and of opportunity;
and to promote among them all;

FRATERNITY assuring the dignity of the individual and the unity and integrity of the Nation;

2 *Dr. Pradeep Jain* v *Union of India* (1984)3 SCC 654.
AUTHORS' NOTE: The Judgment of the Court was delivered by Bhagwati, J. for himself, A.N. Sen and Ranganath Misra, JJ.

IN OUR CONSTITUENT ASSEMBLY this twenty-sixth day of November, 1949, do HEREBY ADOPT, ENACT AND GIVE TO OURSELVES THIS CONSTITUTION.

These words, says Justice Bhagwati, embody the hopes and aspirations of the people and capture and reproduce the social, economic and political philosophy underlying the Constitution and running through the warp and woof of its entire fabric. It is significant to note, points out Justice Bhagwati,[2] that the Preamble emphasises that the people who have given to themselves this glorious document are the people of India, the people of this great nation called India and it gives expression to the resolve of the people of India to constitute India into a sovereign socialist secular democratic republic and to promote among all its citizens fraternity assuring the dignity of the individual and the unity and integrity of the nation. The Constitution makers were aware of the past history of the country and they were also conscious that the divisive forces of regionalism, linguism and communalism may one day raise their ugly head and threaten the unity and integrity of the nation, particularly in the context of the partition of India and the ever present danger of the imperialist forces adopting new stratagems, apparently innocuous, but calculated to destabilise India and re-establish their hegemony and, therefore, they laid great emphasis on the unity and integrity of the nation in the very Preamble of the Constitution.

Article 1 of the Constitution proceeds to declare that India shall be a Union of States but emphasizes that though a Union of States, it is still on nation with one citizenship.

The Constitution recognizes only one domicile. Article 5 of the Constitution is clear and explicit on this point and it refers only to one domicile, namely, "domicile in the territory of India".

Part II dealing with citizenship recognises only Indian citizenship: it does not recognise citizenship of any State forming part of the Union.

Then follow Articles 14 and 15 which are intended to strike against discrimination and arbitrariness in State action, whether legislative or administrative. They read as follows:

Article 14. The State shall not deny to any person equality before the law or the equal protection of the laws within the territory of India.

Article 15. (1) The State shall not discriminate against any citizen on grounds only of religion, race, caste, sex, place of birth or any of them.

(2) No citizens shall, on grounds only of religion, race, caste, sex, place of birth or any of them, be subject to any disability, liability, restriction or condition with regard to—

- (*a*) access to shops, public restaurants, hotels and places of public entertainment; or
- (*b*) the use of wells, tanks, bathing ghats, roads and places of public resort maintained wholly or partly out of State funds or dedicated to the use of the general public.

(3) Nothing in this article shall prevent the State from making any special provision for women and children.

(4) Nothing in this article or in clause (2) of Article 29 shall prevent the State from making any special provision for the advancement of any socially and educationally backward classes of citizens or for the Scheduled Castes and the Scheduled Tribes.

Article 19(1) again recognises the essential unity and integrity of the nation and reinforces the concept of one nation by providing in clauses (*d*) and (*e*) that every citizen shall have the right to move freely throughout the territory of India and to reside and settle in any part of the territory of India.

Article 301 declares that subject to the other provisions of Part XIII, trade, commerce and intercourse throughout the territory of India shall be free.

Then there are situations envisaged in certain articles of the Constitution such as Articles 353 and 356 where the executive power of a State forming part of the Union is exercisable by the Central Government or subject to the directions of the Central Government.

Thus, the entire country, emphasizes Justice Bhagwati, is taken as one nation. There is only one citizenship, namely, citizenship of India, and every citizen has a right to move freely throughout the territory of India and to reside and settle in any part of India, irrespective of the place where he is born or the language which he speaks or the religion which he professes and he is guaranteed freedom of trade, commerce and intercourse throughout the territory of India and is entitled to equality before the law and equal protection of the law with other citizens in every part of the territory of India. Every effort of the Constitution makers is directed towards emphasizing, maintaining and preserving the unity and integrity of the nation.

India has also one single unified legal system which extends throughout the country. It is not possible to say that a distinct and separate system of law prevails in each State forming part of the Union of India. The legal system which prevails throughout the territory of India is one single indivisible system with a single unified justicing system having the Supreme Court of India at the apex of the hirarchy, which lays down the law for the entire country. It is true that with respect to subjects set out in List II of the Seventh Schedule to the Constitution, the States have the power to make laws and subject to the overriding power of Parliament, the States can also make laws with respect to subjects enumerated in List III of the Seventh Schedule to the Constitution, but the legal system under the rubric of which such laws are made by the States is a single legal system which may truly be described as the Indian legal system. It would be absurd to suggest that the legal system varies from State to State or that the legal system of a State is different from the legal system of the Union of India, merely because with respect to the subjects within their legislative competence, the State have power to make laws.'

2 Nation's integrity in peril Justice Bhagwati laments that today the integrity of the country is threatened by the forces of linguism and communalism and regional, linguistic and communal loyalties are gaining ascendancy in national life and seeking to tear apart and destroy national integrity. Owing to the emergence of narrow parochial loyalties fostered by interested parties with a view to gaining advantage for themselves, a serious threat has developed to the unity and integrity of the nation and the very concept of India as a nation is in peril. The threat is obtrusive at some places while at others it is still silent and is masquerading under the guise of apparently innocuous and rather attractive claptrap. The reason is that, says Justice Bhagwati,[3] when the Constitution came into operation, we took the spirit of nationhood for granted and paid little attention to nourish it, unmindful of the fact that it was a hard-won concept. Justice Bhagwati pinpoints[3] 'sons of the soil' claim as one of the demands that threatens the integrity of the nation. We allowed "sons of the soil' demands to develop claiming special treatment on the basis of residence in the concerned State, because recognising and conceding such demands had a populist appeal. The result is that 'sons of the soil' claims, though not altogether

3 *Dr. Pradeep Jain* v *Union of India* (1984)3 SCC 654.
AUTHORS' NOTE: The Judgment of the Court was delivered by Bhagwati, J. for himself, A.N. Sen and Ranganath Misra, JJ.

illegitimate if confined within reasonable bounds, are breaking as under the unity and integrity of the nation by fostering and strengthening narrow parochial loyalties based on language and residence within a State.

3 Caution We tend to forget, cautions Justice Bhagwati,[4] that India is one nation and we are all Indians first and Indians last. It is time we remind ourselves what the great visionary and builder of modern India, Jawaharlal Nehru said, "Who dies if India lives; who lives if India dies?" We must realise, and this is unfortunate that many in public life tend to overlook, sometimes out of ignorance of the forces of history and sometimes deliberately with a view to promoting their self-interest, that national interest must inevitably and for ever prevail over any other considerations proceeding from regional, linguistic or communal attachments.

What Justice Bhagwati observed and said 24 years ago has even greater force in the context of the present day situation in the country.

4 *Dr. Pradeep Jain* v *Union of India* (1984)3 SCC 654.
AUTHORS' NOTE: The Judgment of the Court was delivered by Bhagwati, J. for himself, A.N. Sen and Ranganath Misra, JJ.

"Ours is a socialist republic with social justice as the signature tune of our Constitution."

P. N. BHAGWATI[1]

5

Constitution–A Living Organism

SYNOPSIS

1 *Hussainara Khatoon* v *Home Secretary, State of Bihar* AIR 1979 SC 1360.

1 Introduction The Constitution is neither a dry parchment nor a mere sterile document. It does not even consist merely of paragraphs in a written instrument which are to be mechanically interpreted. The Constitution, on the contrary, says Justice Bhagwati, is a living organism, a document vibrant with a socio-economic mission. It is supreme lex, the paramount law of the land, and there is no department or branch of Government above or beyond it. Every organ of Government, asserts Justice Bhagwati, derives its authority from the Constitution.

2 Indian Constitution not a colourless document The Indian Constitution has not a non-aligned character; it is not a colourless document. It is a document, says Justice Bhagwati, of social revolution. Its every word and letter speaks the language of a new social order; it is a document which has positive tilt in favour of the weaker sections of Indian humanity; the majority of its provisions are either directly aimed at furthering the goals of the socio-economic revolution or attempt to foster this revolution by establishing the conditions necessary for its achievement; it proclaims through its Preamble and Fundamental Rights and more particularly through the Directive Principles of State Policy, the great ideal and noble vision of social justice and it casts an obligation on every instrumentality of the State including the judiciary which is a separate but equal branch of the State, to transform the *status quo ante* into a new human order in which there will be justice, social, economic and political, for all. Despite the permeation of the entire Constitution by the aim of national renaissance, "the core of the commitment to the social revolution", in the words of Granville Austin, "lies ..... in the Fundamental Rights and the Directive Principles of State Policy."[2] These are the conscience of the Constitution and they are designed to be the chief instruments in bringing about the great reforms of the socio-economic revolution and realizing the constitutional goals of social, economic and political justice for all.

3 Aims and objectives in framing the Constitution The Objectives Resolution which set out the Aims and Objectives before the Constituent Assembly in framing the Constitution and which was passed by the Constituent Assembly in January 1947 before embarking upon the actual task of Constitution making, expressed the resolve of the Constituent Assembly to frame a Constitution wherein shall be

2 Granville Austin: *The Indian Constitution, Cornerstone of a Nation*, p. 50.

guaranteed and secured to all the people of India justice-social, economic and political, equality of status and of opportunity before the law; freedom of thought, expression, belief, faith, worship, vocation, association and action subject to law and public morality and wherein adequate safeguards shall be provided for minority, backward and tribal areas and depressed and other backward classes. These objectives, says Justice Bhagwati, were incorporated by the Constitution makers in the Preamble of the Constitution and they were sought to be secured by enacting Fundamental Rights in Part III and Directive Principles in Part IV.[3]

4 Part III—Fundamental Rights—The Backbone of the Constitution

A. *Influence of Universal Declaration of Human Rights in framing Part III on Fundamental Rights* The U.N. General Assembly adopted on 10 December 1948 the Universal Declaration of Human Rights.[4] But the Universal Declaration operated merely as a statement of ideals which was not of the nature of a legally binding covenant and had no machinery for its enforcement. The deficiency was sought to be removed by the U.N. General Assembly by adopting on 16 December 1966 two covenants for the observance of human rights, namely, (*a*) the International Covenant on Civil and Political Rights, and (*b*) the International Covenant on Economic, Social, and Cultural Rights. While the former formulated legally enforceable rights of the individuals called 'Fundamental Rights', the latter was addressed to the States to implement them by legislation and the rights covered by that covenant are known as the 'Directive Principles of State Policy'. The two covenants came into force in December 1976.

When the Universal Declaration of Human Rights was adopted by the U.N. General Assembly in December 1948, debates were going on in the Indian Constituent Assembly on incorporation of Fundamental Rights in the Constitution. It is not surprising, therefore, that the framers of the Indian Constitution were influenced by the provisions of the Universal Declaration in framing Part III on the Fundamental Rights.

B. *Rights under seven heads in Part III wide ranging and comprehensive* Part III of the Constitution, observed Justice Bhagwati in a trend setting case,[5] confers certain fundamental rights which had their roots deep in the struggle for independence. They "were included in the

3 *Minerva Mills Ltd.* v *Union of India* AIR 1980 SC 1789 at p. 1844, para 110.
4 Vide resolution 217A (III).
5 *Maneka Gandhi* v *Union of India* AIR 1978 SC 597: (1978) 1 SCC 248 (Judgment by Bhagwati, J. expressing majority view).

Constitution in the hope and expectation that one day the tree of true liberty would bloom in India." They were indelibly written in the subconscious memory of the race which fought for well-nigh 30 years for securing freedom from British rule and they found expression in the form of fundamental rights when the Constitution was enacted. These fundamental rights represent the basic values cherished by the people of India since the Vedic times and they are calculated to protect the dignity of the individual and create conditions in which every human being can develop his personality to the fullest extent. They weave a 'pattern of guarantees on the basic structure of human rights' and impose on most occasions negative obligations on the State not to encroach on individual liberty in its various dimensions. It is apparent from the enunciation of these rights that the respect for the individual and his capacity for individual volition which finds expression there is not a self-fulfilling prophecy. Its purpose is to help the individual to find his own viability, to give expression to his creativity and to prevent governmental and other forces from 'alienating' the individual from his creative impulses. These rights are wide ranging and comprehensive and they, observes Justice Bhagwati, fall under seven heads, namely, (*i*) right to equality, (*ii*) right to freedom, (*iii*) right against exploitation, (*iv*) right to freedom of religion, (*v*) cultural and educational rights, (*vi*) right to property, and (*vii*) right to constitutional remedies.[6] Of the seven heads, right to property has been omitted from the provisions of Part III with effect from 20th June 1979. These rights were enacted in the background of the long years of the freedom struggle inspired by the dynamic spiritualism of Mahatma Gandhi and were conceived by the constitution makers in the background of the entire cultural and spiritual history of India not in a narrow limited spirit but in their widest sweep, for the aim and objective was to build a new social order where man will not be a mere plaything in the hands of the State or a few privileged persons but there will be full scope and opportunity for him to achieve the maximum development of his personality and the dignity of the individual will be fully assured.

C. *'Unenumerated fundamental rights' deduced as supplemental to those specified in Part III* The Supreme Court led by Justice Bhagwati also deduced 'Unenumerated fundamental rights' as supplemental to those specified in Part III, as for example, the right to human dignity in general.[7] From this general right, as formulated, cropped up various

6 *Ibid* 5.
7 *Ibid* 5.

corollaries, namely, a guarantee against torture or cruel and unusual punishment or inhuman and degrading treatment of an accused or prisoner flowing from Article 21;[8] right of an accused not to be subjected to third-degree or uncivilised methods to extort confession;[9] right of an accused to speedy trial;[10] right to travel abroad;[11] right to healthy environment;[12] right to free legal aid where conviction for an offence may involve loss of life or personal liberty.[13] In the group of corollaries joined other rights since 1990s onward. Thus, came in right to have pollution free water and air;[14] right to protection against hazardous industries;[15] right to have free education up to 14 years of age;[16] right to health;[17] right to shelter;[18] and many other rights.

The fundamental rights as enshrined in Part III are enforceable against the State. It has sometimes been said that the fundamental rights deal with negative obligations of the State not to encroach on individual freedom. But Justice Bhagwati finds it difficult to subscribe to this limited proposition. The learned Judge says that it is not wholly correct to say that the fundamental rights impose only negative obligations of the State. There are a few fundamental rights which have also a positive content. There are four Articles, namely, Articles 15(2), 17, 23 and 24 which are designed to protect the individual against the action of other private citizens and seem to impose positive obligations on the State to ensure the protection to the individual. Justice Bhagwati observes[19] that whenever any fundamental right which is enforceable also against private individuals, such as, for example, a fundamental right enacted in Article 17 or 23 or 24 is being

8 *Francis Coralie Mullin* v *Administrator, Union Territory of Delhi* (1981)1 SCC 608.

9 *Sunil Batra* v *Delhi Administration* AIR 1980 SC 1579: 1980 Cr LJ 1099: (1980)2 SCR 557; *Kishor Singh* v *State of Rajasthan* AIR 1981 SC 625.

10 *Kadra Pehadiya* v *State of Bihar* AIR 1981 SC 939.

11 *Maneka Gandhi* v *Union of India* AIR 1978 SC 597: (1978)1 SCC 248.

12 *Bandhua Mukti Morcha* v *Union of India* AIR 1984 SC 802; *M.C. Mehta* v *Union of India* AIR 1987 SC 1086.

13 *M.H. Hoskot* v *State of Maharashtra* AIR 1978 SC 1548.

14 *B.L. Wadhera* v *Union of India* AIR 1996 SC 2969; *Indian Council for Enviro-legal Action* v *Union of India* AIR 1996 SC 1446.

15 *Vellore Citizens Welfare Forum* v *Union of India* AIR 1996 SC 2715.

16 *J.P. Unnikrishnan* v *State of Andhra Pradesh* AIR 1993 SC 2178.

17 *State of Punjab* v *Mohinder Singh Chawla* AIR 1997 SC 1225.

18 *U.P. Avas Avam Vikas Parishad* v *Friends Co-operative Housing Society Ltd.* AIR 1996 SC 114, para 7.

19 *People's Union for Democratic Rights* v *Union of India* AIR 1982 SC 1473: 1982 Lab IC 1646: (1982)3 SCC 235.

violated, it is the constitutional obligation of the State to take necessary steps for the purpose of interdicting such violation and ensuring observance of the fundamental right by the private individual who is transgressing the same. Of course, Justice Bhagwati says, the person whose fundamental right is violated can always approach the court for the purpose of enforcement of his fundamental right, but that cannot absolve the State from its constitutional obligation to see that there is no violation of the fundamental right of such person, particularly when he belongs to the weaker section of the humanity and is unable to wage a legal battle against a strong and powerful opponent who is exploiting him.

It is pertinent to note in this context that though the fundamental rights as contained in Part III seek to impose restrictions upon the authority of the State and its power to refrain from encroaching upon the liberty of the individual or a social or economic group, these rights are enforceable not only against the acts of the officers of the State but also its agents. An 'agent' is a person, says Justice Bhagwati, who acts in the name of or for the State, or is clothed with the powers of the State or is invested with governmental functions or authority. Gradually, the doctrine, according to Justice Bhagwati, came to be applied even to acts of a private person or body where its action is supported by the Government even without legislative sanction or in abuse of its legislative authority or when the State has become involved in such private action. The courts in India have an easier task in introducing the doctrine of 'State action' because (*i*) most of the fundamental rights included in Part III are addressed to the 'State', and (*ii*) Part III starts with the definition of the word 'State' in Article 12 which included 'other authorities'.

D. *Right to Equality* Articles 14 to 18 of the Constitution appear under the heading 'Right to Equality' which has since been declared by the Supreme Court as the basic feature of the Constitution. While Article 14 outlaws discrimination in a general way and guarantees equality before the law and equal protection of the laws to all persons, Article 15 prohibits discrimination against citizens on such specific grounds as religion, race, caste, sex or place of birth. Article16 guarantees to the citizens of India equality of opportunity in matters of public employment. Article 17 abolishes untouchability, and Article 18 abolishes titles other than a military or an academic distinction. In situations not covered by Articles 15 to 18, the general principle of equality, says Justice Bhagwati, embodied in Article 14 is attracted where anti-discrimination is the core issue. Article 14 thus is the genus while other articles under the group 'Right to Equality' are the species. Article 14 having been given a highly activist magnitude by Justice Bhagwati in his various judgments and judicial thinking, the present discussion under the head 'Right to Equality' centers round the said Article.

ARTICLE 14

(I) ARTICLE AT PAR WITH THE PROVISIONS OF UNIVERSAL DECLARATION OF HUMAN RIGHTS. Article 7 of the Universal Declaration of Human Rights 1948, declares that all are equal before the law and are entitled without any discrimination to equal protection of the law. By and large the same concept of equality inheres in Article 14 of the Constitution which provides: "The State shall not deny to any person equality before the law or the equal protection of the laws within the territory of India." This provision in Article 14, says Justice Bhagwati, corresponds to the equal protection clause of the 14th Amendment of the U.S. Constitution which declares: "No State shall deny to any person within its jurisdiction the equal protection of the laws."

(II) CONCEPTS OF ARTICLE 14. Two concepts are involved in Article 14, viz., 'equality before the law', and 'equal protection of the laws'. 'Equality before the law', says Justice Bhagwati, is a dynamic concept having many facets. One facet is that there shall be no privileged person or class, i.e., there is no special privilege in favour of any one and that all are equally subject to the ordinary law of the land and that no person, whatever be his rank or condition, is above the law. This is equivalent to the second corollary of the Dicean concept of the rule of law in Britain. The second concept 'equal protection of laws' postulates the application of the same laws alike and without discrimination to all persons similarly situated. It implies that amongst equals the law should be equal and equally administered, that the like should be treated alike without any distinction whatsoever. Justice Bhagwati says that the Constitution of the country being wedded to the concept of equality, in other words, equality being recognised as a basic feature of the Constitution, any treatment of equals unequally or unequals as equals will be violation of the basic structure doctrine.

Describing Article 14 as a founding faith of the Constitution, Justice Bhagwati unfolds his conception on the article thus: "It is indeed the pillar on which rests securely the foundation of our democratic republic. And, therefore, it must not be subjected to a narrow, pedantic or lexicographic approach. No attempt should be made to truncate its all-embracing scope and meaning, for to do so would be to violate its activist magnitude. Equality is a dynamic concept with many aspects and dimensions and it cannot be imprisoned within traditional and doctrinaire limits".[20]

(III) ARBITRARINESS IN STATE ACTION AND ARTICLE 14. Justice Bhagwati developed a new dimension of Article 14 which transcended the classificatory principle and laid down in *Maneka Gandhi's* case[20] that "Article 14 strikes at arbitrariness in State action and ensures fairness and equality in treatment. The principle of reasonableness, which legally as well as philosophically, is an essential element of equality or non-arbitrariness, pervades Article 14 like a brooding omnipresence .....". Thus, Justice Bhagwati evolved the principle that Article 14 is primarily a guarantee against arbitrariness in State action and the doctrine of classification stands only as a subsidiary rule for testing whether a particular State action is arbitrary or not. The Constitution Bench of the Supreme Court speaking through Justice Bhagwati in a concurring judgment in *E.P. Royappa's* case,[21] observed: "Equality is a dynamic concept with many aspects and dimensions and it cannot be 'cribbed, cabined and confined" within traditional and doctrinaire limits. From a positivistic point of view, equality is antithetic to arbitrariness. In fact equality and arbitrariness are sworn enemies, one belongs to the rule of law in a republic, while the other, to the whim and caprice of an absolute monarch. Where an act is arbitrary, it is implicit in it that it is unusual both according to political logic and constitutional law and is therefore violative of Article 14". The view as expressed in *E.P. Royappa's* case (supra) was approved by the Constitution Bench of the apex court in *Ajay Hasia's* case.[22] In *Bachan Singh* v *State of Punjab*,[1] Justice Bhagwati explained that Rule of law which permeates the entire fabric of the Indian Constitution excludes arbitrariness. "Wherever we find arbitrariness or unreasonableness there is denial of rule of law." Article 14 enacts primarily a guarantee against arbitrariness and inhibits state action, whether legislative or executive, which suffers from the vice of arbitrariness. "Every state action must be non-arbitrary and reasonable. Otherwise, the Court would strike it down as invalid."

20 *Maneka Gandhi* v *Union of India* AIR 1978 SC 597 at p. 624: per Bhagwati, J. (as His Lordship then was).

21 *E.P. Royappa* v *State of Tamil Nadu* AIR 1974 SC 555: (1974)2 SCR 348.

22 *Ajay Hasia* v *Khalid Mujib Sehravardi* AIR 1981 SC 487.
AUTHORS' NOTE: Judgement of the Court was delivered by Bhagwati, J. on behalf of himself, Y.V. Chandrachud, CJ., V.R. Krishna Iyer, S. Murtaza Fazal Ali and A.D. Koshal, JJ.

1 AIR 1982 SC 1325.

The entire position of Article 14 vis-a-vis arbitrariness in State action was summarized by Desai, J. in *A.L. Kalra* v *The Project and Equipment Corporation of India Ltd.*[2] thus: "It thus appears well settled that Article 14 strikes at arbitrariness in executive/ administrative action because any action that is arbitrary must necessarily involve the negation of equality. One need not confine the denial of equality to a comparative evaluation between two persons to arrive at a conclusion of discriminatory treatment. An action *per se* arbitrary itself denies equality of protection by law. The Constitution Bench (of the Supreme Court) pertinently observed in *Ajay Hasia's* case[3] and put the matter beyond controversy when it said 'wherever, therefore, there is arbitrariness in State action whether it be of the legislature or of the executive or of an "authority" under Article 12, Article 14 immediately springs into action and strikes down such action.' This view was further elaborated and affirmed in *D.S. Nakara* v *Union of India*."[4]

(IV) UNCANALISED AND UNFETTERED DISCRETION—PERMISSIBILITY OF. Since Article 14 strikes at arbitrariness in administrative action, a law cannot confer unguided and unrestricted power on an authority. In *Sheo Nandan Paswan* v *State of Bihar*,[5] Justice Bhagwati observed: "The law always frowns on uncanalised and unfettered discretion conferred on any instrumentality of the State".

In adjudging the constitutionality of a statute on the touchstone of Article 14, Justice Bhagwati in *Maneka Gandhi's* case[6] said "that the law is well settled that when a statute vests unguided and unrestricted power in an authority to affect the rights of a person without laying down any policy or principle which is to guide the authority in exercise of this power, it would be affected by the vice of discrimination" and thus be violative of Article 14 "since it would leave it open to the Authority to discriminate between persons and things similarly situated".

In *Suman Gupta* v *State of J&K*,[7] Pathak, J. (as his Lordship then was) observed: "We think it beyond dispute that the exercise of all administrative power vested in public authority must be structured within a system of controls informed by both relevance and reason–relevance in relation to the object which it attempts to do so. Wherever

2 AIR 1984 SC 1361.
3 *Ibid* 22.
4 (1983)1 SCC 305: AIR 1983 SC 130.
5 AIR 1987 SC 877 at p. 895: (1987)1 SCC 288.
6 *Maneka Gandhi* v *Union of India* AIR 1978 SC 597 at p. 631, para 65.
7 AIR 1983 SC 1235.

the exercise of such power affects individual rights, there can be no greater assurance protecting its valid exercise than its governance by these twin tests. A stream of case law radiating from the now well know decision of this Court (Supreme Court) in *Maneka Gandhi* v *Union of India* (1978)2 SCR 621: AIR 1978 SC 597 has laid down in clear terms that Article 14 of the Constitution is violated by powers and procedures which in themselves result in unfairness and arbitrariness. It must be remembered that our entire constitutional system is founded on the Rule of law, and in any system so designed it is impossible to conceive of legitimate power which is arbitrary in character and travels beyond the bounds of reason." Justice Pathak continued in *Suman Gupta's* case (supra): "We do not doubt that in the realm of administrative power the element of discretion may properly find place, where the statute or the nature of the power intends so. But there is a well recognised distinction between an administrative power to be exercised within defined limits in the reasonable discretion of designated authority and the vesting of an absolute and uncontrolled power in such authority. One is power controlled by law countenanced by the Constitution, the other falls outside the Constitution altogether". Justice Bhagwati unequivocally supports the view of Pathak, J. as expressed in *Suman Gupta's* case (supra).

(v) PRINCIPLES OF NATURAL JUSTICE—AN INTEGRAL PART OF ARTICLE 14. The decision of Justice Bhagwati in *Maneka Gandhi* v *Union of India*[8] is an authority for the propostion that the principles of natural justice are an integral part of the guarantee of equality enshrined in Article 14. *Audi alteram partem, i.e.*, hear both sides, which is one of the two principal rules of natural justice, the other being *nemo debet esse judex in propria causa, i.e.*, no one shall be a judge in his own cause, is a highly effective tool, says Justice Bhagwati, devised by the courts to enable a statutory authority to arrive at a just decision and it is calculated to act as a healthy check on abuse or misabuse of power.

In *Mohinder Singh Gill* v *The Chief Election Commissioner*,[9] V.R. Kirshna Iyer, J. delivering the judgment for himself and on behalf of Beg, C.J. and Bhagwati, J. (as his Lordship then was) observed that "natural justice is a pervasive facet of secular law where a spiritual touch enlivens legislation, administration and adjudication to make fairness a creed of life. It has many colours and shades, many forms and

8 AIR 1978 SC 597: (1978)1 SCC 248.
9 AIR 1978 SC 851: (1978)1 SCC 405.

shapes and, save where valid law excludes, it applies when people are affected by acts of authority." Justice Bhagwati fully concurs with the view of Mathew, J. in *Indira Gandhi Nehru* v *Raj Narain*,[10] where the learned judge observed that "if a power is given to a body without specifying that the rules of natural justice should be observed in exercising it, the nature of the power would call for its observance."

E. Right to freedom Articles 19 to 22 of the Constitution find place under the heading "Right to Freedom". These articles provide for different aspects of freedom. Of these articles, Articles 19(1)(*a*) and (*g*), 21 and 22 have been discussed in this chapter since the views of Justice Bhagwati can be known from judgments delivered by him on these articles.

ARTICLE 19

(I) SEVEN LAMPS OF FREEDOM. Clause (1) of Article 19, according to Justice Bhagwati's observation made in a leading case,[11] enshrines what may be described as the seven lamps of freedom. It provides that all citizens shall have the right—(*a*) to freedom of speech and expression; (*b*) to assemble peaceably and without arms; (*c*) to form associations or unions; (*d*) to move freely throughout the territory of India; (*e*) to reside and settle in any part of the territory of India; (*f*) to acquire, hold and dispose of property; and (*g*) to practise any profession, or to carry on any occupation, trade or business. Of the seven lamps of freedom, one lamp has been taken out of the provisions of Article 19(1), *i.e.*, right to acquire, hold and dispose of property contained in Article 19(1)(*f*) by the Constitution (Forty-fourth Amendment) Act 1978 with effect from 20.6.1979. But these freedoms though necessary to promote certain basic rights of the citizens, certain democratic values in and the oneness and unity of the country cannot make them absolute, says Justice Bhagwati, for absolute and unrestricted freedom of one may be destructive of the freedom of another and in a well-ordered civilized society freedom can only be regulated freedom. For this reason, clauses (2) to (6) of Article 19 permit reasonable restrictions to be imposed on the exercise of the fundamental rights guaranteed under clause (1) of that article. It needs to be emphasized here that such restrictions can be imposed only by law and not through a mere administrative direction or departmental instructions which have no statutory force.

10 AIR 1975 SC 2299: 1975 (Supp) SCC 1: (1976)2 SCR 347.
11 *Maneka Gandhi* v *Union of India* AIR 1978 SC 597 at p. 620.

(II) RIGHT NOT SPECIFICALLY NAMED IN ARTICLE 19—WHETHER BE COVERED BY ANY CLAUSE OF THE ARTICLE. Justice Bhagwati then considers a question which is very pertinent to Article 19(1) and the question is: "If a right is not specifically named in Article 19(1), whether it may still be a fundamental right covered by some clause of that article. He answers the question thus:[12] "even if a right is not specifically named in Art. 19(1), it may still be a fundamental right covered by some clause of that Article, if it is an integral part of a named fundamental right or partakes of the same basic nature and character as that fundamental right. It is not enough that a right claimed .... flows or emanates from a named fundamental right or that its existence is necessary in order to make the exercise of the named fundamental right meaningful and effective. Every activity which facilitates the exercise of a named fundamental right is not necessarily comprehended in that fundamental right nor can it be regarded as such merely because it may not be possible otherwise to effectively exercise that fundamental right." Justice Bhagwati refuses to accept the theory that a peripheral or concomitant right which facilitates the exercise of a named fundamental right or gives its meaning and substance or makes its exercise effective, is itself a guaranteed right included within the named fundamental right. Acceptance of that theory would lead to incongruous results and the entire scheme of Article 19(1) which confers different rights and sanctions different restrictions according to different standards depending upon the nature of the right will be upset, so says Justice Bhagwati.

(III) ARTICLE 19(1)(a)—FREEDOM OF SPEECH AND EXPRESSION. This subject has been dealt with in Chapter 7.

(IV) ARTICLE 19(1)(g)—RIGHT TO PRACTISE ANY PROFESSION OR TO CARRY ON ANY OCCUPATION, TRADE OR BUSINESS. Justice Bhagwati says that the right guaranteed by the clause is intended to ensure that the citizens' right to any profession, occupation, trade or business does not depend upon grant by the State and that the State cannot prevent a citizen from carrying on any profession, occupation, trade or business, except by a law imposing a reasonable restriction in the interest of the general public. The article uses four different expressions—profession, occupation, trade and business—so as to make the guarantee in the article as comprehensive as possible and to include all avenues and modes through which a person earns his livelihood.

(*a*) *Nature of 'reasonable restriction' in the context of the article.* The phrase 'reasonable restriction' as used in Article 19(6) to limit a person

12 *Ibid* 11 at p. 640, para 77.

in enjoyment of the rights guaranteed under Article 19(1)(*g*), views Justice Bhagwati, should not be arbitrary or of an excessive nature beyond what is required in the interest of the public. The word 'reasonable' implies intelligent care and deliberation, i.e., the choice of a course that reason dictates.

(*b*) *Manner of determination of 'reasonable restriction' in the context of the article.* It bears mentioning here that the reasonableness of restriction is to be determined in an objective manner and from the standpoint of the interests of general public and not from the standpoint of the interest of the persons upon whom the restrictions are imposed or upon abstract consideration. Legislation which arbitrarily or excessively invades the right cannot be said to be 'reasonable' and unless it strikes a proper balance between the freedom guaranteed in Article 19(1)(*g*) and the social control permitted by Article 19(6), it must be held to be wanting in that quality. Similarly, an administrative order not authorised by law under which it is made and imposing a restriction on the right to carry on profession, occupation, trade or business is void being violative of the provisions of Article 19(1)(*g*). Generally speaking, Justice Bhagwati says, administrative discretion is not to be regarded as arbitrary if the circumstances in, or the grounds on, which it can be exercised are stated with clarity and precision and are not arbitrary or unrelated to the object and purpose for which the discretion is conferred, or if the law lays down the policy to achieve which the discretion is to be exercised and such policy is constitutionally valid, or if there are enough procedural safeguards in the law to provide security against abuse or misuse of discretion. In case of trade or business which is illegal, dangerous, immoral or injurious to the health, morality and welfare of the public, it would be legitimate for the State in the exercise of its wider discretionary power to prohibit such activity.

Another matter which calls for attention with reference to Article 19(1)(*g*) is regulation of trade or business through a licensing system which is now the order of the day. Grant of license, views Justice Bhagwati, depends upon the policy prevailing as on the date of the grant of the license. An applicant has no vested right to have license. If on account of the change in policy an applicant is refused grant of license, such refusal cannot be questioned unless the refusal is *mala fide* or is an abuse of the power in which event it is for the applicant to plead and prove to the satisfaction of the court that the refusal was vitiated by the above factors. However, Justice Bhagwati says, judicial expectation from persons who are called upon to exercise the functions of granting licenses is that since such persons to a great extent exercise quasi-judicial functions, it is their duty to hear and determine according to law, and they must bring to that task a fair and unbiased mind. According to the modern approach, since such persons act administratively, they must act fairly and the court will see that they do so. Where a license is due for renewal, duty to act fairly and justly becomes stronger because in cases of discretionary grant of licenses, permits or the like, carries with it a reasonable expectation, though not a legal right, to renewal or non-revocation. Justice Bhagwati, however, cautions that where power is entrusted to an administrative agency to grant or withhold a permit or license in its uncontrolled discretion, the law *ex facie* infringes the fundamental right guaranteed under Article 19(1)(*g*).

(*c*) *Right to go abroad—whether a part of right covered by the Article.* Linked with the issue, a question arises: whether the right to go abroad can be treated as part of the right to carry on trade, business or profession guaranteed under Article 19(1)(*g*). Justice Bhagwati views that the right to go aboard is not a guaranteed right under Article 19(1)(*g*). The said right cannot also be regarded as included in the said article on the theory of peripheral or concomitant right. So, if any restriction is imposed on the right to go abroad by impounding of passport under the provisions of a statute, the same cannot be held to be void as offending Article 19(1)(*g*), as its direct and inevitable impact is on the right to go abroad and not on the right to carry on trade, business, profession of calling. On the same breath, Justice Bhagwati, however, says that even where a statutory provision empowering an authority to take action is constitutionally valid, action taken under it may offend a fundamental right and in that event though the statutory provision is valid, the action may be void. The direct and inevitable effect of an order impounding a passport may, in a given case, be to abridge or take away the right to carry on a profession and where such is the case, Justice Bhagwati says, the order would be invalid, unless saved by Article 19(6). To illustrate the case, Justice Bhagwati cites an example. A pilot with international-flying licence, international flying is his profession and if his passport is impounded, it would directly interfere with his right to carry on his profession and unless the order can be justified on the ground of public interest under Article19(6), it would be void as offending Article 19(1)(*g*). Again, if a correspondent of a newspaper is given a foreign assignment and he is refused passport or his passport is impounded, it would be direct interference with his freedom to carry on his profession.[13]

ARTICLE 21

(I) RIGHT TO LIFE AND PERSONAL LIBERTY—A POSITIVE OBLIGATION ON THE STATE. The Article provides: "No person shall be deprived of his life or personal liberty except according to procedure established by law". Couched in negative terms, the article confers the fundamental right to life and personal liberty. Though the article appears to be negative in its grammatical form, it has, in reality, been given a positive effect by judicial interpretation. The right is a fundamental right enforceable against the State; and judicial decisions have imposed on the State several positive obligations. Under the canopy of Article 21, so many rights have found shelter, growth and nourishment. Right to life and personal liberty enshrined in Article 21 stands on an altogether different footing from other fundamental rights. Justice Bhagwati says: "I do not wish to express any definite opinion, but I may point out that if this fundamental right is violated by any legislation, it may be difficult to sustain a constitutional amendment which seeks to protect such legislation against challenge under Article 21".[14]

(II) POSITION PRIOR TO MANEKA GANDHI'S CASE. Until the decision of the Supreme Court in *Maneka Gandhi's* case,[15] a very narrow and constricted meaning was given to the guarantee embodied in Article 21 and that article was understood to embody only that aspect of the rule of law, which requires that no one shall be deprived of his life or personal liberty without the authority of law. It was construed only as a guarantee against executive action unsupported by law. So long as there was some law, which prescribed a procedure authorising deprivation of life or personal liberty, it was supposed to meet the requirement of Article 21.

Thus, the Supreme Court in *A.K. Gopalan* v *State of Madras*,[16] observed that in Article 21, the expression "procedure established by law" meant the procedure as laid down in the law as enacted by the legislature and nothing more. A person could thus be deprived of his "life" or "personal liberty" in accordance with the procedure as laid down in the relevant law. The court was not concerned as to whether the procedure was fair or reasonable, or according to natural justice.

13 *Maneka Gandhi* v *Union of India* AIR 1978 SC 597.
14 *Minerva Mills Ltd.* v *Union of India* AIR 1980 SC 1789 at p. 1832.
15 *Maneka Gandhi* v *Union of India* AIR 1978 SC 597.
16 AIR 1950 SC 27: 1950 SCR 88.

Gopalan's case was characterised as the "high-water mark of legal positivism". Court's approach was very static, mechanical, purely literal and too much coloured by the positivist or imperative theory of law. Former Chief Justice of India K. Subba Rao remarked about *Gopalan* thus: "The preponderance of view among the jurists is that it is wrongly decided. It has in effect destroyed one of the greatest of the Fundamental Rights, i.e., personal liberty".[17] *Gopalan*, however, held the field for almost three decades, *i.e.*, 1950 to 1978.

(III) ALTERED POSITION SINCE MANEKA GANDHI'S CASE. In *Maneka Gandhi* v *Union of India*, which is a landmark decision of the post-emergency period and can be regarded as a highly creative judicial pronouncement on the part of the Supreme Court, Justice Bhagwati showed that Article 21 as interpreted in *Gopalan* could not play any role in providing protection against any harsh law seeking to deprive a person of his life or personal liberty. The Supreme Court through Justice Bhagwati in *Maneka Gandhi's* case (supra) reinterpreted Article 21 and practically overruled *Gopalan* and laid down that Article 21 is not only a guarantee against executive action unsupported by law, but is also a restriction on law making. It is not enough to secure compliance with the prescription of Article 21 that there should be a law prescribing some semblance of a procedure for depriving a person of his life or personal liberty, but the procedure prescribed by law must be reasonable, fair and just and if it is not so, the law would be void as violating the guarantee of Article 21.

The Supreme Court through its majority view expressed by the judgment of Justice Bhagwati in *Maneka Gandhi's* case thus expanded the scope and ambit of the right to life and personal liberty enshrined in Article 21 and sowed the seed for future development of the law enlarging this most fundamental of Fundamental Rights. This decision in *Maneka Gandhi's* case became the starting point and spring-board for a most spectacular evolution of the law culminating in the decisions in *M.H. Hoskot's* case,[18] *Hussainara Khatoon's* case,[19] the first *Sunil Batra's* case,[1] and the second *Sunil Batra's* case.[2] It can be said that a burst of creative decisions of the Supreme Court fast on the heels of

17 Rao: *Some Constitutional Problems,* 115 (1970).

18 *M.H. Hoskot* v *State of Maharashtra* 1978 Cr LJ 1978: (1979)1 SCR 192.

19 *Hussainara Khatoon* v *Home Secretary, State of Bihar* (1980)1 SCC 81: 1979 Cr LJ 1036: AIR 1979 SC 1360.

1 *Sunil Batra* v *Delhi Administration* (1978)4 SCC 494: AIR 1978 SC 1675: 1978 Cr LJ 1741: (1979)1 SCR 392.

2 *Sunil Batra* v *Delhi Administration* 1980 Cr LJ 1099: (1980)2 SCR 557: AIR 1980 SC 1579.

Maneka Gandhi gave a new meaning to the Article and expanded its content and connotation.

The position now is that Article 21 as interpreted in *Maneka Gandhi's* case requires that no one shall be deprived of his life or personal liberty except by procedure established by law and this procedure must be reasonable, fair and just and not arbitrary, whimsical or fanciful and it is for the court to decide in the exercise of its constitutional power of judicial review whether the deprivation of life or personal liberty in a given case is by procedure, which is reasonable, fair and just or it is otherwise. Justice Bhagwati says that Article 21 "embodies a constitutional value of supreme importance in a democratic society"[3] and Justice Krishna Iyre has characterised the article as "the procedural *magna carta* protective of life and liberty".[4]

(IV) RIGHT TO LIFE—MEANING BROADENED. Justice Bhagwati recognised 'right to life' as enshrined in Article 21 as the most precious human right and interpreted the expression not in a narrow and constricted sense but in a wide and liberal manner so as to invest it with significance and vitality which may endure for years to come and enhance the dignity of the individual and the worth of the human person. While recognising that every limb or faculty through which life is enjoyed is protected by Article 21 and a *fortiori*, this would include the faculties of thinking and feeling, Justice Bhagwati went beyond that and observed in *Francis Coralie Mullin's* case[5] that right to life is not limited only to protection of limb or faculty but it goes further and embraces something more. The right to life, says Justice Bhagwati in *Francis Coralie Mullin's* case (supra), includes the right to live with human dignity and all that goes along with it, namely, the bare necessaries of life such as adequate nutrition, clothing and shelter over the head and facilities for reading, writing and expressing oneself in diverse forms, freely moving about and mixing and commingling with fellow human beings. Though the magnitude and content of the components of this right would depend upon the extent of the economic development of the country, it must according to Justice Bhagwati, in any view of the matter, include the right to the basic necessities of life and also the right to carry on such functions and activities as constitute the bare minimum expression of the human-self.

3 *Francis Coralie Mullin* v *Administrator, Union of Territory of Delhi* (1981)1 SCC 608: (1981)2 SCR 516: 1981 Cr LJ 306: AIR 1981 SC 746.
4 *P.S.R. Sadhanantham* v *Arunachalam* AIR 1980 SC 856: (1980)3 SCC 141.
5 *Francis Coralie Mullin* v *Administrator, Union of Territory of Delhi* (1981)1 SCC 608: (1981)2 SCR 516: 1981 Cr LJ 306: AIR 1981 SC 746.

(V) PERSONAL LIBERTY—COVERS A VARIETY OF RIGHTS. The expression 'personal liberty' occurring in Article 21 has been given a broad and liberal interpretation by Justice Bhagwati in *Maneka Gandhi's* case[6] and it has been held in that case that the expression 'personal liberty' used in that article is the widest amplitude and it covers a variety of rights which go to constitute the personal liberty of a man and it also includes rights which have been raised to the status of distinct Fundamental Rights and given additional protection under Article 19. The expression 'personal liberty' in Article 21, asserts Justice Bhagwati, must not be so interpreted as to avoid overlapping between that Article and Article 19(1). The law must now be taken to be well settled, says Justice Bhagwati, that Article 21 does not exclude Article 19 and that even if there is a law prescribing a procedure for depriving a person of 'personal liberty' and there is consequently no infringement of the fundamental right conferred by Article 21, such law, in so far as it abridges or takes away any fundamental right under Article 19, would have to meet the challenge of that article.[7]

(VI) EXPRESSION 'DEPRIVATION'—MEANING. With regard to the expression 'deprivation' as used in Article 21, Justice Bhagwati says,[8] it is every kind of deprivation that is hit by Article 21, whether such deprivation be permanent or temporary and furthermore, deprivation is not an act which is complete once and for all: it is a continuing act and so long as it lasts, it must be in accordance with procedure established by law.

(VII) RIGHT TO PROTECTION AGAINST TORTURE—IMPLICIT IN ARTICLE 21. Justice Bhagwati affirms[8] that there is implicit in Article 21 the right to protection against torture or cruel, inhuman or degrading treatment which is enunciated in Article 5 of the Universal Declaration of Human Rights and guaranteed by Article 7 of the International Covenant on Civil and Political Rights. The right to live which is comprehended within the broad connotation of the right to life can conceivably be abridged only if it is done according to just, fair and reasonable procedure established by law. Refering to the case of a prisoner or

6 *Maneka Gandhi* v *Union of India* AIR 1978 SC 597: (1978)1 SCC 248.

7 AUTHOR'S NOTE: The proposition of Justice Bhagwati that the expression 'personal liberty' in Article 21 must not be so interpreted as to avoid overlapping between that Article and Article 19(1) cannot be disputed after the decisions in *R.C. Cooper* v *Union of India* AIR 1970 SC 564: (1970)3 SCR 530; *Shambhu Nath Sarkar* v *State of West Bengal* AIR 1973 SC 1425; *Haradhan Saha* v *State of West Bengal* AIR 1974 SC 2154.

detenu, Justice Bhagwati says,[8] he would, as a necessary component of the right to life, be entitled to have interviews with the members of his family and friends and no prison regulation or procedure laid down by prison regulation regulating the right to have interview with the members of the family and friends can be upheld as constitutionally valid unless it is reasonable, fair and just. The same consequence would follow, asserts Justice Bhagwati,[8] even if this problem is considered from the point of view of the right to personal liberty enshrined in Article 21, for the right to have interviews with the members of the family and friends is clearly part of personal liberty guaranteed under that article. Likewise, the right of a detenu to consult a legal adviser of his choice for any purpose not necessary limited to defence in a criminal proceeding but also for securing release from preventive detention or filing a writ petition or prosecuting any claim or proceeding, civil or criminal, is obviously included in the right to live with human dignity and is also part of personal liberty and the detenu cannot be deprived of this right nor can this right of the detenu be interfered with except in accordance with reasonable, fair and just procedure established by a valid law.[8]

(VIII) RIGHT TO SPEEDY TRIAL—IMPLICIT IN ARTICLE 21. Under our Constitution, says Justice Bhagwati,[9] though speedy trial is not specifically enumerated as a fundamental right, it is implicit in the broad sweep and content of Article 21 as interpreted by the Supreme Court in *Maneka Gandhi's* case. As said earlier, in *Maneka Gandhi's* case it has been held that Article 21 confers a fundamental right on every person not to be deprived of his life or liberty except in accordance with the procedure prescribed by law and it is not enough to constitute compliance with the requirement of that article that some semblance of a procedure should be prescribed by law, but that the procedure should be 'reasonable, fair and just'. If a person is deprived of his liberty under a procedure which is not 'reasonable, fair or just', such deprivation would be violative of his fundamental right under Article 21 and he would be entitled to enforce such fundamental right and secure his release. Now, obviously procedure prescribed by law for depriving a person of his liberty cannot be 'reasonable, fair or just' unless that

8 *Francis Coralie Mullin* v *Administrator, Union Territory of Delhi* (1981)1 SCC 608: (1981)2 SCR 516: 1981 Cr LJ 306: AIR 1981 SC 746.

9 *Hussainara Khatoon* v *Home Secretary, State of Bihar* AIR 1979 SC 1360; followed in *Kadra Pehadiya* v *State of Bihar* AIR 1981 SC 939: 1981 Cr LJ 481: (1983)2 SCC 104.

procedure ensures a speedy trial for determination of the guilt of such person. No procedure, affirms Justice Bhagwati,[9] which does not ensure a reasonably quick trial can be regarded as 'reasonable, fair or just' and it would fall foul of Article 21. Speedy trial, meaning thereby reasonably expeditious trial, is, therefore, an integral and essential part of the fundamental right to life and liberty enshrined in Article 21.

(IX) RIGHT OF AN ACCUSED TO FREE LEGAL SERVICE—IMPLICIT IN ARTICLE 21. The Supreme Court in *M.H. Hoskot's* case[10] observed: "Judicial justice, with procedural intricacies, legal submissions and critical examination of evidence, leans upon professional expertise, and a failure of equal justice under the law is on the cards where such supportive skill is absent for one side. Our judicature, moulded by Anglo-American models and our judicial process, engineered by kindred legal technology, compel the collaboration of lawyer-power for steering the wheels of equal justice under the law." It is not possible, views Justice Bhagwati, to reach the benefits of the legal process to the poor, to protect them against injustice and to secure to them their constitutional and statutory rights unless there is a nationwide programme to provide legal services to them. It is now well settled, as a result of the decision in *Maneka Gandhi's* case, that the procedure under which a person may be deprived of his life or liberty under Article 21 should be 'reasonable, fair and just'. A procedure, holds Justice Bhagwati,[11] which does not make available legal services to an accused person who is too poor to afford a lawyer and who would, therefore, have to go through the trial without legal assistance, cannot possibly be regarded as 'reasonable, fair and just.' It is an essential ingredient of 'reasonable, fair and just' procedure to a prisoner who is to seek his liberation through the court's process that he should have legal services available to him. The right to free legal services, holds Justice Bhagwati,[11] must be held implicit in the guarantee of Article 21. This is a constitutional right of every accused person who is unable to engage a lawyer and secure legal services on account of reasons such as poverty, indigence or incommunicado situation and the State is under a mandate to provide a lawyer to an accused person if the circumstances of the case and the needs of the justice so required, provided of course the accused person does not object to the provision of such lawyer.

10 *M.H. Hoskot* v *State of Maharashtra* AIR 1978 SC 1548: (1978)3 SCC 544 per Krishna Iyer, J.

11 *Hussainara Khatoon* v *Home Secretary, State of Bihar* AIR 1979 SC 1360; followed in *Kadra Pehadiya* v *State of Bihar* AIR 1981 SC 939: 1981 Cr LJ 481: (1983)2 SCC 104.

Justice Bhagwati says[12] that legal assistance to a poor or indigent accused who is arrested and put in jeopardy of his life or personal liberty is a necessary *sine qua non* of justice and where it is not provided, injustice is likely to result and undeniably every act of injustice corrodes the foundations of democracy and rule of law, because nothing rankles more in the human heart than a feeling of injustice and those who suffer and cannot get justice because they are priced out of the legal system, lose faith in the legal process and feeling begins to overtake them that democracy and rule of law are merely slogans or myths intended to perpetuate the domination of the rich and the powerful and to protect the establishment and vested interests. Imagine the helpless condition, says Justice Bhagwati, of a prisoner who is lodged in a jail who does not know to whom he can turn for help in order to vindicate his innocence or defend his constitutional or legal rights or to protect himself against torture and ill-treatment or oppression and harassment at the hands of his custodians. It is also possible that he or the members of his family may have other problems where legal assistance is required but by reason of his being incarcerated, it may be difficult if not impossible for him or the members of his family to obtain proper legal advice or aid. It is, therefore, absolutely essential that legal assistance must be made available to prisoners in jails, whether they are under-trial or convicted prisoners.

ARTICLE 22

(I) PROTECTION AGAINST ARREST AND DETENTION IN CERTAIN CASES. Article 22, observes Justice Bhagwati,[13] provides various safeguards calculated to protect personal liberty against arbitrary restraint without trial. These safeguards cannot be regarded as substantial. They are essentially procedural in character and their efficacy depends on the care and caution and the sense of responsibility with which they are observed by the detaining authority.

The article consists of two parts. Clauses (1) and (2) apply to persons arrested or detained under a law otherwise than a preventive detention law. Clauses (4) to (7) apply to persons arrested or detained under a preventive detention law. Our discussion in this topic remains limited and confined to Article 22(5).

12 *Sheela Barse* v *State of Maharashtra* (1983)2 SCC 96.

13 *Khudiram Das* v *State of West Bengal* AIR 1975 SC 550.
AUTHOR'S NOTE: The Judgment of the Court was delivered by Bhagwati, J. on behalf of himself and P. Jaganmohan Reddy, P.K. Goswami and S.R. Sarkaria, JJ.

(II) PROCEDURAL REQUIREMENTS OF ARTICLE 22(5). Article 22(5), says Justice Bhagwati,[13] introduces two procedural requirements embodying the rule of *audi alteram partem* to a limited but a crucial and compulsive extent by providing that: "when a person is detained in pursuance of an order made under any law providing for preventive detention, the authority making the order shall, as soon as may be, communicate to such person the grounds on which the order has been made and shall afford him the earliest opportunity of making a representation against the order." The constitutional imperatives enacted in Article 22(5) accordingly are two-fold: (*a*) that the detaining authority must, as soon as may be, that is, as soon as practicable after the detention, communicate to the detenue the grounds on which the order of detention has been made, and (*b*) the detaining authority must afford the detenue the earliest opportunity of making a representation against the order of detention. These are the barest minimum safeguards which, Justice Bhagwati says, must be observed before an executive authority can be permitted to preventively detain a person and thereby drown his right of personal liberty in the name of public good and social security.

The requirement of communication of grounds of detention as the first safeguard acts as a check against arbitrary and capricious exercise of power, observes Justice Bhagwati.[13] The detaining authority cannot whisk away a person and put him behind bar at its own sweet will. It must have grounds for doing so and those grounds must be communicated to the detenu, so that, not only the detenu may know what are the facts and materials before the detaining authority on which he is being deprived of his personal liberty, but he can invoke the power of judicial review, howsoever limited and peripheral it may be. The communication of the grounds of detention is also intended to subserve the purpose of enabling the detenu to make an effective representation. But, what does the word 'grounds' mean? Justice Bhagwati answers that 'grounds' mean all the basic facts and materials which have been taken into account by the detaining authority in making the order of detention and on which the order of detention is based.[13] 'Grounds' does not merely mean a recital or reproduction of a ground of satisfaction of the authority; nor is its connotation restricted to a bare statement of conclusions of fact. It means something more. That 'something' is the factual constituent of the 'grounds' on which the subjective satisfaction of the authority is based. The basic facts and material particulars, therefore, which are the foundation of the order of detention, will be covered by 'grounds' within the contemplation of Article 22(5). This has always been the view consistently taken by the Supreme Court in a series of decisions, says Justice Bhagwati.

The second safeguard in Article 22(5) requires that the detenu shall be afforded the earliest opportunity of making a representation against the order of detention. No avoidable delay, no short fall in the materials communicated shall stand in the way of the detenu in making an early, yet comprehensive and effective, representation in regard to all basic facts and materials which may have influenced the detaining authority in making the order of detention depriving him of his freedom. These are legal bulwarks, says Justice Bhagwati,[13] enacted by the Constitution makers against arbitrary or improper exercise of the vast powers of preventive detention which may be vested in the executive by a law of preventive detention.

(III) SUBJECTIVE SATISFACTION FAVOURING AN ORDER OF DETENTION SUBJECT TO JUDICIAL SCRUTINY. The courts, says Justice Bhagwati, have, by judicial decisions, carved out an area, limited though it be, within which the validity of the subjective satisfaction favouring an order of detention can be subjected to judicial scrutiny. The basic postulate on which the courts have proceeded is that the subjective satisfaction being a condition precedent for the exercise of the power conferred on the executive, the court can always examine whether the requisite satisfaction is arrived at by the authority: if it is not, the condition precedent to the exercise of the power would not be fulfilled and the exercise of the power would be bad.[13]

Where the liberty of the subject is involved, says Justice Bhagwati, it is the bounden duty of the court to satisfy itself that all the safeguards provided by the law have been scrupulously observed and the subject is not deprived of his personal liberty otherwise than in accordance with law.

(IV) LAW OF PREVENTIVE DETENTION—TO SATISFY THE REQUIREMENTS OF ARTICLES 14, 19 AND 21. A question is often asked in this context whether a law of preventive detention is to satisfy the requirements of Articles 14, 19 and 21. The view taken by the majority in *A.K. Gopalan* v *State of Madras*[14] was that Article 22 is a self-contained Code, and therefore, a law of preventive detention does not have to satisfy the requirements of Articles 14, 19 and 21. The minority view of Fazal Ali, J., in *Gopalan's* case (supra), on the other hand, was that preventive detention was a

14 AIR 1950 SC 27: 1950 SCR 88.

direct breach of the right under Article 19(1)(*a*) and (*d*) and that a law providing for preventive detention had to be subject to such judicial review as is obtainable under clause (5) of that article. It was in *Cooper's* case,[15] the aforesaid premise of the majority in *Gopalan's* case was disapproved and it was held by a majority of judges, only Ray, J., as he then was, dissenting, that though a law of preventive detention may pass the test of Article 22, it has yet to satisfy the requirements of other fundamental rights such as Article 19. Therefore, the majority view in *Gopalan's* case, says Justice Bhagwati, no longer holds the field.

F. ***Rights against exploitation*** Articles 23 and 24 of the Constitution appear under the head 'Right against Exploitation'. While Article 23 contains prohibition of traffic in human beings and forced labour, Article 24 prescribes prohibition of employment of children in factories, etc.

ARTICLE 23

(I) PROHIBITION OF TRAFFIC IN HUMAN BEINGS AND FORCED LABOUR. The article which is a right against exploitation guaranteed by the Constitution is not limited in its application against the State but it prohibits "traffic in human beings and begar and other similar forms of forced labour" practised by any one else. Thus, Article 23 is clearly designed to protect the individual not only against the State but also against other private citizens. Insofar as its area of operation is concerned, the sweep of the article is wide and unlimited and it strikes at "traffic in human beings and begar and other similar forms of forced labour" wherever they are found. The prohibition contained in the article is clearly intended to be a general prohibition total in its effect and all pervasive in its range. Justice Bhagwati traced down the reason for enacting this provision in the Chapter of Fundamental Rights in the socio-economic condition of the people at the time when the Constitution came to be enacted.[16] The Constitution makers, when they set out to frame the Constitution, Justice Bhagwati says, had enormous task before them of changing the socio-economic structure of the country and bringing about socio-economic regeneration with a view to reaching social and economic justice to the common man. Large masses of people, bled white by well-neigh two centuries of foreign rule, were living in abject poverty and destitution with ignorance and illiteracy accentuating

15 *R.C. Cooper* v *Union of India* AIR 1970 SC 564: (1970)3 SCR 530.

16 *People's Union for Democratic Rights* v *Union of India* AIR 1982 SC 1473: (1982)3 SCC 235: 1982 SCC (L&S) 275.

their helplessness and despair. The society had degenerated into a status-oriented hierarchical society with little respect for the dignity of the individual who was in the lower rungs of the social ladder or in an economically impoverished condition. The political revolution was completed and it had succeeded in bringing freedom to the country. But freedom was not an end in itself, it was only a means to an end, the end being the raising of the people to higher level of achievement and bringing about their total advancement and welfare. Political freedom had no meaning unless it was accompanied by social and economic freedom and it was, therefore, necessary to carry forward the social and economic revolution with a view to creating socio-economic condition in which everyone would be able to enjoy basic human rights and participate in the fruits of freedom and liberty in an egalitarian social and economic framework. It was with this end in view that the Constitution makers enacted the Directive Principles of State Policy in Part IV of the Constitution setting out the constitutional goal of a new socio-economic order. There persisted, however, one feature of our national life which was ugly and shameful and which cried for urgent attention and that was the existence of bonded or forced labour in large parts of the country. This evil was the relic of a feudal exploitative society and it was totally incompatible with the new egalitarian socio-economic order which "We the people of India" were determined to build and constituted a gross and most revolting denial of basic human dignity. It was, therefore, necessary to eradicate this pernicious practice and wipe it out altogether from the national scene and this had to be done immediately because with the advent of freedom such practice could not be allowed to continue to blight the national life any longer. Obviously, it would not have been enough merely to include abolition of forced labour in the Directive Principles of State Policy because then outlawing this practice would not have been legally enforceable and it would have continued to plague our national life in violation of the basic constitutional norms and value until some appropriate legislation could be brought by the legislature forbidding such practice. The Constitution makers, therefore, decided to give teeth to their resolve to obliterate and wipe out this evil practice by enacting constitutional prohibition against it in the chapter on Fundamental Rights, so that abolition of such practice may become enforceable and effective as soon as the Constitution came into force. That is the reason, says Justice Bhagwati, why the provisions enacted in Article 23 was included in the chapter of Fundamental Rights.

(II) TRUE SCOPE AND MEANING OF THE EXPRESSION TRAFFIC IN HUMAN BEINGS AND BEGAR AND OTHER SIMILAR FORMS OF FORCED LABOUR. When the

Constitution makers enacted Article 23 they had before them Article 4 of the Universal Declaration of Human Rights but they deliberately departed from its language and employed words which would make the reach and content of Article 23 much wider than that of Article 4 of the Universal Declaration of Human Rights. They banned "traffic in human beings" which is an expression of much larger amplitude than "slave trade" and they also interdicted "begar and other similar forms of forced labour". The word 'begar' in Article 23 is not a word of common use in English language. It is a word of Indian origin which, like many other words, has found its way in the English vocabulary. It is very difficult to formulate a precise definition of "begar" but there can be no doubt that it is a form of forced labour under which a person is compelled to work without receiving any remuneration. Molesworth describes 'begar' as "labour or service exacted by a Government or person in power without giving remuneration for it." Wilson's Glossery of Judicial and Revenue Terms gives the following meaning of the word 'begar': "a forced labourer, one pressed to carry burthens for individuals or the public". Under the old system, when pressed for public service, no pay was given. The Begary though still liable to be pressed for public objects, now receives pay. Forced labour for private service is prohibited." "Begar" may, therefore, be loosely described as labour or service which a person is forced to give without receiving any remuneration for it. That was the meaning of the word 'begar' accepted by a Division Bench of the Bombay High Court in *S. Vasudevan* v *S.D. Mital.*[17] 'Begar' is thus clearly a form of forced labour.

It is not merely 'begar' which is prohibited by Article 23 but also all other similar forms of forced labour. This article strikes at forced labour in whatever form it may manifest itself because it is violative of human dignity and is contrary to basic human values. The practice of forced labour is condemned in almost every international instrument dealing with human rights. As far back as in 1930, long before the Universal Declaration of Human Rights came into being, International Labour Organisation adopted Convention No. 29 laying down that every member of the International Labour Organisation which ratifies this Convention shall "suppress the use of forced or compulsory labour in all its forms" and this prohibition was elaborated in Convention No. 105 adopted by International Labour Organisation in 1957. The words "forced or compulsory labour" in Convention No. 29 had of course a limited meaning but that was so on account of the restricted definition

17 AIR 1962 Bom 53.

of these words given in Article 2 of the Convention. Article 4 of the European Convention of Human Rights and Article 8 of the International Covenant on Civil and Political Rights also prohibit forced or compulsory labour. Article 23 of the Constitution of India is in the same strain and it enacts a prohibition against forced labour in whatever form it may be found.

In making prohibition in the article, the Constitution makers did not intend to strike only at certain forms of forced labour leaving it open to the socially or economically powerful section of the community to exploit the poor and the weaker section by resorting to other forms of forced labour. Article 23 cannot be reduced to a mere rope of sand with the logic or reasoning that if a person is forced to give labour or service to another without receiving any remuneration at all, it should be regarded as a pernicious practice sufficient to attract the condemnation of Article 23 but if some remuneration is paid for it, then it should be outside the inhibition of that article. If such interpretation is extended, Justice Bhagwati says, it would then be the easier thing in an exploitative society for a person belonging to socially or economically dominant class to exact labour or service from a person belonging to the deprived and vulnerable section of the community by paying a negligible amount of remuneration and thus escape the rigour of Article 23.

Justice Bhagwati warns that it would not be right to place on the language of Article 23 an interpretation which would emasculate its beneficent provisions and defeat the very purpose of enacting them. Justice Bhagwati expressed his views very clearly to the effect that Article 23 is intended to abolish every form of forced labour. The words "other similar form of forced labour" are used in Article 23 not with a view to importing the particular characteristic of 'begar' that labour or service should be exacted without payment of any remuneration but with a view to bringing within the scope and ambit of that article all other forms of forced labour and since 'begar' is one form of forced labour, the Constitution makers used the words "other similar form of forced labour." If the requirement that labour or work should be exacted without any remuneration were imported in other form of forced labour, they would straightway come within the meaning of the word 'begar' and in that event there would be no need to have the additional words "other similar forms of forced labour." The object of adding the words "other similar forms of forced labour" was clearly, according to Justice Bhagwati, to expand the reach and content of Article 23. Every form of forced labour, 'begar' or otherwise, is, in the opinion of Justice Bhagwati, within the inhibition of Article 23 and it makes no difference whether the person who is forced to give his labour or service to another is remunerated or not. Even if remuneration is paid, labour supplied by a person would be hit by this Article if it is forced labour, that is, labour supplied not willingly but at the result of force or compulsion. As example, Justice Bhagwati cited a case where a person has entered into a contract of service with another for a period of three years and he wishes to discontinue serving such other person before the expiration of the period of three years. If a law were to provide that in such a case the contract shall be specifically enforced and he shall be compelled to serve for the full period of three years, it would clearly amount to forced labour and such a law would be void as offending Article 23. That is why, Justice Bhagwati opines, specific performance of a contract of service cannot be enforced against an employee and an employee cannot be forced by compulsion of law to continue to serve the employer. Of course, Justice Bhagwati says, if there is a breach of contract of service, the employee would be liable to pay damages to the employer but he cannot be forced to continue to serve the employer without breaching the injunction of Article 23.

Article 23 asserts Justice Bhagwati, strikes at every form of forced labour even if it has its origin in a contract voluntarily entered into by the person obligated to provide labour or service. The reason is that it offends against human dignity to compel a person to provide labour or service to another if he does not wish to do so, even though it may result in the breach of the contract entered into by him. There should be no serfdom or involuntary servitude, in a free democratic India which respects the dignity of the individual and the worth of the human person. Moreover, Justice Bhagwati says, in a country like India where there is so much poverty and unemployment and there is no equality of bargaining power, a contract of service may appear on its face voluntary but it may, in reality, be involuntary because while entering into the contract, the employee, by reason of his economically helpless condition, may have been faced with Hobson's choice, either to starve or to submit to the exploitative terms dictated by the powerful employer. Justice Bhagwati strongly asserts that it would be a travesty of justice to hold the employee in such a case to the terms of the contract and to compel him to serve the employer even though he may not wish to do so. That would aggravate the inequality and injustice from which the employee even otherwise suffers on account of his economically disadvantaged position and lend the authority of law to the exploitation of the poor, helpless employee by the economically powerful employer. Article 23, therefore, says that no one shall be forced to provide labour or service against his will even though it be under a contract of service.

Comes with this a relevant question whether there is any breach of Article 23 when a person provides labour or service to the State or to any person at a pay less than the minimum wage for it. In answering this question, Justice Bhagwati says that ordinarily no one would willingly supply labour or service to another for less than the minimum wage when he knows that under the law he is entitled to get minimum wage for the labour or service provided by him. It may, therefore, be legitimately presumed, says Justice Bhagwati, that when a person provides labour or service to another against receipt or remuneration which is less than the minimum wage, he is acting under the force or some compulsion which drives him to work though he is paid less than what he is entitled under the law to receive. What Article 23 prohibits, says Justice Bhagwati, is "forced labour" i.e. labour or service which a person is forced to provide and "force" which would make such labour or service "forced labour" may arise in several ways. It may be physical force which may compel a person to provide labour or service to another or it may be force exerted through a legal provision, such as, a provision for imprisonment or fine in case the employee fails to provide labour or service or it may even be compulsion arising from hunger and poverty, want and destitution. Any factor which deprives a person of a choice of alternative and compels him to adopt one particular course of action may properly be regarded as 'force' and if labour or service is compelled as a result of such 'force', it would be "forced labour".

Justice Bhagwati further says where a person is suffering from hunger or starvation, when he has no resources at all to fight disease or to feed his wife and children or even to hide their nakedness, where utter grinding poverty has broken his back and reduced him to a state of helplessness and despair and where no other employment is available to alleviate the rigour of his poverty, he would have no choice but to accept any work that comes his way even if the remuneration offered to him is less than the minimum wage. He would be in no position, in that event, to bargain with the employer; he would have to accept what is offered to him. And in doing so, says Justice Bhagwati, he would be acting not as a free agent with a choice between alternative but under compulsion of economic circumstances and the labour or service provided by him would be clearly "forced labour".

The word 'force' must, therefore, be construed, asserts Justice Bhagwati, to include not only physical or legal force but also force arising from the compulsion of economic circumstances which leaves no choice of alternative to a person in want and compels him to provide labour or service even though the remuneration received for it is less than the minimum wage. Justice Bhagwati, therefore, concludes with the view that where a person provides labour or service to another for remuneration which is less than the minimum wage, the labour or service provided by him clearly falls within the scope and ambit of the words "forced labour" under Article 23. Such a person would be entitled in that event to come to the court for enforcement of his fundamental right under Article 23 by asking the Court to direct payment of the minimum wage to him so that the labour or service provided by him ceases to be "forced labour" and the breach of Article 23 is remedied.

Justice Bhagwati is so much firm in implementing the prohibition of Article 23 in its letter and spirit that in a case[18] he opined that whenever any labour or service is taken by the State from any person, whether he be affected by drought or scarcity condition or not, the State must pay, at the least, minimum wage to such person on pain of violation of Article 23. The State, says Justice Bhagwati, cannot be permitted to take advantage of the helpless condition of the affected persons and extract labour or service from them on payment of less than the minimum wage. No work of utility and value can be allowed to be constructed, asserts Justice Bhagwati, on the blood and sweat of persons who are reduced to a state of helplessness on account of drought and scarcity condition.

ARTICLE 24

In consonance with Convention No. 59 adopted by the International Labour Organisation and ratified by India, we have Article 24 which provides that no child below the age of 14 years shall be employed to work in any factory or mine or engaged in any other hazardous employment. This is a constitutional prohibition which Justice Bhagwati says,[19] even if not followed up by appropriate legislation, must operate *proprio vigore*. So far as Article 24 is concerned, it embodies a fundamental right which is plainly and indubitably enforceable against every one and the mandate is compulsive in nature. Following this constitutional prohibition, Justice Bhagwati called for prohibition of employment of children under the age of 14 years in every type of construction work, the same being clearly a hazardous occupation, notwithstanding the absence of specification of construction industry in the Schedule to the Employment of Children Act 1938.[19]

18 *Sanjit Roy* v *State of Rajasthan* AIR 1983 SC 328: (1983)1 SCC 525.
19 *People's Union for Democratic Rights* v *Union of India* AIR 1982 SC 1473: 1982 Lab IC 1646.

G. ***Right to constitutional remedies*** Articles 32 to 35 of the Constitution appear under the head "Right to Constitutional Remedies". Of the said articles, Article 32 which deals with remedies for enforcement of rights conferred by Part III of the Constitution is taken up for discussion with views of Justice Bhagwati reflected on the said article.

ARTICLE 32

(I) REMEDIES FOR ENFORCEMENT OF RIGHTS CONFERRED BY PART III. Article 32 is so frequently used by lawyers and judges for enforcement of fundamental rights without any objection against its invocation being raised on behalf of the State, that the Supreme Court had rarely any occasion to examine its language and consider how large is the width and amplitude of its dimension and reach. It was only in *Bandhua Mukti Morcha's* case[20] that this aspect was considered by the apex court in details.

(II) OLD CONCEPT OF INVOKING THE ARTICLE YIELDING PLACE TO THE NEW. We are, says Justice Bhagwati, so much accustomed to the concepts of Anglo-Saxon jurisprudence which requires every legal proceeding including a proceeding for a high prerogative writ to be cast in a rigid or definitive mould and insist on observance of certain well-settled rules of procedure, that we implicitly assume that the same sophisticated procedural rules must also govern a proceeding under Article 32 and the Supreme Court cannot permit itself to be freed from the shackles of these rules even if that be necessary for enforcement of a fundamental right. It was on the basis of this impression fostered by long association with the Anglo-Saxon system of administration of justice that for a number of years the Supreme Court had taken the view that it is only a person whose fundamental right is violated who can approach the Supreme Court for relief under Article 32 or in other words, he must have a cause of action for enforcement of his fundamental right. It was only in the year 1981 in the Judges' Appointment and Transfer case[1] that the Supreme Court expressing its majority view through Justice Bhagwati for the first time observed that where a person or class of persons to whom legal injury is caused by reason of violation of a fundamental right is unable to approach the Court for judicial redress on account of poverty or disability or socially or economically disadvantaged position, any member of the public acting *bona fide* can move the Court for relief under Article 32 and a *fortiorari*, also under Article 226, so that the fundamental rights may become meaningful not

20 *Bandhua Mukti Morcha* v *Union of India* (1984)3 SCC 161.
1 *S.P. Gupta* v *Union of India* (1982)2 SCR 365: 1981 (Supp) SCC 87.

only for the rich and the well-to-do who have the means to approach the Court but also for the large messes of people who are living a life of want and destitution and who are by reason of lack of awareness, assertiveness and resources unable to seek judicial redress.

The above view which the apex court took in the Judges' Appointment and Transfer case[2] is clearly within the terms of Article 32, says Justice Bhagwati, if only we look at the language of this article uninfluenced and uninhibited by any preconceptions and prejudices or any preconceived notions. Article 32, in so far as it is material, runs thus: Article 32 "(1) the right to move the Supreme Court by appropriate proceedings for the enforcement of the rights conferred by this Part is guaranteed. (2) The Supreme Court shall have power to issue directions or orders or writs, including writs in the nature of *habeas corpus*, *mandamus*, prohibition, *quo warranto* and *certiorari*, whichever may be appropriate, for the enforcement of any of the rights conferred by this part."

While interpreting Article 32, it must be borne in mind, says Justice Bhagwati,[2] that our approach must be guided not by any verbal or formalistic canons of construction but by the paramount object and purpose for which this article has been enacted as a fundamental right in the Constitution and its interpretation must receive illumination from the trinity of provisions which permeate and energise the entire Constitution, namely, the Preamble, the Fundamental Rights and the Directive Principles of State Policy.

Clause (1) of Article 32 confers the right to move the Supreme Court for enforcement of any of the fundamental rights, but it does not say as to who shall have this right to move the Supreme Court nor does it say by what proceedings the Supreme Court may be so moved. There is no limitation, asserts Justice Bhagwati,[2] in the words of Clause (1) of Article 32 that the fundamental right which is sought to be enforced by moving the Supreme Court should be one belonging to the person who moves the Supreme Court nor does it say that the Supreme Court should be moved only by a particular kind of proceeding. It is clear, says Justice Bhagwati,[2] on the plain language of Clause (1) of Article 32 that whenever there is a violation of a fundamental right, any one can move the Supreme Court for enforcement of such fundamental right. Of course, the Court would not, in exercise of its descretion, intervene at the instance of a meddlesome interloper or busybody and would ordinarily insist that only a person whose fundamental right is violatited should be allowed to activise the Court, but there is no fetter upon the

2 *Bandhua Mukti Morcha* v *Union of India* (1984)3 SCC 161: AIR 1984 SC 802.

power of the Court to entertain a proceeding initiated by any person other than the one whose fundamental right is violated. Justice Bhagwati says that when we have the case of a person or class of persons whose fundamental right is violated but who cannot have resort to the Court on account of his or their poverty or disability or socially or economically disadvantaged position, the Court, in such a case, can and must allow any member of the public acting *bona fide* to espouse the case of such person or class of persons and move the Court for judicial enforcement of the fundamental right of such person or class of persons. This does not violate, in the slightest measure, says Justice Bhagwati, the language of the Constitutional provision enacted in Clause (1) of Article 32.

Then again Clause (1) of Article 32 says that the Supreme Court can be moved for enforcement of a fundamental right by any 'appropriate' proceeding. Justice Bhagwati says that there is no limitation in regard to the kind of proceeding envisaged in Clause (1) of Article 32 except that the proceeding must be 'appropriate' and this requirement of appropriateness must be judged in the light of the purpose for which the proceeding is to be taken, namely, enforcement of a fundamental right. The Constitution makers deliberately did not lay down any particular form of proceeding, says Justice Bhagwati for enforcement of a fundamental right nor did they stipulate that such proceeding should conform to any rigid pattern or strait-jacket formula as, for example, in England, because they knew that in a country like India where there is so much of poverty, ignorance, illiteracy, deprivation and exploitation, any insistence on a rigid formula of proceeding for enforcement of a fundamental right would become self-defeating because it would place enforcement of fundamental rights beyond the reach of the common man and the entire remedy for enforcement of fundamental rights which the Constitution makers regarded as so precious and invaluable that they elevated it to the status of a fundamental right, would become a mere rope of sand so far as the large masses of the people in this country are concerned. The Constitution makers, therefore, advisedly provided in Clause (1) of Article 32 that the Supreme Court may be moved by any 'appropriate' proceeding, 'appropriate' not in terms of any particular form but 'appropriate' with reference to the purpose of the proceeding. That is the reason, says Justice Bhagwati, why it was held by the Supreme Court in the Judges' Appointment and Transfer case[3] that where a member of the public acting *bona fide* moves the Court for enforcement of a fundamental right on behalf of a person or

3 *S.P. Gupta* v *Union of India* (1982)2 SCR 365: 1981 (Supp) SCC 87.

class of persons who on account of poverty or disability or socially or economically disadvantaged position cannot approach the Court for relief, such member of the public may move the Court even by just writing a letter because it would not be right or fair to expect a person acting *pro bono publico* to incur expenses out of his own pocket for going to a lawyer and preparing a regular writ petition for being filed in Court for enforcement of a fundamental right of the poor and deprived sections of the community and in such a case, a letter addressed by him can legitimately be regarded as an 'appropriate' proceeding.

Justice Bhagwati then raises a question as to what is the power which may be exercised by the Supreme Court when it is moved by an 'appropriate' proceeding for enforcement of a fundamental right. Justice Bhagwati answered the question thus:[4] 'The only provision made by the Constitution makers in this behalf is to be found in Clause (2) of Article 32 which confers power on the Supreme Court "to issue directions or orders or writs including writs in the nature of *habeas corpus*, *mandamus*, prohibition, *quo warranto* and *certiorari*, whichever may be appropriate, for enforcement of any of the fundamental rights". It will be seen that the power conferred by Clause (2) of Article 32 is in the widest terms. It is not confined to issuing the high prerogative writs of *habeas corpus*, *mandamus* prohibition, *certiorari* and *quo warranto*, which are hedged in by strict conditions differing from one writ to another and which to quote the words spoken by Lord Atkin in *United Australia Ltd.* v *Barclays Bank Ltd.*[5] in another context often "stand in the path of justice clanking their medieval chains". But it is much wider and includes within its matrix, power to issue any directions, orders or writs which may be appropriate for enforcement of the fundamental right in question and this is made amply clear by the inclusive clause which refers to (writs) in the nature of *habeas corpus*, *mandamus*, prohibition, *quo warranto* and *certiorari*.' It is not only the high prerogative writs of *mandamus*, *habeas corpus*, prohibition, *quo warranto* and *certiorari* which can be issued by the Supreme Court but it can also issue directions or orders and writs in the nature of these high prerogative writs and therefore even if the conditions for issue of any of these high prerogative writs are not fulfilled, the Supreme Court would not be constrained to fold its hands in despair and plead its inability to help the citizen who has come before it for judicial redress, but would have power to issue any direction, order or writ including a

4 *Bandhua Mukti Morcha* v *Union of India* (1984)3 SCC 161: AIR 1984 SC 802.
5 [1941] AC 1: [1939]2 KB 53.

writ in the nature of any high prerogative writ. This provision conferring on the Supreme Court power to enforce the fundamental rights in the widest possible terms, says Justice Bhagwati,[6] shows the anxiety of the Constitution makers not to allow any procedural technicalities to stand in the way of enforcement of fundamental rights. The Constitution makers clearly intended that the Supreme Court should have the amplest power to issue whatever direction, order or writ may be appropriate in a given case for enforcement of a fundamental right.[7] But as regards the procedure to be followed by the Supreme Court in exercising the power to issue such direction, order or writ, the Constitution is silent because the Constitution makers never intended to fetter the discretion of the Supreme Court to evolve a procedure appropriate in the circumstances of a given case for the purpose of enabling it to exercise its power of enforcing a fundamental right. Justice Bhagwati asserts that neither Clause (2) of Article 32 nor any other provision of the Constitution requires that any particular procedure shall be followed by the Supreme Court in exercising its power to issue an appropriate direction, order or writ. The purpose for which the power to issue an appropriate direction, order or writ is conferred on the Supreme Court, opines Justice Bhagwati, is to secure enforcement of a fundamental right and obviously, therefore, whatever procedure is necessary for fulfilment of that purpose must be permissible to the Supreme Court. It is not at all obligatory, says Justice Bhagwati, that adversarial procedure, where each party produces his own evidence tested by cross-examination by the other side and the judge sits like an umpire and decides the case only on the basis of such material as may be produced before him by both parties, must be followed in a proceeding under Article 32 for enforcement of a fundamental right. In fact, there is no such Constitutional compulsion enacted in Clause (2) of Article 32 or in any other part of the Constitution. It is only because we have been following the adversarial procedure for over a century owing to the

6 *Bandhua Mukti Morcha* v *Union of India* (1984)3 SCC 161: AIR 1984 SC 802.

7 AUTHOR'S NOTE: In exercise of this wide power, the Supreme Court in *Bandhua Mukti Morcha* v *Union of India* (1984)3 SCC 161: AIR 1984 SC 802 not only directed quick rehabilitation of bonded labourers who had been released from bondage in pursuance of the court's direction to make the release meaningful to them but also issued a number of positive suggestions to improve upon the functioning of the Bonded Labour System (Abolition) Act 1976. In another case, *Upendra Baxi* v *State of UP* (1986)4 SCC 106: AIR 1987 SC 191 the apex court issued elaborate directions for the welfare of the inmates of a protective home for girls, including a direction to the State Government to put up a direct rehabilitation programme for these inmates who might be released from the protective home.

introduction of the Anglo-Saxon system of jurisprudence under the British Rule that it has become a part of our conscious as well as subconscious thinking that every judicial proceeding must be cast in the mould of adversarial procedure and that justice cannot be done unless the adversarial procedure is adopted. But Justice Bhagwati says that there is nothing sacrosanct about the adversarial procedure and in fact it is not followed in many other countries where the civil system of law prevails. The adversarial procedure with evidence led by either party and tested by cross-examination by the other party and the judge playing a passive role has become a part of our legal system because it is embodied in the Code of Civil Procedure and the Indian Evidence Act. But these statutes, Justice Bhagwati says, obviously have no application where a new jurisdiction is created in the Supreme Court for enforcement of a fundamental right. It would not be justified, says Justice Bhagwati, to impose any restriction on the power of the Supreme Court to adopt such procedure as it thinks fit in exercise of its new jurisdiction, by engrafting adversarial procedure on it, when the Constitution makers have deliberately chosen not to insist on any such requirement and instead, left it open to the Supreme Court to follow such procedure as it thinks appropriate for the purpose of securing the end for which the power is conferred, namely, enforcement of a fundamental right. There is a considerable body of juristic opinion in our country which believes that strict adherence to the adversarial procedure can sometimes lead to injustice, particularly where the parties are not evenly balanced in social or economic strength. Where one of the parties to a litigation belongs to a poor and deprived section of the community and does not possess adequate social and material resources, he is bound to be at a disadvantage position as against a strong and powerful opponent under the adversary system of justice, because of his difficulty in getting competent legal representation and more than anything else, his inability to produce relevant evidence before the court. Therefore, when the poor come before the Court, particularly for enforcement of their fundamental rights, it is necessary, says Justice Bhagwati, to depart from the adversarial procedure and to evolve a new procedure which will make it possible for the poor and the weak to bring the necessary material before the Court for the purpose of securing enforcement of their fundamental rights. Justice Bhagwati cautions that the problems of the poor which are now coming before the Court are qualitatively different from those which have hitherto occupied the attention of the Court and they need a different kind of lawyering skill and a different kind of judicial approach. If we blindly follow the adversarial procedure in their case, Justice Bhagwati says, they would never be able to enforce their fundamental rights and the result would be nothing but a mockery of the Constitution. We have, therefore, to abandon the *laissez faire* approach in the judicial process particularly where it involves a question of enforcement of fundamental rights and forge new tools, devise new methods and adopt new strategies for the purpose of making fundamental rights meaningful for the large masses of people. And this is clearly permissible on the language of Clause (2) of Article 32 because the Constitution makers while enacting that clause have deliberately and advisedly not used any words restricting the power of the Court to adopt any procedure which it considers appropriate in the circumstances of a given case for enforcing a fundamental right. It is true that the adoption of this non-traditional approach, says Justice Bhagwati, is not likely to find easy acceptance from the generality of lawyers because their minds are conditioned by constant association with the existing system of administration of justice which has become ingrained in them as a result of long years of familiarity and experience and become part of their mental make-up and habit and they would, therefore, always have an unconscious predilection for the prevailing system of administration of justice. But Justice Bhagwati says, if we want the fundamental rights to become a living reality and the Supreme Court to become a real sentinel on the *qui vive*, we must free ourselves from the shackles of outdated and outmoded assumptions and bring to bear on the subject fresh outlook and original unconventional thinking.

Justice Bhagwati lays emphasis on the fact that the poor and the disadvantaged cannot possibly produce relevant material before the Court in support of their case and equally where an action is brought on their behalf by a citizen acting *pro bono publico*, it would be almost impossible for him to gather the relevant material and place it before the Court. In the face of such situation, Justice Bhagwati throws two questions: What is the Supreme Court to do in such a case? Would the Supreme Court not be failing in discharge of its constitutional duty of enforcing a fundamental right if it refuses to intervene because the petitioner belonging to the underprivileged segment of society or a public spirited citizen espousing his cause is unable to produce the relevant material before the Court? If the Supreme Court adopts a passive approach and declines to intervene in such a case because relevant material has not been produced before it by the party seeking its intervention, the fundamental rights would remain merely a teasing illusion so far as the poor and disadvantaged sections of the community are concerned. It is for this reason, asserts Justice Bhagwati, that the Supreme Court has evolved the practice of appointing commissioners for the purpose of gathering facts and data in regard to a complaint of breach of a fundamental right made on behalf of the weaker sections of the society. The report of the commissioner would furnish *prima facie* evidence of the facts and data gathered by the commissioner and that is why the Supreme Court is careful to appoint a responsible person as commissioner to make an enquiry or investigation into the facts relating to the complaint. It may be of interest to note that in the past the Supreme Court has appointed sometimes a district magistrate, sometimes a district judge, sometimes a professor of law, sometimes a journalist, sometimes an officer of the Court and sometimes an advocate practising in the Court, for the purpose of carrying out an enquiry or investigation and making report to the Court because the commissioner appointed by the Court must be a responsible person who enjoys the confidence of the Court and who is expected to carry out his assignment objectively and impartially without any predilection or prejudice. Once the report of the commissioner is received, copies of it would be supplied to the parties so that either party, if it wants to dispute any of the facts or data stated in the report, may do so by filing an affidavit and the Court then consider the report of the commissioner and the affidavits which may have been filed and proceed to adjudicate upon the issue arising in the writ petition. It would be entirely for the Court to consider what weight to attach to the facts and data stated in the report of the commissioner and to what extent to act upon such facts and data. But it would not be correct to say that the report of the commissioner has no evidentiary value at all, since the statements made in it are not tested by cross-examination. To accept this contention would be to introduce the adversarial procedure in a proceeding where in the given situation, it is totally inapposite. Sometimes reliance is placed on Order XXVI of the Code of Civil Procedure and Order XLVI of the Supreme Court Rules, 1966 for the purpose of contending that a commissioner can be appointed by the Supreme Court only for the purpose of examining witnesses, making legal investigations and examining accounts and the Supreme Court has no power to appoint a commissioner for making an inquiry or investigation into facts relating to a complaint of violation of a fundamental right in a proceeding under Article 32. It is true, says Justice Bhagwati, that Order XLVI of the Supreme Court Rules, 1966 makes the provisions of Order XXVI of the Code of Civil Procedure, except Rules 13, 14, 19, 20, 21 and 22, applicable to the Supreme Court and lays down the procedure for an application for issue of a commissioner, but Order XXVI is not exhaustive and does not detract from the inherent power of the Supreme Court to appoint a commissioner, if the appointment of such commissioner is found necessary for the purpose of securing enforcement of a fundamental right in exercise of its constitutional jurisdiction under Article 32. Order XLVI of the Supreme Court Rules, 1966 cannot in any way militate against the power of the Supreme Court under Article 32 and in fact Rule 6 of Order XLVII of the Supreme Court Rules, 1966 provides that nothing in those rules "shall be deemed to limit or otherwise affect the inherent powers of the Court to make such orders as may be necessary for the ends of justice."[8]

5 Part IV—Directive Principles of State Policy—the conscience of the Constitution

A. *Theme of Directive Principles* The Directive Principles, says Justice Bhagwati, aim at making the Indian masses free in the positive sense, free from the passivity engendered by centuries of coercion by society and by nature, free from the abject physical conditions that had prevented them from fulfilling their best salves. To create socio-economic conditions in which there can be social and economic justice to everyone is the theme of Directive Principles. It is the Directive Principles which nourish the roots of our democracy, provide strength and vigour to it and attempt to make it a real participatory democracy which does not remain merely a political democracy but also becomes social and economic democracy with fundamental rights available to all irrespective of their power, position or wealth. The dynamic provisions of the Directive Principles fertilise the static provisions of the Fundamental Rights. The object of the Fundamental Rights is to protect individual liberty, but individual liberty cannot be considered in isolation from the socio-economic structure in which it is to operate. Under the present socio-economic system, it is the liberty of the few which is in conflict

8 AUTHOR'S NOTE: What has been said in regard to the exercise of jurisdiction by the Supreme Court under Article 32 must apply equally in relation to the exercise of jurisdiction by the High Courts under Article 226, for the latter jurisdiction is also a new constitutional jurisdiction and it is conferred in the same wide terms as the jurisdiction under Article 32 and the same powers can and must, therefore, be exercised by the High Courts while exercising jurisdiction under Article 226. In fact, the jurisdiction of the High Courts under Article 226 is much wider, because the High Courts are required to exercise this jurisdiction not only for enforcement of a fundamental right but also for enforcement of any legal right and there are many rights conferred on the poor and the disadvantaged which are the creation of statute and they need to be enforced as urgently and vigoriously as fundamental rights. *Bandhua Mukti Morcha* v *Union of India* (1984)3 SCC 161, per Bhagwati, J.

with the liberty of the many. The Directive Principles, says Justice Bhagwati, impose an obligation on the State to take positive action for creating socio-economic conditions in which there will be an egalitarian social order with social and economic justice to all, so that individual liberty will become a cherished value and the dignity of the individual a living reality, not only for a few privileged persons but for the entire people of the country. Directive Principles, in the opinion of Justice Bhagwati, enjoy a very high place in the Constitutional scheme and it is only in the framework of the socio-economic structure envisaged in the Directive Principles that the Fundamental Rights are intended to operate, for it is only then they can become meaningful and significant for the millions of our poor and deprived people who do not have even the bare necessities of life and who are living below the poverty level.

B. ***Article 37 of the Indian Constitution and Article 45 of the Irish Constitution—a comparative analysis*** The Directive Principles set out in Part IV of the Constitution starts with Article 37 which, to Justice Bhagwati's mind, is an article of crucial importance. It says: "The provisions contained in this Part shall not be enforceable by any court, but the principles therein laid down are nevertheless fundamental in the governance of the country and it shall be the duty of the State to apply these principles in making laws." It is necessary, in order to appreciate the full implications of this article, to compare it with the corresponding provision in the Irish Constitution which provided to some extent the inspiration for introducing Directive Principles in the Constitution. Article 45 of the Irish Constitution provides: "The principles of social policy set forth in this Article are intended for the general guidance of the Direchtas. The application of those principles in the making of laws shall be the care of the Direchtas exclusive and shall not be cognizable for any court under any of the provisions of the Constitution".[9]

It is interesting to note, says Justice Bhagwati,[9] that Article 37 of the Constitution of India makes three significant departures form the language of Article 45 of the Irish Constitution; first whereas Article 45 provides that the application of the principles of social policy shall not be cognizable by any court, Article 37 says that the Directive Principles shall not be enforceable by any court; secondly whereas Article 45 provides that the principles of social policy are intended for the general guidance of the Direchtas, Article 37 makes the Directive Principles fundamental in the governance of the country; and lastly, whereas Article 45 declares that

9 *Minerva Mills Ltd.* v *Union of India* AIR 1980 SC 1789 at p. 1847, para 114.

the application of principles of social policy in the making of laws shall be the care of the Direchtas exclusively, Article 37 enacts that it shall be the duty of the State to apply the Directive Principles in making laws. The changes made by the framers of the Constitution are vital and they have the effect of bringing about a total transformation or metamorphosis of this provision, fundamentally altering its significance and efficacy.

C. ***Directive Principles not of subordinate importance to any other part of the Constitution*** Justice Bhagwati opines that merely because Directive Principles are not enforceable by the judicial process does not mean that they are of subordinate importance to any other part of the Constitution. At one time a view was taken by the Supreme Court[10] to the effect that because Fundamental Rights are made enforceable in a court of law and Directive Principles are not, "the Directive Principles have to conform to and run as subsidiary to the chapter on Fundamental Rights." This view, says Justice Bhagwati, was patently wrong and within a few years an opportunity was found by the apex court in Re, *Kerala Education Bill*[11] to introduce a qualification by stating that: "Nevertheless in determining the scope and ambit of the Fundamental Rights relied on by or on behalf of any person or body, the court may not entirely ignore these Directive Principles of State Policy laid down in Part IV of the Constitution but should adopt the principle of harmonious construction and should attempt to give effect to both as much as possible." But even this observation, according to Justice Bhagwati, seemed to give greater importance to Fundamental Rights as against Directive Principles and that was primarily because the Fundamental Rights are enforceable by the judicial process while the Directive Principles are expressly made non-enforceable. Justice Bhagwati is, however, of the opinion which found its expression in *Minerva Mill's* case[12] that: "Whether or not a particular mandate of the Constitution is enforceable by the court has no bearing on the importance of that mandate. The Constitution contains many important mandates which may not be enforceable by the courts of law. That does not mean that those Articles must render subsidiary to the Chapter on Fundamental Rights ...... it would be wrong to say that those positive mandates", that is the positive mandates contained in the Directive Principles, "are of lesser significance than the mandates under Part III."

10 *State of Madras* v *Champakam Dorairajan* AIR 1951 SC 226: 1951 SCR 525.
11 AIR 1958 SC 956: 1959 SCR 995.
12 *Minerva Mills Ltd.* v *Union of India* AIR 1980 SC 1789 at p. 1848.

Justice Bhagwati says that we are so much obsessed by the Hohfeldian Classification that we tend to think of rights, liberties, powers and privileges as being invariably linked with the corresponding concept of duty, liability and immunity. We find it difficult to conceive of obligations or duties which do not create corresponding rights in others. But the Hohfeldian concept does not provide a satisfactory analysis in all kinds of jural relationships and breaks down in some cases where it is not possible to say that the duty in one creates an enforceable right in another. There may be a rule which imposes an obligation on an individual or authority and yet it may not be enforceable in a court of law and therefore not give rise to a corresponding enforceable right in another person. But it would still be a legal rule because it prescribes a norm of conduct to be followed by such individual or authority. The law may provide a mechanism for enforcement of this obligation, but the existence of the obligation does not depend upon the creation of such mechanism. The obligation exists prior to and independent of the mechanism of enforcement. A rule imposing an obligation or duty would not, therefore, cease to be a rule of law because there is no regular judicial or quasi-judicial machinery to enforce its command. Such a rule would exist despite of any problem relating to its enforcement. Otherwise the conventions of the Constitution and even rules of international law would no longer be liable to be regarded as rules of law.

"It is, therefore, to my mind, clear", says Justice Bhagwati,[13] "beyond doubt that merely because the Directive Principles are not enforceable in a court of law, it does not mean that they cannot create obligations or duties binding on the State. The crucial test which has to be applied is whether the Directive Principles impose any obligations or duties on the State; if they do, the State would be bound by a constitutional mandate to carry out such obligations or duties, even though no corresponding right is created in any one which can be enforced in a court of law."

D. ***Two significant aspects of the Principles*** Two significant things are required to be noted in this context. First is that Article 37 says that Directive Principles are "nevertheless fundamental in the governance of the country and it shall be the duty of the State to apply those principles in making laws." There could not have been more explicit language used by the Constitution makers, says Justice Bhagwati, to

13 *Ibid* 12.

make the Directive Principles binding on the State and there can be no doubt that the State is under a constitutional obligation to carry out this mandate contained in Article 37. In fact, the learned Judge says, non-compliance with the Directive Principles would be unconstitutional on the part of the State and it would not only constitute a breach of faith with the people who imposed this constitutional obligation on the State but it would also render a vital part of the Constitution meaningless and futile. The second significant aspect to note is that for the purpose of Directive Principles, the "State" has the same meaning as given to it under Article 13 for the purpose of the Fundamental Rights. This would mean that the same State which is injuncted from taking any action in infringement of the fundamental rights is told in no uncertain terms that it must regard the Directive Principles as fundamental in the governance of the country and is positively mandated to apply them in making laws. This, according to Justice Bhagwati, gives rise to a paradoxical situation and its implications are far-reaching. The State is, on the one hand, prohibited by the Constitutional injunction in Article 13 from making any law or taking any executive action which would infringe any Fundamental Right and on the other hand is directed by the constitutional mandate in Article 37 to apply the Directive Principles in the governance of the country and to make laws for giving effect to the Directive Principles. Both are constitutional obligations of the State and the question is, asks Justice Bhagwati, as to which one must prevail when there is a conflict between the two. In answering the question, Justice Bhagwati says that "the intention of the Constitution makers was that the Fundamental Rights should operate within the socio-economic structure or a wider continuum envisaged by the Directive Principles, for then only would the Fundamental Rights become exercisable by all and a proper balance and harmony between Fundamental Rights and Directive Principles secured".[14] "The Constitution makers", says the learned Judge, "never contemplated that a conflict would arise between the constitutional obligation in regard to Fundamental Rights and the constitutional mandate in regard to Directive Principles".[14] But if a conflict does arise between these two constitutional mandates of equal fundamental character, the path of resolving the same has not been shown in the Constitution. The Constitution did not provide any answer because such a situation was not anticipated by the Constitution makers and this problem has to be solved by Parliament and some *modus operandi*

14 *Minerva Mills Ltd.* v *Union of India* AIR 1980 SC 1789 at p. 1851.

has to be evolved in order to eliminate the possibility of conflict howsoever remote it might be. The way, says Justice Bhagwati was shown in no uncertain terms by Jawaharlal Nehru when he said in the Lok Sabha in the course of discussion on the Constitution (First Amendment) Bill:[15]

"The Directive Principles of State Policy represent a dynamic move towards a certain objective. The Fundamental Rights represent something static, to preserve certain rights which exist. Both again are right. But somehow and sometime it might so happen that that dynamic movement and that static standstill do not quite fit into each other.

The dynamic movement towards a certain objective necessarily means certain changes taking place: that is the essence of movement. Now it may be that in the process of dynamic movement certain existing relationships are altered, varied or affected. In fact, they are meant to affect those settled relationships and yet if you come back to the Fundamental Rights they are meant to preserve, not indirectly, certain settled relationships. There is a certain conflict in the two approaches, not inherently, because that was not meant, I am quite sure. But there is that slight difficulty and naturally when the courts of the land have to consider these matters they have to lay stress more on the Fundamental Rights than on Directive Principles. The result is that the whole purpose behind the Constitution, which was meant to be a dynamic Constitution leading to a certain goal step by step, is somewhat hampered and hindered by the static element being emphasized a little more than the dynamic element .... If in the protection of individual liberty you protect also individual or group inequality, then you come into conflict with that Directive Principle which wants, according to your own Constitution, a gradual advance, or let us put it in another way, not so gradual but more rapid advance, whenever possible to a State where there is less and less inequality and more and more equality. If any kind of an appeal to individual liberty and freedom is construed to mean as an appeal to the continuation of the existing inequality, then you get into difficulties. Then you become static, unprogressive and cannot change and you cannot realize the ideal of an egalitarian society which I hope most of us aim at."

Parliament by constitutional amendment took the view that the constitutional obligation in regard to Directive Principles should have precedence over the constitutional obligation in regard to the Fundamental Rights in Articles 14 and 19, because Fundamental Rights

15 *Ibid* 14 at p. 1851-52.

though precious and valuable for maintaining the democratic way of life have absolutely no meaning for the poor, down trodden and economically backward classes of people who unfortunately constitute the bulk of the people of India and the only way in which Fundamental Rights can be made meaningful for them is by implementing the Directive Principles, for the Directive Principles are intended to bring about a socio-economic revolution and to create a new socio-economic order where there will be social and economic justice for all and every one, not only a fortunate few but the teeming millions of India, would be able to participate in the fruits of freedom and development and exercise the Fundamental Rights.

Justice Bhagwati in this context quoted Chandrachud, J. (as he then was) who in *Kesavananda Bharati's* case[16] said that 'the Constitution accords a place of pride to Fundamental Rights and place of permanence to the Directive Principles. .... As I look at the provisions of Parts III and IV, I feel no doubt that the basic object of conferring freedoms on individuals is the ultimate achievement of the ideas set out in Part IV. A circumspect use of the freedoms guaranteed by Part III is bound to subserve the common good but voluntary submission to restraints is a philosopher's dream. Therefore, Article 37 enjoins the State to apply the Directive Principles in making laws. The freedom of a few have then to be abridged in order to ensure the freedom of all. ...... The Nation stands today at the cross-roads of history and exchanging the time honoured place of the phrase, may I say that the Directive Principles of State of Policy should not be permitted to become "a mere sand of the rope". If the State fails to create conditions in which the fundamental freedoms could be enjoyed by all, the freedom of the few will be at the mercy of the many and then all freedoms will vanish. In order, therefore, to preserve their freedom, the privileged few must part with a portion of it.'

E. *Role of the Supreme Court in enforcing Directive Principles* In its zeal to enforce justiciable human rights, the Indian Supreme Court has been indirectly enforcing non-justiciable human rights. In infusing dynamism into these non-justiciable human rights, the Court has been prompted by the philosophy of social justice or social rights, which are a counterpart of justiciable individual rights. The task of national reconstruction, says Justice Bhagwati, has brought about enormous increase in development activities and law is being utilised for the purpose of development, social and economic. It is creating more and more a new category of rights in favour of a large section of people and imposing a

16 *Kesavananda Bharati* v *State of Kerala* (1973) Supp SCR 1.

new category of duties on the State with a view to reaching social justice to the common man. This is not to say that individual rights have ceased to have a vital place in our society but it is recognised that these rights are meaningless in today's setting unless accompanied by the social rights necessary to make them effective and really accessible to all.

The new social and economic rights which are sought to be created in pursuance of the Directive Principles of State Policy essentially require active intervention of the State. In these cases, the duty which is breached giving rise to the injury is owed by the State not to any specific or determinate class or group of persons, but to the general public. Now if breach of such public duty were allowed to go unredressed because there is no one who has received a specific legal injury, the failure to perform such public duty would go unchecked. It would also make the new social collective rights and interests created for the benefit of the deprived sections of the community meaningless and ineffectual.

Thus, to enforce the obligation of the State under Article 39A of the Constitution, to ensure that opportunities for securing justice are not denied to any citizen by reason of economic or other disabilities, the Court directed[17] that the State Government shall extend its cooperation and support to certain categories of voluntary organisations and social action groups in running the legal aid programme and organising legal aid camps and lok adalats or *niti melas*. In another case,[18] the Court directed the State Government to offer minimum wages to workers engaged in drought relief operations (Article 43), at the same time wishing the Central Government to provide necessary financial assistance to the State Government to enable it to bear the expenditure involved. In yet another case,[19] the Court issued directions to enforce the obligation of the State, under Article 48A, to protect and improve the environment and to safeguard the forests and wild life of the country. For the same purpose, the Court in another case[20] issued directions as to the workings of an industry manufacturing hazardous chemicals and gases. In order to ensure that the State carries out its obligation under Article 39(1) to protect children, the Court in a case

17 *S.P. Gupta* v *Union of India* AIR 1982 SC 149.
18 *Special Works* v *State of Rajasthan* (1986) Supp SCC 561.
19 *Rural Litigation and Entitlemeent Kendra, Dehradun* v *State of UP* AIR 1985 SC 652: (1985)2 SCC 431: AIR 1987 SC 2426: (1989)3 SCC 615.
20 *M.C. Mehta* v *Union of India* (1986)2 SCC 176.

directed that a State Government should bring into force its Children Act without delay.

6 Fundamental Rights in Part III and Directive Principles in Part IV of the Constitution—both part of the broad spectrum of human rights 'It is not possible', says Justice Bhagwati[21] 'to fit Fundamental Rights and Directive Principles in two distinct and strictly defined categories, but it may be stated broadly that Fundamental Rights represent civil and political rights while Directive Principles embody social and economic rights. Both are clearly part of the broad spectrum of human rights. If we look at the Universal Declaration of Human Rights adopted by the General Assembly of the United Nations on 18th December 1948, we find that it contains not only rights protecting individual freedom (Articles 1 to 21) but also social and economic rights intended to ensure socio-economic justice to every one (Articles 22 to 29). There are also two International Covenants adopted by the General Assembly for securing human rights, one is the International Covenant on Civil and Political Rights and the other is the International Covenant on Economic, Social and Cultural Rights. Both are international instruments relating to human rights. It is ...... not correct to say that Fundamental Rights alone are based on human rights while Directive Principles fall in some category other than human rights. The socio-economic rights embodied in the Directive Principles are as much a part of human rights as the Fundamental Rights. Hegde and Mukherjea, JJ. were, to my mind, right in saying in *Kesavananda Bharati's* case[22] that "the Directive Principles and the Fundamental Rights mainly proceed on the basis of human rights". Together, they are intended to carry out the objective set out in the Preamble of the Constitution and to establish an egalitarian social order informed with political, social and economic justice and ensuring dignity of the individual not only to a few privileged persons but to the entire people of the country including the have-nots and the handicapped, the lowliest and the lost.'

Justice Bhagwati says that[23] 'although Fundamental Rights and Directive Principles appear in the Constitution as distinct entities, there was no such demarcation made between them during the period prior to the framing of the Constitution. ...... They were both placed on the same pedestal and treated as falling within the same category

21 *Minerva Mills Ltd.* v *Union of India* AIR 1980 SC 1789 at p. 1844, para 111.
22 *Kesavananda Bharati* v *State of Kerala* (1973) Supp SCR 1: AIR 1973 SC 1461.
23 *Minerva Mills Ltd.* v *Union of India* AIR 1980 SC 1789 at p. 1845, para 112.

compendiously described as "Fundamental Rights". The Sapru Committee in its Constitutional Proposals made in 1945, recommended that the declaration of Fundamental Rights in its wider sense was absolutely necessary and envisaged these rights as falling in two classes; one justiciable and the other non-justiciable—the former being enforceable in Courts of law and the latter, not. The Committee, however, felt difficulty in dividing the Fundamental Rights into these two classes and, left the whole issue to be settled by the Constitution-making body with the observation that though the task was difficult, it was by no means impossible. This suggestion of the Sapru Committee perhaps drew its inspiration from the Irish Constitution of 1937, which made a distinction between justiciable and non-justiciable rights and designated the former as Fundamental Rights and the latter as Directive Principles of Social Policy. ...... Sir B.N. Rau, who was the Constitutional Adviser to the Government of India, was considerably impressed by these ideas and he suggested that the best way of giving effect to the objectives set out in the Objectives Resolution was to split-up the objectives into Fundamental Rights and Fundamental Principles of State Policy, the former relating to personal and political rights enforceable in Courts of Law and the latter relating to social and economic rights and other matters, not so enforceable and proposed that the Chapter on Fundamental Rights may be split-up into two parts; Part A dealing with the latter kind of rights under the heading "Fundamental Principles of Social Policy" and Part B dealing with the former under the heading "Fundamental Rights". The Fundamental Rights Sub-Committee also recommended that "the list of fundamental rights should be prepared in two parts, the first part consisting of rights enforceable by appropriate legal process and the second consisting of Directive Principles of Social Policy." A week later, while moving for consideration, the Interim Report on Fundamental Rights, Sardar Vallabhbhai Patel said:

"This is a preliminary report or an interim report because the Committee when it sat down to consider the question of fixing the fundamental rights and its incorporation into the Constitution, came to the conclusion that the Fundamental Rights should be divided into two parts—the first part justiciable and the other non-justiciable."

This position was reiterated by Sardar Vallabhbhai Patel when he said while presenting the Supplementary Report: "There were two parts of the Report; one contained Fundamental Rights which were justiciable and the other part of the Report referred to Fundamental Rights which were not justiciable but were directives ......".'

'It will, therefore, be seen', continues Justice Bhagwati,[24] 'that from the point of view of importance and significance, no distinction was drawn between justiciable and non-justiciable rights and both were treated as forming part of the rubric of Fundamental Rights, the only difference being that whereas the former were to be enforceable in Courts of Law, the latter were not to be so enforceable. ... And the reason for this is obvious. It has been expressed succinctly by the Planning Commission in the following words:

"The non-justiciability clause only provides that the infant State shall not be immediately called upon to account for not fulfilling the new obligations laid upon it. A State just awakened to freedom with its many pre-occupations might be crushed under the burden unless it was free to decide the order, the time, the place and the mode of fulfilling them."

The social and economic rights and other matters dealt with in the Directive Principles are by their very nature incapable of judicial enforcement and moreover, the implementation of many of those rights would depend on the state of economic development in the country, the availability of necessary finances and the Government's assessment of priority of objectives and values and that is why they are made non-justiciable. But merely because the Directive Principles are non-justiciable, it does not follow that they are in any way subservient or inferior to the Fundamental Rights.'

24 *Minerva Mills Ltd.* v *Union of India* AIR 1980 SC 1789 at p. 1846, para 112.

[I]n testing the validity of the State action with reference to fundamental rights, what the court must consider is the direct and inevitable consequence of State action.

— P.N. BHAGWATI*

6

State Action and the Constitutional Implications

SYNOPSIS

1 Introduction To enforce human rights, the courts in India expanded their jurisdiction by innovating the strategy of 'public interest' litigation as regards the petitioner. An indepth study on the importance of the strategy of public interest litigation in the legal history of the country has been made in Chapter 9. But the courts' responsibility did not end there. The category of respondent has similarly been enlarged by the courts by applying the doctrine of 'State action.'

2 Origin of the doctrine The doctrine of 'State action' had its origin in the USA, nearly a century after the adoption of its Constitution. While the First Amendment, adopted in 1791, was couched in the form of a prohibition against the Legislature alone by using the word 'Congress', the Fourteenth Amendment, adopted in 1869, extended the prohibition

* *Maneka Gandhi* v *Union of India* AIR 1978 SC 597: (1978)1 SCC 248.

in the "due process" and "equal protection" clauses to the 'State'. In interpreting the word 'State' in these clauses, the US Supreme Court first held[1] that it included all the organs and acts of the State- legislative, executive and judicial. Soon, however, it was realized[2] that, in order to be effective, the Fundamental Rights should be enforced not only against the acts of the officers of the State but also its "agents". An "agent" was a person who acted in the name of and for the State, or is clothed with the powers of the State[3] or endowed with governmental functions.[4] Gradually, the doctrine has come to be applied even to acts of a private person or body,[5] where its action is supported by the Government even without legislative sanction or in abuse of its legislative authority;[6] or where the State has become involved in such private action.[7] The test to be applied is: whether the infringement of the petitioner's right is 'fairly attributable to the State'.[8]

3 Essence of the doctrine The essence of the doctrine is that the State cannot get rid of constitutional limitations or restraints by simply delegating its powers or functions to some private individual or group. Since such a person acts as the agent or the instrumentality of the State, he must be subject to the same limitations, such as the fundamental rights, that the Constitution imposes upon the State itself. Thus, under the doctrine of 'State action', remedy for infringement of a fundamental right would be available against a non-government body which acts as an 'agency or instrumentality' of the State, and, to that extent, it becomes an organ of the State.

4 Application of the doctrine in India In India, Justice Bhagwati says, the Supreme Court had an easier task in introducing the doctrine of 'State action' because (*i*) most of the Fundamental Rights included in Part III of the Constitution of India are addressed to the 'State', and (*iii*) Part III starts with the definition of the word 'State' in Article 12 of the Constitution which includes 'other authorities'.

Article 12 of the Constitution defines 'State' for the purpose of Part III of the Constitution thus: 12. Definition. 'In this part, unless the

1 *Strauder* v *W. Virginia* [1879]100 US 303.
2 Ex p. *Virginia* [1880]100 US 339.
3 *Pennsylvania* v *Board of Trust* [1957]353 US 230; *Steele* v *L.N.R.* [1944]323 US 192.
4 *Evans* v *Newton* [1966]382 US 296; *Blum* v *Yaretsky* [1982]457 US 991.
5 *Pruneyard Shopping Centre* v *Robins* [1980]447 US 74.
6 *Screws* v *U.S.* [1945]325 US 91.
7 *Sniadach* v *N.G.F.* [1975]419 US 601.
8 *Lugar* v *Edmondson* (1982)457 US 922; *Rendell-Baker* v *Kohn* [1982]457 US 830.

context otherwise requires, "the State" includes the Government and Parliament of India and the Government and the Legislature of each of the States and all local or other authorities within the territory of India or under the control of the Government of India.'

Article 12 contains a special definition with a broader goal and by a liberal interpretation of the word 'authority' as used in Article 12 the court has made the Fundamental Rights enforceable against numerous private bodies by treating such bodies as 'agencies' or instrumentalities' of the State.

5 Corporation as an 'agency' or 'instrumentality' of the State In John Marshall's view a corporation is an artificial being invisible, intangible and existing only in the contemplation of the law. Being the mere creature of the law, it possesses only those properties which the charter of its creation confers on it either expressly, or as incidental to its very existence. Those are such as are best calculated to effect the object for which it was created. Among the most important are immortality and individuality.[9]

Although corporate personality is not a modern invention, its adaptation, says Justice Bhagwati, to embrace the wide range of industry and commerce, has a modern flavour. Welfare States like ours called upon to execute many economic projects readily resort to this resourceful legal contrivance because of its practical advantages without a wee-bit of diminution in ownership and control of the undertaking. The true owner is the State, the real operator is the State and accountability for its actions to the community and to Parliament is of the State.[10] It is thus important to note that in case of corporations called upon to discharge economic projects of an welfare State, while the formal ownership is cast in the corporate mould, the reality boils down to state control.

So far as India is concerned, said Justice Bhagwati in *International Airport Authority of India's* case,[11] the genecies of the emergence of corporations as instrumentalities or agencies of government is to be found in the Government of India Resolution on Industrial Policy dated 6th April 1948, where it was stated *inter alia* that "management of State enterprise will as a rule be through the medium of public

9 *Dartmouth College* v *Woodward* [1819]4 Wheat 518.
10 *Som Prakash Rekhi* v *Union of India* AIR 1981 SC 212, per Krishna Iyer, J.
11 *R.D. Shetty* v *The International Airport Authority of India* AIR 1979 SC 1628.

corporation under the statutory control of the Central Government who will assume such powers as may be necessary to ensure this". It was in pursuance of the policy envisaged in this and subsequent resolutions on industrial policy, says Justice Bhagwati, that corporations were created by Government for setting up and management of public enterprises and carrying out other public functions. Ordinarily, says Justice Bhagwati, these functions could have been carried out by Government departmentally through its service personnel, but the instrumentality or agency of the corporations was resorted to in these cases having regard to the nature of the task to be performed. Today with increasing assumption by the Government of commercial ventures and economic projects, the corporation, Justice Bhagwati says in *Ajay Hasia's* case,[12] has become an effective legal contrivance in the hands of the Government for carrying out its activities, for it is found that this legal facility of corporate instrument provides considerable flexibility and elasticity and facilitates proper and efficient management with professional skills and on business principles and it is blissfully free from "departmental rigidity, slow motion procedure and hierarchy of officers."

A corporation may be created, says Justice Bhagwati,[13] in one of two ways. It may be either established by statute or incorporated under a law such as the Companies Act, 1956 or the Societies Registration Act, 1860.

The concept of instrumentality or agency of the government, said Justice Bhagwati,[14] is not limited to a corporation created by a statute but is equally applicable to a company or society and in a given case, it would have to be decided on a consideration of the relevant factors, whether the company or society is an instrumentality of the government so as to come within the meaning of the expression "authority" in Article 12.

6 Tests to determine whether a corporation is an instrumentality or agency of Government. What are the tests to determine whether a corporation established by statute or incorporated under law is an instrumentality or agency of government? Justice Bhagwati himself answered the question thus[13]: "It is not possible to formulate an all inclusive or exhaustive test which would adequately answer this question. There is

12 *Ajay Hasia* v *Khalid Mujib* AIR 1981 SC 487.
13 *R.D. Shetty* v *The International Airport Authority of India* AIR 1979 SC 1628.
14 *Ajay Hasia* v *Khalid Mujib* AIR 1981 SC 487.

no cut and dried formula which would provide the correct division of corporations into those which are instrumentalities or agencies of Government and those which are not". He, however, laid down[15] detailed guideline in determining the question as to whether a corporation established by statute or incorporated under law is an instrumentality or agency of government.

Where a corporation is wholly controlled by government not only in its policy making but also in carrying out the functions entrusted to it by the law establishing it or by the Charter of its incorporation, there can be no doubt that it would be an instrumentality or agency of government.[16]

But ordinarily where a corporation is established by statute, it is autonomous in its working, subject only to a provision, often times made, that it shall be bound by any directions that may be issued from time to time by government in respect of policy matters. So also a corporation incorporated under law is managed by a board of directors or committee of management in accordance with the provisions of the statute under which it is incorporated. Such a corporation becomes an instrumentality or agency of government in the following circumstances:[16]

(*a*) If the entire share capital of the corporation is held by government, it would go a long way towards indicating that the corporation is an instrumentality or agency of government.

(*b*) Where the financial assistance of the State is so much as to meet almost entire expenditure of the corporation, it would afford some indication of the corporation being impregnated with governmental character.

(*c*) A finding of State financial support plus an unusual degree of control over the management and policies might lead one to characterize an operation as State action.

(*d*) It may be a relevant factor to consider whether the corporation enjoys monopoly status which is State conferred or State protected. There can be little doubt that the State conferred or State protected monopoly status would be highly relevant in assessing the aggregate weight of the corporations' ties to the State.

15 *R.D. Shetty* v *The International Airport Authority of India* AIR 1979 SC 1628.
16 *Ibid* 15.

(*e*) If the functions of the corporation are of public importance and closely related to governmental functions, it would be a relevant factor in classifying the corporation as an instrumentality or agency of government. In other words, the public nature of the function, if impregnated with governmental character or 'tied or entwined with Government' or fortified by some other additional factor, may render the corporation an instrumentality or agency of government. Specifically, if a department of government is transferred to a corporation, it would be a strong factor supportive of this inference.

Justice Bhagwati, however, cautioned[17] that in the following spheres a corporation is not to be treated as an instrumentality or agency of government:

(*a*) A mere finding of some control by the State would not be determinative of the question that the corporation is an instrumentality or agency of government "since a State has considerable measure of control under its police power over all types of business opportunities."

(*b*) Where financial assistance is not so extensive, it may not by itself, without anything more, render the corporation an instrumentality or agency of government, for there are many private institutions which are in receipt of financial assistance from the State and merely on that count, they cannot be classified as State agencies.

Justice Bhagwati further expressed the view[17] that the particularization of the relevant factors in determining that a corporation is an instrumentality or agency of government is not exhaustive and by its very nature it cannot be, because with increasing assumption of new tasks, growing complexities of management and administration and the necessity of continuing adjustment in relations between the corporation and government calling for flexibility, adaptability and innovative skills, it is not possible to make an exhaustive enumeration of the tests which would invariably and in all cases provide an unfailing answer to the questions whether a corporation is governmental instrumentality or agency. Moreover, even amongst the factors which have been described, no one single factor will yield a satisfactory answer to the question and the court will have to consider the cumulative

17 *R.D. Shetty* v *The International Airport Authority of India* AIR 1979 SC 1628.

effect of those various factors and arrive at its decision on the basis of a particularized inquiry into the facts and circumstances of each case.

7 Corporations' limitation in constitutional and administrative law Justice Bhagwati expressed the view in *Airport Authority's* case[18] that the corporations acting as instrumentality or agency of government would obviously be subject to the same limitations in the field of constitutional and administrative law as government itself, though in the eye of the law, they would be distinct and independent legal entities. If government acting through its officers is subject to certain constitutional and public law limitations, it must follow a fortiori that government acting through the instrumentality or agency of corporations should equally be subject to the same limitations. The same view was expressed by Justice Bhagwati in *Ajay Hasia's* case.[19]

If a corporate body is but an instrumentality or agency of government, Part III of the Constitution dealing with Fundamental Rights will trammel its operation, asserts Justice Bhagwati. The State has an expansive role to play under Part IV of the Constitution in the form of undertaking a multitude of socio-economic operations keeping in mind the welfare of the people. "Having regard to the directive in Article 38 and the amplitude of other Articles in Part IV, Government may appropriately embark upon almost any activity", so remarks Justice Bhagwati quoting V.R. Krishna Iyer, J. in *Som Prakash's* case.[20] This expansive role of State is not, however, played at the expense of the cherished rights of the people entrenched in Part III. The Fundamental Rights, views Justice Bhagwati, cannot be forbidden access to corporations, companies, institutions and kindred bodies, which act as agencies of administration. If the access of Fundamental Rights is so forbidden, it will lead to a complete break-down of the rule of law and the constitutional order in a large sector of governmental activity carried on under the guise of 'jural persons'. It will hold no bar to tyranny by arbitrary administrators operated from behind by government but unaccountable to Part III of the Constitution. The court has to take the stand that corporations cannot be exonerated from the need to have constitutional conscience, they must be amenable to constitutional limitations as against the alternative of permitting them to flourish as an '*imperium in imperio*'. The view was urged

18 *R.D. Shetty* v *The International Airport Authority of India* AIR 1979 SC 1628.

19 *Ajay Hasia* v *Khalid Mujib* AIR 1981 SC 487.

20 *Som Prakash* v *Union of India* AIR 1981 SC 212.

strongly by Justice Bhagwati in *Ajay Hasia's* case[1] when he observed: "If such a corporation were to be free from the basic obligation to obey the Fundamental Rights, it would lead to considerable erosion of the efficiency of the Fundamental Rights, for in that event the Government would be enabled to override the Fundamental Rights by adopting the stratagem of carrying out its functions through the instrumentality or agency of a corporation, while remaining control over it. The Fundamental Rights would then be reduced to little more than an idle dream or a promise of unreality. It must be remembered that the Fundamental Rights are constitutional guarantees given to the people of India and are not merely paper hopes or fleeting promises and so long as they find a place in the Constitution, they should not be allowed to be emasculated in their application by a narrow and constricted judicial interpretation. The courts should be anxious to enlarge the scope and width of the Fundamental Rights by bringing within their sweep every authority which is an instrumentality or agency of the Government or through the corporate personality of which the Government is acting, so as to subject the Government in all its myriad activities, whether through natural persons or through corporate entitities, to the basic obligation of the Fundamental Rights."

Speaking about the application of the equality clause of the Constitution in the matter of employment in corporations set up or owned by the government and in its dealings with the employees, Justice Bhagwati expressed the view that the functions of the State has long since ceased to be confined to the preservation of the public peace, the exaction of taxes and the defence of its frontiers. It is now the function of the State to secure 'social, economic, and political justice', to preserve 'liberty of thought, expression, belief, faith and worship,' and to ensure 'equality of status and of opportunity'. That is the proclamation of the people in the Preamble to the Constitution. The desire to attain these objectives has necessarily resulted in intense governmental activity in manifold ways. Legislative and executive activities have reached very far and have touched very many aspects of a citizen's life. The government directly or through the corporations set up by it or owned by it, now owns or manages a large number of industries and institutions. It is the biggest builder in the country. Mammoth and minor irrigation projects, heavy and light engineering projects, projects of various kinds are undertaken by the government. The government is also the biggest trader in the country. The State and the multitudinous agencies and

1 *Ajay Hasia* v *Khalid Mujib* AIR 1981 SC 487.

corporations set up by it are the principal purchasers of the produce and the products of our country and they control a vast and complex machinery of distribution. The government, its agencies and instrumentalities, corporations set up by the government under the statutes and corporations incorporated under the Companies Act but owned by the government have thus become the biggest employers in the country. There is no good reason, views Justice Bhagwati, why if government is bound to observe the equality clause of the Constitution in the matter of employment and in its dealings with the employees, the corporations set up or owned by the government should not be equally bound and why, instead, such corporations could become citadels of patronage of arbitrary action. In a country like ours which teems in population, where the State, its agencies, its instrumentalities and its corporations are the biggest employers and where millions seek employment and security, to confine the applicability of the equality clauses of the Constitution, in relation to matters of employment, strictly to direct employment under the government is perhaps to mock at the Constitution and the people, asserts Justice Bhagwati. Some element of public employment is all that is necessary to take the employee out of the mischief of the rule that denies him access to a court to enforce a contract of employment and the protection of Articles 14 and 16 of the Constitution. After all, employment in the public sector has grown to vast dimensions and employees in the public sector often discharge as onerous duties as civil servants and participate in activities vital to our country's economy. In growing realization of the importance of employment in the public sector, Parliament and the Legislatures of the States have declared persons in the service of local authorities, government companies and statutory corporations as public servants and, extended the same to civil servants for the purpose of suits and prosecution. According to Justice Bhagwati, it is, therefore, right that the independence and integrity of those employed in the public sector should be secured as much as the independence and integrity of government servants. The compulsion of this reasoning in the Indian setting and constitutional matrix cannot be missed.

8 Juristic entity — not 'State' for the purpose of Part XIV of the Constitution

Merely because a juristic entity may be an "authority" and, therefore, 'State' within the meaning of Article 12, it may not be elevated to the position of "State" for the purpose of Articles 209, 310 and 311 which find a place in Part XIV of the Constitution. The definition of "State" in Article 12 which includes an "authority" within the territory of India or under the control of the Government of India is not limited in its application to Part III only but by virtue of Article 36, it extends to Part IV. It does not, however, extend to other provisions of the Constitution. Hence, a juristic entity, says Justice Bhagwati in *Ajay Hasia's* case,[2] which may be "State" for the purpose of Parts III and IV would not be so for the purpose of Part XIV or any other provision of the Constitution.

9 State action—constitutional validity with reference to Fundamental Rights—Test of determination Justice Bhagwati says that the law on this point has undergone radical change since the days of *A.K. Gopalan's* case.[3] That was the earliest decision of the Supreme Court on the subject, following almost immediately upon the commencement of the Constitution. The decision in *A.K. Gopalan's* case followed by *Ram Singh's* case[4] gave rise to the theory that the object and form of State action determine the extent of protection which may be claimed by an individual and the validity of such action has to be judged by considering whether it is "directly in respect of the subject covered by any particular article of the Constitution or touches the said article only incidentally or indirectly." The test to be applied for determining the constitutional validity of State action with reference to fundamental rights was: What is the object of the authority in taking the action; what is the subject matter of the action and to which fundamental right does it relate?

This theory that "the extent of protection of important guarantees, such as the liberty of person and right to property, depend upon the form and object of the State action and not upon its direct operation upon the individual's freedom" held sway, says Justice Bhagwati, for a considerable time and was applied in *Naresh Shridhar Mirajkar* v *State of Maharashtra*.[5]

In between 1950 (*A.K. Gopalan's* case) and 1967 (*Mirajkar's* case), there were two decisions given by the apex court which seemed to denote and strike, however, a different note. In *Express News Papers (P) Ltd.* v *Union of India*,[6] N.H. Bhagwati, J., speaking on behalf of the Court formulated the test of direct and inevitable effect for the purpose of adjudging whether a statute offends a particular fundamental right. In *Sakal Paper (P) Ltd.* v *Union of India*,[7] the test of direct and immediate effect was applied by the apex court and it was pointed out that "it is the substance and the practical result of the act of the State

2 *Ajay Hasia* v *Khalid Mujib* AIR 1981 SC 487.
3 *A.K. Gopalan* v *State of Madras* AIR 1950 SC 27: 1950 SCR 88.
4 *Ram Singh* v *State of Delhi* AIR 1951 SC 270: 1951 SCR 451.
5 AIR 1967 SC 1: (1966)3 SCR 744.
6 AIR 1958 SC 578: 1959 SCR 12.
7 AIR 1962 SC 305: (1962)3 SCR 842

that should be considered rather than its purely legal aspect" and "the correct approach in such cases should be to enquire as to what in substance is the loss or injury caused to the citizen and not merely what manner and method has been adopted by the State in placing the restriction".

It was *Cooper's* case,[8] says Justice Bhagwati, that turned the table upside down and the prevalent doctrine that the object and form of the State action alone determine the extent of protection that may be claimed by an individual and that the effect of the State action on the fundamental right of the individual is irrelevant was rejected and thrown overbroad. Speaking on behalf of the majority, Shah, J., in *Cooper's* case pointed out: " .... it is not the object of the authority making the law impairing the right of a citizen nor the form of action that determine the protection he can claim; it is the effect of the law and of the action upon the right which attract the jurisdiction of the Court to grant relief. If this be the true view, and we think it is, in determining the impact of State action upon constitutional guarantees which are fundamental, it follows that the extent of protection against impairment of a fundamental right is determined not by the object of the Legislature nor by the form of the action, but by its direct operation upon the individual's rights." "We are of the view", continued Shah, J. in *Cooper's* case, "that the theory that the object and form of the State action determine the extent of protection which the aggrieved party may claim not consistent with the constitutional scheme ......". Taking cue from Cooper's case, Justice Bhagwati said in *Maneka Gandhi's* case[9] that "in testing the validity of the State action with reference to fundamental rights, what the Court must consider is the direct and inevitable consequence of State action. Otherwise, the protection of the fundamental rights would be subtly but surely eroded."

8 *R.C. Cooper* v *Union of India* AIR 1970 SC 564: (1970)3 SCR 530 (a decision given by the Full Court consisting of eleven judges).

9 *Maneka Gandhi* v *Union of India* AIR 1978 SC 597: (1978)1 SCC 248.

"My love for freedom is my greatest love"
— P.N. BHAGWATI

7

Freedom of Speech and Press

SYNOPSIS

FREEDOM OF SPEECH

1 Freedom of speech—a necessary condition of survival 'Open up, maintain, and preserve the integrity of the channels of communication by which, men convey to one another what they perceive, feel, and desire', so said Lon L. Fuller.[1] Freedom of speech or expression,[2] a necessary condition of survival and a means of enriching and expanding

1 Lon L. Fuller: *The Morality of Law*, 185-6, rev. edn. (New Haven, Conn., 1969).
2 The terms 'freedom of speech' and 'freedom of expression' are used interchangeably throughout this chapter, unless the context indicates otherwise.

the meaning and scope of life, itself is, in the words of Justice Bhagwati, the first principle of natural law. It is not a cultural grace of the constitution but an ubiquitous right of the people of all strata.

The degree to which speech or expression should be granted constitutional protection and the precise justification for such a guarantee are controversial questions. But Justice Bhagwati defends the view of free speech that embodies the manifestation of its role as the servant of truth in the limited, but supremely important, sphere of truth and justice. From this perspective, freedom of speech or expression is an intrinsic feature of any genuine constitutional democracy. Again, freedom of speech is seen as an integral aspect of each individual's right to self-development and fulfillment. Restrictions on what we say and write, or hear and read inhibit a person's personality and his growth. Thus, self-fulfillment arguments do justify a constitutional guarantee of free speech.

The protection of freedom of expression in most modern constitutions is probably more closely connected with allowing all citizens an equal right to engage in open public discourse. T.R.N. Allan in his essay "Common Law Constitutionalism and Freedom of Speech"[3] said: "At the heart of the freedom of speech, in its positive aspect, lies the citizens' right to participate, as a contributor to political debate, in the collective pursuit of justice. A constitutional guarantee of freedom of speech ensures his ability to assist in the operation and development of institutional arrangements that serve the common good, enabling all members of the community to pursue their various ends in reasonable harmony and co-operation. Since the requirements of justice are invariably contested, reflecting divergent conceptions of the common good, they cannot simply be imposed on selfish and recalcitrant individuals by a wise and benevolent ruler : in a decent society, that acknowledges the equal dignity of all members of the community, the requirements of justice must be determined, and regularly reassessed, by means of well-informed reflection and debate. Freedom of speech serves the end of justice by denying government the ability to stifle moral and political discussion, especially where it concerns the merit of the current conduct of government or the legitimacy of the prevailing distribution of power."

Freedom of speech is usually regarded as a liberty against the State, or a negative freedom. In its negative aspect, Justice Bhagwati says, the principle of freedom of speech curtails the State's authority to

3 *Freedom of Expression and Freedom of Information*—Essays in Honour of Sir David Williams, Edited by Jack Beatson and Yvonne Cripps, Oxford University Press, p. 17.

deprive someone of the information necessary to judge its coercive acts. Freedom of speech is a necessary consequence of the view that "a legitimate government is one whose authority citizens can recognise while still regarding themselves as equal, autonomous, rational, agents".[4]

Freedoms of thought and conscience, as per the view of Justice Bhagwati, should be regarded as absolute intrinsic components of human dignity and communications between persons may not be restricted in a way that seriously impairs these fundamental freedoms.

2 Freedom of speech instrumental in facilitating and enhancing representative democracy The maintenance of a confident democracy is best guaranteed by protecting freedom of speech in all circumstances. Freedom of speech, says Justice Bhagwati, is often prized chiefly for its instrumental value in facilitating and enhancing representative democracy: its preservation enables citizens to participate in government by supporting or opposing political programmes and policies, and by choosing between candidates for election on the basis of adequate knowledge of their opinions and abilities. The standard view of democracy gives pride of place to political debate. It is in the wider political sphere that freedom of speech is all-important, giving citizens access to the public forum and enabling all interests to be represented in a manner that permits the legislative product to claim democratic legitimacy.

Regarded as the first condition of liberty, freedom of speech is the bulwark of democratic government and essential for the proper functioning of democratic process. It plays an important role in the formation of public opinion on social, economic and political matters. Emphasizing the significance of the freedom of speech and expression, Bhagwati, J. in *Maneka Gandhi* v *Union of India*[5] observed: "Democracy is based essentially on free debate and open discussion, for that is the only corrective of government action in a democratic set up. If democracy means government of the people, by the people, it is obvious that every citizen must be entitled to participate in the democratic process and in order to enable him to intelligently exercise his right of making a choice, free and general discussion of public matters is absolutely essential."

4 T. Scanlon: *A Theory of Freedom of Expression*, in R.M. Dworkin (Ed), the Philosophy of Law (Oxford, 1977), at 161.
5 AIR 1978 SC 597: (1978)1 SCC 248.

The core of the freedom of speech, in a constitutional democracy, is the liberty to argue in favour of a specific conception of justice, or more concretely, in support of the particular decisions or arrangements that conception requires. At the political level, it encompasses the freedom to speak in defence of any principle or policy that is consistent with the constitution, or even in favour of constitutional amendment and is a means indispensable to the discovery and spread of political truth. In particular cases, which must be determined by existing law, freedom of speech is secured for those directly affected by the denial of principles of natural justice. A person must be free to argue, not merely in support of a view of the relevant facts of his case, but in favour of a specific interpretation of the law that officials or judges are bound to apply.

3 Freedom of speech—an integral requirement of the rule of law Freedom of speech is as much an integral requirement of the rule of law as of democratic governance. Freedom of speech, conscience and association are all intrinsic to the rule of law: they protect and foster rational criticism of government and support the requirement that laws should be morally justifiable, consistent with justice and the common good.

It is only when freedoms of speech and conscience are secure that the law can be regarded as legitimate, in the critical sense that it can be intelligibly treated as our law — that of the community to which we belong and to which we owe duties of loyalty. In his essay, On Liberty, John Stuart Mill treated freedom of thought and expression as preconditions of the advance of truth and understanding, which in turn promoted happiness and well-being by enabling people to reject traditional modes of life in favour of more satisfactory alternatives.

4 Freedom of speech or expression—a fundamental human right The right to freedom of speech or expression is a fundamental human right.[6] Recognising this fundamental human right, Article 10 of the European Convention for the Protection of Human Rights and Fundamental Freedoms 1950 reads:

> "1. Everyone has the right to freedom of expression. This right shall include freedom to hold opinions and to receive and impart information and ideas without interference by public authority and regardless of frontiers .....
>
> 2. The exercise of these freedoms, since it carries with it duties and responsibilities, may be subject to such formalities,

6 *R (Singh)* v *West Midlands Police* per Hallett, LJ. in [2007]2 All ER 297 (CA).

> conditions, restrictions or penalties as are prescribed by law and are necessary in a democratic society, in the interest of national security, territorial integrity or public safety, for the prevention of disorder or crime, for the protection of health or morals, for the protection of the reputation or rights of others, for preventing the disclosure of information received in confidence, or for maintaining the authority and impartiality of the judiciary."

Written constitutions and bills of rights invariably protect freedom of speech as one of the fundamental liberties guaranteed against State suppression or regulation. It is also guaranteed by Article 19 of the Universal Declaration of Human Rights which reads:

> "Every one has the right to freedom of opinion and expression; this right includes freedom to hold opinions without interference and to seek, receive and impart information and ideas through any media and regardless of frontiers."

5 Freedom of speech in U.S.A. The First Amendment of the U.S. Constitution says: "Congress shall make no law ..... abridging the freedom of speech or of the press, or the right of the people peaceably to assemble, and to petition the Government for a redress of grievances." The provision of the U.S. Constitution has two notable features: viz., (*i*) Freedom of speech is recognised without any restriction imposed thereon; and (*ii*) freedom of press is specifically mentioned. The purpose of the First Amendment was explained by Louis Brandeis, J., on his classic statement of the freedom of speech in *Whitney* v *California*[7] thus: "Those who won our independence believed that the final end of the State was to make men free to develop their faculties; and that in its government the deliberative forces should prevail over the arbitrary. They believed liberty to be the secret of happiness and courage to be the secret of liberty. They believed that the freedom to think as you will and to speak as you think are means indispensable to the discovery and spread of political truth; that without free speech and assembly discussion would be futile; that the greatest menace to freedom is an inert people; that public discussion is a political duty; and that this should be a fundamental principle of American Government." In *Associated Press* v *US*,[8] the U.S. Supreme Court observed: "It is the purpose of the First Amendment to preserve an uninhibited market

7 274 US 357 (1927).
8 326 US 1 (1945).

place of ideas in which truth will ultimately prevail, rather than to countenance monopolization of that market whether it be by the Government itself or a private licensee."

The argument for democracy has been the popular positive justification for the place of freedom of speech in U.S. constitutional law, its influence being shown by the particularly strong protection given to political speech. In comparison, the court has been more willing to countenance restriction on commercial speech and advertising, while hard-core pornography still falls entirely outside the scope of free speech coverage. Despite the frequent promptings of Black, J., a member of the Supreme Court since 1937 to 1971, the Court has never taken literally the injunction as contained in the First Amendment of the U.S. Constitution that "Congress shall make no law .... abridging the freedom of speech ....' The absolutist position advocated by Black and Douglas, JJ. was not accepted because the Courts are aware of the vital interest that may be threatened by unrestricted speech. Holmes, J. pointed out in the first Supreme Court case *Schenk* v *U.S.*[9] to consider First Amendment principles that the 'most stringent protection of free speech would not protect a man in falsely shouting fire in a theatre and causing a panic.' The United States Supreme Court balances free speech and other important rights and interests on the basis of principles it has developed over a long period without guidance from the text of the Constitution. Other interests, such as public order and decency, national security, the rights to reputation and a fair trial are weighed in the scales with free speech. If these interests are found 'compelling, or in some circumstances 'substantial', they may justify restriction on the exercise of speech rights, at least if the government or other authority seeking to justify the limit shows that the restriction has been narrowly formulated, so that it does not restrict more speech than the compelling interest warrants. One form of balancing test is 'clear and present danger' formula.

6 Freedom of speech in U.K. Courts in England have often invoked common law principles of freedom of speech to limit the scope of other common law rules which inhibit the exercise of this freedom. This has been particularly true in libel, breach of confidence, and contempt of court cases. The defences of fair comment and privilege to libel actions have been formulated and applied to promote freedom of speech. In some contexts, courts recognise that it is more important to protect that

9 249 US 47, 52 (1919).

freedom than the interest of the individual in safeguarding the reputation.

A classic example is Lord Reid's observation in *Cozens* v *Brutus*[10] construing the word 'insulting' in the public order legislation not to cover a demonstration which offended and affronted spectators, but did not abuse them personally. In defence of freedom of speech, the courts in many cases developed new rules of law or exercised discretionary powers in a novel way. Thus, In re *X (A Minor) (Wardship: Jurisdiction)*,[11] the Court of Appeal refused to grant an injunction to restrain the publication of a book containing details of the degrading conduct of the ward's father. Again, in *R* v *Central Independent Television*[12] when an application was made to stop the showing of a television documentary on the work of the obscene Publications Squard, unless the broadcasting deleted pictures of a man identified as a convicted paedophile and it was argued that without their removal the programme would be distressing to his wife and five-year old daughter, the Court of Appeal rejected the application doubting whether it had power to stop a broadcast or other exercise of free speech rights in the circumstances of the case when the programme would not have prejudiced any legal proceedings, nor did it relate to upbringing of a child under court supervision. Hoffman, LJ. in the said case observed that in 'an area of human rights like freedom of speech, I respectfully doubt the wisdom of creating judge-made exceptions, particularly, when they require a judicial balancing of interests.'

In 1980s and 1990s judges had begun to develop the law on free speech in the light of the European Convention of Human Rights and Fundamental Freedoms (ECHR) by U.K.'s participation in ECHR although its provisions were not binding in English law at that time. It may be noted that English free speech law has in principle been transformed by the incorporation of the ECHR into United Kingdom law by the Human Rights Act 1998. Courts are required by the Human Rights Act 1998, to interpret legislation, whether primary or delegated, as far as possible compatibly with convention rights.[13]

The importance of the speech when balancing the exercise of freedom of expression against the right to respect for private life guaranteed by

10 [1973] AC 854 (HL).
11 [1975] Fam 47.
12 [1994] Fam 192, 203 (CA).
13 *Ghaidan* v *Mendoza* [2004]3 All ER 411 (HL).

the ECHR was determined by the House of Lords in *Campbell* v *MGM.*[14] In the said case, the House of Lords by a 3-2 majority upheld the right of the supermodel, Naomi Campbell, to keep details of her therapy from Narcotics Anonymous (NA) private. The Daily Mirror infringed this right when they published that information and photographs of her leaving a meeting of NA. The majority did not think the publication merited strong free speech protection. Baroness Hale was particularly clear on this point. Political speech in particular, but also intellectual, educational, and artistic speech and expression are important, because they are crucial for a democracy or a dynamic society, which values individual originality and development. No claim of this kind could be made for the publication of details of a celebrity's private life. It was, therefore, not entitled to much weight when balanced against Ms. Campbell's private life.

7 Freedom of speech in India Article 19(1)(*a*) of the Constitution of India guarantees that all citizens stall have the right to freedom of speech and expression. The right to freedom of speech and expression enshrined in the article is one of the cherished freedoms, says Justice Bhagwati, in a democracy. It occupies a preferred position in the hierarchy of liberties giving succour and protection to all other liberties. The freedom of speech under the article includes the right to express one's views and opinions at any issue through any medium, e.g., by words of mouth, writing, printing, picture, film, movie, or in any other manner. It thus includes the freedom of communication and the right to propagate or publish opinion. Referring to *Madhu Limaye's*[15] case and the case of *K.A. Abbas*,[16] Justice Bhagwati says, freedom of speech and expression includes freedom to circulate views and ideas by books, magazines, leaflets and other media of mass communication. Referring to an English decision,[17] Justice Bhagwati further says that free speech includes not only the inoffensive but the irritating, the contentious, the eccentric, the heretical, the unwelcome and the provocative provided it does not tend to provoke violence. Freedom only to speak inoffensively is not worth having.

A. ***Scope and Ambit of Freedom of Speech and Expression under Article 19(1)(a)*** Public debate in India and other liberal democracies about free speech

14 [2004]2 AC 457.
15 *Madhu Limaye* v *Sub-Divisional Magistrate* (1970)3 SCC 746.
16 *K.A. Abbas* v *Union of India* AIR 1971 SC 481 (on Pre-censorship of Films).
17 *Redmond-Bate* v *DPP* (1999)7 BHRC 375 at 382-383, per Sedley, LJ. as referred to in *R (Singh)* v *West Midlands Police* [2007]2 All ER 297 (CA).

is usually more concerned with the scope of the freedom than with the issue whether the freedom should be protected at all. There are questions how far hard-core pornography or commercial advertising, say, for cigarettes, are covered by freedom of speech. Other subjects of controversy are how much weight should be given to freedom of speech and press freedom when a newspaper article discloses details of a celebrity's private life and whether it is right to limit media publicity before legal proceedings. These matters raise questions of constitutional law. About the scope and ambit of this right, Justice Bhagwati's thought is reflected thus: "Freedom of speech and expression carries with it the right to gather information as also to speak and express oneself at home and abroad and to exchange thoughts and ideas with others not only in India but also outside".[18] It is pointed out by Justice Bhagwati that only a shortwhile before the Constitution was brought into force and whilst the constitutional debate was still going on the Universal Declaration of Human Rights was adopted by the General Assembly of the United Nations on 10th December 1948 and most of the fundamental rights which we find included in Part III were recognised and adopted by the United Nations as the inalienable rights of man in the Universal Declaration of Human Rights. Article 19 of the Universal Declaration declared: "Every one has the right to freedom of opinion and expression; this right includes freedom to hold opinions without interference and to seek, receive and impart information and ideas through any media and regardless of frontiers." This was the glorious declaration of the fundamental freedom of speech and expression—noble in conception and universal in scope – which was before them when the Constitution makers enacted Article 19(1)(*a*). We have, therefore, no doubt that freedom of speech and expression guaranteed by Article 19(1)(*a*) is exercisable not only in India but also outside.[18] Justice Bhagwati asserts that the State cannot by any legislative or executive action interfere with the exercise of this right, except in so far as permissible under Article 19(2). The State action would necessarily be taken in India but it may impair or restrict the exercise of this right elsewhere. Today in the modern world, Justice Bhagwati says, with vastly developed science and technology and highly improved and sophisticated means of communication, a person may be able to exercise freedom of speech and expression abroad by doing something within the country and if this is prohibited or restricted, his freedom of speech and expression

18 *Maneka Gandhi* v *Union of India* AIR 1978 SC 597: (1978)1 SCC 248.

would certainly be impaired and Article 19(1)(*a*) violated. Therefore, merely because the State action is restricted to the territory of India, it does not necessarily follow that the right of free speech and expression is also limited in its operation to the territory of India and does not extend outside.[18] This thesis can also be substantiated by looking at the question from a slightly different point of view, so says Justice Bhagwati. It is obvious that the right of free speech and expression guaranteed under Article 19(1)(*a*) can be subjected to restriction permissible under Article 19(2). Such restriction, imposed by a statute or an order made under it, if within the limits provided in Article 19(2), would, says Justice Bhagwati, clearly bind the citizen not only when he is within the country but also when he travels outside. As an example, Justice Bhagwati cites a case where, either under the Passports Act 1967 or as a condition in the passport issued under it, an arbitrary, unreasonable and wholly unjustifiable restriction is placed upon the citizen that he may go abroad, but he should not make any speech there. This would, asserts Justice Bhagwati, plainly be a restriction which would interfere with his freedom of speech and expression outside the country, for, if valid, it would bind him wherever he may go. He would be entitled to say that such a restriction imposed by State action is impermissible under Article 19(2) and is accordingly void as being violative of Article 19(1)(*a*). Justice Bhagwati, therefore, views that freedom of speech and expression guaranteed under Article 19(1)(*a*) is exercisable not only inside the country, but also outside. There are no geographical limitations to freedom of speech and expression guaranteed under Article 19(1)(*a*), says Justice Bhagwati.

B. Communication and Receipt of Information—Two Sides of the same Coin—Named Freedom of Speech Guranteed under Article 19(1)(a) Justice Bhagwati reminds that the Supreme Court has given a broad definition to Article 19(1)(*a*) by laying down the proposition that freedom of speech involves not only communication, but also receipt of information. Right to know is a basic right of the citizens of a free country and Article 19(1)(*a*) protects this right. Justice Bhagwati wholly concurs with the view as expressed by the Supreme Court in *State of Uttar Pradesh* v *Raj Narain*[19] where the Court observed that the "people of this country have a right to know every public act, everything that is done in a public way, by their public functionaries. They are entitled to know the particulars of every public transaction in all its bearings. The right to

19 AIR 1975 SC 865: (1975)4 SCC 428.

know, which is derived from the concept of freedom of speech, though not absolute, is a factor which should make one wary, when secrecy is claimed for transactions which can, at any rate, have no repercussion on public security." To the same effect, Justice Bhagwati agrees with the view as expressed in *Reliance Petrochemicals Ltd.* v *Indian Express*[20] where the apex court observed: "We must remember that the people at large have a right to know in order to be able to take part in a participatory development in the industrial life and democracy. Right to know is a basic right which citizens of a free country aspire in the broaden horizon of the right to live in this age on our land under Article 21 of the Constitution. That right has reached new dimensions and urgency. That right puts greater responsibility upon those who take upon the responsibility to inform." It is important to note that in later decisions, the Supreme Court reiterated the principle in the same vein. While in *Secretary, Ministry of Information and Broadcasting, Govt. of India* v *Cricket Association of Bengal*,[21] the Supreme Court reiterated the proposition that the freedom of speech and expression guaranteed under Article 19(1)(*a*) includes the right to acquire information and disseminate the same, in *Dinesh Trivedi* v *Union of India*,[1] the Court observed that "in modern constitutional democracies, it is axiomatic that citizens have a right to know about the affairs of the government which, having been elected by them, seek to formulate sound policies of governance aimed at their welfare". It is worthwhile to note that the Right to Information Act is the direct outcome of the views expressed by the apex court in the right to know theory springing from the right to freedom of speech and expression enshrined in Article 19(1)(*a*).

C. ***Right to go abroad—Whether included in Freedom of Speech and Expression under Article 19(1)(a)*** Corelated with the issue comes a question: whether right to go abroad, which is not specifically named as a fundamental right, is included in freedom of speech and expression under Article 19(1)(*a*). Justice Bhagwati views that the right to go abroad cannot in all circumstances be regarded as included in freedom of speech and expression. The learned Judge elaborates his views thus: "Freedom of movement at home and abroad is a part of our heritage and .... it is a highly cherished right essential to the growth and development of the human personality and its importance cannot be

20 AIR 1989 SC 190: (1988)4 SCC 592.
21 AIR 1995 SC 1236.
1 (1997)4 SCC 306: (1997)1 SCJ 697.

over-emphasised. But it cannot be said to be part of the right of free speech and expression. It is not of the same basic nature and character as freedom of speech and expression. When a person goes abroad, he may do so for a variety of reasons and it may not necessarily and always be for exercise of freedom of speech and expression. Every travel abroad is not an exercise of right of free speech and expression and it would not be correct to say that whenever there is a restriction on the right to go abroad, ex necessitae it involves violation of freedom of speech and expression. It is no doubt true that going abroad may be necessary in a given case for exercise of freedom of speech and expression, but that does not make it an integral part of the right of free speech and expression. Every activity that may be necessary for exercise of freedom of speech and expression or that may facilitate such exercise or make it meaningful and effective cannot be elevated to the status of a fundamental right as if it were part of the fundamental right of free speech and expression. Otherwise, practically every activity would become part of some fundamental right or the other and the object of making certain rights only as fundamental rights with different permissible restrictions would be frustrated".[2]

Though, however, the right to go abroad is not in itself a fundamental right, the denial of the right to go abroad may in truth and in effect in some cases restrict, so views Justice Bhagwati, freedom of speech and expression so as to contravene Article 19(1)(*a*). As example, Justice Bhagwati cites the case of an evangelist who has made it a mission of his life to preach his faith to people all over the world and for that purpose, set up institutions in different countries. If an order is made impounding his passport, it would directly affect his freedom of speech and expression and the challenge to the validity of the order under Article 19(1)(*a*) would be unanswerable unless it is saved by Article 19(2). Again, a musician may want to go abroad to sing, a dancer to dance, visiting professor to teach and a scholar to participate in a conference or seminar. If in such cases his passport is denied or impounded, it would directly interfere with his freedom of speech and expression.[3] There may thus be may such cases where the restriction imposed, says Justice Bhagwati, is apparently only on the right to go abroad but the direct and inevitable consequence is to interfere with the freedom of speech and expression.

2 *Maneka Gandhi* v *Union of India* AIR 1978 SC 597 at p. 641, para 77: (1978)1 SCC 248.

3 *Maneka Gandhi* v *Union of India* AIR 1978 SC 597: (1978)1 SCC 248.

D. ***Rights forming part of Free Speech and Expression under Article 19(1)(a)*** Justice Bhagwati cites a number of instances where the rights though not named as fundamental rights are recognised as part of the right of free speech and expression. Thus, freedom of circulation is necessarily involved in freedom of speech and expression and hence enjoys the protection of Article 19(1)(*a*).[4] Similarly, the right to paint or sing or dance or to write poetry or literature is also covered by Article 19(1)(*a*), because the common basic characteristic in all these activities is freedom of speech and expression, or to put it differently, each of these activities is an exercise of freedom of speech and expression.[4]

E. ***Criticising judgments of Court—Whether a feature of Free Speech under Article 19(1)(a)*** The right of the public to criticize judgments is certainly an important feature of free speech under Article 19(1)(*a*), says Justice Bhagwati. In the free market place of ideas, criticism about the judicial system or judges should be welcome so long as such criticism does not impair or hamper administration of justice. In a free democracy, everybody is entitled to express his opinion about the correctness or legality of a judgment or sentence or an order of a court objectively and with detachment in a language dignified and respectable tone with moderation. The liberty of expression, cautions Justice Bhagwati, should not be a licence to make personal attack on a judge. Subject to that, an honest criticism of the administration of justice is welcome since justice is not a cloistered virtue and is entitled to respectful scrutiny.

F. ***Conflict between Freedom of Speech and the Privilege of Parliament or a State Legislature—stand to be taken*** A question often crops up: in case of a conflict between freedom of speech and the privilege of Parliament or a State Legislature – which one shall prevail? Justice Bhagwati answered the question thus: "In case of a conflict between the freedom of speech under Article 19(1)(*a*) and the privilege of Parliament or a State Legislature under Article 105 or 194 respectively, the freedom of speech will give way to accommodate the legislative privilege". Justice Bhagwati's view on the issue finds support in the apex court decision in *P.V. Narasimha Rao* v *State*,[5] where it has been held that freedom of speech available to a Member of Parliament under Article 105(1) as well as to a Member of a State Legislature under Article 194(1) is wider in amplitude than the right to freedom of speech and expression guaranteed under Article 19(1)(*a*) since the freedom of speech of the

4 *Maneka Gandhi* v *Union of India* AIR 1978 SC 597: (1978)1 SCC 248.
5 AIR 1998 SC 2120: (1998)4 SCC 626.

members of Legislature on the floor of the House under Article 105(1) is not subject to the limitations contained in Article 19(2). It bears mentioning here, asserts Justice Bhagwati, that the totality of rights enjoyed by a legislator including the freedom to speak on the floor of the House are privileges governed by Article 105 and not Fundamental Rights. In case of clash of two values- freedom of speech and promotion and strengthening of democratic fabric-the Court has to give preference to promotion of democracy. This view of Justice Bhagwati finds support in *Kihota Hollohon* v *Zachilhu*.[6]

8 Freedom of Speech not absolutely free from restrictions Nothing is more certain in modern society than the principle that there are no absolutes. Speech, according to Justice Bhagwati, is not an absolute, above and beyond control by the legislature. A free speech principle need not entail absolute protection for any exercise of freedom of expression. Most proponent of strong free speech guarantees concede that its exercise may probably be restricted in some circumstances.

The freedom of speech which is secured by the Constitution does not, therefore, confer an absolute right to speak, without responsibility, whatever one may choose, or an unrestricted and an unbridled license giving immunity for every possible use of language and preventing the punishment of those who abuse this freedom; and that a State in the exercise of its police power may punish those who abuse this freedom by utterances inimical to the public welfare, tending to incite to crime, disturb the public peace, or endanger the foundations of organised government and threaten its overthrow by unlawful means. Article 19(2) of the Indian Constitution imposes reasonable restrictions on the right to freedom of speech for certain purposes. Any limitation on the exercise of the right under Article 19(1)(*a*) not falling within the four corners of Article 19(2) is not sustainable in law.

A. ***Limitation in case of overthrow of Government*** Justice Bhagwati views that overthrow of the Government by force and violence is certainly a substantial enough interest for the Government to limit speech. Indeed, this is the ultimate value of any society, for if a society cannot protect its very structure from armed internal attack, it must follow that no subordinate value can be protected.

Justice Bhagwati, however, believes that the demands of free speech in a democratic society as well as the interest in national security are

6 AIR 1993 SC 412: 1992 Supp (2) SCC 651.

better served by candid and informed weighing of the competing interests. But how are the competing interests to be assessed? Since they are not subject to quantitative ascertainment, the issue necessarily resolves itself into asking, who is to make the adjustment? Who is to balance the relevant factors and ascertain which interest is in the circumstances to prevail? Justice Bhagwati answers the questions in an interview with the authors thus: "Full responsibility for the choice cannot be given to the courts. Courts are not representative bodies. They are not designed to be a good reflex of a democratic society. Their judgment is best informed, and therefore most dependable, within narrow limits. Their essential quality is detachment, founded on independence. History teaches that the independence of the judiciary is jeopardized when courts become embroiled in the passions of the day and assume primary responsibility in choosing between competing political, economic and social pressures. Primarily responsibility for adjusting the interests which compete in the situation of necessity belongs to the legislature."

B. *Limitation in case of right to life* Freedom of speech cannot have priority over right to life. Thus, groups who believe that the only valuable form of life is one devoted to committing spectacular murders or to the consumption of dangerous drugs cannot be allowed to propagate their views of life since the spread of these beliefs does put life in danger. So, it will be right to curtail their propagation.

C. *Limitation in case of human dignity* Protection of human dignity should trump any free speech claim. Thus, where the racist leaflets are distributed in a neighbourhood where tensions exist between the majority and minority ethnic groups, and many of those who looking at the leaflets feel vulnerable and threatened as a result while members of the majority group get confirmation of their racist outlook, respect for human dignity will legitimize the proscription of racist speech, rather than an argument for its tolerance.

D. *Limitation in case of inflammatory speech* Freedom of speech can be restrained in case of inflammatory speech, where the state can show that as a result imminent disorder is likely to occur. A prior restraint is not permissible unless the state can show that without such an order, it would suffer direct, immediate and irreparable damage. The state must show a compelling or substantial reason to justify the restriction. Further, it must show that it could not have achieved this aim by 'less restrictive means'.

E. *Restriction inappropriate as the means of averting trival harm to society* Justice Bhagwati, however, cautions that prohibition of free speech is a measure so stringent that it would be inappropriate as the means for averting a relatively trival harm to society. To justify suppression of free speech, there must be a reasonable ground to fear that serious harm will result if free speech is in the particular circumstances of situation allowed to be practiced. Whenever the fundamental right of free speech is alleged to have been invaded, it must remain open to aggrieved citizens to present the issue whether there actually did exist at the time a clear danger; whether the danger, if any, was imminent; and whether the evil apprehended was one so substantial as to justify the restriction interposed by the legislature or the executive authority of the State in exercise of its police power.

9 Court's responsibility in the disposition of free speech cases When freedom of speech or freedom of expression provisions are contained in bills or charters of rights, it is clear that those are rights entitled to protection. Courts need not explore further the philosophical character of the said right. Unlike philosophers, Courts do not have to worry whether the best arguments for free speech are utilitarian in character or are instead deontological, that is, that free speech is a natural moral right. Moreover, guidance on the scope of free speech may be provided by the constitutional text. Arguments of political theory are often central to the disposition of free speech cases. They are particularly relevant when courts determine the meaning of speech and the scope of the freedom. Courts must decide, for instance, the extent to which freedom of expression covers commercial advertising, sexually explicit material, and expressive conduct such as the desecration of a national flag. They must also determine whether the protection of hate speech directed at racial or religious groups is required by freedom of expression in the light of the underlying moral arguments for guarantee of that freedom, or alternatively whether human dignity supports its proscription. They must rule whether freedom of speech is only a negative liberty, guaranteed against interference by government, or whether it also embodies some positive rights, for example, to use public property for speech or to acquire information from public authorities (freedom of information). Answers to these questions are rarely provided by the text of the Constitution. Judges, therefore, must decide them on the basis of a creative, dynamic interpretation of the Constitution in the light of the international human rights instruments.

FREEDOM OF PRESS

1 Meaning By the freedom of press is meant the right of citizens to speak and publish and express their views. It embodies the right of the people to read and it is not antithetical to the right of the people to speak and express. The expression 'freedom of press' means freedom from interference from any authority, immunity from previous restraints or censorships over what shall be published and exemption from control as to what shall appear in print.

2 Freedom of press—a cherished right in a democratic country Freedom of press is always placed on a higher footing than other enterprises and has always been a cherished right in all democratic countries. It is described as the Fourth Estate. The democratic credentials of a State are judged today by the extent of freedom the press enjoyed in that State. Douglas, J., of the US Supreme Court observed that "acceptance by Government of a dissident press is a measure of the maturity of the nation".[7] A great upholder of the freedom of press, Justice Bhagwati views that the true measure of the health and vigour of a democracy is always to be found in its press. Suppression of belief, opinion or other expressions is an affront to the dignity of man and negation of man's essential nature. If the voice of the underdog is not heard, aspirations of millions of hungry naked people are not reflected in the press, democracy will be in peril, says Justice Bhagwati.

3 Connection between press freedom and freedom of speech David Feldman in his book 'Civil Liberties and Human Rights' stated: The obvious connection between press freedom and freedom of speech is that the press is a medium for broadcasting information and opinion. Firstly, media freedom as a tool of self-expression is a significant instrument of personal autonomy. Secondly, as a channel of communication, it helps to allow the political discourse in a democracy. Thirdly, it helps to provide one of the essential conditions in scholarships making possible the exchange and evaluation of theories, explanations and discoveries; and lastly, it helps to promulgate a society's cultural values and facilitates the debate about them, advancing the development and survival of civilization.

4 Constitutional position of press freedom in USA The First Amendment of the U.S. Constitution specifically protects a free press. The view developed by U.S. Supreme Court is that freedom of the press includes

7 *Terminiello* v *Chicago* [1948]93 L.ed 1131: 337 US 1.

more than merely serving as a "neutral conduit of information between the people and their elected leaders or as a neutral form of debate."

The position of law on freedom of speech and press in U.S.A. has been explained in American Jurisprudence[8] thus: "The liberty of the press was initially a right to publish without a license that which formerly could be published only with one, and although this freedom from previous restraint upon publication could not be regarded as exhausting the guaranty of liberty, the prevention of that restraint was a leading purpose in the adoption of the First Amendment. It is well established that liberty of the press historically considered and taken up by the Federal Constitution, means principally, although not exclusively, immunity from previous restraints or censorships. Stated differently, the rule is that an essential element of the liberty of the press is its freedom from all censorships over what shall be published and exemption from control, in advance, as to what shall appear in print.

* * * * * *

The freedom of speech and press embraces the right to distribute literature, and necessarily protects the right to receive literature which is distributed. It is said that liberty in circulating is as essential to the freedom as liberty of publishing, since publication without circulation would be of little value.

The right or privilege of free speech and publication guaranteed by the Constitutions of the United States and of the several States, has its limitations and is not an absolute right, although limitations are recognised only in exceptional cases.

* * * * * *

The question of when the right of free speech or press becomes wrong by excess is difficult to determine. Legitimate attempts to protect the public, not from the remote possible effects of noxious ideologies, but from present excesses of direct, active conduct are not presumptively bad because they interfere with and in some of their manifestations restrain the exercise of the First Amendment rights. The issue in every case is whether the words used are used in such circumstances and are of such a nature as to create a clear and present danger that they will bring about substantive evils which the Federal or State Legislatures have a right to prevent; it is a question of proximity and degree.

* * * * * *

8 16 Am Jur 2d 343.

The freedoms of speech and press are not limited to particular media of expression. Verbal expression is, of course, protected, but the right to express one's views in an orderly fashion extends to the communication of ideas by handbills and literature as well as by the spoken word. Picketing carried on in a non-labor context, when free from coercion, intimidation, and violence, is constitutionally guaranteed as a right of free speech."

5 Constitutional position of press freedom in India Freedom of press is not expressly guaranteed as a fundamental right in the Indian Constitution. Though not specifically named as a fundamental right, freedom of press is recognised as part of the right of free speech and expression and is implicitly covered by Article 19(1)(*a*). The reason, according to Justice Bhagwati, is that it 'is the most cherished and valued freedom in a democracy: indeed democracy cannot survive without a free press. Democracy is based essentially on free debate and open discussion, for that is the only corrective of governmental action in a democratic set up. If democracy means government of the people, by the people, it is obvious that every citizen must be entitled to participate in the democratic process and in order to enable him to intelligently exercise his right of making a choice, free and general discussion of public matters is absolutely essential. Manifestly, free debate and open discussion, in the most comprehensive sense, is not possible unless there is a free and independent press. Indeed the true measure of the health and vigour of a democracy is always to be found in its press. Look at its newspapers—do they reflect diversity of opinions and views, do they contain expression of dissent and criticism against governmental policies and actions, or do they obsequiously sing the praises of the government or lionize or defy the ruler. The newspapers are an index of the true character of the Government—whether it is democratic or authoritarian. It was Mr. Justice Potter Stewart who said: "Without an informed and free press, there cannot be an enlightened people." Thus, freedom of the press constitutes, one of the pillars of democracy and indeed lies at the foundation of democratic organisation.'[9] Freedom of press thus partakes of the same basic nature and character and is indeed an integral part of free speech and expression and perhaps it would not be so incorrect to say that it is the same right applicable in relation to the press.

In *Sakal Papers* v *Union of India*,[10] the Supreme Court described the freedom of the press as a "species of which freedom of expression is

9 *Maneka Gandhi* v *Union of India* AIR 1978 SC 597 at p. 640, para 77: (1978)1 SCC 248.

10 AIR 1962 SC 305: (1962)3 SCR 842.

a genus". The press, Justice Bhagwati says, seeks to advance public interest by publishing facts and opinions without which a democratic electorate cannot make responsible judgments. It acts as the fourth estate outside the government as an additional check on the three official branches – executive, legislative and the judiciary. It is the primary function of the press to provide comprehensive and objective information on all aspects of the country's social, economic and political life. It serves as a powerful antidote to any abuse of power by government officials and as a means for keeping the elected officials responsible to the people. Freedom of the press is the heart of social and political intercourse and has to be maintained not so much for the benefit of the press as for the benefit of the general community because the community has a right to be supplied with information and the government owes a duty to educate the people within the limits of its resources.

The expression 'freedom of the press' as comprehended in Article 19(1)(*a*) means a freedom from interference from any authority. The freedom ensures freedom of circulation of a publication, since a publication is of little value without circulation. If any ban is, therefore, imposed upon entry and circulation of a journal within a State, this will be regarded as a restriction on Article 19(1)(*a*). Again, imposition of pre-censorship on a newspaper or prohibiting it from publishing its views or those of its correspondents on a burning topic of the day will constitute an encroachment on the freedom of speech and expression.

Freedom of speech covering press freedom vis-a-vis the interest of the security of the state and public order Article 19(2) permits reasonable restrictions to be imposed on freedom of speech and expression *inter alia* in the interest of the security of the State and public order. Freedom and security in their pure form are antagonistic poles: one pole represents the interest of the individual in being afforded the maximum right of self-assertion free from Governmental and other interference while the other represents the interest of the politically organized society in its self-preservation. It is impossible to extend to either of them absolute protection for, as observed by Mr. Justice Frankfurter, "absolute rules would inevitably lead to absolute exceptions and such exceptions would eventually corrode the rules". It is now, in the view of Justice Bhagwati, a generally accepted postulate that freedom of speech and expression which includes within its fold freedom of propagation of ideas lies at the foundation of all democratic organizations, for without free political discussion, no public education so essential for the proper functioning of the processes of popular Government is possible.

It is the matrix, the indispensable condition, of nearly every other form of freedom and because it has the capacity of upholding the truth, it is indispensable to the democratic process. Freedom of such amplitude might, however, involve risk of abuse but, as pointed out by Patanjali Shastri, J., in *Ramesh Thapper* v *State of Madras*,[11] the framers of the Constitution may well have reflected, with Madison who was the leading spirit in the preparation of the First Amendment of the Federal Constitution, that "it is better to leave a few of its noxious branches to their luxuriant growth, than, by pruning them away, to injure the vigor of those yielding fruits".[12] While conceding the imperative necessity of freedom of speech and expression in its full width and amplitude, it is necessary at the same time to remember that the first and most fundamental duty of every Government is the preservation of order, since order is a condition precedent to all civilization and the advance of human happiness. The security of the State and organized Government, views Justice Bhagwati, are the very foundation of freedom of speech and expression which maintains the opportunity for free political discussion to the end that Government may be responsive to the will of the people and it is, therefore, essential that the end should not be lost sight of in an over-emphasis of the means. The protection of freedom of speech and expression,asserts Justice Bhagwati, should not be carried to an extent where it may be permitted to disturb law and order or create public disorder with a view to subverting Government established by law. It is, therefore, necessary to strike a proper balance between the competing claims of freedom of speech on the one hand and security of the State on the other.[13]

Criticism of public measures or comment on Government action, however strongly worded, would be expression and would not be penal. It is only when the words, written or spoken, etc., which have the pernicious tendency or intention of creating public disorder or disturbance of law and order that the law steps in to prevent such activities in the interest of public order under section 124A of the Indian Penal Code

11 AIR 1950 SC 124.
12 *Near* v *Minnesotta* [1930]283 US 607.
13 *Manubhai Tribhovandas Patel* v *State of Gujarat* (1971) Guj Law Report, Vol. XII, p. 968.

1860[14] and section 95(1) read with section 95(2)[15] of the Criminal Procedure Code 1973 (old section 99A of the Criminal Procedure Code 1898).

In quashing and setting aside an order made by the Gujarat State Government forfeiting the book "Extracts from Mao-Tse-Tung" which contained 184 passages from different speeches given by Mao-Tse-Tung at different times between 1926 and 1957, Justice Bhagwati in *Manubhai Tribhovandas Patel* v *State of Gujarat*,[16] explained the principle of law relating to freedom of speech and expression as emphasized in Article 19(1)(*a*) *vis-a-vis*, the action prescribed in

14 124A. *Sedition.* Whoever, by words, either spoken or written, or by signs, or by visible representation, or otherwise, brings or attempts to bring into hatred or contempt, or excites or attempts to excite disaffection towards, the Government established by law in India, shall be punished with imprisonment for life, to which fine may be added, or with imprisonment which may extend to three years, to which fine may be added, or with fine.

Explanation 1. The expression "disaffection" includes disloyalty and all feelings of enmity.

Explanation 2. Comments expressing disapprobation of the measures of the Government with a view to obtain their alteration by lawful means, without exciting or attempting to excite hatred, contempt or disaffection, do not constitute an offence under this section.

Explanation 3. Comments expression disapprobation of the administrative or other action of the Government without exciting or attempting to excite hatred, contempt or disaffection, do not constitute an offence under this section.

15 Section 95(1) & (2) of the Criminal Procedure Code 1973 provide as under:

"95. (1) Where—

(*a*) any newspaper, or book, or

(*b*) any document,

wherever printed, appears to the State Government to contain any matter the publication of which is punishable under section 124A or section 153A or section 153B or section 292 or section 293 or section 295A of the Indian Penal Code (45 of 1860), the State Government may, by notification, stating the grounds of its opinion, declare every copy of the issue of the newspaper containing such matter, and every copy of such book or other document to be forfeited to Government, and thereupon any police officer may seize the same wherever found in India and any Magistrate may be warrant authorise any police officer not below the rank of Sub-Inspector to enter upon and search for the same in any premises where any copy of such issue or any such book or other document may be or may be reasonably suspected to be.

(2) In this section and in section 96,—

(*a*) "newspaper" and "book" have the same meaning as in the Press and Registration of Books Act 1867 (25 of 1867);

(*b*) "document" includes any painting, drawing or photograph, or other visible representation.

16 (1971) Guj Law Report, Vol. XII, p. 968.

section 124A of the Indian Penal Code and Section 99A of the Criminal Procedure Code 1898, (new section 95(1) and (2) of the Criminal Procedure Code, 1973) thus: "These passages are intended to acquaint the reader with the principles and practice of Communism as understood and explained by Mao-Tse-Tung in various speeches delivered by him to the Chinese people over a period of thirty years. They are not exhortations to our public to resort to violence or create public disorder with a view to subverting Government by law established in India. There is not a word in these passages which even remotely suggests that people should overthrow lawfully established Government in India by force or by violence. These passages expound the philosophy of Mao-Tse-Tung with a view to its academic study and they cannot possibly by any stretch of language be regarded as seditious.

To condemn them as seditious would be to close the doors of knowledge, to ostracise a philosophy because it challenges values cherished and held dear by our present day society and holds up for acceptance a new way of life vastly different from that to which our people are presently accustomed. It is not for the Government of the day nor for the Judges presiding over our Courts to decide what doctrine or philosophy is good for our people. It is for the people to choose what is best for them and in order that they may be able to make a wise and intelligent choice, free propagation of ideas is an essential requisite. The ideas propagated may be unorthodox and unconventional: they may disturb the complacency of a handful minority or they may challenge deep seated, sacred beliefs and question the most fundamental postulates of our social, political or economic thinking. That should be no ground for anxiety or apprehension, particularly in a country like ours which has always believed in the pursuit of truth and in its unending search for truth, never hesitated to receive new ideas and absorb them, if found acceptable. There can indeed be no real freedom unless thought is free and unchecked, not free thought for those who agree with us but freedom for the thought that we hate. It is only from clash of ideas that truth can emerge, for the best test of truth is the power of the thought to get itself accepted in the competition of the market. If, therefore, the publisher of this forfeited book wants to propagate the philosophy of Communism as expounded by Mao-Tse-Tung amongst the people, there is no reason why he should not be free to do so. Let the people decide what doctrine or philosophy they wish to adopt". Expressing faith in the commonsense of our people, Justice Bhagwati in the said case observed: "We have no doubt that with the sound unerring instinct which has guided them over the years, our people will choose a doctrine or philosophy true to their genius and reject the rest. If the people want to adopt the philosophy of Communism as expounded by Mao-Tse-Tung, confiscation of a book like this is not going to stop them from doing so. The reasons for their choice would be much deeper and if the Government wants to repel the onslaught of Communist ideology, it is through an elimination of these reasons that the Government may well address itself rather than proscribe a book like this which propagates the principles and practice of Communism as expounded by one of its chief exponents, with a view to their academic study by the people". Justice Bhagwati, however, made it clear in the said case that "when we say this, we do not wish to suggest, that if any words or writings incite violence or disturb law and order or create public disorder with a view to overthrowing Government established by law, the State would have no power to forfeit a book containing such words or writings in order to prevent disturbance of public tranquility or public order."

6 To act responsibly and maintain balance—a duty of the press Laws of the land, says Justice Bhagwati, should be governed by two fundamental principles : "open justice" and "freedom of the press". The basic rule of Indian law is that court hearings shall be open to the public, and that, unless otherwise restricted by specific order when faced with the risk of prejudice to the administration of justice, the press can freely and fairly report on all proceedings. Though the three great institutions, Parliament, the Press and the Judiciary are regarded as safeguards of justice and liberty and they embody the spirit of the Constitution yet the press should keep the right balance between freedom and the abuse of it. A balance of the public interest must be determined as between the interest of the parties in a fair trial without unfair pressure, and the public interest in being informed of matters of national concern and the freedom of the press to make fair comments on such matters.

Justice Bhagwati cautions that all gagging injunctions in the name of safeguarding the administration of justice seeking to prevent true and fair comment by the press should fail. Again only when there is a pressing social need for restraint of publication of information on moral, social grounds with a substantial risk of grave injustice and such as to outweigh the public right to know would Justice Bhagwati concede that an injunction could be given in advance. Justice Bhagwati treats national security, and threatened publication of discovered documents on high-level policy as coming under this exception.

Prior restraints, regardless of their form, on press freedom are, however, frowned upon as threats to freedom of expression since they contain within themselves forces which if released have the potential of imposing arbitrary and at times direct conflict with the right of another citizen.

Justice Bhagwati, however, cautions that the press has a duty to act responsibly. If they show irresponsible conduct, they may find that curbs have been put upon their freedom, if by none else then by the judiciary. 'I have throughout my career upheld the freedom of the press, and of the media, and it is only out of deep regard for it that I would urge that it be not misused', said Justice Bhagwati at an interview with the authors.

'The satisfaction of the President is a condition precedent to the exercise of power under Article 352, Cl. (1) and if it can be shown that there is no satisfaction of the President at all, the exercise of the power would be constitutionally invalid ....'

— P.N. BHAGWATI*

8

Declaration of Emergency– Constitutional Implications

(With Special Emphasis on 44th Constitutional Amendment)

SYNOPSIS

1 Introduction The issue of a proclamation of emergency makes serious in roads into the principle of federalism and emasculates the operation and efficacy of the fundamental rights. The power of declaring an emergency is, therefore, a power fraught with grave consequences and it has the effect of disturbing the entire power structure under the Constitution. But it is a necessary power given to the Central Government with a view to arming it adequately to meet an exceptional situation arising out of threat to the security of the country on account of war or external aggression or internal disturbance or imminent danger of any such calamity. It is, therefore, a power which has to be exercised with the greatest care and caution and utmost responsibility.

2 Constitutional implications Prior to 30th April 1979, the President could proclaim emergency under Clause (1) of Article 352 of the

* *Minerva Mills Ltd.* v *Union of India* AIR 1980 SC 1789.

Constitution if he was satisfied that a grave emergency existed whereby the security of India or any part of the territory thereof was threatened, whether by war or external aggression or internal disturbance. The situation somewhat changed with effect from 30th April 1979 when the Constitution (Forty-fourth Amendment) Act 1978 came into force. The expression 'internal disturbance' as used in Article 352(1) as a ground of proclaiming emergency was too vague and broad. The 44th Constitutional amendment substituted the words 'armed rebellion' for 'internal disturbance' with a view to exclude the possibility of an emergency being proclaimed on the ground of 'internal disturbance' only not involving 'armed rebellion'. This change has restricted the scope of what may be called as internal emergency. Justice Bhagwati cautions that while 'internal disturbance', though serious in nature, may not pose a threat to the security of the country, 'armed rebellion' is likely to pose such a threat. According to the Statement of Objects and Reasons of the Constitution (Forty-fourth Amendment) Act 1978, internal disturbance not amounting to armed rebellion would not be a ground for the issue of a proclamation. The satisfaction of the President that a grave emergency exists whereby the security of India is threatened whether by war or external aggression or armed rebellion now substituted for internal disturbance is a condition precedent which must be fulfilled before the President can issue a proclamation under Article 352, Clause (1) of the Constitution.

The Constitutional implications of a declaration of emergency under Clause (1) of Article 352, according to Justice Bhagwati, are vast and they are provided in Articles 83(2), 250, 353, 354, 358 and 359.[1]

The emergency being an exceptional situation arising out of a national crisis, certain wide and sweeping powers have been conferred on the Central Government and Parliament with a view to combating the situation and restoring normal conditions. One such power is that given by Article 83(2) of the Constitution, which provides that while a proclamation of emergency is in operation, Parliament may by law extend its duration for a period not exceeding one year at a time.[1]

The power conferred under Article 250 says that while a proclamation of emergency is in operation, Parliament shall have the power to make laws for the whole or any part of the territory of India with respect to any of the matters enumerated in the State List. The effect of this

1 *Minerva Mills Ltd.* v *Union of India* AIR 1980 SC 1789 at p. 1837, para 104.

provision is that the federal structure based on separation of powers is put out of action for the time being.[1]

Another power of a similar kind is given by Article 353 which provides that during the time when a proclamation of emergency is in force, the executive powers of the Union shall extend to the giving of directions to any State as to the manner in which the executive power thereof is to be exercised. This provision also derogates from the federal principle which forms the basis of the Constitution.[1]

Then comes Article 354 which confers powers on the President during the operation of proclamation of emergency to direct that the provisions relating to distribution of revenues under Articles 268 to 270 shall have effect subject to such modifications or exceptions as he thinks fit.[1]

Another drastic consequences of the proclamation of emergency is that provided in Article 358 which suspends the operation of the Fundamental Rights guaranteed under Article 19 while a proclamation of emergency remains in operation.[1]

Article 359(1) empowers the President during the operation of a proclamation of emergency to make an order suspending the enforcement of any of the Fundamental Rights conferred by Part III.[1]

3 Constitutionality of a proclamation of emergency—limitation on the court's power to review The competence of the court to examine the question of validity of a proclamation of emergency is often questioned on two grounds. One is that the issue whether a grave emergency exists whereby the security of India or any part thereof is threatened by war or external aggression or armed rebellion (substituted for 'internal disturbance' by the 44th Constitutional amendment) is essentially a political question entrusted by the Constitution to the Union Executive and on that account, it is not justiciable before the court. The other objection is that in any event by reason of Clauses (4) and (5) of Article 352, the court has no jurisdiction to question the satisfaction of the President leading to the issue of a proclamation of emergency or to entertain any question regarding the validity of the proclamation of emergency or its continued operation. Both these objections are, in the view of Justice Bhagwati, unfounded. Justice Bhagwati's view in this respect was clearly expressed in *Minerva Mills* case[1] where the learned Judge referring to *State of Rajasthan* v *Union of India*[2] observed:

> 'I pointed out in my judgment in that case and I still stand by it, that merely because a question has a political colour, the court

2 (1977)3 SCC 592: AIR 1977 SC 1361.

> cannot fold its hands in despair and declare "Judicial hands off". So long as the question is whether an authority under the Constitution has acted within the limits of its power or exceeded it, it can certainly be decided by the court. Indeed it would be its constitutional obligation to do so. I have said before, I repeat again, that the Constitution is suprema lex, the paramount law of the land, and there is no department or branch of Government above or beyond it. Every organ of Government, be it the executive or the legislature or the judiciary, derives its authority from the Constitution and it has to act within the limits of its authority and whether it has done so or not is for the court to decide. The court is the ultimate interpreter of the Constitution and when there is manifestly unauthorised exercise of power under the Constitution, it is the duty of the court to intervene. .... It would not, therefore, be right for the court to decline to examine whether in a given case there is any constitutional violation involved in the President issuing a Proclamation of Emergency under Cl. (1) of Art. 352.'

Justice Bhagwati did not stop there. In *Minerva Mills* case,[3] he further observed:

> 'But when I say this, I must make it clear that the constitutional jurisdiction of this Court (the Supreme Court) does not extend further than saying whether the limits on the power conferred by the Constitution on the President have been observed or there is transgression of such limits. Here the only limit on the power of the President under Article 352, Cl. (1) is that the President should be satisfied that a grave emergency exists whereby the security of India or any part thereof is threatened whether by war or external aggression or internal disturbance (now substituted by 'armed rebellion' by the 44th Constitutional amendment). The satisfaction of the President is a subjective one and cannot be decided by reference to any objective tests. It is deliberately and advisedly subjective because the matter in respect to which he is to be satisfied is of such a nature that its decision must necessarily be left to the Executive Branch of Government.[4] There may be a

3 *Minerva Mills Ltd.* v *Union of India* AIR 1980 SC 1789 at p. 1838, para 105.

4 AUTHORS' NOTE: The 44th Constitutional Amendment has introduced a clause, viz., Article 352(3), to the effect that the President shall not issue a proclamation of emergency under Article 352(1), or a proclamation varying the same, unless the decision of the Union Cabinet (i.e., the Council consisting of the Prime Minister and other Ministers of Cabinet rank appointed under Article 75) that

wide range of situations which may arise and their political implications and consequences may have to be evaluated in order to decide whether there is a situation of grave emergency by reason of the security of the country being threatened by war or external aggression or internal disturbance (now substituted by 'armed rebellion' by the 44th Constitutional amendment). It is not a decision which can be based on what the Supreme Court of the United States has described as "judicially discoverable and manageable standards". It would largely be a political judgment based on assessment of diverse and varied factors, fast-changing situations, potential consequences and a host of other imponderables. It cannot, therefore, by its very nature, be a fit subject matter for adjudication by judicial methods and materials and hence it is left to the subjective satisfaction of the Central Government which is best in a position to decide it. The court cannot go into the question of correctness or adequacy of the facts and circumstances on which the satisfaction of the Central Government is based. That would be a dangerous exercise for the court, both because it is not a fit instrument for determining a question of this kind and also because the court would thereby usurp the function of the executive and in doing so, enter the "political thicket" which it must avoid, if it is to retain its legitimacy with the people. But one thing is certain that if the satisfaction is *mala fide* or is based on wholly extraneous and irrelevant grounds, the court would have jurisdiction to examine it, because in that case there would be no satisfaction of the President in regard to the matter on which he is required to be satisfied. The satisfaction of the President is a condition precedent to the exercise of power under Article 352, Cl. (1) and if it can be shown that there is no satisfaction of the President at all, the exercise of the power would be constitutionally invalid ......'.

The question whether or not a proclamation of emergency can be judicially reviewed on the ground that it is *mala fide* or an abuse of

---

such a proclamation may be issued has been communicated to him in writing. This means that the decision to issue such a proclamation has to be arrived at collectively by the Cabinet and not by the Prime Minister alone without consulting the Cabinet. It may be of interest to note here that in 1975 the President proclaimed emergency on the advice of the Prime Minister alone and the Council of Ministers was later presented with a *fait accompli*. It is to avoid any such situation in future that Article 352(3) has been introduced in the Constitution.

power of the President did arise before the Supreme Court in *Ghulam Sarwar* v *Union of India*,[5] but the Court declined to express any opinion on this question since no material was placed before the Court making out a case for *mala fides* or abuse of power. In the subsequent decision of the Supreme Court in *Bhutnath Mato* v *State of West Bengal*,[6] there are one or two observations which might seem to suggest at first blush that a proclamation of emergency being a political matter is "*de hors* our ken", but if one looks closely at the judgment of Krishna Iyer, J., in that case, it will be apparent, says Justice Bhagwati, that he did not lay down that a proclamation of emergency cannot be reviewed by the judiciary even on a limited ground and has left that question open. There is thus no decision of the Supreme Court holding that a proclamation of emergency is beyond the judicial ken and Justice Bhagwati says: "I am not fettered by any such decision compelling me to take a view different from the one which I have expounded ......".[7]

4 Proclamation of Emergency—whether continues to be in force until revoked by another proclamation

• ***Position prior to the 44th Constitutional amendment*** The answer to this question, says Justice Bhagwati, depended on the interpretation of Clause (2) of Article 352. Sub-clause (*a*) of Clause (2) of Article 352 provided that a proclamation of emergency issued under Clause (1) might be revoked by a subsequent proclamation. Sub-clause (*b*) of that clause required that a proclamation issued under Clause (1) be laid before each House of Parliament and under Sub-clause (*c*), such a proclamation would cease to operate at the expiration of two months, unless it was approved by both Houses of Parliament before the expiration of two months. It is clear from the provisions of Clause (2) of Article 352 (as existed prior to the 44th Constitutional amendment came into force) that a proclamation of emergency validly issued under Clause (1) would continue to operate at least for a period of two months and if before the expiration of that period, it was approved by resolutions of both Houses of Parliament, it would continue to operate further even beyond the period of two months, and the only way in which it could be brought to an end was by revoking it by another proclamation issued under Clause (2)(*a*). There was no otherway in which it could cease to operate. Justice Bhagwati asserts that neither Article 352 nor any other article of the Constitution contained any provision saying that a proclamation of emergency validly issued under

5 (1967)2 SCR 271: AIR 1967 SC 1335.
6 (1974)1 SCC 645: AIR 1974 SC 806.
7 *Minerva Mills Ltd.* v *Union of India* AIR 1980 SC 1789.

Clause (1) would cease to operate as soon as the circumstances warranting its issuance ceased to exist. Justice Bhagwati pointed out that this interpretation of the provision of Clause (2) of Article 352 was supported by the decision of the Supreme Court in *Lakhan Pal* v *Union of India*[8] where dealing with a similar contention urged on behalf of the petitioner that the continuance of the emergency which was declared on 26th October 1962 was a fraud on the Constitution, the apex court speaking through Sarkar, CJ. pointed out that "the only way a proclamation ceases to have effect is by one of the events mentioned in this clause" and since neither had happened, the proclamation must be held to have continued in operation. The petitioner urged in that case that armed aggression which justified the issue of the proclamation of emergency had come to an end and the continuance of the proclamation was therefore unjustified. But his contention was negatived on the ground that the proclamation having been approved by the two Houses of Parliament within a period of two months of its issuance, it could cease to have effect only if revoked by another proclamation and that not having happened, the proclamation continued to be in force. It is true that the power to revoke a proclamation of emergency was vested only in the Central Government and it was possible that the Central Government might abuse this power by refusing to revoke a proclamation of emergency even though the circumstances justifying the issue of proclamation ceased to exist and thus prolonged baselessly the state of emergency obliterating the fundamental rights. But the primary and real safeguard of the citizen against such abuse of power lay in "the good sense of the people and in the system of representative and responsible Government" which was provided in the Constitution. Additionally, it was possible for the citizen in a given case to move the court for issuing a writ of *mandamus* for revoking the proclamation of emergency if he was able to show by placing clear and cogent material before the court that there was no justification at all for the continuance of the proclamation of emergency. But this was a very heavy onus because it was entirely for the executive Government to be satisfied whether a situation had arisen where the proclamation of emergency could be revoked. This was not a matter which was a fit subject matter for judicial determination and the court would not interfere with the satisfaction of the executive Government in that regard unless it was clear on the material on record that there was absolutely no justification for the continuance of the proclamation of emergency and the

8 (1966) Supp SCR 209; AIR 1967 SC 243.

proclamation was being continued *mala fide* or for a collateral purpose. The court might in such a case, if satisfied beyond doubt, grant a writ of *mandamus* directing the Central Government to revoke the proclamation of emergency. But until that was done, the proclamation of emergency would continue in operation and it could not be said that, though not revoked by another proclamation, it still ceased to be in force.

• ***Post Constitution (Forty-forth Amendment) Act 1978 position*** The 44th Constitutional Amendment which came into force on 30th April 1979, says Justice Bhagwati, brought about a sea change in the matter. Under Article 352(2), a proclamation issued under Article 352(1) may be varied or revoked by a subsequent proclamation.

The 44th Amendment has introduced a clause, viz., Article 352(3) which provides that the decision to issue a proclamation has to be arrived at collectively by the Cabinet and not by the Prime Minister alone without consulting the Cabinet.

Article 352(4) provides that every proclamation issued under Article 352(1) is to be laid before each House of Parliament and it ceases to operate (except when it is a proclamation revoking the previous proclamation) at the expiration of one month, unless in the meantime, it has been approved by resolutions of both Houses of Parliament. Thus, a proclamation now will automatically cease after one month if not approved by Parliament in the meantime. Formerly, it may be noted, the period allowed for parliamentary approval of the proclamation was two months. Under the proviso to Article 352(4) if, however, at the time of the issue of the proclamation or thereafter, Lok Sabha is dissolved without approving the proclamation, and the Rajya Sabha approves it, then the proclamation ceases to operate 30 days after the Lok Sabha sits again after fresh elections, unless in the meantime the new Lok Sabha passes a resolution approving the proclamation.

Previously, once approved by the two Houses of Parliament, the proclamation could remain in force as long as the executive desired. There was no provision for periodical parliamentary review of the need for continuance of the emergency. But the Constitution's 44th Amendment now provides that once approved by Parliament,[9] the

9 AUTHORS' NOTE: Effect of 44th Constitutional Amendment. A resolution approving the proclamation of emergency or one varying it has to be passed by each House by a majority of the total membership of each House and not less than two-thirds of the majority of the members present and voting in each House. [Article 352(6)]. Before the 44th Amendment, passage of such a resolution by a simple majority in each House was sufficient.

proclamation remains in force, unless revoked earlier, only for six months from the date of the passing of the later of the resolutions. This provision is contained in Article 352(5) of the Constitution. For continuance of the emergency beyond that period, parliamentary approval is needed again. Thus, now each time Parliament approves the proclamation, its life is extended for six months.

Again, by the 44th Amendment of the Constitution, Article 352(7) has been inserted which requires that the President is obliged to revoke a proclamation of emergency issued under Article 352(1) or one varying the same, if the Lok Sabha passes a resolution disapproving the same. This resolution is to be passed by a simple majority of the members of the House present and voting.

Now, therefore, says Justice Bhagwati, continuance of emergency is no longer an executive privilege. The power to revoke the proclamation does not vest in the executive. The question whether the emergency should continue or not must periodically come forward before both Houses of Parliament. The executive has to withdraw the emergency if the Lok Sabha so desires.

"[L]earn what is true in order to do what is right".
—THOMAS HUXLEY

9

Public Interest Litigation

A Stratagic Instrument of Legal Aid

SYNOPSIS

1 History The concept of 'Public Interest Litigation', or 'PIL', as it is in short called, had its origin in the United States. The period of 1960s in USA was the important period of social embroilment during which not only manifold changes to many institutions took place but also significant reforms, of which public interest litigation was one, were proposed and tried. Over the years, the concept of PIL has passed through various vicissitudes and modifications in the country of its origin. Suffice it to say, the strict requirement of legal interest has been watered down, diluted and attenuated in that country. Its vibration was felt in England too.

PIL in the United States and England were characterized by typical industrial capitalistic tendencies and did not deal with issues of repression on governmental lawlessness not did it focus attention to the suffering of the rural poor and had little to do with justice in the real sense. However, there emanated spontaneously from PIL in United States and England one very significant development of enduring value and lasting contribution to jurisprudence in general and to the legal doctrine of *locus standi* in particular which is of vital significance for the study of social action legislation in India. The result of this development was liberalization of the *locus standi* rule in law.

In India, a solid foundation of PIL as a means of easy access to justice was laid by Justice Bhagwati. In this task, he was ably supported by one of his esteemed colleagues on the Bench Justice V.R. Krishna Iyer. PIL in India focused in various ways the suffering of the poor masses who, in the words of Justice Bhagwati, 'constitute the low visibility area of humanity'; gave the judges greater participatory role in the trial placing the poor on a footing of equality with the rich in the administration of justice; and started affecting the behaviour of persons who felt themselves immune from legal control. The noble intention of PIL has, however, been suffering consequent to frequent filing of frivolous PILs now-a-days and this has alarmed the court so much so that it has been dismissing such PILs with stern warning and reminder to its applicants as to its meaning and purpose.

2 **Meaning** A matter of 'public or general interest', observed Campbell, CJ.[1] "does not mean that which is interesting as gratifying curiosity or a love of information or amusement; but that in which a class of the community have a pecuniary interest, or some interest by which their legal rights or liabilities are affected."

Black's *Law Dictionary* (8th Edition) defines 'public interest' thus "(1) The general welfare of the public that warrants recognition and protection. (2) Something in which the public as a whole has a stake; esp., an interest that justifies governmental regulation."

The meaning of the words 'public interest' is defined in the *Oxford English Dictionary*[2] as "the common well being ... also public welfare."

The expression 'litigation', as observed by the Supreme Court in *Janata Dal's* case,[3] means a legal action including all proceedings therein initiated in a court of law with the purpose of enforcing a right or seeking a remedy.

1 *R.* v *Bedfordshire* 24 LJQB 84.
2 2nd Edition, Vol. XII.
3 *Janata Dal* v *H.S. Chowdhary* (1992)4 SCC 305: 1993 SCC (Cri) 36: AIR 1993 SC 892.

The expression 'public interest litigation', in Justice Bhagwati's view, lexically means a legal action initiated in a court of law for the general welfare of the public that warrants recognition and protection; "a legal action initiated in a court of law for the enforcement of public interest or general interest in which the public or a class of the community have pecuniary interest or some interest by which their legal rights or liabilities are affected."[4]

The Council for Public Interest Law set up by the Ford Foundation in USA, says Justice Bhagwati, defined 'public interest litigation' in its Report of Public Interest Law, USA, 1976, thus: "Public interest law is the name that has recently been given to efforts which provide legal representation to previously unrepresented groups and interests. Such efforts have been undertaken in the recognition that ordinary marketplace for legal services fail to provide such services to significant segments of the population and to significant interests. Such groups and interests include the proper environmentalists, consumers, racial and ethnical minorities and others."

The definition of PIL, asserts Justice Bhagwati, emerged from historical context in which the commonality of the various forms of legal representation involving the basic and fundamental rights of a significant segment of the public demanding vindication of its rights has been recognised in various parts of the world.

3 Position of the concept in India It is the product of judicial activism of the Supreme Court of India and primarily Judge-led and it represents the exercise of the power of judicial review vested by the Constitution. The strategy of the public interest litigation, says Justice Bhagwati, has been devised to face numerous challenges arising from poverty, ignorance and illiteracy of large masses of our people. The problems of the poor of the country are very often not individual problems but class problems and they cannot be effectively solved by dealing with them on a case to case basis. This, affirms Justice Bhagwati, necessitated that "the Courts must become a great debating forum where the claims of the poor can be agitated and rights which are struggling to be born are actualized for the benefit of the weaker section. Legal and judicial process must become the vehicle for establishing the claims and demands of the haves and have-nots which are struggling to find expression". The result was the birth of public interest litigation.

4 *Janata Dal* v *H.S. Chowdhary* (1992)4 SCC 305: 1993 SCC (Cri) 36: AIR 1993 SC 892.

PIL, says Justice Bhagwati, has thus become a strategic arm of the Legal Aid Movement and is intended to bring justice within the reach of the poor masses forming the low visibility area of humanity. It is a totally different kind of litigation from the ordinary traditional litigation which is essentially of an adversary character where there is a dispute between the two litigating parties, one making claim or seeking relief against the other and that other opposing such claim or resisting such relief. PIL is brought before the court not for the purpose of enforcing the right of one individual against another as happens in the case of ordinary litigation but it is intended to promote and vindicate public interest which demands that violations of constitutional or legal rights of large number of people who are poor, ignorant or in a socially or economically disadvantaged position should not go unnoticed and un-redressed. That would be destructive of the rule of law which forms one of the essential elements of public interest in any democratic form of government. The rule of law, Justice Bhagwati views, does not mean that protection of the law must be available only to a fortunate few or that the law should be allowed to be prostituted by the vested interest for protecting and upholding the *status quo* under the guise of enforcement of their civil and political rights. The poor too have civil and political rights and the rule of law is meant for them also.

PIL, according to Justice Bhagwati, is essentially a cooperative or collective effort on the part of the petitioner, the State or public authority and the court to secure observance of the constitutional or legal rights, benefits and privileges conferred upon the vulnerable section of the community and to reach social justice to them. The State or public authority against whom public interest litigation is brought should be as much interested in ensuring basic human rights, constitutional as well as legal, to those who are in a socially and economically disadvantaged position as the petitioner who brings public interest litigation before the court. The State or public authority which is arrayed as a respondent in public interest litigation should welcome it as it would give it an opportunity to correct a wrong or to redress an injustice done to the poor and weaker section of the community whose welfare is and must be the prime concern of the State or the public authority.

4 PIL as a strategic instrument of legal aid While in Gujarat High Court, in a report on legal aid in 1971, Justice Bhagwati observed 'even while retaining the adversary system, some changes may be effected whereby the judge is given greater participatory role in the trial so as to place the poor, as far as possible, on a footing of equality with the rich in administration of justice'.[5]

Another report of the Committee on Legal Aid presided by Justice Krishna Iyer in 1973, while he was in Kerala High Court, dealt with the nexus between law and poverty, and spoke of public interest litigation in this context. It emphasized the need for an active and widespread legal system that enabled law to reach the people, rather than requiring people to reach the law.[6]

The two judges joined forces as a two-member committee on juridicare, which released its final report in August 1977. The report, while emphasizing the need for a new philosophy of legal services programme, cautioned that it 'must be framed in the light of the socio-economic conditions prevailing in our country'.[7] It further noted that 'the traditional legal services programme which is essentially court or litigation oriented, cannot meet the specific needs and the peculiar problems of the poor in our country'.[7] The report also included draft legislation for legal services and referred to social action legislation, a synonym for public interest litigation (PIL). PIL, where the role held by the court is more assertive than in traditional actions, was seen as a strategic arm of the legal aid movement intended to bring justice within the reach of those who, on account of their indigency, illiteracy, and lack of resources, were unable to reach the courts.

After the germination of the seeds of the concept of PIL in the soil of our judicial system, the rule of PIL has been carefully nourished, nurtured and developed by the courts of India led by the apex court of the land. PIL gained momentum day by day, took its root firmly in the Indian judiciary and fully blossomed with fragrance in *S.P. Gupta* v *Union of India*.[8] Fostered by judicial activism, PIL has become an increasingly important instrument with a valuable and respectable record in the arena of constitutional and legal strategy for the 'unrepresented and under-represented.'

Justice Bhagwati says that "the transition from a traditional captive agency with a low social visibility into a liberated agency with a high social-political visibility is a remarkable development in the career of

5 *Supreme Court on Public Interest Litigation*, Vol. 1, SCALE, A-43 at p. A-53, Jagga Kapur (ed.).

6 *Report of the Expert Committee on Legal Aid: Processual Justice to the People*, May 1973, 208-10.

7 *Report on National Judicare: Equal Justice-Social Justice*, August 1977, 128.

8 AIR 1982 SC 149: 1981 (Supp) SCC 87.

the Indian Appellate judiciary. People of India now know that the court has constitutional power of intervention which can be invoked to ameliorate their miseries arising from repression, governmental lawlessness and administrative deviance. Under-trial as well as convicted persons, women in protective custody, children in juvenile institutions, bonded and migrant labourers, unrecognized labourers, untouchables and schedule tribes, hapless agricultural labourers who fall prey to faulty mechanization, women who are bought and sold, slum dwellers and pavement dwellers, kins of victim of extra-judicial execution—these and many more groups now flock to the Supreme Court under Article 32 and the High Courts under Article 226 of the Constitution seeking justice".

5 PIL and the liberalization of the locus standi rule *Locus standi* is understood to mean legal capacity to challenge an act or decision. The requirement of *locus standi* of a party to litigation is mandatory; because the legal capacity of the party to any litigation whether in private or public action in relation to any specific remedy sought for has to be primarily ascertained at the threshold. The traditional rules of procedure in the adversarial system of law permit only a person whose rights are directly affected to approach the court. Under the Common Law, a person claiming the writ of *mandamus* had to show that he was enforcing his own personal right. It has been held, says Justice Bhagwati, in a number of cases in the United States of America that no one except those whose rights are directly affected by a law can raise the question of the constitutionality of that law. This principle has been very clearly stated by Hughes, J. in *McCabe* v *Atchison*[9] thus: "It is an elementary principle that in order to justify the granting of this extra-ordinary relief, the complainant's need of it and the absence of an adequate remedy at law must clearly appear. The complainant cannot succeed because someone else may be hurt. Nor does it make any difference that other persons who may be injured are persons of the same race or occupation. It is the fact, clearly established, of injury to the complainant—not to others—which justifies judicial interference".

On the statement of law propounded by Hughes, J. of USA in *McCabe's* case (supra) Fazal Ali, J., entirely agreed in *Charanjit Lal* v *Union of India*.[10] B.K. Mukherjee, J. in *Charanjit Lal's* case (supra) observed that the rights that could be enforced under Article 32 of the Constitution must ordinarily be the rights of the petitioner himself who

9 [1914]235 US 151.
10 1950 SCR 869: AIR 1951 SC 41.

complains of infraction of such rights and approach the Court for relief. For the exercise of the extra-ordinary jurisdiction by the Court under the Constitution, the Supreme Court held in *D. Nagaraj* v *State of Karnataka*,[11] the existence of the right implicit. It is well established that a person who is not aggrieved cannot maintain a writ petition.

The rule of *locus standi*, says Justice Bhagwati, thus insists that only a person who has suffered a specific legal injury by reason of actual or threatened violation of his legal right or legally protected interest can bring an action for judicial redress. It is only the holder of the right who can sue for actual or threatened violation of such right and no other person can file an action to vindicate such right. This rule of standing was obviously evolved to deal with right duty pattern which is to be found only in private law litigation. But it effectively barred the door of the court to large masses of people who on account of poverty and ignorance were unable to avail of the judicial process.

In *Municipal Council, Ratlam* v *Shri Vardi Chand*,[12] the Court reacted for the first time to this approach and observed: "The truth is that a few profound issues of processual jurisprudence of great strategic significance to our legal system face us and we must zero in on them as they involve problems of access to justice for the people beyond the blinkered rules of 'standing' of British-Indian vintage. If the centre of gravity of justice is to shift, as the Preamble of our Constitution mandates, from the traditional individualism of *locus standi* to the community orientation of public interest litigation, these issues must be considered."

The need for shifting the centre of gravity from the traditional individualism of *locus standi* was felt in an unreported judgment of Gandhi, J., of the Bombay High Court in a writ filed by a public spirited citizen Mr. Piloo Mody. In *Piloo Modi* v *State of Maharashtra,* Gandhi, J. adopted the modified view on *locus standi*. Piloo Modi complained that the government—through three ministers—had leased out valuable plots of land at a gross undervalue. Gandhi, J. rejected the respondents' contention that the petitioner had no *locus standi*. He upheld the petitioner's contention that the leases were granted *mala fide* at a gross undervalue.

Later, Justice Bhagwati developed the concept of participatory justice promoted through mass based organization in widening the rules of

11 (1977)2 SCC 148.
12 (1980)4 SCC 162, 163.

locus standi and in *S.P. Gupta* v *Union of India*[13] observed: "today a vast revolution is taking place in the judicial process; the theatre of law is fast changing and the problems of the poor are coming to the forefront. The Court has to innovate new methods and devise new strategies for the purpose of providing access to justice to large masses of people who are denied their basic human rights and to whom freedom and liberty have no meaning. The only way in which this can be done is by entertaining writ petitions and even letters from public-spirited individuals seeking judicial redress for the benefit of persons who have suffered a legal wrong or a legal injury or whose constitutional and legal rights have been violated but who by reason of their poverty or socially or economically disadvantaged position are unable to approach the Court for relief". Justice Bhagwati in *S.P. Gupta's* case (supra) continued "where a legal wrong or a legal injury is caused to a person or to a determinate class of persons by reason of violation of any constitutional or legal right or any burden is imposed in contravention of any constitutional or legal provision or without authority of law or any such legal wrong or legal injury or legal burden is threatened and such person or determinate class of persons is by reasons of poverty, helplessness or disability or socially or economically disadvantaged position, unable to approach the Court for any relief, any member of the public can maintain an application for an appropriate direction, order or writ in the High Court under Article 226 and in case of breach of any fundamental right of such person or class of persons, in this Court (Supreme Court) under Article 32 seeking judicial redress for the legal wrong or injury caused to such person or determinate class of persons". In such case, the Court will allow any member of the public acting in a *bona fide* manner to espouse the cause of such person or class of persons.[14]

Justice Bhagwati, however, cautioned in *S.P. Gupta's* case (supra) which was later on echoed in *Janata Dal's* case[15] that only a person acting *bona fide* and having sufficient interest in the proceeding of PIL will alone have *locus standi* and can approach the Court to wipe out the tears of the poor and the needy, suffering from violation of their fundamental rights, but not a person for personal gain or private profit or political motive or any oblique consideration.

13 1981 (Supp) SCC 87: AIR 1982 SC 149.

14 *Bandhua Mukti Morcha* v *Union of India* (1984)3 SCC 161, 186.

15 *Janata Dal* v *H.S. Chowdhary* (1992)4 SCC 305: 1993 SCC (Cri) 36: AIR 1993 SC 892 followed in *Kushum Lata* v *Union of India* (2006)6 SCC 180.

It may be of interest to note, says Justice Bhagwati, that the Australian Law Commission in its Discussion Paper No. 4[16] strongly supported the wider basis for access to justice and viewed that class actions will activise the legal process where individuals cannot approach the court for many reasons. The Commission warned that "if the courts cannot, or will not, give relief to the people who are in fact concerned about a matter then they will resort to self-help, with grave results for other persons and the rule of law."

Over the recent years, continues Justice Bhagwati, successive decisions of the United States Supreme Court have liberalized standing so as to afford a hearing to any person with a real interest in the relevant controversy. Prof. K.E. Scott in his book 'Standing in the Supreme Court: A Functional Analysis (1973)' pointed out that the liberalized standing rules had caused no significant increase in the number of actions brought, arguing that parties will not litigate at considerable personal cost unless they have a real interest in the matter.

Effective access to justice, asserts Justice Bhagwati, should be seen as the most basic requirement—the most basic human right—of a system which purports to guarantee legal rights.

6 Letter as petition under the broadened rule of locus standi in PIL The broadened legal principle enunciated by the apex court through Justice Bhagwati in the rules of *locus standi* helped establishing another issue also—the issue of admitting a letter as a writ petition. Taking queue from the American Supreme Court's decision in *Gidern* v *Wainwright*,[17] where a postcard from a prisoner was treated as a petition, Justice Bhagwati in *S.P. Gupta* v *Union of India*[18] ruled that a public spirited person could move the court even by writing a letter.

In *State of Himachal Pradesh* v *A Parent of a Student of Medical College, Shimla*,[19] Justice Bhagwati observed: "it is settled law that this Court (Supreme Court) under Article 32 of the Constitution and the High Courts under Article 226 of the Constitution can treat a letter as a writ petition and take action upon it". Justice Bhagwati, however, made it clear in the said case that "it is not every letter which may be treated as a writ petition by the Supreme Court or the High Court. It

16 Discussion Paper No. 4—Access to the Court-1, Standing: Public Interest suits.
17 [1963]372 US 335.
18 1981 (Supp) SCC 87: AIR 1982 SC 149.
19 AIR 1985 SC 910.

is only where a letter is addressed by an aggrieved person or by a public spirited individual or a social action group for enforcement of the constitutional or legal rights of a person in custody or of a class or group of persons who by reason of poverty, disability or socially or economically disadvantaged position find it difficult to approach the court for redress that the Supreme Court or the High Court would be justified, nay bound, to treat the letter as a writ petition. There may also be cases where even a letter addressed for redressal of a wrong done to an individual may be treated as a writ petition where the Supreme Court or the High Court considers it expedient to do so in the interests of justice". "This is an innovative strategy", observed Justice Bhagwati in the case referred to above, "which has been evolved by the Supreme Court for the purpose of providing easy access to justice to the weaker sections of Indian humanity and it is a powerful tool in the hands of public spirited individuals and social action groups for combating exploitation and injustice and securing for the under privileged segments of society their social and economic entitlements. It is a highly effective weapon in the armoury of the law for reaching social justice to the common man."

The Court thus accepted a letter as petition in *Sunil Batra (II)* v *Delhi Administration*[20] dealing with the rights of prisoners to humane treatment within prison walls; *Dr. Upendra Baxi* v *State of U.P.*[1] concerning the functioning of the Agra Protective Home regarding shelter and rehabilitation of women rescued from prostitution; *Veena Sethi* v *State of Bihar*[2] concerning the plight of mentally ill locked away in the jails of Bihar; *People's Union for Democratic Rights* v *Union of India*[3] concerning the payment of minimum wages to construction labourers. At later stage, even a telegram has been accepted as petition as in *Paramjit Kaur* v *State of Punjab*[4] where the CBI at the instance of the Supreme Court unearthed the facts of mass cremation of thousands of persons by the Punjab Police by labeling them 'unidentified.'

Justice R.S. Pathak in *Bandhua Mukti Morcha's* case[5] objected to the addressing of the letter to a particular judge and observed: "When jurisdiction of the Court is invoked, it is the jurisdiction of the entire court ... No such communication can be properly addressed to a particular

20 (1980)3 SCC 488.
1 (1983)2 SCC 308.
2 (1982)2 SCC 583.
3 AIR 1982 SC 1473: 1982 Lab IC 1646: (1982)3 SCC 235: 1982 SCC (L&S) 275.
4 (1996)7 SCC 20.
5 *Bandhua Mukti Morcha* v *Union of India* (1984)3 SCC 161.

judge ... Which judge or judges will hear the case is exclusively a matter concerning the internal regulation of the business of the Court, interference with which by a litigant or a member of the public constitutes the grossest impropriety".

Justice Bhagwati, however, disapproved the objection raised by Justice R.S. Pathak in *Bandhua Mukti Morcha's* case (supra) on the issue of addressing a letter to a particular Judge. A five Judges Bench headed by Bhagwati as the Chief Justice of the apex court in *M.C. Mehta* v *Union of India*[6] specifically dealing with the issue observed: "We do not think that it would be right to reject a letter addressed to an individual justice of the Court merely on the ground that it is not addressed to the Court or to the Chief Justice and his companion by poor and disadvantaged persons or by social action groups who may not know the proper form of address. They may know only a particular Judge who comes from their State and they may therefore address the letters to him. If the Court were to insist that the letters must be addressed to the Court or to the Chief Justice and his companion Judges, it would exclude from the judicial ken a large number of letters and in the result, deny access to justice to the deprived and vulnerable sections of the community. We are therefore of the view that even if a letter is addressed to an individual Judge of the Court, it should be entertained, provided of course it is by or on behalf of a person in custody or on behalf of a woman or a child or a class of deprived or disadvantaged persons. We may point out that now there is no difficulty in entertaining letters addressed to individual Justice of the Court, because this Court (Supreme Court) has a Public Interest Litigation Cell to which all letters addressed to the Court or to the individual Justices are forwarded and the staff attached to this cell examines the letters and it is only after scrutiny by the staff members attached to this cell that the letters are placed before the Chief Justice and under his direction, they are listed before the Court. We must therefore hold that letters addressed to individual Justice of the Court should not be rejected merely because they fail to conform to the preferred form of address. Nor should the Court adopt a rigid stance that no letters would be entertained unless they are supported by an affidavit. If the Court were to insist on an affidavit as a condition of entertaining the letters, the entire object and purpose of epistolary jurisdiction would be frustrated because most of the poor and disadvantaged persons will then not be able to have any easy access to the Court and even the

6 AIR 1987 SC 1086 at p. 1090.

social action groups will find it difficult to approach the Court. We may point out that the Court has so far been entertaining letters without an affidavit and it is only in a few rare cases that it has been found that the allegations made in the letters were false. But that might happen also in cases where the jurisdiction of the Court is invoked in a regular way."

7 Access to justice revolutionized with the liberalisation of locus standi rule With the liberalisation of the rule of *locus standi* under which writ petitions and even letters from public-spirited individuals were entertained as said above, the process of providing access to justice to large masses of people started.

On the legal strength of the principle enunciated by Justice Bhagwati in *S.P. Gupta's* case (supra), researchers and social scientists,[7] lawyers,[8] social welfare organizations,[9] journalists,[10] law professors,[11] and medical practitioners,[12] amongst many others, started bringing representative actions. The process thus started till continues unabated. It requires mentioning, says Justice Bhagwati, that the intervention of social welfare organizations in litigative processes has been recognised as a healthy mediation between the people and the rule of law. Wisely permitted, participative justice, promoted through mass-based organizations with special concern to combat injustice has a democratic potential for the little men and the law.

In *People's Union for Democratic Rights* v *Union of India*[13] Justice Bhagwati observed that "the traditional rule of standing which confines access to the judicial process only to those to whom legal injury is caused or legal wrong is done has now been jettisoned by this Court (Supreme Court) and the narrow confines within which the rule of standing was imprisoned for long years as a result of inheritance of the Anglo-Saxon system of jurisprudence have been broken and a new dimension has been given to the doctrine of *locus standi* which has revolutionized the whole concept of access to justice in a way not known before to the western system of jurisprudence ..."

7 *Kadra Pehadiya* v *State of Bihar* (1981)3 SCC 671.
8 *R.K. Garg* v *Union of India* (1981)4 SCC 675.
9 *People's Union for Democratic Rights* v *Union of India* AIR 1982 SC 1473: 1982 Lab IC 1646: (1982)3 SCC 235: 1982 SCC (L&S) 275.
10 *Sheela Barse* v *Union of India* (1983)2 SCC 96.
11 *Dr. Upendra Baxi (I)* v *State of U.P.* (1983)2 SCC 308.
12 *Dr. Shiva Rao Shantaram Ram Wagle* v *Union of India* (1988)2 SCC 115.
13 *People's Union for Democratic Rights* v *Union of India* AIR 1982 SC 1473: 1982 Lab IC 1646: (1982)3 SCC 235: 1982 SCC (L&S) 275.

Thus, the 19th century concept of *locus standi* that dominated the Indian scenario for a long time was altered at the end of the 20th century. There is now much wider concept of *locus standi* when complaint is made against a public authority. It extends to any one who is not a mere busy body but is coming to the Court on behalf of the public at large. Now every responsible citizen has an interest in seeing that the law is enforced and that is considered as sufficient interest in itself to warrant his applying for *Mandamus* or *Certiorari* to see that it is enforced. Now every responsible citizen has a sufficient interest, such as, to entitle him to be heard if he complains that the law is not being enforced in the way as it should be.

Justice Bhagwati views that for the liberalisation of the *locus standi* rule as a land mark in the history of jurisprudence and as a source for redressal of grievance, we owe an immense and invaluable debt to Lord Denning who in 1973 in a leading decision[14] observed that "if there is good ground for supposing that a Government department or a public authority is transgressing the law, or is about to transgress it, in a way which offends or injures thousands of Her Majesty's subject, then in the last resort any one of those offended or injured can draw it to the attention of the Courts of law and seek to have the law enforced."

8 Liberalisation of locus standi rule not extended to criminal and service matters The Court, says Justice Bhagwati, has, however, been careful not to liberalize the concept of standing in criminal and service matters. In *Panchi* v *State of U.P.*[15] refusing permission to the National Commission for Women to intervene in a case of death sentence awarded to a woman, the Court said that this was 'for the obvious reason that under the Code of Criminal Procedure, the National Commission of Women or any other organization cannot have *locus standi* in this murder case'. In *Janata Dal* v *H.S. Chowdhary*[16] the apex court observed: 'Even if a million questions of laws were to be deeply gone into and examined in a criminal case of this nature registered against specified accused persons, it is for them and them alone to raise all such questions and challenge the proceedings initiated against them at the appropriate time before the proper forum and not for third parties under the garb of public interest litigants'. In *Janata Dal* v *H.S. Chowdhary,*[17] the Court held that the lawyer petitioner was concerned with the private

14 *Attorney General (on the relation of McWhirter)* v *Independent Broadcasting Authority* [1973]1 All ER 689.
15 (1988)1 SCC 177.
16 (1991)3 SCC 756, 768.
17 (1992)4 SCC 305: 1993 SCC (Cri) 36: AIR 1993 SC 892.

interest of the accused and therefore lacked *locus standi* to pursue the case as a public interest litigation.

Similarly, in service matters, the Court has held that a third party cannot challenge the appointment of a person.[18] The Court has held that PIL cannot be maintained by a meddlesome interloper or busybody,[19] wayfarers,[20] or officious interveners having no public interest except for personal gain either for themselves or for the glare of publicity.[1]

9 PIL in enforcement of human rights PIL has contributed substantially in facilitating judicial activism in the area of human rights of the poor, down-trodden, ignorant and illiterate. In *People's Union for Democratic Rights* v *Union of India*,[2] Justice Bhagwati alerted that millions of persons belonging to the deprived and vulnerable sections of humanity are looking to the courts for improving their life conditions and making basic human rights meaningful for them. They have been crying for justice but their cries have so far been in the wilderness. They have been suffering injustice silently with the patience of a rock, without the strength even to shed any tears. The legal aid movement and public interest litigation seek to bring justice to these forgotten specimens of humanity who constitute the bulk of the citizens of India and who are really and truly the "People of India", who gave to themselves the magnificent Constitution.

In *Veena Sethi* v *State of Bihar,*[3] Justice Bhagwati observed that the rule of law does not exist merely for those who have the means to fight for their rights and very often for the perpetuation of the *status quo* which protects and preserves their dominance and permits them to exploit large sections of the community but it exists also for the poor and the down-trodden, the ignorant and the illiterate who constitute the large bulk of humanity in this country. It is the solemn duty of the Supreme Court to protect and uphold the basic human rights of the weaker sections of the society, and it is this duty the Court is trying to discharge in entertaining the public interest litigation.

18 *R.K. Jain* v *Union of India* (1993)4 SCC 119; *Dr. Duryodhan Sahu* v *Jitandra Kumar Mishra* AIR 1999 SC 114.

19 *Bandhua Mukti Morcha* v *Union of India* (1984)3 SCC 161.

20 *Janata Dal's* case (1992)4 SCC 305, 349.

1 *Kumar* v *State of Bihar* (1991)1 SCC 598; *Ramsharan Autyanuprashi* v *Union of India* 1989 Supp (1) SCC 251; *Chhetriya Pazdushan Mukti Sanaghrsh Samiti* v *State of U.P.* (1990)4 SCC 449.

2 *People's Union for Democratic Rights* v *Union of India* AIR 1982 SC 1473: 1982 Lab IC 1646: (1982)3 SCC 235: 1982 SCC (L&S) 275.

3 (1982)2 SCC 583.

The responsibility of the court to the same effect was also echoed by Justice Bhagwati in *People's Union for Democratic Rights* v *Union of India*[4] where he observed that social justice is the signature tune of our Constitution, and it is the solemn duty of the Courts under the Constitution to enforce the basic human rights of the poor and vulnerable sections of the community and actively help in the realization of the constitutional goals. This new change has to come if the judicial system is to become an effective instrument of social justice, for without it, it cannot survive for long.

Justice Bhagwati, however, took solace in the fact that the change as contemplated has taken place and public interest litigation has played a large part in bringing about this change. It is through public interest litigation that the problems of the poor are now coming to the forefront and the entire theatre of the law has thereby changed. In public interest litigations, the Court has expressed its views firmly to the effect that since constitutional guarantees are non-negotiable, human rights entrenched in the National Charter shall not be held hostages by any authority. The Court's active concern has been focused on different occasions on the rights of detenus and under-trials, police excesses, custodial violence, conditions in prisons and other custodial institutions based upon postcards, letters, articles in newspapers, press reports, and petitions from a cross-section of citizens. Before the Supreme Court, the Court's action starts by converting the facts brought before it into a petition under Article 32; it would then issue directions to the concerned State agency to provide information, and, when that is not forthcoming, it would appoint a commissioner to investigate and collect the facts. When the Court becomes convinced on the basis of facts before it that the matter required its intervention, it would issue a *Mandamus* or any appropriate writ or direction to State agencies to carry out its directives within a specified time frame.

In *Hussainara Khatoon* v *Home Secretary*,[5] the attention of the apex court was drawn on the basis of a news report to the incredible situation of Bihar under-trials who had been detained pending trials for periods far in excess of the maximum sentence for the offences they were charged with. Attacking the highly unsatisfactory bail system, Justice Bhagwati in the said case observed that 'it is a travesty of justice that many poor accused, "little Indians, are forced into long cellular servitude for little offences" because the bail procedure is beyond their meager

4 AIR 1982 SC 1473.
5 (1980)1 SCC 81.

means and trials don't commence and even if they do, they never conclude. There can be little doubt, after the dynamic interpretation placed by this Court (Supreme Court) on Article 21 in *Maneka Gandhi* v *Union of India*[6] that a procedure which keeps such large numbers of people behind bars without trial so long cannot possibly be regarded as 'reasonable, just or fair' so as to be in conformity with the requirement of that Article. It is necessary, therefore, that the law as is enacted by the legislature and as administered by the courts must radically change its approach to pre-trial detention and ensure 'reasonable, just and fair' procedure which received creative interpretation and connotation in *Maneka Gandhi's* case'.

Making speedy trial as the central issue, Justice Bhagwati in *Hussainara Khatoon's* case (supra) observed that speedy trial is an integral and essential part of the fundamental right to life and liberty enshrined in Article 21 of the Constitution of India. No procedure, observed Justice Bhagwati, which does not ensure a reasonably quick trial can be regarded as 'reasonable, fair and just' which is the basis of Article 21. If a person is deprived of his liberty under a procedure which is not "reasonable, fair or just", such deprivation would be violative of his fundamental right under Article 21 and he would be entitled to enforce such fundamental right and secure his release.[7]

Justice Bhagwati minced no words in criticizing our legal and judicial system which permits men and women languishing in jails for years without trial and expressed his anguish in this respect in *Hussainara Khatoon's* case (supra) thus: "It is a crying shame on the judicial system which permits incarceration of men and women for such long periods of time without trial. We are shouting from housetops about the protection and enforcement of human rights. We are talking passionately and eloquently about the maintenance and preservation of basic freedoms. But, are we not denying human rights to these nameless persons who are languishing in jails for years for offences which perhaps they might ultimately be found not to have committed? Are we not withholding

6 AIR 1978 SC 597: (1978)2 SCR 621: (1978)1 SCC 248.

7 AUTHORS' NOTE: In *Kadra Pahadiya* v *State of Bihar* (1983)2 SCC 104, Justice Bhagwati drawing reference to *Hussainara Khatoon's* case also observed that speedy trial is a fundamental right implicit in the guarantee of life and personal liberty enshrined in Article 21 of the Constitution and any accused who is denied this right of speedy trial is entitled to approach the Supreme Court for the purpose of enforcing such right and the Supreme Court in discharge of its constitutional obligation has the power to issue necessary directions to the State Governments and other appropriate authorities for securing this right to the accused.

basic freedoms from these neglected and helpless human beings who have been condemned to a life of imprisonment and degradation for years on end? Are expeditious trial and freedom from detention not part of human rights and basic freedoms? Many of these unfortunate men and women must not even be remembering when they entered the jail and for what offence. They have over the years ceased to be human beings: they are mere ticket-numbers. It is high time that the public conscience is awakened and the government as well as the judiciary begin to realise that in the dark cells of our prisons there are large numbers of men and women who are waiting patiently, impatiently perhaps, but in vain, for justice—a commodity which is tragically beyond their reach and grasp. Law has become for them an instrument of injustice and they are helpless and despairing victims of the callousness of the legal and judicial system. The time has come when the legal and judicial system has to be revamped and restructured so that such injustices do not occur and disfigure the fair and otherwise luminous face of our nascent democracy." Justice Bhagwati in this context referred to data given by the Union Home Minister in 2007 in response to a question in the Rajya Sabha which highlights that at the end of 2005 there were 2,37,076 under-trials in different jails in India. Of the over two lakhs under-trials, 45,249 had been languishing in jails for more than a year and 1,884 for more than five years. Of the total number, 96% were males and there were 9,070 females waiting for justice.

In *Kadra Pehadiya* v *State of Bihar*,[8] where a letter was addressed to the Court by a researcher and social scientist highlighting the conditions of four young boys who were detained in Pakud sub-jail in Santhal Parganas of Bihar for a period of about eight years without their trial having made any progress, Justice Bhagwati questioned the tolerance of a civilized society for a legal and judicial system which keeps a person in jail for years without commencing his trial and decried and deprecated the tendency that once a person accused of an offence is lodged in the jail, everyone forgets about him and no one bothers to care what is happening to him. He becomes a mere ticket number—a forgotten specimen of humanity—cut off and alienated from the society, an unfortunate victim of a heartless legal and judicial system which consigns him to long unending years of oblivion in jail. It is a crying shame, said Justice Bhagwati, upon our adjudicatory system which keeps men in jail for years on end without a trial. In the said case, Justice Bhagwati made a number of observations in protecting

8 (1983)2 SCC 104.

the human rights of under-trial prisoners. He said that (*i*) an under-trial prisoner shall have to be provided legal representation by a fairly competent lawyer at the cost of the State, since legal aid in a criminal case is a fundamental right implicit in Article 21 of the Constitution; (*ii*) the jail authorities cannot exact work from a person who has not been convicted but is merely an under-trial prisoner since that would be a flagrant violation of prison regulations and contrary to the I.L.O. Conventions against Forced Labour; and (*iii*) no convicted or under-trial prisoner shall be kept long in irons except in accordance with the ratio of the decision in *Sunil Batra (I)* v *Delhi Administration*.[9]

In *Veena Sethi* v *State of Bihar*,[10] where the Free Legal Aid Committee, Bihar, addressed a letter to the Court drawing the Court's attention to unjustified and illegal detention of certain prisoners in Hazaribagh Central Jail for almost two or three decades, Justice Bhagwati observed that personal liberty is one of the most precious rights of a human being and it cannot be allowed to be smothered by bureaucratic or judicial inadequacy or inefficiency.

If it is so done, says Justice Bhagwati, one day the cry and despair of large number of people will shake the very foundations of the society and imperil the entire democratic structure of our polity and if that happens, we shall only have ourselves to blame. Justice Bhagwati asked the government to take note of the provisions of Section 428 of the Code of Criminal Procedure 1973, which provide that the period during which an accused has been in jail as an under-trial prisoner should be taken into account for the purpose of computing the period of the sentence and the maximum imprisonment which an accused is ordinarily required to undergo even in case of sentence of life imprisonment is not more than 14 years.

Expressing his concern for the mentally sick prisoners who were detained in jail for years and in some cases 30 or 40 years at a stretch because of non-availability of adequate institutions for treatment of the mentally sick, Justice Bhagwati in *Veena Sethi's* case (supra) observed that in a large State there must be adequate number of institutions for looking after the mentally sick and the practice of sending lunatics or persons of unsound mind to the jail for safe custody is not at all a healthy or desirable practice, because jail is hardly a place for treating those who are mentally sick. The difficulty, said Justice Bhagwati, is

9 (1978)4 SCC 494: 1979 SCC (Cri) 155.
10 (1982)2 SCC 583.

that "when a person is lodged in jail on the ground that he is of unsound mind, and, therefore, required to be kept in safe custody, the custody becomes so safe that the prisoner has no opportunity of ever getting out of it even though he has become sane and the raison *d'etre* of his custody has disappeared".

In *Sheela Barse* v *State of Maharashtra*,[11] where a letter was addressed by journalist Sheela Barse complaining of custodial violence to women prisoners whilst confined in the police lock-up in the city of Bombay, Justice Bhagwati issued a number of directions having meaningful bearing on human rights and the directions included, amongst others: (*i*) Female suspects should not be kept in police lock-up in which male suspects are detained. Female suspects should be kept in female lock-ups by female constables. (*ii*) Interrogation of females should be carried out solely in the presence of female police officers/constables. (*iii*) Whenever a person is arrested by police without warrant, he must be immediately informed of the grounds of his arrest and in case of every arrest it must be immediately made known to the arrested person that he is entitled to apply for bail. (*iv*) Whenever a person is arrested by the police and taken to the police lock-up, the police will immediately give intimation of the fact of such arrest to the nearest Legal Aid Committee and such Legal Aid Committee will take immediate steps for the purpose of providing legal assistance to the arrested person at State cost provided he is willing to accept such legal assistance.[12] (*v*) As soon as a person is arrested, the police must immediately obtain from him the name of any relative or friend whom he would like to be informed about his arrest and the police should get in touch with such relative or friend and inform him about the arrest. (*vi*) The magistrate before whom an arrested person is produced shall

11 (1983)2 SCC 96.

12 AUTHORS' NOTE: Justice Bhagwati in *Sheela Barse* v *State of Maharashtra* (1983)2 SCC 96 observed that legal assistance to a poor or indigent accused who is arrested and put in jeopardy of his life or personal liberty is a constitutional imperative mandated not only by Article 39A but also by Articles 14 and 21 of the Constitution. It is a necessary *sine qua non* of justice and where it is not provided, injustice is likely to result and undeniably every act of injustice corrodes the foundation of democracy and rule of law, because nothing rankles more in the human heart than a feeling of injustice and those who suffer and cannot get justice because they are priced out of legal system, lose faith in the legal process and a feeling begins to overtake them that democracy and rule of law are merely slogans or myths intended to perpetuate the domination of the rich and the powerful and protect the establishment and the vested interests. It is absolutely essential that legal assistance must be made available to prisoners in jails whether they be under-trial or convicted prisoners.

enquire from the arrested person whether he has any complaint of torture or maltreatment in police custody and inform him that he has right under section 54 of the Code of Criminal Procedure 1973, to be medically examined.

In *Sunil Batra (II)* v *Delhi Administration*,[13] where by a letter the attention of the Court was drawn by a prisoner of Tihar Jail about the inhuman torture to which another life convict had been subjected to by jail warder, Justice V.R. Krishna Iyer, a brother Judge of Justice Bhagwati, said that the rule of law meets with its Waterloo when the State's minions become law-breakers and so the Court, as the sentinel of the nation and the voice of the Constitution, runs down the violators with its writ and secures compliance with human rights even behind iron bars and by prison warders. Where injustice, verging on inhumanity, emerges from hacking human rights guaranteed in Part III of the Constitution and the victim beseeches the Court to intervene and relief, the Supreme Court will be a functional futility as a constitutional instrumentality if its guns do not go into action until the wrong is righted. The Court has power and responsibility to intervene and protect the prisoner against mayhem, crude or subtle, and may use *habeas corpus* for enforcing in prison humanism and forbiddance or harsher restraints and heavier severities than the sentence carries. In deciding *Sunil Batra's* case (supra), Krishna Iyer, J., referred to *Maneka Gandhi's* case,[14] where in a passage Justice Bhagwati, observed: "The principle of reasonableness, which legally as well as philosophically, is an essential element of equality, of non-arbitrariness pervades Article 14 like a brooding omnipresence and the procedure contemplated by Article 21 must answer the test of reasonableness in order to be in conformity with Article 14. It must be 'right, just and fair' and not arbitrary, fanciful or oppressive; otherwise, it would be no procedure at all and the requirement of Article 21 would not be satisfied." Whether inside prison or outside, a person, says Justice Bhagwati, shall not be deprived of his guaranteed freedom save by methods 'right, just and fair.'

In *People's Union for Democratic Rights* v *Union of India,*[15] where the organization People's Union commissioned the services of three social scientists for the purpose of investigating and inquiring into the conditions under which the workmen engaged in the various Asiad Projects had been working and based on their report addressed a letter

13 (1980)3 SCC 488: AIR 1980 SC 1579.

14 *Maneka Gandhi* v *Union of India* (1978)1 SCC 248: (1978)2 SCR 621: AIR 1978 SC 597.

15 AIR 1982 SC 1473: 1982 Lab IC 1646: (1982)3 SCC 235: 1982 SCC (L&S) 275.

to the Court to ensure the observance of the provisions of various labour laws in relation to workmen employed in the construction work of various projects connected with the Asian Games, Justice Bhagwati, treating the letter of People's Union as a writ petition and the matter as a public interest litigation, characterised and earmarked in the said case 'construction work' as a hazardous occupation and called for prohibition of employment of children under the age of 14 years in every type of construction work and also called for amendment of the Schedule of the Employment of Children Act, 1938 by including construction industry in it. In support of his call, Justice Bhagwati referred to Convention No. 59 adopted by the International Labour Organization and ratified by India. But apart altogether from the requirement of Convention No. 59, Justice Bhagwati also referred to Article 24 of the Constitution of India which provides that no child below the age of 14 years shall be employed to work in any factory or mine or engaged in any other hazardous employment. This is a constitutional prohibition which, even if not followed up by appropriate legislation, must operate *proprio vigore* and construction work being plainly and indubitably a hazardous employment, it is clear that, by reason of this constitutional prohibition, no child below the age of 14 years can be allowed to be engaged in a construction work. It may be of interest to note that pursuant to the observation of Justice Bhagwati so made, the Schedule to Section 3(3) of the Employment of Children Act, 1938, was amended by adding to the schedule 'Building and Construction industry' as an area where employment of children below 14 is prohibited.[16] Again, Part B of the Schedule to section 3 of the Child Labour (Prohibition and Regulation) Act 1986, also includes 'Building and Construction Industry' as an area where employment of children has been prohibited.

In *People's Union for Democratic Rights*,[17] the Court became also concerned with the welfare of labourers engaged in construction work. In deciding the case, Justice Bhagwati issued a number of directions which, *inter alia*, stated: (*i*) Whenever any contracts are given by the government or any other governmental authority including a public sector corporation, it should be ensured by introducing a suitable provision in the contracts that wage shall be paid by the contractors to the workmen directly without the intervention of any jamadars or thekadars and that the contractors shall ensure that no amount by way of commission or otherwise is deducted or recovered by the jamadars

16 Vide: Notification No. S.O. 594 (E), dated 12.8.1983.
17 AIR 1982 SC 1473.

from wage of the workmen. (*ii*) Whenever any construction work is being carried out either departmentally or through contractors, the government or any other governmental authority including a public sector corporation which is carrying out such work must take great care to see that the provision of the labour laws are being strictly observed and they should not wait for any complaint to be received from the workmen in regard to non-observance of any such provisions before proceeding to take action against the erring officers or contractors but they should institute an effective system of periodic inspections coupled with occasional surprise inspections by the higher officers in order to ensure that there are no violations of the provisions of labour laws and the workmen are not denied the rights and benefits to which they are entitled under such provisions.

In interpreting Article 23 of the Constitution of India which prohibits 'traffic in human beings and forced labour,' Justice Bhagwati in *People's Union for Democratic Rights* (supra) observed that the Article is clearly designed to protect the individual not only against the State but also against other private citizens. Under the article, no one shall be forced to provide labour or service against his will, even though it be under a contract of service. When a person provides labour or service to another against receipt of remuneration which is less than the minimum wage, he is acting under the force of some compulsion which drives him to work though he is paid less than what he is entitled under law to receive. This is prohibited under Article 23.[18]

It requires mentioning here that at the time when Justice Bhagwati was fighting relentlessly to protect the human rights of the downtrodden and the oppressed section of the community, a helping hand was equally extended to him by his brother Judge on the Bench V.R. Krishna Iyer. In *Sunil Batra* v *Delhi Administration*,[19] Justice Iyer fighting for the rights of a prisoner observed that for a prisoner all fundamental rights are an enforceable reality, though restricted by the fact of imprisonment. The ratio in *A.K. Gopalan's* case,[20] said Justice Iyer, where the Court,

18 AUTHORS' NOTE: In *Sanjit Roy* v *State of Rajasthan* (1983)1 SCC 525, Justice Bhagwati observed that every person who provides labour or services to another is entitled at least to the minimum wage under the Minimum Wages Act, 1948 and if anything less than the minimum wage is paid to him, he can complain of violation of his fundamental right under Article 23 of the Constitution and ask the Court to direct payment of the minimum wage to him so that the breach of Article 23 may be abated.

19 AIR 1978 SC 1675: (1978)4 SCC 494.

20 *A.K. Gopalan* v *State of Madras* AIR 1950 SC 27: 1950 SCR 88.

by a majority, adopting a restrictive construction ruled out the play of fundamental rights for anyone under valid detention, was upturned in *R.C. Cooper's* case.[1] In *Maneka Gandhi*[2] the Supreme Court, through Justice Bhagwati highlighted this principle in the context of Article 21 itself. "The martyrdom of *Gopalan* and resurrection by Cooper paved the way for Maneka where the potent invocation of the Part III was affirmed in indubitable breadth", said Justice Iyer in *Sunil Batra's* case. Justice Krishna Iyer, in *Sunil Batra's* case also expressed himself strongly against 'solitary confinement' and viewed that the court should reject 'solitary confinement' as horrendous. Speaking about the rights of the condemned prisoners, Justice Iyer said that they shall be merely kept in custody and shall not be put to work like those sentenced to rigorous imprisonment. They shall be entitled to amenities of ordinary inmates in the prison like games, books, newspapers, reasonably good food, the right to expression and normal clothing and bed.

Justice Bhagwati strongly believes that if human rights are necessary in promoting the individual development of human beings, healthy environment becomes equally necessary to safeguard conditions conducive to such individual development, there being a natural link between environment development and human rights. The sweep of the right to life conferred by Article 21 is wide and far reaching after the interpretation given by Justice Bhagwati in *Francis Coralie Mullin's* case.[3] The right to life in its wider connotation now includes the right to live in healthy environment, says Justice Bhagwati. The learned Judge laments that pollution which has the effect of endangering human life and continuous destruction of nature are slowly but steadily destroying environment, thereby denying the citizens' right to live in healthy environment. Our natural resources and wealth of bio-diversity are being depleted unchecked, rivers polluted, air contaminated, and soil toxicated. Humanity must, as matter of pririty, maintain, clean air, potable water and non-noxious soil and prevent deforestation. Otherwise, wounded nature will recoil and avenge itself against its destruction by the mindless humanity. The jurisprudence of healthy environment and the constitutional law of the country insist on ecological justice and environmental protection as a *sine qua non* of the human rights for survival, asserts Justice Bhagwati. In *Rural Litigation and Entitlement Kendra* v *State of Uttar Pradesh*[4] which was the first case

1 *Rustom Cavasjee Cooper* v *Union of India* AIR 1970 SC 1318: (1970)2 SCC 298.
2 *Maneka Gandhi* v *Union of India* AIR 1978 SC 597: (1978)2 SCR 621: (1978)1 SCC 248.
3 *Francis Coralie Mullin* v *Union Territory of Delhi* AIR 1981 SC 746: (1981)1 SCC 608.
4 AIR 1987 SC 359.

in the country invoking the issues relating to environment and ecological balance, a Division Bench of Bhagwati, CJ. and Ranganath Misra, J., observed: "Preservation of the environment and keeping the ecological balance unaffected is a task which not only Governments but also every citizen must undertake. It is a social obligation and let us remind Indian citizen that it is his fundamental duty as enshrined in Article 51A(*g*) of the Constitution."

Justice V.R. Krishna Iyer in *Municipal Council, Ratlam* v *Vardichand*[5] observed: "Public nuisance, because of pollutants being discharged by big factories to the detriment of the poorer sections, is a challenge to the social justice component of the rule of law". Keeping that thing in mind, Justice Bhagwati in *M.C. Mehta* v *Union of India*[6] observed that "an enterprise which is engaged in a hazardous or inherently dangerous industry which poses a potential threat to the health and safety of the persons working in the factory and residing in the surrounding areas owes an absolute and non-delegable duty to the community to ensure that no harm results to anyone on account of hazardous or inherently dangerous nature of the activity which it has undertaken. The enterprise must be held to be under an obligation to provide that the hazardous or inherently dangerous activity in which it is engaged must be conducted with the highest standards of safety and if any harm results on account of such activity, the enterprise must be absolutely liable to compensate for such harm and it should be no answer to the enterprise to say that it had taken all reasonable care and that the harm occurred without any negligence on its part. Since the persons harmed on account of the hazardous or inherently dangerous activity carried on by the enterprise would not be in a position to isolate the process of operation from the hazardous preparation of substance or any other related element that caused the harm, the enterprise must be held strictly liable for causing such harm as a part of the social cost for carrying on the hazardous or inherently dangerous activity. If the enterprise is permitted to carry on an hazardous or inherently dangerous activity for its profit, the law must presume that such permission is conditional on the enterprise absorbing the cost of any accident arising on account of such hazardous or inherently dangerous activity as an appropriate item of its overheads." "This principle," observed further Justice Bhagwati in *M.C. Mehta's* case (supra), "is also sustainable on the ground that the enterprise alone has the resource to discover and

5 AIR 1980 SC 1622: 1980 Cr LJ 1075.
6 AIR 1987 SC 1086.

guard against hazards or dangers and to provide warning against potential hazards." Justice Bhagwati in fixing the strict liability of the enterprise did not allow his judicial thinking to be constricted by reference to the law as it prevails in England. The English rule of *Rylands* v *Fletcher* evolved in 1868 laid down a principle of liability that if a person who brings on to his land and collects and keeps there anything likely to do harm and such thing escapes due to his negligence and causes damage to another, he is liable to compensate for the damage caused. This rule, however, applies to non-natural user of the land. It does not apply to things naturally on the land or where the escape is due to act of God and an act of a stranger or the default of the person injured or where the thing which escapes is present by the consent of the person injured or in certain cases where there is statutory authority.

Court orders of Justice Bhagwati and Justice Krishna Iyer in PILs helped improving the live conditions of thousand and thousand of persons belonging to the deprived and vulnerable section of humanity and made the basic human rights meaningful to them.

Judicial activism that got its steam in PIL in protecting the human rights of the poor, down-trodden, ignorant and the illiterate continued also without any sign of diminution in post-Bhagwati era. Decisions on such matters as the right against handcuffing as in *TVS Vatheeswaran* case,[7] the right against custodial violence as in *Nilabati Behara's* case,[8] the rights of the arrestee as in *D.K. Basu* case,[9] the right of the female employees not to be sexually harassed at the place of work as in *Bisakha's* case[10] were rendered during post-Bhagwati era in public interest litigations by expanding the ambit and scope of Article 21 so as to include within its fold the right to live with human dignity because the "dignity of man supersedes all other considerations," a concept developed by Justice Bhagwati in *Frances Coralie Mullin's* case.[11]

10 PIL in enforcement of public accountability The trust reposed in persons holding public positions and exercising public power is abused

7 *TVS Vatheeswaran* v *State of Tamil Nadu* AIR 1983 SC 361: (1983)2 SCC 68. AUTHORS' NOTE: The Supreme Court condemned the handcuffs and chaining prisoners in *Prem Shankar Shukla* v *Delhi Administration* AIR 1980 SC 1535: (1980)3 SCC 526: 1980 Cr LJ 930. In the said case, Justice Bhagwati concurred with the view as expressed by V.R. Krishna Iyer, J.

8 *Nilabati Behara* v *State of Orissa* AIR 1993 SC 1960: (1993)2 SCC 746.

9 *D.K. Basu* v *State of West Bengal* AIR 1997 SC 610: (1997)1 SCC 416.

10 *Visakha* v *State of Rajasthan* AIR 1997 SC 3011: (1997)6 SCC 241.

11 *Francis Corlie Mullin* v *Union Territory of Delhi* AIR 1981 SC 746: (1981)1 SCC 608.

when discretion is exercised irregularly and sometimes even for collateral considerations. The Supreme Court acting through Justice Bhagwati in various PILs has dealt with the issue and laid down elaborate guideline in limiting uncanalised exercise of discretionary power.

In *R.D. Shetty* v *The International Airport Authority of India*,[12] Justice Bhagwati laid down that an executive authority must hold rigorously to the standards by which it professes its actions to be judged and it must scrupulously observe those standards on pain of invalidation of an act done in violation of them. This is a rule of administrative law, said Justice Bhagwati, which has been judicially evolved as a check against exercise of arbitrary power by the executive authority. Every action of the executive government must be informed with reason and should be free from arbitrariness.

In *State of Himachal Pradesh* v *A Parent of a Student of Medical College, Shimla*,[13] Justice Bhagwati observed: "If the executive is not carrying out any duty laid upon it by the Constitution or the law, the Court can certainly require the executive to carry out such duty and this is precisely what the Court does when it entertains public interest litigation. Where the Court finds, on being moved by an aggrieved party or by any public spirited individual or social action group, that the executive is remiss in discharging its obligations under the Constitution or the law, so that the poor and the underprivileged continue to be subjected to exploitation and injustice or are deprived of their social and economic entitlements or that social legislation enacted for their benefit is not being implemented thus depriving them of the rights and benefits conferred upon them, the Court certainly can and must intervene and compel the executive to carry out its constitutional and legal obligations and ensure that the deprived and vulnerable sections of the community are no longer subjected to exploitation or injustice and they are able to realise their social and economic rights."

In the matter of largess, observed Justice Bhagwati, in *International Airport Authority's* case,[14] the power of the government is not unlimited in that the government cannot give or withhold largess in its arbitrary discretion or at its sweet will. The power of discretion of the government in the matter of grant of largess including award of jobs, contract quotas, licenses, etc. must be confined and structured by rational, relevant and non-discriminatory standard or norm and if the government

12 AIR 1979 SC 1628.
13 AIR 1985 SC 910.
14 AIR 1979 SC 1628.

departs from such standard and norm in any particular case or cases, the action of the government would be liable to be struck down unless it can be shown that the departure was not arbitrary, but was based on some valid principle which in itself was not irrational, unreasonable or discriminatory. In post-Bhagwati era, such type of issue resurfaced before the Supreme Court in *Centre for Public Interest Litigation* v *Union of India*[15] where the problem of discretionary quota vested in the minister concerned for allotment of petrol pumps and oil and gas dealerships was considered. The Supreme Court, in the said case, requested the Attorney-General to submit draft guidelines and then set them down in its judgment as norms that would govern all future allotments of dealerships under the discretionary quota.

In the view of Justice V.R. Krishna Iyer which had the concurrence of Justice Bhagwati in *Fertilizer Corporation Kamnagar Union* v *Union of India*[16] it is not part of the judicial process to examine entrepreneurial activities of public bodies like government companies to ferret out flaws. The court is least equipped for such oversights. Nor, is it the function of the judges in our constitutional scheme. The internal management, business activity or institutional operation of public bodies cannot be subjected to inspection by the Court. To do so is incompetent and improper and, therefore, out of bounds. If the directorate of a government company has acted fairly, even if it has faltered in its wisdom, the court cannot, as a super-auditor, take the board of directors to task. The court's function is limited to testing whether the administrative action has been fair and free from taint of unreasonableness and has substantially complied with the norms of procedures set for it by rules of public administration. The broad parameters of fairness in administration, *bona fides* in action, and the fundamental rules of reasonable management of public business, if breached, will become justiciable.

Justice Bhagwati agrees with the view as expressed by Chinnappa Reddy, J., in *Chaitanya Kumar* v *State of Karnataka*[17] where the learned Judge observed: "When arbitrariness and perversion are writ large and brought out clearly, the Court cannot shirk its duty and refuse its writ. Advancement of the public interest and avoidance of the public mischief are the paramount considerations. As always, the Court is concerned with the balancing of interest."

15 1995 Supp (3) SCC 382.
16 AIR 1981 SC 344: 1980 Lab IC 1367.
17 AIR 1986 SC 825.

Noteworthy in this respect is the observation of Y.V. Chandrachud, CJ., in *Fertilizer Corporation Kamagar Union's* case[18] which had the concurrence of the other two Judges sitting in the Bench with him, namely, V.R. Krishna Iyer and Bhagwati, JJ., when the Chief Justice said: 'If public property is dissipated, it would require a strong argument to convince the Court that representative segments of the public which is directly interested and affected would have no right to complain of the infraction of public duties and obligations. Public enterprises are owned by the people and those who run them are accountable to the people. The accountability of the public sector to the Parliament is ineffective because the parliamentary control of the public enterprises is "diffuse and haphazard".'

11 PIL and judicial review of administrative and legislative action The 'Indian Constitution', observed the Supreme Court in *Ram Jawaya Kapur* v *State of Punjab,*[19] 'has not ... recognised the doctrine of separation of powers in its absolute rigidity but the functions of the different parts or branches of the government have been sufficiently differentiated and consequently it can very well be said that our Constitution does not contemplate assumption, by one organ or part of the State, of functions that essentially belong to another.' In line with that principle, Justice V.R. Krishna Iyer in *Fertilizer Corporation Kamagar Union, Sindri* v *Union of India*[20] observed to which Justice Bhagwati had the concurrence that judicial interference with the administration cannot be meticulous in our Montesquien system of separation of powers. The court cannot usurp or abdicate, and the parameters of judicial review must be clearly defined and never exceeded. In *State of Himachal Pradesh* v *A Parent of a Student of Medical College, Shimla*[21] Justice Bhagwati observed that though the court cannot usurp the functions assigned to the executive and the legislature under the Constitution and it cannot even indirectly require the executive to introduce a particular legislation or the legislature to pass it or assume to itself a supervisory role over the law making activities of the executive and the legislature yet if the executive is not carrying out any duty laid upon it by the Constitution or the law, the court can certainly require the executive to carry out such duty and this is precisely what the court does in exercise of its power of judicial review

18 *Fertilizer Corporation Kamagar Union, Sindri* v *Union of India* AIR 1981 SC 344: (1981)1 SCC 568: 1980 Lab IC 1367.
19 (1955)2 SCR 225.
20 (1981)1 SCC 568: AIR 1981 SC 344: 1980 Lab IC 1367.
21 AIR 1985 SC 910: (1985)3 SCC 169.

when it entertains public interest litigation. Thus, continued Justice Bhagwati, where the court finds, on being moved by an aggrieved party or by any public spirited individual or social action group, that the executive is remiss in discharging its obligations under the Constitution or the law, so that the poor and the underprivileged continue to be subjected to exploitation and injustice or are deprived of their social and economic entitlements or that social legislation enacted for their benefit is not being implemented thereby depriving them of the rights and benefits conferred upon them, the court certainly, in exercise of its power of judicial review, can and must intervene and compel the executive to carry out its constitutional and legal obligations and ensure that the deprived and vulnerable sections of the community are no longer subjected to exploitation or injustice and they are able to realise their social and economic rights.

It is an established principle of law, says Justice Bhagwati, that policy-making and implementation thereof belong to the exclusive domain of the executive and the legislature. But the concept has undergone radical modification in PIL to the extent that when the implementation or non-implementation of the policy results in violation of fundamental rights, the court, through judicial review, may interdict the violation and issue orders.

In the legislative field, if the legislatures step beyond the areas assigned to them under the three lists set out in the Seventh Schedule of the Constitution or trespass, while acting within their respective areas, on the fundamental rights of the citizens in a manner not justified by the relevant articles dealing with the said fundamental rights, the Supreme Court under Article 32 and the High Courts under Article 226 of the Constitution in exercise of the power of judicial review in a PIL action can strike down such legislative actions. The issue has been dealt with elaborately in Chapter 10 on 'Judicial Review.'

12 PIL and the role of Commissioner Lack of access to information is a problem which a petitioner often faces in case of PIL. Often the government in its defence cites the Official Secrets Act 1923 under which it may not be possible for any member of the public to access information which the government regards as being a secret for various reasons. One method by which the court could gather facts is by the appointment of commissioners. The court appoints commissioners when the information sought for by the court from the State authority is not forthcoming. The Commissioner in that case investigates; collects the facts and reports to the court. The use of commissioners, says Justice Bhagwati, has enabled the court to check the facts alleged by the petitioner as well as the State after proper scrutiny without affecting its role as an adjudicator. It may be noted that even in case of Official Secrets Act 1923, barring an exceptional situation where the government may claim privilege, the courts can always require the former to provide the necessary information either to it directly or to its Commissioners. It requires mentioning here that while the power to appoint commissioners in matters of civil nature is found in Order XXVI of the Civil Procedure Code and Order XLVI of the Supreme Court Rules, the powers under Article 32 read with Article 142 are wide enough to permit such a course of action in any matter before the Supreme Court. The court in many cases appointed lawyers, journalists, district judges, mental health professionals, bureaucrats, and expert bodies as Commissioners. Thus, in *Sheela Barse* v *State of Maharashtra*[1] the Director of Social Work, Nirmala Niketan, Bombay, was appointed to investigate the ill-treatment of women prisoners; Dr. L. Misra, Joint Secretary, Government of India, was appointed Commissioner in *Bandhua Mukti Morcha* v *Union of India*;[2] a district judge was appointed in *Kamaladevi Chattopadhyay* v *State of Punjab*[3] to report on the women and children detained in Ludhiana jails. The precedence in the matter of appointment of Commissioner was set by Justice Bhagwati. In post-Bhagwati era, the trend continued. Thus, to mention only a few, Kishan Mahajan of the Indian Express was appointed Commissioner along with Upendra Baxi, Law Professor, in *Gulshan* v *Zila Parishad*;[4] Gopal Subramanium was appointed Commissioner in *Sheela Barse* v *Union of India*[5] to visit Assam and carry out the orders of the Court in regard to the release of the mentally-ill held in the jails there; Dr. Srinivasa Murthy, Professor of Psychiatry and Dr. Amita Dhandha, Assistant Professor of Law, were appointed Commissioners to visit jails in West Bengal and report on the mentally-ill held there in *Sheela Barse* v *Union of India*.[6] In environmental matters, the court has relied upon expert bodies like the Central Pollution Control Board.[7]

13 PIL and the petitioner's responsibility Justice Bhagwati perceived a PIL petitioner as one who must be a public spirited individual 'seeking

1 (1983)2 SCC 96.
2 (1984)3 SCC 161.
3 (1985)1 SCC 41.
4 (1987) Supp 619.
5 1994(4) SCALE 493.
6 (1993)4 SCC 204.
7 *M.C. Mehta* v *Union of India* 1999(4) SCALE 196.

judicial redress for the benefit of persons who have suffered a legal wrong or a legal injury or whose constitutional and legal rights have been violated but who by reason of their poverty or socially or economically disadvantaged position are unable to approach the court for relief.[8] The learned Judge cautioned in *S.P. Gupta's* case[9] that only a person acting *bona fide* and having sufficient interest in the proceeding of PIL will alone have *locus standi* and can approach the court to wipe out the tears of the poor and the needy, suffering from violations of their fundamental rights. The view as expressed by Justice Bhagwati has been reiterated by the Supreme Court in later cases[10] where the court in no uncertain term observed that a writ petitioner who comes to the court for relief in public interest litigation must come not only with clean hands like any other writ petitioner but also with a clean heart, clean mind, and clean objective.

In PIL cases, Justice Bhagwati mentions, the petitioner is not entitled to withdraw his petition at his sweet will unless the court sees reasons to permit withdrawal. In granting the permission, the court would be guided by considerations of public interest and would also ensure that it does not result in abuse of the process of law.[11]

14 Guidelines entertaining letters/petitions as PIL application Justice Bhagwati views that in granting permission to entertain a letter or petition as PIL, the court would be guided by considerations of public interest and would also ensure that it does not result in abuse of the processes of the law.[12] To ensure the same, the Court has to be satisfied about (*a*) the credentials of the applicant; (*b*) the *prima facie* correctness or nature of information given by him; (*c*) the information being not vague and indefinite. The information should show gravity and seriousness involved. Court has to strike balance between two conflicting interests: (*i*) nobody should be allowed to indulge in wild and reckless allegations besmirching the character of others; and

8 *S.P. Gupta* v *Union of India* 1981 (Supp) SCC 87: AIR 1982 SC 149.

9 *S.P. Gupta* v *Union of India* (supra).
AUTHORS' NOTE: This view of Justice Bhagwati as expressed in *S.P. Gupta's* case was echoed by the apex court in *Janata Dal* v *H.S. Chowdhary* (1992)4 SCC 305: 1993 SCC (Cri) 36: AIR 1993 SC 892.

10 *Ramjas Foundation* v *Union of India* 1993 Supp (2) SCC 20: AIR 1993 SC 852; *K.R. Srinivas* v *R.M. Premchand* (1994)6 SCC 620.

11 AUTHORS' NOTE: Justice Bhagwati's view in this field finds support in *S.P. Ananda* v *H.D. Deve Gowda* (1996)6 SCC 734.

12 AUTHORS' NOTE: The view of Justice Bhagwati finds support in the decision of the Supreme Court in *S.P. Ananda* v *H.D. Deve Gowda* (1996)6 SCC 734.

(*ii*) avoidance of public mischief and to avoid mischievous petitions seeking to assail, for oblique motives, justifiable executive actions. It has to be extremely careful to see that under the guise of redressing a public grievance, it does not encroach upon the sphere reserved by the Constitution to the executives and the legislature. Justice Bhagwati cautions that public interest litigation is a weapon in the armory of law which has to be used with great care and circumspection and the judiciary has to be extremely careful to see that behind the veil of public interest an ugly private malice, vested interest and/or publicity seeking is not lurking. It is to be used as an effective weapon in the armory of law for delivering social justice to the citizens. The attractive brand name of public interest litigation should not be allowed to be misused for ulterior and mischievous purposes. It should be aimed at redressal of genuine public wrong or public injury and should not be publicity oriented or founded on personal malice or vendetta.[13]

As said earlier, the court has barred the PIL in criminal and service matters. The court, says Justice Bhagwati, may also refuse to entertain a PIL if it finds that the issues raised are not within the judicial ambit or capacity. Thus, in rejecting a petition seeking directions to the Central Government to preserve and protect the Gyanvapi Masjid and the Vishwanath Temple at Varanasi as well as Krishna temple and Idgah at Mathura, the Court in *Mohd. Aslum* v *Union of India,*[14] observed that 'the matter is eminently one for appropriate evaluation and action by the executive, and may not have an adjudicative disposition or judicially manageable standards as the pleadings now stand'.

It may be noted in this context that the Supreme Court, on its administrative side, issued on 1st December, 1988, guidelines to be followed in letters/petitions received in the Court as public interest litigation. The full Court decided that letters/petitions received under the following categories alone would ordinarily be entertained as public interest litigations:

(1) bonded labour matters;

(2) neglected children;

(3) non-payment of minimum wages to workers and exploitation of casual workers and of labour laws (except in individual cases);

13 AUTHORS' NOTE: In *Neetu* v *State of Punjab* 2007 SCCL. COM 14, the apex court has also expressed the same view.

14 (1994)2 SCC 48.

(4) petitions from jails complaining of harassment, for pre-mature release and seeking release after having completed 14 years in jail, transfer, release on personal bond, speedy trial as a fundamental right;

(5) petitions against police for refusing to register a case, harassment by police and death in police custody;

(6) petitions against atrocities on women, in particular harassment of bride, bride-burning, rape, murder, kidnapping, etc.;

(7) petitions complaining of harassment or torture of villagers by co-villagers or by police from persons belonging to Schedule Castes and Schedule Tribes and economically backward classes;

(8) petitions pertaining to environmental pollutions, disturbance of ecological balance, drugs, food adulteration, maintenance of heritage and culture, antiques, forest and wildlife and other matters of public importance;

(9) petitions from riot-victims; and

(10) family pension.

All letter-petitions received in the PIL Cell (Public Interest Litigation Cell) in the Supreme Court will first be screened in the Cell and only such petitions as are covered by the above mentioned categories will be placed before a Judge to be nominated by the Hon'ble Chief Justice of India for directions after which the case will be listed before the Bench concerned. To begin with, only one Hon'ble Judge might be assigned this work and the number may be increased to two or three later depending on the workload.

It was also decided that the cases falling under the following categories would not be entertained as public interest litigation and these might be returned to the petitioners or filed in the PIL Cell as the case may be:

(1) landlord-tenant matters;

(2) service matter and those pertaining to pension and gratuity;

(3) complaint against Central/State Government Departments and Local Bodies except those relating to item Nos. (1) to (10) above;

(4) admission to medical and other educational institutions; and

(5) petitions for early hearing of cases pending in High Courts and Subordinates Courts.

In regard to the petitions concerning maintenance of wife, children and parents, the petitioners may be asked to file a petition under section 125 of Criminal Procedure Code 1973 or a Suit in the Court of competent jurisdiction and for that purpose to approach the nearest Legal Aid Committee for legal aid and advice.

The guidelines issued by the Supreme Court in 1988 were reiterated in 2008 by the apex court. While reiterating the guidelines of 1988, the Supreme Court advised (based on order dated 19.8.1993 of the then Chief Justice of India) that petitions for premature release, parole etc. are not matters which deserve to be treated as petitions under Article 32 as they can effectively be dealt with by the concerned High Court. To save time Registry may simultaneously call for remarks of the Jail Superintendent and ask him to forward the same to High Court. The main petition may be forwarded to the concerned High Court for disposal in accordance with law. Even in regard to petitions containing allegations against Jail Authorities, there is no reason, the apex court said, why it cannot be dealt with by the High Court. But petitions complaining of torture, custody death and the like may be entertained by the Supreme Court directly if the allegations are of a serious nature.

In so far as the guideline speaks about the non-eligibility of admission to medical and other educational institutions as PIL, Justice Bhagwati views that PIL would certainly lie if there is violation of Articles 14, 16 or 21 of the Constitution in the matter of such admission.

15 Criticisms surrounding PIL Taking advantage of the courts' pro-poor approach, some people started filing frivolous PILs much to the discomfort of the courts. A few examples may give an idea as to the frivolous nature of such PILs. The day the Supreme Court reopened after the summer vacation in 2007, it found itself deluged by a rash of frivolous PILs. One petition wanted India rechristened 'Hindustan', another wanted the Arabian sea renamed 'Sindhu Sagar' and yet another petitioner read out a self-composed alternative to the national anthem and demanded that 'Jana Gana Mana' be discarded as it was a 'eulogy' to British Monarch George V. One petitioner wanted all traditional incandescent bulbs to be replaced with power-saving CFL lamps to save electricity. "What is the cost of a CFL bulb compared to an ordinary one? How will poor people afford it?" asked the Bench of Chief Justice of India K.G. Balakrishnan and Justice R.V. Raveendran before dismissing it.

The advent of frivolous PILs so much disturbed the legislature that a private member Suresh Pachouri tabled in the Rajya Sabha a Bill titled 'Public Interest Litigation (Regulation) Bill, 1996'. The Statement of Objects and Reasons of the said Bill stated that while the objective of PIL, particularly those intended to benefit the poorer sections of society, was laudable, it was being misused. Moreover, PIL cases were being given priority over other cases, which had remained pending in the courts for years. It was urged that if a PIL petition failed or was shown to be *mala fide*, the petitioner should be 'put behind bars and pay the damages.' Although the Bill lapsed, Parliament witnessed sharp criticism of PIL actions.

At a conference of Chief Ministers and Chief Justices held on 8th April 2007, Dr. Manmohan Singh, the Prime Minister of India, criticised PILs on the ground that PILs are often misused and argued that these should be subjected to filter. Though PILs have great utilities for initiating corrective action, they should not become vehicles for settling political and other scores, observed the Prime Minister. "We need standards to screen PILs so that only PILs with a justifiable cause of action based on judicially manageable standards are taken up", he said, adding that the Supreme Court should frame rules in this regard.

The judiciary also took note of the misuse. In *Neetu* v *State of Punjab*,[15] a Bench of the apex court comprising Dr. Justice Arijit Pasayat and Justice S.H. Kapadia, observed that a time has come to weed out the petitions, which though titled as public interest litigations are in essence something else. It is shocking to note that courts are flooded with large number of so called public interest litigations where even a minuscule percentage can legitimately be called as public interest litigations. The court expressed its anguish to such efforts and observed that on account of such trumpery proceedings initiated before the courts, innumerable days are wasted, which time otherwise could have been spent for the disposal of cases of the genuine litigants. Though we spare no efforts in fostering and developing the laudable concept of PIL and extending our long arm of sympathy to the poor, the ignorant, the oppressed and the needy whose fundamental rights are infringed and violated and whose grievance go unnoticed, un-presented and unheard, yet we cannot avoid but express our opinion that while genuine litigants with legitimate grievances relating to civil matters involving properties worth hundreds of millions of rupees of substantial rights and criminal cases with persons sentenced to death facing gallows under untold agony and persons sentenced to life imprisonment and kept in incarceration for long years, persons suffering from undue delay in

15 2007 SCCL. COM 14.

service matters-government or private, persons awaiting the disposal of tax cases wherein huge amounts of public revenue or unauthorized collection of tax amounts are locked up, detenu expecting their release from the detention orders etc. etc. are all standing in a long serpentine queue for years with the fond hope of getting into the courts and having their grievances redressed, the busy bodies, meddlesome interlopers, wayfarers or officious interveners having absolutely no real public interest except for personal gain or private profit either of themselves or as a proxy of others or for any other extraneous motivation or for glair of publicity break the queue muffing their faces by wearing the mask of public interest litigations and get into the courts by filling vexatious and frivolous petitions of luxury litigants who have nothing to loose but trying to gain for nothing and thus criminally waste the valuable time of the courts and as a result of which the queue standing outside the doors of the court never moves, which piquant situation creates frustration in the minds of the genuine litigants. To thwart any such attempt, it was suggested that it would be desirable for the courts to filter out the frivolous petitions and dismiss them with exemplary costs so that the message goes in the right direction that petitions filed with oblique motive do not have the approval of the courts.

Justice Bhagwati fully endorses the concern of the Supreme Court as expressed in respect of frivolous PILs. In *S.P. Gupta* v *Union of India*[16] he clearly cautioned that only a person acting *bona fide* and having sufficient interest in the proceeding of PIL will alone have *locus standi* and can approach the court. The *locus standi* will be lacking when the person is motivated by personal gain or private profit or any oblique consideration. We must not, however, forget what V.R. Krishna Iyer, J., said in *Fertilizer Corporation Kamnagar Union* v *Union of India*:[17] "Law is a social auditor and this audit function can be put into action only when some one with real public interest ignites the jurisdiction." "We cannot be," continued V.R. Krishna Iyer, J., to which Justice Bhagwati, had the concurrence, "scared by the fear that all and sundry will be litigation happy and waste their time and money and the time of the Court through false and frivolous cases. In a society where freedoms suffer from atrophy and activism is essential for participative public justice, some risks have to be taken and more opportunities opened for the public-minded citizen to rely on the legal process and not be repelled from it by narrow pedantry now surrounding *locus standi*".

16 1981 (Supp) SCC 87: AIR 1982 SC 149.
17 AIR 1981 SC 344: 1980 Lab IC 1367.

Schwartz and H.W.R. Wade wrote in Legal Control of Government:[18] "Restrictive rules about standing are in general inimical to a healthy system of administrative law. If a plaintiff with a good case is turned away, merely because he is not sufficiently affected personally, that means that some government agency is left free to violate the law, and that is contrary to the public interest. Litigants are unlikely to expend their time and money unless they have some real interest at stake. In the rare cases where they wish to sue merely out of public spirit, why should they be discouraged?"

Black said:[19] "... today it is unreal to suggest that a person looks to the law solely to protect his interests in a narrow sense. It is necessary to do no more than read the newspapers to see the breadth of the interests that today's citizen expects the law to protect and he expects the Court where necessary to provide that protection. He is interested in results, not procedural niceties".

Effective access to justice is now seen as the most basic requirement, the most basic human right of a system which purports to guarantee legal rights.

16 Conclusion There is no denying the fact that public interest litigation, described by some as an engine of destruction and by others as a mighty force for good, is part of the process of participative justice and 'standing' in civil litigation of that pattern must have liberal reception at the judicial doorsteps, so said V.R. Krishna Iyer, J., which had the concurrence of Bhagwati, J., in *Fertilizer Corporation of India Kamagar Union* v *Union of India*.[20] If the Courts cannot, or will not, give relief to people who are in fact concerned about a matter, cautioned V.R. Krishna Iyer, J., then they will resort to self-help, with grave results for other persons and the rule of law.

So far as the placement of PIL in Indian legal system is concerned, we can be proud of saying that tremendous development and dynamic progress have taken place in the cosmos of PIL in spite of multiple criticisms leveled against its various aspects. We can loudly say that our dynamic activism in the field of PIL is by no means less than that of other activist judicial systems in other parts of the world.

18 Professors Bernerd Schwartz and H.W.R. Wade, O.C. in *Legal Control of Government*, (1972), p. 291.
19 Black—"*The Right to be Heard*", New Zealand LJ., No. 4, 1977, 66.
20 AIR 1981 SC 344.

'The power of judicial review is a constituent power and it cannot be abrogated without affecting the basic structure of the Constitution'.

—P.N. BHAGWATI

10

Judicial Review

SYNOPSIS

1 Basic structure of the Constitution Judicial review, a basic and fundamental feature of the Constitution of India, is not concerned with the merits of the decision but with the authority by which and the manner in which the decision was taken. The power of judicial review is a constituent power and it cannot be abrogated without affecting the basic structure of the Constitution. Parliament, observed Justice Bhagwati in *P. Sambamurthy* v *State of Andhra Pradesh,*[1] however, can certainly without in any way violating the basic structure doctrine amend the Constitution so as to set up an effective alternative institutional mechanism or arrangement for judicial review.[2]

1 (1987)1 SCC 362.

2 AUTHORS' NOTE: The basic and constitutional feature of judicial review cannot be dispensed with but it would be within the competence of Parliament to amend the Constitution so as to substitute in place of the High Court, another

In the early years, the Supreme Court interpreted the role of the judiciary merely as determining the lis before it in accordance with narrow procedural rules. In *A.K. Gopalan* v *State of Madras,*[3] the Court remarked: "In India the position of the judiciary is somewhere in between the Courts in England and the United States .... But our Constitution, unlike the American Constitution, does not recognise the absolute supremacy of the Court over the legislative authority in all respects, for outside the restricted field of constitutional limitations our Parliament and the State Legislatures are supreme in their respective legislative fields and in that wider field there is no scope for the Court in India to play the role of the Supreme Court of the United States."

This perception changed since the *Golak Nath* case[4] where the Court declared that fundamental rights could not be derogated from even by an amendment to the Constitution. Six years later, in *Kesavananda Bharati's* case,[5] while overruling Golak Nath, the Court evolved another far-reaching doctrine under which Parliament was denied the power to amend the Constitution in a matter that violated its 'basic structure'. The Supreme Court also identified the power of judicial review as being part of such basic structure. Thus, the legislature cannot take away judicial review even by a constitutional amendment.

The court's power of judicial view was widened further in *Maneka Gandhi's* case[6] decided by Justice Bhagwati.

---

alternative judicial mechanism or arrangement for judicial review, provided it is no less efficacious than the High Court [*S.P. Sampath Kumar* v *Union of India* (1987)1 SCC 124, per Bhagwati, CJ.]. If "any constitutional amendment made by Parliament takes away from the High Court the power of judicial review in any particular area and vests it in any other institutional mechanism or authority, it would not be violative of the basic structure doctrine, so long as the essential condition is fulfilled, namely, that the alternative institutional mechanism or authority set up by the parliamentary amendment is no less effective than the High Court" [*S.P. Sampath Kumar* v *Union of India,* supra].

3 (1950) SCR 88 at 286-87.

4 *Golak Nath* v *State of Punjab* (1967)2 SCR 762.

5 *Kesavananda Bharati* v *State of Kerala* (1973)4 SCC 225.

6 *Maneka Gandhi* v *Union of India* (1978)2 SCC 248.

2 Legislative action and scope of judicial interference

A. ***Legislative action subject to constitutional limitations*** In the constitutional scheme that has been adopted in India, the legislatures enjoy plenary powers but such powers, says Justice Bhagwati, are controlled by the structure of the Constitution and can be exercised only within the legislative fields allotted to them under the three lists set out in the Seventh Schedule of the Constitution of India. Beyond the lists specified under the Seventh Schedule, the legislatures cannot travel. The plenary legislative authority and discharge of that function by the legislatures are thus controlled by the relevant provisions of the Constitution and more particularly by the provisions contained in Part III of the Constitution. If the legislatures step beyond the legislative fields assigned to them or trespass, while acting within their respective fields, on the fundamental rights of the citizens in a manner not justified by the relevant articles dealing with the said fundamental rights, their legislative actions are liable to be struck down by the courts in India, asserts Justice Bhagwati.

Thus, the legislative action under our Constitution is subject only to the limitations prescribed by the Constitution and to no other. Any law made by the legislature, which it is not competent to pass or which is violative of the provisions in Part III of the Constitution or any other constitutional provision, is ineffective.

Every provision of the law which is violative of the provisions contained either in Article 14 or 21 of the Constitution can be subjected to judicial scanner through judicial review. In *Bachan Singh* v *State of Punjab*,[7] it was held that Article 14 enacts primarily a guarantee against arbitrariness and inhibits State action, whether legislative or executive, which suffers from the vice of arbitrariness. It was similarly held in *Bachan Singh's* case (supra) that Article 21 affords protection not only against executive action but also against legislation and any law which deprives a person of his life or personal liberty would be invalid unless it prescribes a procedure for such deprivation which is reasonable, fair and just. The concept of reasonableness, says Justice Bhagwati, runs through the entire fabric of the Constitution. The courts can declare a statute unconstitutional when it transgresses constitutional limits. They are, however, precluded from inquiring into the propriety of the exercise of the legislative power. It has to be kept in mind, cautions Justice Bhagwati, that the motive of the legislature

7 AIR 1982 SC 1325: (1982)3 SCC 24.

in passing a statute is beyond the scrutiny of courts. It is beyond the jurisdiction of the courts also to examine whether the legislature has applied its mind to the provisions of the statute before passing it.

B. *Claim of any power, privilege or immunity by Legislature—Court's role* Hidayatullah, CJ. in *Rustom Cavasjee Cooper* v *Union of India*[8] observed: "The supremacy of a legislature under a written Constitution is only within what is in its power but what is within its power and what is not, when any specific act is challenged, it is for the Courts to say. If that were realised much of the misunderstanding would be avoided and the organs of Government would function truly in their own spheres."

Whenever Parliament, or for that matter any State Legislature claims any power or privilege or immunity in terms of the provisions contained in Article 105(3) or Article 194(3), as the case may be, it is the Court, reminds Justice Bhagwati, which has the authority and the jurisdiction to examine, on grievance being brought before it, to determine if the particular power or privilege that has been claimed or asserted by the legislature is one that was contemplated by the said constitutional provisions.

It has to be borne in mind, says Justice Bhagwati, that neither the Parliament nor the Legislative Assemblies in India discharge any judicial function. The constitutional background also does not support the claim that they can be regarded as Courts of Record in any sense. Thus, a House of Parliament or State Legislature cannot try anyone or any case directly as a Court of Justice can, but it can proceed quasi-judicially in cases of contempt of its authority and take up motions concerning its "privileges" or "immunities" because in doing so, it only seeks removal of obstruction to the due performance of its legislative functions. If, however, any question of jurisdiction arises as to whether a matter falls here or not, it has to be decided by the courts in appropriate proceedings. This view of Justice Bhagwati finds support in *State of Karnataka* v *Union of India*.[9]

C. *Legislative action through Article 31B read with the Ninth Schedule of the Constitution and scope of judicial review* A question often arises: whether on or after 24th April 1973, when basic structure doctrine was propounded, it is permissible for the Parliament under Article 31B to immunize legislations from fundamental rights by inserting them into

8 AIR 1970 SC 1318: (1970)2 SCC 298.
9 (1977)4 SCC 608: AIR 1978 SC 68.

the Ninth Schedule; and, if so, what is its effect on the power of judicial review of the Court.

Article 31B was not part of the original Constitution. It was inserted in the Constitution by the Constitution (First Amendment) Act 1951, to assist the process of legislation to bring about agrarian reforms and confer on such legislative measures immunity from possible attack on the ground that they contravene the fundamental rights of the citizens. Article 31B reads thus: "Without prejudice to the generality of the provisions contained in Article 31A, none of the Acts and Regulations specified in the Ninth Schedule nor any of the provisions thereof shall be deemed to be void, or ever to have become void, on the ground that such Act, Regulation or provision is inconsistent with or takes away or abridges any of the rights conferred by any provisions of this Part (Part III), and notwithstanding any judgment, decree or order of any court or tribunal to the contrary, each of the said Acts and Regulations shall, subject to the power of any competent legislature to repeal or amend it, continue in force."

The First Amendment of the Constitution in 1951 also added the Ninth Schedule to the Constitution containing thirteen items, all relating to land reform laws, immunizing these laws from challenge on the ground of contravention of Article 13 which, *inter alia*, provides that the State shall not make any law which takes away or abridges the rights conferred by Part III and any law made in contravention thereof, shall to the extent of the contravention, be void. It may be noted that when Jawharlal Nehru was the Prime Minister, K.T. Chari, the then Advocate General of Madras, by his letter dated 14th March 1950, addressed to Law Secretary K.V.K. Sundaram proposed that to exempt land tenure laws from judicial reach they should be included in a separate schedule to the Constitution.[10] This resulted in bringing into existence the Ninth Schedule to the Constitution by the Constitution's First Amendment. Thus, Parliament, to meet the spate of challenges to land reform laws, brought into existence, through the First Amendment to the Constitution, the Ninth Schedule as an enclave where laws could be placed beyond judicial challenge on the ground of violation of any of the fundamental rights.

The constitutional validity of the First Amendment which inserted Article 31B was upheld in *Sri Shankari Prasad Singh Deo* v *Union of India*[11] where it was held that Article 13(2) does not affect amendments

10 Law Ministry File No. F34/51C, National Archives of India.

11 (1952) SCR 89.

to the Constitution made under Article 368 because such amendments are made in the exercise of constituent power. The Court further observed that to make a law which contravenes the Constitution constitutionally valid is a matter of constitutional amendment and as such it falls within the exclusive power of Parliament.

After the First Amendment of the Constitution, several Acts were further added to the Ninth Schedule by the Constitution (Seventeenth Amendment) Act 1964. It may be noted in this context that in 1964 by the Seventeenth Amendment of the Constitution, the Government proposed to place 124 State land laws in the Schedule. A Joint Parliamentary Committee deleted 88 of these laws after widespread criticism of the amending bill and the confession of the Law Ministry officials that they had not read many of the laws proposed for inclusion. The constitutional validity of the Acts added to the Ninth Schedule by the Constitution (Seventeenth Amendment) Act 1964 was challenged in *Sajjan Singh* v *State of Rajasthan*[12] which upheld the law declared in *Sri Shankari Prasad Singh Deo* v *Union of India*.[13]

The correctness of the view taken in *Sri Shankari Prasad Singh Deo* v *Union of India*[14] and *Sajjan Singh* v *State of Rajasthan*[15] was considered by a Bench of 11 Judges of the Supreme Court in *Golak Nath* v *State of Punjab*.[16] By majority of six to five, the decisions in *Shankari Prasad and Sajjan Singh* (supra) were overruled in *Golak Nath* case and it was held that the constitutional amendment is 'law' within the meaning of Article 13 of the Constitution and, therefore, if it takes away or abridges the rights conferred by Part III thereof, it is void. It was further observed in

12 AIR 1965 SC 845: (1965)1 SCR 973.
13 (1952) SCR 89: AIR 1951 SC 418.
14 (1952) SCR 89: AIR 1951 SC 418.
15 AIR 1965 SC 845: (1965)1 SCR 973.
16 AIR 1967 SC 1643: (1967)2 SCR 762.
AUTHORS' NOTE: In the *Golak Nath* case, a Bench of eleven Judges was constituted to consider the power of Parliament to amend the fundamental rights, and more specifically in relation to the 1st, 4th and 17th Amendments. The amendments were effected by Parliament acting under its amending power provided by Article 368 of the Constitution. There was Article 13 which prevented the State from making any law that takes away or abridges the fundamental rights and which states that any law so made shall be void. In February 1967, by a majority of 6 : 5, the Court held that Article 368 could not override the specific provision of Article 13(2) and that Parliament was not competent to amend the chapter on fundamental rights in the Constitution so as to take away or abridge those rights. To avoid chaos, the Court held that the decision would not govern amendments that had been made in the past but would only be prospective, based on the doctrine of 'prospective overruling'.

Golak Nath's case (supra) that the Parliament will have no power from the date of the decision, i.e., 27th February 1967, to amend any of the provisions of Part III of the Constitution so as to take away or abridge the fundamental rights enshrined therein.

After the judgment of the Supreme Court in *Golak Nath's* case was pronounced, a national debate followed discussing about the merits of the decision in the said case. In this debate, advocates of the view propounded by the majority in *Golak Nath's* case as well as those who are critical of that view used strong words, such as, the supremacy of the judiciary, encroachment on fundamental rights, introduction of totalitarian concepts in the democratic set-up of our country, or tyranny of the judiciary. The introduction of such political overtones in this national debate, says Justice Bhagwati, created an appearance of confrontation between the Parliament and the Supreme Court.

Soon after *Golak Nath's* case, two vital amendments of the Constitution came into force. By the Constitution (Twenty-fourth Amendment) Act 1971, Article 13 was amended and after Clause (3), Clause (4) was inserted thus: "13(4). Nothing in this article shall apply to any amendment of this Constitution made under Article 368." Article 368 was also amended by the Constitution (Twenty-fourth Amendment) Act 1971 and in Article 368(1), the words "in exercise of its constituent powers" were inserted. Thus, the Twenty-fourth Amendment gave Parliament full constituent power over the Constitution for 'addition, variation or repeal'.

Then came the Constitution (Twenty-fifth Amendment) Act 1971, inserting Article 31C which read thus: "31C Notwithstanding anything contained in Article 13, no law giving effect to the policy of the State towards securing the principles specified in clause (*b*) or clause (*c*) of Article 39 shall be deemed to be void on the ground that it is inconsistent with, or takes away or abridges any of the rights conferred by Article 14, Article 19 or Article 31; and no law containing a declaration that it is for giving effect to such policy shall be called in question in any court on the ground that it does not give effect to such policy: Provided that where such law is made by the Legislature of a State, the provisions of this article shall not apply thereto unless such law, having been reserved for the consideration of the President, has received his assent".[17]

17 The Constitution (Forty-second Amendment) Act 1976, brought about an amendment to Article 31C. By section 4 of the Constitution (Forty-second Amendment) Act 1976, for the words "the principles specified in clause (*b*) or clause (*c*) of Article 39", the words "all or any of the principles laid down in

The Twenty-fifth Amendment brought into force Article 31C whereby the two most classically socialist provisions in the Directive Principles—clauses (*b*) and (*c*) of Article 39[18] were given precedence over the fundamental right to equality before the law and equal protection of the law (Article 14), the 'freedoms' provided in Article 19, and Article 31 dealing with property. Furthermore, Article 31C provided that a law declared as giving effect to this policy could not be questioned in court because it did not further the policy. The Law Commission of India, led by former Chief Justice of India P.B. Gajendragadkar, in its Forty-sixth Report on the Constitution (Twenty-fifth Amendment) Bill 1971, assailed the portion of Article 31C which provided that if a law made by Parliament or a State Legislature by virtue of Article 31C declares that it is for giving effect to the policy enunciated by Article 39, Clause (*b*) or (*c*), the said law shall not be called in question in any court on the ground that it does not give effect to such policy. The Commission observed that "the effect of this provision is that any question as to whether there is any rational nexus or connection between the provisions of the law passed by Parliament or State Legislature and the object intended to be achieved by them will be completely excluded from judicial scrutiny." The Commission opined that "the whole object of Article 31C ... is to enable Parliament and State Legislatures to pass laws with the object of implementing the Directive Principles in question. If that is so, we see no justification for excluding judicial inquiry into the question about the existence of any rational nexus between the law and the object intended to be achieved by it". The Commission accordingly recommended very strongly that the relevant part in question should be deleted from Article 31C. Gajendragadkar had such 'serious misgivings' about the provision that he expressed them to the Prime Minister personally in a letter.[19]

Part IV" were substituted. Section 4 of the Constitution (Forty-second Amendment) Act 1976, which brought about the aforesaid amendment by way of substitution has been declared invalid by the majority decision of the Supreme Court in *Minerva Mills Ltd.* v *Union of India* AIR 1980 SC 1789: (1980)2 SCC 591.

The Constitution (Forty-fourth Amendment) Act 1978, brought about further amendment to Article 31C. By section 8 of the Constitution (Forty-fourth Amendment) Act 1978, for the words "Article 14, Article 19 or Article 31", the words "Article 14 or Article 19" were substituted.

18 Clauses (*b*) and (*c*) of Article 39 provide:
"The State shall, in particular, direct its policy towards securing—(*b*) that the ownership and control of the material resources of the community are so distributed as best to subserve the common good;
(*c*) that the operation of the economic system does not result in the concentration of wealth and means of production to the common detriment."

19 Gajendragadkar—Indira Gandhi letter dated 18th October 1971—vide Nehru Memorial Museum and Library, Gajendragadkar Papers, Subject file 1.

The Twenty-fourth and Twenty-fifth Amendments of the Constitution, amongst others, were challenged in *Kesavananda Bharati* v *State of Kerala.*[20] The decision in *Kesavananda Bharati's* case was rendered by a 13 Judges Bench on 24th April 1973. The majority opinion, though held valid the Constitution Twenty-fourth Amendment, did not accept the unlimited power of the Parliament to amend the Constitution and instead held that Article 368 has implied limitations and does not enable the Parliament to alter the basic structure or framework of the Constitution.

In the same case, though the majority opinion again upheld the first part of Article 31C inserted by the Constitution Twenty-fifth Amendment, the second part of Article 31C that "no law containing a declaration that it is for giving effect to such policy shall be called in question in any court on the ground that it does not give effect to such policy" was declared unconstitutional. *Kesavananda Bharati* decision thus struck down the provision regarding exclusion of judicial enquiry and strengthened the court's power of judicial review by enunciating the basic structure doctrine.

In *Smt. Indira Gandhi* v *Raj Narain,*[1] a Bench of five Judges of the Supreme Court accepted the majority view in *Kesavananda Bharati's* case to be that the amending power conferred under Article 368 does not enable Parliament to alter the basic structure or framework of the Constitution.[2]

20 AIR 1973 SC 1461: (1973)4 SCC 225.

1 AIR 1975 SC 2299: (1976)2 SCR 347.

2 LOOKING THROUGH THE EYES OF JUSTICE BHAGWATI: IMPACT OF INDIRA GANDHI'S CASE ON KESAVANANDA BHARATI: In *Kesavananda Bharati's* case, six out of thirteen learned Judges (S.M. Sikri, CJ., J.M. Shelat, A.N. Grover, K.S. Hegde, P. Jaganmohan Reddy and S. Mukherjea, JJ.) accepted the contention of the petitioners that though Article 368 conferred power to amend the Constitution, there were inherent and implied limitations on the power of amendment and therefore Article 368 did not confer power on Parliament to amend the Constitution so as to destroy or emasculate the essential or basic elements of features of the Constitution. The fundamental rights, according to the view taken by these six learned Judges, constituted basic or essential features of the Constitution and they could not be, therefore, abrogated or emasculated in the exercise of the amending power conferred by Article 368 though a reasonable abridgment of those rights could be effected in the public interest.

Six other Judges (A.N. Ray, D.G. Palekar, K.K. Mathew, S.N. Dwivedi, M.H. Beg and Y.V. Chandrachud, JJ.) took the view that there were no limitations of any kind on the power of amendment, though three of them seemed willing to foresee the limitation that the entire constitution could not be abrogated, leaving behind a State without a Constitution.

Article 368 of the Constitution went for a second amendment[3] by the Constitution (Forty-second Amendment) Act 1976 by insertion of clauses (4) and (5) which ran thus:

> "368(4). No amendment of this Constitution (including the provisions of Part III) made or purporting to have been made under this article whether before or after the commencement of

---

The remaining Judge (H.R. Khanna, J.) held that the power to amend does not include the power to abrogate the Constitution, that the word 'amendment' postulates that the existing constitution must survive without loss of identity, that it must be retained though in an amended form, and, therefore, the power of amendment does not include the power to destroy or abrogate the basic structure or framework of the Constitution.

The summary of judgments given by nine out of the thirteen Judges after the delivery of the judgments states *inter alia* the majority view to be that "Article 368 does not enable Parliament to alter the basic structure or framework of the Constitution".

Justice Bhagwati in *Minerva Mills Ltd.* v *Union of India* [AIR 1980 SC 1789: (1980)2 SCC 591] opposing the statement of the majority view contained in the summary given at the end of the judgments in *Kesavananda Bharati's* case said : "in my view this summary signed by nine Judges has no legal effect at all and cannot be regarded as law declared by the Supreme Court under Article 141. It is difficult to appreciate what jurisdiction or power these nine Judges had to give a summary setting out the legal effect of the eleven judgments delivered in the case. Once the judgments were delivered, these nine judges as also the remaining four became *functus officio* and thereafter they had no authority to cull out the ratio of the judgments or to state what, on a proper analysis of the judgments, was the view of the majority. What was the law laid down was to be found in the judgments and that task would have to be performed by the Court before whom the question would arise as to what is the law laid down in *Kesavananda Bharati's* case. The Court would then hear the arguments and dissect the judgments as was done in *Smt. Indira Gandhi's* case and then decide as to what is the true ratio emerging from the judgments which is binding upon the Court as law laid down under Article 141. But here it seems that the nine Judges set out in the summary what according to them was the majority view without hearing any arguments. This was a rather unusual exercise, though well-intentioned. But quite apart from the validity of this exercise embarked upon by the nine Judges, it is a little difficult to understand how a proper and accurate summary could be prepared by these judges when there was not enough time, after the conclusion of the arguments, for an exchange of draft judgments amongst the Judges and many of them did not even have the benefit of knowing fully the views of others". In giving his opinion in *Minerva Mill's* case, Justice Bhagwati, therefore, did not rely on the statement of the majority view contained in the summary given at the end of the judgments in *Kesavananda Bharati's* case, but proceeded on the basis of the view taken in *Smt. Indira Gandhi's* case as regards the ratio of the majority decision in *Kesavananda Bharati's* case.

3 The first amendment of Article 368 was made by the Constitution (Twenty-fourth Amendment) Act 1971.

section 55 of the Constitution (Forty-second Amendment) Act 1976 shall be called in question in any court on any ground.

(5) For the removal of doubts, it is hereby declared that there shall be no limitation whatever on the constituent power of Parliament to amend by way of addition, variation or repeal the provisions of this Constitution under this article."

The Forty-second Amendment thus, says Justice Bhagwati, reversed the Kesavananda Bharati verdict bringing into existence again the Parliament's unlimited constituent power to amend the constitution and left no room for judicial review of exercise of such power. This condition lasted until the Supreme Court in 1980 in the *Minerva Mills* case[4] struck down Clauses (4) and (5) of the Constitution (Forty-second Amendment) Act 1976 finding that they violated the basic structure of the Constitution thus reducing Parliament's power of amendment to that in the Twenty-fourth Amendment as interpreted in *Kesavananda Bharati's* case.

Justice Bhagwati is of the view that the doctrine of basic structure, which as a principle has now become axiomatic, has been propounded to protect the basic features of the Constitution from the vigories of parliamentary majority and it contemplates that there are certain parts or aspects of the Constitution including Articles 14, 15, 19 and 21 which constitute the core values which if allowed to be abrogated would change completely the nature and character of the Constitution. It is premised on the basis that certain freedoms are vital to the existence and survival of democracy and are inviolable and their violation cannot be justified under any circumstances.

Equality, rule of law and separation of powers form parts of the basic structure of the Constitution. So also is judicial review. These concepts, says Justice Bhagwati, are intimately connected with each other. The power of judicial review being a constituent power, it cannot be abrogated by legislation or judicial process of interpretation. It is a cardinal principle of Constitution of India that no one can claim to be the sole judge of the power given under the Constitution and that its actions are within the confines of the powers given by the Constitution. It is the duty and function of the Supreme Court to uphold the constitutional values and enforce constitutional limitations as the ultimate interpreter of the Constitution.[5] Constitution of India has

4 *Minerva Mills Ltd.* v *Union of India* AIR 1980 SC 1789: (1980)2 SCC 591.
5 *S.R. Bommai* v *Union of India* (1994)3 SCC 1: AIR 1994 SC 1918.

been framed by a Constituent Assembly which was not the Parliament. It is in the exercise of a law making power of the Constituent Assembly that we have a controlled Constitution. The principle of constitutionalism which has since been recognised as a legal principle requires control over the exercise of Governmental power to ensure that it does not destroy the democratic principles upon which it is based. These democratic principles include the protection of fundamental rights. The principle of constitutionalism advocates a check and balance model of the separation of powers, it requires a diffusion of powers, necessitating different independent centres of decision making. The principle of constitutionalism, according to Justice Bhagwati, underpins the principle of legality which requires the courts to interpret legislation on the assumption that Parliament would not wish to legislate contrary to fundamental rights. The Legislature can restrict fundamental rights to the extent permissible under the Constitution but it is impossible for laws protecting fundamental rights to be impliedly repealed by future legislation. Articles 14, 19, and 21 represent the foundational values which form the basis of the rule of law. These are the principles of constitutionalism which form the basis of judicial review apart from the rule of law and separation of powers.

Fundamental rights occupy a unique place in the life of civilised societies and have often been described as "transcendental", "inalienable" and "primordial". They constitute the ark of the Constitution. If the protection of fundamental rights and more specifically those provided in Articles 14, 19 and 21 is withdrawn in respect of an un-catalogued variety of laws, fundamental freedoms will become a 'teasing illusion and a promise of unreality'. The observations of Justice Bhagwati in *Minerva Mills* case[6] show how Clause (4) of Article 368 would have resulted in enlarging the amending power of the Parliament contrary to the dictum in *Kesavananda Bharati's* case. The learned Judge in declaring Section 4 of the Constitution (Forty-second Amendment) Act 1976, dealing with Article 368(4) beyond the amending power of the Parliament and void, observed in *Minerva Mills* case (paragraph 85): "So long as clause (4) stands, an amendment of the Constitution ... would be unchallengeable in a court of law. The consequence of this exclusion of the power of judicial review would be that, in effect and substance, the limitation on the amending power of Parliament would, from a practical point of view, become non-existent and it would not be incorrect to say that, covertly and indirectly, by the exclusion of judicial

6 AIR 1980 SC 1789: (1980)2 SCC 591.

review, the amending power of Parliament would stand enlarged, contrary to the decision of this Court in *Kesavananda Bharati* case. This would undoubtedly damage the basic structure of the Constitution, because there are two essential features of the basic structure which would be violated, namely, the limited amending power of Parliament and the power of judicial review with a view to examining whether any authority under the Constitution has exceeded the limits of its powers."

In early years, the scope of the guarantee provided by fundamental rights was considered to be very narrow. Individuals could only claim limited protection against the State. This position has changed since long. Over the years, the development of jurisprudence of fundamental rights has made it clear that they are not limited, narrow rights but provide a broad check against the violations or excesses by the State authorities. The fundamental rights have in fact proved to be the most significant constitutional control on the Government, including its legislative power. This transition from a set of independent narrow rights to broad check on State power, says Justice Bhagwati, is demonstrated by a series of cases that have been decided by the Supreme Court. In *State of Bombay* v *Bhanji Munji*,[7] relying on the ratio of *A.K. Gopalan* v *State of Madras*,[8] it was held that Article 31 was independent of Article 19(1)(*f*). However, it was in *Rustom Cavasjee Cooper* v *Union of India*[9] (popularly known as Bank Nationalisation case), the view point of Gopalan was seriously disapproved. While rendering decision in *Cooper's* case (supra), the focus of the Court was on the actual impairment caused by the law, rather than the literal validity of the law. The Court also examined in *Cooper's* case (supra) the relation between Article 19(1)(*f*) and Article 31 and held that they were not mutually exclusive. The view taken in Bank Nationalization case has been reiterated in a number of cases, viz., *Sambhu Nath Sarkar* v *State of West Bengal*,[10] *Haradhan Saha* v *State of West Bengal*,[11] *Khudiram Das* v *State of West Bengal*,[12] and finally the landmark judgment in *Maneka Gandhi* v *Union of India*.[13] After *Maneka Gandhi's* case (supra), it is clear that the development of fundamental rights has been such that it no longer involves the

7 AIR 1955 SC 41: (1955)1 SCR 777.
8 AIR 1950 SC 27: 1950 SCR 88.
9 AIR 1970 SC 564.
10 AIR 1973 SC 1425: (1973)1 SCC 856.
11 AIR 1974 SC 2154: (1975)3 SCC 198.
12 AIR 1975 SC 550: (1975)2 SCC 81.
13 AIR 1978 SC 597: (1978)1 SCC 248.

interpretation of rights as isolated protections which directly arise but they collectively form a comprehensive test against the arbitrary exercise of State power in any area. It is a fallacy, says Justice Bhagwati, to regard fundamental rights as a gift from the State to its citizens. Individuals possess basic human rights independently of any constitution by reason of the basic fact that they are members of the human race. These fundamental rights are important as they possess intrinsic value. Part III of the Constitution does not confer fundamental rights. It confirms their existence and gives them protection.

In *Minerva Mills Ltd.* v *Union of India*,[14] Justice Bhagwati observed: "... all constitutional amendments made after the decision in *Kesavananda Bharati* case would have to be tested by reference to the basic structure doctrine, for Parliament would then have no excuse for saying that it did not know the limitation on its amending power." In *I.R. Coelho (Dead) by Lrs.* v *State of Tamil Nadu*[15] (a judgment on Ninth Schedule), Y.K. Sabharwal, CJ., said: "To us, it seems that the position is correctly reflected in the aforesaid observations of Bhagwati, J. ...". Thus, *Minerva Mills* case showed the way that Acts inserted in Schedule 9 after 25th April 1973, were not unconditionally valid, but would have to stand the test of fundamental rights and would thus be subjected to judicial review.

It thus stands a settled law that the Parliament has power to amend the provisions of Part III so as to abridge or take away fundamental rights, but that power is subjected to the limitation of basic structure doctrine. Whether the impact of any amendment results in violation of basic structure doctrine has to be examined with reference to each individual case by the judiciary.

In this background, if Article 31B only provided restricted immunity and it seems that original intent was to protect a limited number of laws, it would have been only exception to Part III. However, the Supreme Court, Justice Bhagwati says, has rightly pointed in *I.R. Coelho (Dead) by Lrs.* v *State of Tamil Nadu*[15] (a judgment on the Ninth Schedule) that the unchecked and rampant exercise of power amending Schedule 9 forming part of Article 31B, the number having gone from 13 to 284, shows that it is no longer a mere exception. The absence of guidelines for exercise of such power means the absence of constitutional control which results in destruction of constitutional supremacy and creation of parliamentary hegemony and absence of full

14 AIR 1980 SC 1789: (1980)2 SCC 591.
15 (2007)2 SCC 1.

power of judicial review to determine the constitutional validity of such exercise.

It bears mentioning that the power to amend the Ninth Schedule flows from Article 368. This power of amendment has to be compatible with the limits on the power of amendment. This limit came with the *Kesavananda Bharati's* case. By addition of the words 'constituent power' in Article 368 by the Constitution (Twenty-fourth Amendment) Act 1971, the amending body, namely, Parliament does not become the original Constituent Assembly. It remains a Parliament under a controlled Constitution. Even after the words 'constituent power' are inserted in Article 368, the limitations of the doctrine of basic structure would continue to apply to the Parliament. It is on this premise that Clauses (4) and (5) inserted in Article 368 by the Forty-second Amendment of the Constitution were struck down in *Minerva Mill's* case. Therefore, Article 31B after 24th April 1973 despite its wide language cannot confer unlimited or unregulated immunity in respect of laws included after that date.

The judicial view is thus clear that the Ninth Schedule does not provide an escape route to the Parliament to enact any laws violative of fundamental rights apart from those which were already included in that schedule prior to 24th April 1973. Such laws would have to meet the challenge of fundamental rights which form the basic structure of the Constitution notwithstanding the provisions contained in Article 31B. In the immediate period after *Kesavananda Bharati*, there was some confusion over whether any of the fundamental rights could be regarded as forming part of the basic structure. Subsequent decisions have, however, made it abundantly clear that while some fundamental rights such as the right to property would not be part of the basic structure, core values such as the right to equality under Article 14, equal opportunity under Article 15, the freedoms including the freedom of speech under Article 19, the right to life and liberty under Article 21, are part of the basic structure along with other features like federalism, separation of powers, secularism and judicial review.

D. ***Legislative action exercised through Parliament's power of expulsion and scope of judicial review*** A question often arises: Whether under Indian jurisprudence it is open to the court to examine the manner of exercise of power of expulsion by Parliament?

Expulsion from the Legislature of members deemed unfit is a proper exercise of parliamentary privilege under the British system of parliamentary supremacy and the courts have no role to play in monitoring the exercise of parliamentary privilege.

In Canada, this has been altered by the Charter's enunciation of values which may in particular cases conflict with the exercise of such privilege. To prevent abuses cloaked in the guise of privilege from trumping legitimate Charter interests, the courts must inquire into the legitimacy of a claim of parliamentary privilege. The courts in Canada thus may properly question whether a claimed privilege exists or not. This screening roles mean that where it is alleged that a person has been expelled or disqualified on invalid grounds, the courts must determine whether the act falls within the scope of parliamentary privilege. If the court concludes that it does, no further review lies.

In India, the manner of enforcement of privilege by the legislature, according to Justice Bhagwati, can be subjected to judicial scrutiny on the touchstone of Article 20 or 21, though subject to the restrictions contained in the other Constitutional provisions, for example, Article 212(1) in the case of Legislative Assembly of the State corresponding to Article 122 in the case of Parliament. It requires mentioning that the applicability of Articles 20 and 21 in the context of manner of exercise of the powers and privileges of the Legislative Assembly are of general import. The plenitude of powers possessed by the Parliament under the Constitution is always subject to legislative competence and restrictions imposed by fundamental rights and that in case a member's personal liberty is threatened by imprisonment of committal in execution of Parliamentary privilege, Article 21 would be attracted. These principles would apply good not merely in relation to a member of the legislature but also in relation to a non-member who is entitled to the protection when the impugned action entails civil consequences. Justice Bhagwati reminded that the above view has its precedence in India. In the case of *Pandit M.S.M. Sharma* v *Shree Krishna Sinha*,[16] the manner of exercise of the privilege claimed by the Bihar Legislative Assembly was tested against the "procedure established by law" and thus on the touch-stone of Article 21. It is a different matter that the requirements of Article 21, as at that time understood in its restrictive meaning, were found satisfied. The point that deserves to be noted is that Article 21 was found applicable and the procedure of the legislature was tested on its anvil. This view was followed in the case of Special Reference No. 1 of 1964,[17] known as U.P. Assembly case, which added the enforceability of Article 20 to the determination of the issue.

16 AIR 1959 SC 395: 1959 Supp (1) SCR 806.
17 (1965)1 SCR 413.

When the cases of *Pandit M.S.M. Sharma* v *Shree Krishna Sinha*[18] and Special Reference No. 1 of 1964 (U.P. Assembly case)[19] were decided, Article 21 was construed in a limited sense, mainly on the strength of the law laid down in *A.K. Gopalan* v *State of Madras*[20] in which a Constitution Bench of the Supreme Court held that the operation of each Article of the Constitution and its effect on the protection of fundamental rights was required to be measured independently. The case of *Rustom Cavasjee Cooper* v *Union of India*[1] decided by a Constitution Bench of 11 Judges of the Supreme Court brought about a total transformation in the law as laid down in *A.K. Gopalan's* case (supra) and held that all the provisions of the Constitution are required to be read conjointly to understand the effect and operation of fundamental rights of the citizens when the State action infringed the rights of the individual. Then came *Maneka Gandhi's* case (*Maneka Gandhi* v *Union of India*)[2] where the apex court led by Justice Bhagwati held that different Articles in the Chapter of Fundamental Rights of the Constitution must be read as an integral whole. With possible overlapping of the subject-matter of what is sought to be protected by its various provisions particularly by Articles relating to the Fundamental Rights contained in Part III of the Constitution, they do not represent entirely separate streams of rights. They are all parts of an integrated scheme in the Constitution.

The Fundamental Rights protected by Part III of the Constitution in general and those covered by Articles 14, 19 and 21 in particular are most frequently invoked to test the validity of executive as well as legislative actions when these actions are subjected to judicial scrutiny.

The enforceability of Article 21 in relation to the manner of exercise of Parliamentary privilege as affirmed in *Pandit M.S.M. Sharma* v *Shree Krishna Sinha*[3] and Special Reference No. 1 of 1964 (U.P. Assembly case)[4] has thus to be understood in the light of the expanded scope of the said fundamental right as interpreted in *Rustam Cavasji Cooper* v *Union of India*[5] and *Maneka Gandhi* v *Union of India*.[6]

18 AIR 1959 SC 395: 1959 Supp (1) SCR 806.
19 (1965)1 SCR 413.
20 AIR 1950 SC 27: 1950 SCR 88.
1 AIR 1970 SC 564.
2 AIR 1978 SC 597: (1978)1 SCC 248.
3 AIR 1959 SC 395: 1959 Supp (1) SCR 806.
4 (1965)1 SCR 413.
5 AIR 1970 SC 564.
6 AIR 1978 SC 597: (1978)1 SCC 248.

The exercise of parliamentary privilege having thus been established to be subjected to judicial scrutiny, the next question that arises is: to what extent Parliamentary matters can be judicially reviewed? Article 122(1), says Justice Bhagwati, prohibits "the validity of any proceedings in Parliament" from being "called in question" in a court merely on the ground of any "irregularity of procedure". To put in other words, the procedural irregularities, according to Justice Bhagwati, cannot be used by the court to undo or vitiate what happens within the four walls of the legislature. But 'procedural irregularity', Justice Bhagwati views, stands in stark contrast to "substantive illegality". The touchstone upon which parliamentary actions within the four-walls of the legislature may be examined must be both the constitutional as well as substantive law. The proceedings which may be tainted on account of substantive illegality or unconstitutionality, as opposed to those sufferings from mere irregularity, thus, cannot be held protected from judicial scrutiny by Article 122(1) of the Constitution. This view is also supported by the latest decision of the Supreme Court in *Raja Ram Pal* v *The Hon'ble Speaker, Lok Sabha* (decided on 10.1.2007).

In a country like India governed by the written Constitution, it is the Constitution which is the touchstone of the limits of the powers of the various organs of the State and constitutes the fundamental and, in that sense, a 'higher law'. Judicial review is an incident of and flows from this concept of the fundamental and higher law. The judicial wing is the interpreter of the Constitution and, therefore, in such capacity determines the limits of authority of the executive and the legislature, the two vital organs of the State. As an interpreter of the Constitution, Justice Bhagwati confirms, the judiciary does not exclude itself in determining even the limits of its own authority. As the interpreter of the Constitution and for its meaning, the Supreme Court is final arbiter. Here, the fundamental difference with the British system of governance is required to be mentioned. The British Parliament with the Crown is supreme and its powers are unlimited and the courts have no power of judicial review of legislation.

Article 102 of the Constitution relates to disqualifications for membership of either House of Parliament. The authority to decide the questions arising in the context of the provisions of Article 102(1) is vested in the President whose decision, according to Article 103, "shall be final". Similarly, Article 191 relates to disqualifications for memberships of the State Legislature. The authority to decide the questions arising as a result is vested in the Governor whose decision, according to Article 192(1), "shall be final".

The Tenth Schedule was added to the Constitution by the Constitution (52nd Amendment) Act 1985 with effect from 1st March 1985 to provide for detailed provisions as to disqualification on the ground of defection with reference, *inter alia*, to Article 102 that deals with "disqualifications for membership" of Parliament. Paragraph 6(1), amongst others, of the Tenth Schedule vests the authority to take a decision on the questions of disqualification on the ground of defection unto the Chairman of Rajya Sabha or the Speaker of Lok Sabha, as the case may be. This provision declares that the decision of the said authority "shall be final". It is interesting to note that while paragraph 6(2) of the Tenth Schedule states that all the proceedings relating to decision on the question of disqualification on the ground of defection "shall be deemed to be proceedings in Parliament within the meaning of Article 122," paragraph 7 of the said schedule contains an express bar of jurisdiction of courts in respect of matters connected with the disqualification of a member of a House under this Schedule.

The determinative jurisdiction of the Speaker or the Chairman in the Tenth Schedule read with Article 102(2), in the view of Justice Bhagwati, is a judicial power and it cannot be within the non-justiciable legislative area in the name of "finality". The decision of the apex court in *Kihoto Hollahan* v *Zachillhu*[7] supports this view of Justice Bhagwati. Since the Speaker of the Lok Sabha and the Chairman of the Rajya Sabha, while exercising powers and discharging functions under the Tenth Schedule of the Constitution, act as Tribunal adjudicating rights and obligations under the said schedule, their decisions in that capacity are amenable to judicial review. For the same reason, the determinative jurisdiction of the President under Article 103 read with Article 102(1) cannot remain within the non-justiciable area in the name of "finality". Justice Bhagwati opines that where there is a lis—an affirmation by one party and denial by another—and the dispute necessarily involves a decision on the rights and obligations of the parties to it and the authority is called upon to decide it, there is an exercise of judicial power. That authority is called a Tribunal, if it does not have all the trappings of a Court. When an authority exercises under a finality clause judicial power, in spite of the existence of such clause it remains open to the court to examine whether the impugned action of the authority is *ultra vires* the powers conferred on the said authority. Such an action can be *ultra vires* for the reason that it is in contravention

7 1992 Supp (2) SCC 651.

of a mandatory provision of the law conferring on the authority the power to take such an action. It will also be *ultra vires* the powers conferred on the authority if it is vitiated by *mala fides* or in colourable exercise of power based on extraneous and irrelevant considerations. While exercising their *certiorari* jurisdiction, the courts apply the test whether the impugned action falls within the jurisdiction of the authority taking the action or it falls outside such jurisdiction. An ouster clause attaching finality to a determination, it is to be noted, will be effective in ousting the power of the court to review the decision of an inferior tribunal by *certiorari* if the inferior tribunal has not acted without jurisdiction and has merely made an error of fact and if it is not a nullity for some reason such as breach of rule of natural justice. It can, therefore, be said that the scope of judicial review under Articles 136, 226 and 227 of the Constitution in respect of an order passed by the Speaker of the Lok Sabha or Chairman of the Rajya Sabha under paragraph 6 of the 10th Schedule of the Constitution would be confined only to jurisdictional errors, viz., infirmities based on violation of constitutional mandate, *mala fides*, non-compliance with rules of natural justice and perversity. This view of Justice Bhagwati finds support in the decision of the apex court in *Raja Ram Pal* v *The Hon'ble Speaker, Lok Sabha* decided on 10.01.2007.

Clause (1) of Article 122 of the Constitution of India provides that the validity of any proceedings in Parliament shall not be called in question on the ground of any alleged irregularity of procedure. Similarly, Clause (1) of Article 212 of the Constitution of India lays down that the validity of any proceedings in the Legislature of a State shall not be called in question on the ground of any alleged irregularity of procedure. Justice Bhagwati views that want of legislative competence is not cured either by Article 122 or by 212. Both the Articles, i.e., Article 122(1) and Article 212(1), according to Justice Bhagwati, make it possible for a citizen to call in question in the appropriate court of law the validity of any proceedings inside the legislative chamber if his case is that the said proceedings suffer not from mere irregularity of procedure, but from an illegality. If the impugned procedure is illegal and unconstitutional, it remains open to scrutiny in a court of law, though such scrutiny is prohibited if the complaint against the procedure is no more than an irregularity of procedure. Articles 122(1) and 212(1), Justice Bhagwati says, must, therefore, be found to contemplate the twin test of legality and constitutionality for any proceedings within the four walls of Parliament or the State Legislature, as the case may be. Any attempt to read a limitation into either of the articles so as to restrict the court's jurisdiction to examination of the Parliament's or the State Legislature's procedure in case of unconstitutionality or illegality, would amount to doing violence to the constitutional text. Prohibition against examination on the touchstone of "irregularity of procedure", asserts Justice Bhagwati, does not make taboo judicial review on findings of illegality or unconstitutionality. It deserves mentioning here that though Parliament is a coordinate organ and its views do deserve deference, its acts are still amenable to judicial scrutiny but the same ought not to be tested in the same manner as an ordinary administrative action would be tested.

Parliament's exercise of its privilege in expelling its members for misconduct is thus subject to judicial review but the court limits the review to such grounds as lack of jurisdiction, gross illegality, or it being a nullity for some reason, such as, irrationality, violation of constitutional mandate, *mala fides*, non-compliance with natural justice and perversity etc. Subject to above infirmities, the courts, Justice Bhagwati suggests, would start with the presumption that the powers of Parliament would have been properly and reasonably exercised.

3 Administrative decisions and scope for judicial interference

A. *Judicial activism re: executive action—behind the curtain episode*

"Parliament as the highest representative body should have the unquestioned authority", subject of course to limitation imposed by the Constitution, "to pass laws that it considers appropriate. The executive branch should be accountable to Parliament, and should have full administrative powers to implement laws and programmes as approved by Parliament. And the judiciary should give verdicts and settle legal disputes as per the law of the land. Most of the time, in all mature democracies, there should also be no cause for jurisdictional conflict among different organs of the State."[8] "While there is common agreement among all the organs of the state, i.e., the legislature, the executive, and the judiciary, on their respective powers and jurisdictions, from time to time a dispute arises about whether the judiciary has exceeded

8 *India's Politics—A view from the Backbench* by Bimal Jalan, p. 181, Penguin/ Viking.

its powers in issuing directions to the other branches of the government in the light of its own interpretation of the provisions of the Constitution. The dispute about the judiciary having exceeded its powers becomes intense when the executive branch at the Centre or in the states takes a decision that is apparently in favour of some parties at the expense of other parties. Irrespective of the intrinsic merits or otherwise of the decisions taken in such situations, an appeal to the courts by aggrieved parties and legislators becomes unavoidable. This is precisely what happened after the indecisive electoral verdicts in three states, i.e., Goa, Jharkhand, and Bihar in early 2005. Neither the Governors of these states (who had the final powers to appoint a government) nor the presiding officers of the legislatures (who had the power to conduct the proceedings of the House to test the majority) were considered to be impartial in their decisions. The aggrieved legislators went to the Court, and the Court issued certain interim directions to the executive and/or the legislature as per its interpretation of the Constitution. The directions of the Court, in turn, led to protests by members of the new government as well as the presiding officers about the Court having exceeded its jurisdiction in issuing such directions.

It is no accident that in India's democratic history, the political pressure to limit the powers of the judiciary and declare Parliament as being 'supreme' and representative of the will of the 'people of India' is the strongest when a coalition government of parties with varying agendas is in power, or when the political survival of the undisputed leader of the majority party is threatened (as, for example, was the case in 1975 when the Emergency was imposed). In these circumstances, political survival becomes more important than the legal merits or demerits of a case.

The erosion in the Constitutional principle of collective responsibility, the politicisation of the bureaucracy, and the dispute about the separation of powers between the judiciary and the executive (or legislature) have important implications for the working of India's political system and its institutions."[9]

B. ***Principles of judicial review in general*** As said earlier, there are three main departments of the State amongst which the powers of Government are divided; the Executive, the Legislature and the Judiciary. Under

9 *India's Politics—A view from the Backbench* by Bimal Jalan, pp. 155 to 157, Penguin/Viking.

the Constitution of India, we have no rigid separation of powers as in the United States of America, but there is a broad demarcation, though having regard to the complex nature of governmental functions, certain degree of overlapping is inevitable. The reason for this broad separation of powers is that "the concentration of powers in any one organ may", to quote the words of Chandrachud, J. (as he then was) in *Smt. Indira Gandhi's* case,[10] "by upsetting that fine balance between the three organs, destroy the fundamental premises of a democratic Government to which we are pledged." As an example, Justice Bhagwati cites a case where the executive which is in charge of administration acts to the prejudice of a citizen and a question arises as to what are the powers of the executive and whether the executive has acted within the scope of its powers. Such a question obviously, says Justice Bhagwati, cannot be left to the executive to decide and for two very good reasons. First, the decision of the question would depend upon the interpretation of the Constitution and the laws and this would pre-eminently be a matter fit to be decided by the judiciary, because it is the judiciary which alone would be possessed of expertise in this field and secondly, the constitutional and legal protection afforded to the citizen would become illusory, if it were left to the executive to determine the legality of its own action.

Administrative action is stated to be referable to broad area of Government activities in which the repositories of power may exercise every class of statutory function of executive, quasi-legislative and quasi-judicial nature. Generally, the court will be slow to interfere in matters relating to administrative functions unless the decision of the administrative body is tainted by any vulnerability, such as, illegality, irrationality or procedural impropriety. The decision of an administrative authority must be within the four corners of the law, and a *bona fide* one. It must not be one which no sensible person could have reasonably arrived at. The decision could be one of many choices open to the authority but it would be for that authority to decide upon the choice and not for the court to substitute its view.

The principles of judicial review of administrative action, says Justice Bhagwati, were summarised in 1985 by Lord Diplock in *Council of Civil Service Unions* v *Minister for the Civil Service*[11] as illegality, procedural impropriety and irrationality. He said more grounds could

10 AIR 1975 SC 2299.
11 [1985] AC 374: [1984]3 WLR 1174.

in future become available, including the doctrine of proportionality which has since been followed by certain members of the European Economic Community. This is what Lord Diplock in *Council of Civil Service Union's* case (supra) observed:

"... Judicial review has, I think, developed to a stage today when, without reiterating any analysis of the steps by which the development has come about, one can conveniently classify under three heads the grounds on which administrative action is subject to control by judicial review. The first ground I would call 'illegality', the second 'irrationality' and the third 'procedural impropriety'. That is not to say that further development on a case-by-case basis may not in course of time add further grounds. I have in mind particularly the possible adoption in the future of the principle of 'proportionality' which is recognized in the administrative law of several of our fellow members of the European Economic Community."

By 'irrationality', Lord Diplock meant 'what can be succinctly referred to as Wednesbury unreasonableness'. 'It applies to a decision', observed Lord Diplock in *Council of Civil Service Union's* case (supra), 'which is so outrageous in its defiance of logic or of accepted moral standards that no sensible person who had applied his mind to the question to be decided could have arrived at it.' In other words, to characterize a decision of an administrative authority as 'irrational', the court has to hold on material that it is a decision so outrageous as to be in total defiance of logic or moral standards.

Wednesbury Principles of Reasonableness to which reference has been made above is contained in *Associated Provincial Picture House Ltd.* v *Wednesbury Corporation.*[12] In that case, Lord Greene, MR, observed that a decision of a public authority will be quashed in judicial review proceeding where the court concludes that the decision is such that no authority properly directing itself on the relevant law and acting reasonably could have arrived at it.

In *Huang* v *Secretary of State for the Home Department*,[13] Laws, LJ. observed that "... precisely stated, the test imposed on the decision-maker a duty to make his decision in good faith, to have regard to all and only relevant considerations, and to bring a rational mind to bear on whatever was the issue. This approach informed a judicial review jurisdiction which was largely remote from the merits of the decision

12 [1947]2 All ER 680: [1948]1 KB 223: 63 TLR 623.
13 [2005]3 All ER 435.

under review. The judge might violently disagree with the merits decision; but applying the Wednesbury test he could only strike it down if he were satisfied that it failed to meet the test's relatively undemanding standards".

The Wednesbury Principles were severely criticised by Lord Cooke of Thorndon in *R.* v *Secretary of State for the Home Department ex parte Daly*[14] where the learned Law Lord observed: "... I think that the day will come when it will be more widely recognised that the Wednesbury case was an unfortunately retrogressive decision in English administrative law, in so far as it suggested that there are degrees of unreasonableness and that only a very extreme degree can bring an administrative decision within the legitimate scope of judicial invalidation. The depth of judicial review and the deference due to administrative discretion vary with the subject-matter. It may well be, however, that the law can never be satisfied in any administrative field merely by a finding that the decision under review is not capricious or absurd." This does not mean that there has been a shift to merits review. On the contrary, the respective roles of judges and administrators are fundamentally distinct and will remain so.

Laws LJ. in *R.* v *Secretary of State for the Home Department, ex p. Mahmood*[15] observed "that the intensity of review in a public law case will depend on the subject-matter in law." In *Huang* v *Secretary of State for the Home Department*,[16] Laws LJ. observed (at p. 461): "Wednesbury review consigned the relative weight to be given to any relative factor to the discretion of the decision-maker. In the new world, the decision-maker is obliged to accord decisive weight to the requirements of pressing social need and proportionality." This view of Laws LJ. in *Huang's* case (supra) finds support in the observations of Lord Steyn in *R.* v *Secretary of State for the Home Department ex p. Daly*[17] where the Law Lord said: "... the intensity of the review ... is guaranteed by the twin requirements that the limitation of the right was necessary in a democratic society, in the sense of meeting a pressing social need, and the question whether the interference was really proportionate to the legitimate aim being pursued."

In India, the position, according to Justice Bhagwati, is that the courts will play only a secondary role while the primary judgment as to

14 [2001]3 All ER 433: [2001]2 WLR 1622
15 [2000]1 WLR 840 (CA): [2001]2 FCR 63.
16 [2005]3 All ER 435.
17 [2001]3 All ER 433: [2001]2 WLR 1622.

reasonableness will remain with the executive or administrative authority. The secondary judgment of the court is to be based on the principles laid down in *Associated Provincial Picture House Ltd.* v *Wednesbury Corporation*[18] and *Council of Civil Service Unions* v *Minister for the Civil Service*[19] to find if the executive or administrative authority has reasonably arrived at his decision as the primary authority. Whether in case of administrative or executive action affecting fundamental freedoms, the courts in India will apply the principle of 'proportionality' and assume a primary role, is left open to be decided in an appropriate case where such action is alleged to offend fundamental freedoms. This view of Justice Bhagwati finds support in *Damoh Panna Sagar Rural Regional Bank* v *Munna Lal Jain.*[20]

C. ***Government policy and scope of judicial review*** The courts will generally recognise that democratic powers in the State have a special responsibility. Policy-making is their territory, and not that of the judges. Hence, a certain margin of discretionary decision making should be accorded to the government policy-maker on democratic grounds. The courts should also recognise that government is better equipped than the court to judge how needful the policy is to achieve the aim in view. Justice Bhagwati reminds that the courts should not enter into any field which distinctly lies within the constitutional responsibility of government. This does not mean, however, that the court should altogether abdicate its power to review any policy decision of the government, so says Justice Bhagwati. The court, according to him, should adopt a middle way. If the policy is in violation of a fundamental right, the court will not be satisfied merely upon its being shown that a reasonable decision-maker might consider the policy proportionate, it will require a substantial reasoned justification of the policy in light of the discipline inherent in the kind of case involved. It must not be forgotten, reminds Justice Bhagwati, that in the new world the decision-maker is under an obligation to accord decisive weight to the requirements of pressing social need and proportionality. On the whole, Justice Bhagwati reminds that questions of political wisdom or executive policy cannot be subjected to judicial control so long as it operates within its sphere and constitutional limitations.

D. ***Public contracts and scope for judicial review*** In matters of administrative decisions regarding public contracts, the courts of law,

18 [1947]2 All ER 680: [1948]1 KB 223: 63 TLR 623.
19 [1985] AC 374: [1984]3 WLR 1174.
20 (2005)10 SCC 84.

according to Justice Bhagwati, should not interfere unless there is violation of fundamental rights or allegation of malice or ulterior motive. In this context, Justice Bhagwati refers to Chapter 5 of the U.S. Code 41 which talks about judicial review of administrative decisions regarding public contracts. The said Chapter of the US Code states that the Courts would not interfere in an award process unless it is shown to be manifestly fraudulent, capricious and so grossly erroneous as to imply bad faith. In matters of administrative decisions regarding public contracts, it is the primary duty of the Court, reminds Justice Bhagwati, to confine itself to the question of legality and the court's concern should be to see whether a decision-making authority: (*i*) exceeded its powers; (*ii*) committed an error of law; (*iii*) committed a breach of the rules of natural justice; (*iv*) reached a decision which no reasonable person or authority would have reached; or (*v*) abused its power. This view of Justice Bhagwati finds support in *Tata Cellular* v *Union of India*.[1] It may be noted in this context that in matters of exercise of contractual powers of government bodies, judicial review is intended to prevent arbitrariness or favouritism and it is exercised in the larger public interest. The power of judicial review can also be exercised if it is brought to the notice of the court that in the matter of award of a contract, power has been exercised for any collateral purpose. It is, however, to be noted that while exercising power of judicial review courts should not proceed if two views are possible and one view has been taken and that too without *mala fide* taking one of the views. "It is not every wandering from the precise paths of best practice that lends fuel to a claim for judicial review", so was observed in Queen's Bench decision in *R.* v *Department of Constitutional Affairs*.[2] Only when the Court comes to a conclusion that there is an overwhelming public interest in entertaining a petition, the Court should intervene.

E. ***Order passed under a statute and scope for judicial interference*** It is an established principle of law, says Justice Bhagwati, that though an order passed in exercise of power under a statute cannot be challenged on the ground of propriety or sufficiency, it is liable to be quashed on the ground of *male fides*, dishonesty or corrupt purpose. Even if it is passed in good faith and with the best of intention to further the

1 (1994)6 SCC 651: AIR 1996 SC 11.
2 [2006]2 All ER 993.

purpose of the legislation which confers the power, since the authority has to act in accordance with and within the limits of that legislation, its order can also be challenged if it is beyond those limits or is passed on grounds extraneous to the legislations or if there are no grounds at all for passing it or if the grounds are such that no one can reasonably arrive at the opinion or satisfaction requisite under the legislation. In the event of existence of requisite conditions being challenged, the courts are entitled to examine whether those circumstances were existing when the order was made. In other words, the existence of the circumstances in question is open to judicial review. This view of Justice Bhagwati, it may be noted, finds support in *Barium Chemicals Ltd.* v *Company Law Board.*[3]

F. ***Subjective satisfaction of executive action and scope for judicial review*** The courts, Justice Bhagwati says in *Khudiram Das* v *State of West Bengal,*[4] have by judicial decisions carved out an area, limited though it be, within which the validity of the subjective satisfaction of executive action can be subjected to judicial scrutiny. The basic postulate on which the courts have proceeded is that the subjective satisfaction being a condition precedent for the exercise of a power conferred on the executive, the court can always examine whether the requisite satisfaction is arrived at by the authority; if it is not, the condition precedent to the exercise of the power would not be fulfilled and the exercise of the power would be bad.

Thus, in a case where the authority has not applied its mind at all, it cannot possibly be satisfied as regards the fact in respect of which it is required to be satisfied. Justice Bhagwati, as example, cites *Emperor* v *Shibnath Banerjee,*[5] as a case in point.

Then, there may be a case where the power is exercised dishonestly or for an improper purpose. Such a case would also negative the existence of satisfaction on the part of the authority.

The existence of 'improper purpose', that is, a purpose not contemplated by statute, has been recognised as an independent ground of control in several decided cases.

The satisfaction, views Justice Bhagwati, must be a satisfaction of the authority itself, and, therefore, if, in exercising the power, the authority has acted under the dictation of another body, the exercise of

3 AIR 1967 SC 295: 1966 Supp SCR 311.
4 AIR 1975 SC 550.
5 AIR 1943 SC 75.

the power would be bad. This view of Justice Bhagwati finds support in *Commissioner of Police* v *Gordhandas Bhanji*,[6] and *Simms Motor Units Ltd.* v *Minister of Labour and National Service*.[7]

The exercise of the power by an executive authority would also be vitiated, Justice Bhagwati asserts, where the authority has disabled itself from applying its mind to the facts of each individual case by self created rules of policy or in any other manner.

The satisfaction said to have been arrived at by the authority would again be bad, points out Justice Bhagwati, where it is based on the application of a wrong test or the misconstruction of a statute. Where this happens, the satisfaction of the authority would not be in respect of the thing in regard to which it is required to be satisfied.

Justice Bhagwati views that satisfaction of the executive authority must also be grounded on materials which are of rationally probative value. The grounds on which the satisfaction is based must be such as a rational human being can consider connected with the fact in respect of which the satisfaction is to be based. They must be relevant to the subject-matter of inquiry and must not be extraneous to the scope and purpose of the statute as said earlier. If the authority has taken into account, it may even be with the best of intention, as a relevant factor something which it could not properly take into account in deciding whether or not to exercise the power or the manner or extent to which it should be exercised, the exercise of the power would be bad. Justice Bhagwati in support of his contention refers the case of *Pratap Singh* v *State of Punjab*.[8] If there are to be found in the statute expressly or by implication matters which the authority ought to have regard to, then, in exercising the power, the authority must have regard to those matters. The authority, it bears mentioning, must call its attention to the matters which it is bound to consider.

There is also another ground on which the subjective satisfaction reached by an authority can successfully be challenged and it is of late becoming increasingly important. The genesis of this ground, opines Justice Bhagwati, is to be found in the famous words of Lord Halsbury in *Sharpe* v *Wakefield*[9]: "... when it is said that something is to be done within the discretion of the authorities ... that something is to be done

6 1952 SCR 135: AIR 1952 SC 16.
7 [1946]2 All ER 201.
8 AIR 1964 SC 72.
9 [1891] AC 173.

according to the rules of reason and justice, not according to private opinion ... according to law and not humour. It is to be, not arbitrary, vague, fanciful, but legal and regular." So far as this ground is concerned, Justice Bhagwati says, the courts in the United States have gone much further than the courts in England or in India. The courts of United States are prepared to review administrative findings which are not supported by substantial evidence, that is, by "such relevant findings as a reasonable man may accept adequate to support a conclusion." But in England and India, the courts stop-short at merely inquiring whether the grounds on which the authority has reached its subjective satisfaction are such that any reasonable person could possibly arrive at such satisfaction. "If", to use the words of Lord Greene, M.R. in *Associated Provincial Picture Houses Ltd.* v *Wednesbury Corporation*,[10] "the authority has come to a conclusion so unreasonable that no reasonable authority could ever have come to it, then the Court can interfere." In such a case, Justice Bhagwati says, a legitimate inference may fairly be drawn to the effect either that the authority did not honestly form the view or that in forming it, he could not have applied his mind to the relevant facts. The power of the court to interfere in such a case is not as an appellate authority to override a decision taken by the statutory authority, but as a judicial authority which is concerned, and concerned only, to see whether the statutory authority has contravened the law by acting in excess of the power which the legislature has confided in it.

There is nothing like unfettered discretion immune from judicial review ability, asserts Justice Bhagwati. The truth is that in a government under law, there can be no such thing as unreviewable discretion. "Law has reached its finest moments", said Justice Douglas, "when it has freed man from the unlimited discretion of some ruler, some ... official, some bureaucrat ... Absolute discretion is a ruthless master. It is more destructive of freedom than any man's other inventions".[11] And this is much more so, asserts Justice Bhagwati, in a case where personal liberty is involved. That is why the courts have devised various methods of judicial control so that power in the hands of an individual officer or authority is not misused or abused or exercised arbitrarily or without any justifiable grounds.

G. ***Mere technical irregularity in administrative decision—no ground for judicial review*** Justice Bhagwati views that a court may reject an application for judicial review of an administrative decision taken in exercise of

10 [1948]1 KB 223.
11 *United States* v *Wunderlich* [1951]342 US 98.

statutory power when there is mere irregularity in form or a technical irregularity. Justice Bhagwati's view in this respect finds support in the Judicial Review Procedure Act 1996 of Canada where Section 9 provides that the court may reject an application for judicial review of a statutory power of decision, if there is mere irregularity in form or a technical irregularity, or if the court feels that there has been no miscarriage of justice.

H. ***Rule of law to guide executive action*** Rule of law, reminds Justice Bhagwati, is a basic and essential feature of the Constitution. It is a basic principle of the rule of law that the exercise of power by the executive or any other authority must not only be conditioned by the Constitution but must also be in accordance with law and the power of judicial review is conferred by the Constitution with a view to ensuring that the law is observed and there is compliance with the requirement of law on the part of the executive and other authorities. This view of Justice Bhagwati finds support in his own judgment in *P. Sambamurthy* v *Union of India*.[12]

4 Exercise of power by the President under the Constitution and scope for judicial interference

A. *Power exercised under the finality clause*

ARTICLE 217(3). Article 217(3) vests in the President of India the jurisdiction to decide the question as to the age of a Judge of a High Court, after consultation with the Chief Justice of India and declares that the decision of the President shall be final. The President acting under Article 217(3), views Justice Bhagwati, performs a judicial function of grave importance under the scheme of the Constitution of India. He cannot act on the advice of his Ministers. Notwithstanding the declared finality of the order of the President, the court has jurisdiction in appropriate cases to set aside the order if it appears that it was passed on collateral considerations or the rules of natural justice were not observed, or that the President's judgment was coloured by the advice or representation made by the executive or it was founded on no evidence. Justice Bhagwati's view in this respect finds support in the decision of the Supreme Court in *Union of India* v *Jyoti Prakash Mitter*.[13]

ARTICLE 311. Article 311 relates to the dismissal, removal, etc. of persons employed in civil capacities under the Union or a State. The

12 (1987)1 SCC 124.
13 AIR 1971 SC 1093: (1971)1 SCC 396.

second proviso to Article 311(2) empowers the President or the Governor, as the case may be, to dispense with the enquiry generally required to be held upon satisfaction that in the interest of the security of the State it is not expedient to hold such enquiry. Article 311(3) gives finality to such decision thus: "If, in respect of any such person as aforesaid, a question arises whether it is reasonably practicable to hold such inquiry as is referred to in clause (2), the decision thereon of the authority empowered to dismiss or remove such person or to reduce him in rank shall be final."

Construing the expression "finality" in the provision of Article 311(3), the Supreme Court in *Union of India* v *Tulsiram Patel*[14] observed that the finality given by Clause (3) of Article 311 to the disciplinary authority's decision that it was not reasonably practicable to hold the inquiry is not binding upon the Court. The Court will examine the charge of *mala fides*, if any, made in the writ petition. In examining the relevancy of the reasons, the court will consider the situation which according to the disciplinary authority made it come to the conclusion that it was not reasonably practicable to hold the inquiry. If the court finds that the reasons are irrelevant, then the recording of its satisfaction by the disciplinary authority would be an abuse of power conferred upon.

B. *Power exercised in ordering dissolution of assembly*

ARTICLE 356. The exercise of power by the President under Article 356(1) to issue proclamation ordering dissolution of the Legislative Assembly of a State, assuming to himself the functions of the Government of the State, is subject to judicial review at least to the extent of examining whether the conditions precedent to the issuance of the proclamation have been satisfied or not. For purposes of such examination, Justice Bhagwati opines, the exercise would necessarily involve "the scrutiny as to whether there existed the material" for such a satisfaction being arrived at. It is not "any material" but material "which would lead to the conclusion" that is required to be under scrutiny. It bears mentioning here that although "the sufficiency or otherwise of the material cannot be questioned, the legitimacy of inference drawn from such material is certainly open to judicial review." This was also the view of the majority of the Constitution Bench (9 Judges) of the Supreme Court in *S.R. Bommai* v *Union of India*.[15] It has to be noted that the power vested

14 AIR 1985 SC 1416: (1985)3 SCC 398.
15 AIR 1994 SC 1918: (1994)3 SCC 1.

de jure in the President but *de facto* in the Council of Ministers under Article 356 has all the latent capacity to emasculate the two basic features of the Constitution, namely, democracy and federalism and hence it is necessary to scrutinize the material on the basis of which the advice is given and the President forms his satisfaction more closely and circumspectly. This can be done by the courts while confining themselves to the acknowledged parameters of the judicial review, viz., illegality, irrationality and *mala fides*. Judicial review of the Presidential proclamation on the ground of *mala fide*, it has to be noted, takes in *inter alia* situation where the proclamation is found to be a clear case of abuse of power, or what is sometimes called fraud on power i.e., cases where the power is invoked for a collateral purpose or for achieving oblique ends. Judicial review of the Presidential proclamation is not concerned with the merits of the decision, but to the manner in which the decision had been arrived.

5 Supreme Court's own decision and scope for judicial review The Supreme Court, Justice Bhagwati views, has power to review its earlier decisions or even depart from them and the doctrine of *stare decisis* cannot be permitted to perpetuate erroneous decisions of this Court to the detriment of the general welfare of the public.[16] There is indeed a school of thought which believes with Cardozo that "the precedents have turned upon us and they are engulfing and annihilating us, engulfing and annihilating the very devotees that worshipped at their shrine" and the Court should not be troubled unduly if it has to break away from precedents in order to modify old rules and if need be to fashion new ones to meet the challenges and problems thrown upon by a dynamic society. But at the same time, it must be borne in mind that certainty and continuity are essential ingredients of rule of law. Certainty in applicability of law would be considerably eroded and suffer a serious set-back if the highest court in law were readily to overrule the view expressed by it in earlier decisions even where that view has held the field for a number of years. It is obvious, says Justice Bhagwati, when constitutional problems are brought before the Supreme Court for its decision, complex and difficult questions are bound to arise and since the decision on many of such questions may depend upon choice between competing values, two views may be possible depending upon the value judgment or the choice of values made by the individual judge. Therefore, Justice Bhagwati continues, if one view

16 *Minerva Mills Ltd.* v *Union of India* AIR 1980 SC 1789: (1980)2 SCC 591.

has been taken by the Court after mature deliberation, the fact that another Bench is inclined to take another view would not justify the Court in reconsidering the earlier decision and overruling it. Justice Bhagwati cautioned that the law laid down by the Supreme Court is binding on all courts in the country and the numerous cases all over the country are decided in accordance with the view taken by the apex court. Many people arrange their affairs and large number of transactions also take place on the faith of the correctness of the decision given by the Supreme Court. It would create uncertainty, instability and confusion if the law propounded by the Supreme Court is held to be not the correct law after a number of years. The doctrine of *stare decisis* has, Justice Bhagwati says, evolved from the maxim *"stare decisis et non movere quieta"* meaning "adhere to the decision and do not unsettle things which are established", and it is a useful doctrine intended to bring about certainty and uniformity in the law. But when Justice Bhagwati says this, he makes it clear that he does not regard the doctrine of *stare decisis* as a rigid and inevitable doctrine which must be applied at the cost of justice. There may be cases where it may be necessary to rid the doctrine of its petrifying rigidity. The Court may in an appropriate case overrule a previous decision taken by it, but that should be done only for substantial and compelling reasons. The power of review must be exercised with due care and caution and only for advancing the public well-being and not merely because it may appear that the previous decision was based on an erroneous view of the law. It is only where the perpetuation of the earlier decision would be productive of mischief or inconvenience or would have the effect of deflecting the nation from the course which has been set by the Constitution makers or to use the words of Krishna Iyer, J. in *Ambika Prasad Misra* v *State of U.P*,[17] "where national crisis of great moment to the life, liberty and safety of this country and its millions are at stake or the basic direction of the nation itself is in peril of a shake-up" that the Court would be justified in reconsidering its earlier decision and departing from it. It is fundamental that the nation's Constitution should not be kept in constant uncertainty by judicial review every now and then, because otherwise it would paralyse by perennial suspense all legislative and administrative action on vital issues. The Court should not indulge in judicial destabilization of State action and a view which has been accepted for a long period of time in a series of decisions and on the faith of which millions of people have acted and a large

17 AIR 1980 SC 1762.

number of transactions have been affected, should not be disturbed. Justice Bhagwati reminds: 'Let us not forget the words of Justice Roberts of the United States Supreme Court—words which are equally applicable to the decisions making process of the Supreme Court: "The reason for my concern is that the instant decision overruling that announced about nine years ago, tends to bring adjudications of this tribunal into the same class as a restricted rail road ticket good for this day and train only ... It is regrettable that in an era marked by doubt and confusion, an era whose greatest need is steadfastness of thought and purpose, this Court which has been looked to as exhibiting consistency in adjudication, and a steadiness which would hold the balance even in the face of temporary ebbs and flows of opinion, should now itself become the breeder of fresh doubt and confusion in the public mind as to the stability of our institutions".

6 Courts—the ultimate authority in deciding question of law Any discussion on judicial review will remain inconclusive unless the observations of Lord Hoffmann in *R (on the application of Prolife Alliance)* v *BBC*[18] are taken into consideration and the learned Law Lord in that case observed: "In a society based upon the rule of law and the separation of powers, it is necessary to decide which branch of government has in any particular instance the decision-making power and what the legal limits of that power are. That is a question of law and must therefore be decided by the courts." Justice Bhagwati fully endorses this view of Lord Hoffmann as a correct principle of law laid down in a democratic set up governed by the rule of law.

18 [2003]2 All ER 977: [2004]1 AC 185.

"Judicial activism is nothing but the pro-active role played by the judiciary in ensuring, protecting and preserving the rights and liberties of citizens."

—P.N. BHAGWATI

11

Judicial Activism

(Judge as Law Maker)

SYNOPSIS

1 Introduction Judicial activism, views Justice Bhagwati, is a central feature of every political system that vests adjudicatory power in a free and independent judiciary. If we analyse the true nature of judicial function, it will immediately become apparent that judicial activism, whatever its degree or extent, is an essential part of the judicial process. Judicial activism thus being an undeniable feature of the judicial process in a democracy, the only relevant question is what should be the degree and extent of judicial activism permissible to a judge. The scope of judicial activism, says Justice Bhagwati, varies with the width of the power conferred on the courts. Where the courts have the power of judicial review, there is greater scope for judicial activism, and this scope increases considerably where the power of judicial review extends not only over executive action, as in the United Kingdom, but also over legislative action, as in the United States, and even over constitutional amendments, as in India.

2 Judicial activism and an activist judge—meaning Judicial activism, in the view of Justice Bhagwati, is nothing but the pro-active role played by the judiciary in ensuring, protecting and preserving the rights and liberties of citizens. It is a positive approach to the statute, an active desire to do justice in accordance with the law and the Constitution, with a readiness to stretch the law and the Constitution to a certain degree so that justice may be done in the particular case. Judicial activism, therefore, is a positive approach to the work of a judge, and the words of Edmund Burk, mentions Justice Bhagwati, on Lord Mansfield sum it up: "He sought to effect the amelioration of the law by making its liberality keep pace with justice and the actual concerns of the world". Judicial activism is characterised by bias in favour of justice and the will to stretch the law to achieve it.

In Black's *Law Dictionary*, 6th Ed., "judicial activism" is defined thus: "Judicial philosophy which motivates judges to depart from strict adherence to judicial precedent in favor of progressive and new social policies which are not always consistent with the restraint expected of appellate judges. It is commonly marked by decisions calling for social engineering and occasionally these decisions represent intrusions into legislative and executive matters."

Black's *Law Dictionary*, 7th and 8th Eds., define "judicial activism" thus: "A philosophy of judicial decision-making whereby judges allow their personal views about public policy, among other factors, to guide their decisions, usu. with the suggestion that adherents of this philosophy tend to find constitutional violations and are willing to ignore precedent."

According to Ronald Dworkin,[1] "Judicial activism in its strongest form holds that courts should work out principles of legality, equality, and the rest, revise these principles from time to time in the light of what seems to the court fresh moral insight, and judge the acts of Congress, the states and the President accordingly."

An activist judge, in the words of Justice Bhagwati, is one who plays a pro-active role in ensuring, protecting and preserving the rights and liberties of citizens; one who seeks to adapt the law to the changing needs of the society, one who chooses from the group of possibilities open to him the possibility that accords more with the interests of justice than any other possibility. Lord Scarman in *Duport Steels Limited* v *Sirs*[2] observed: "Great Judges are in their different ways judicial activists".

1 "*Taking Rights Seriously*", p. 137.
2 [1980]1 All ER 529, 551.

3 Forms of judicial activism Judicial activism, according to Justice Bhagwati, can be of different forms, namely, technical activism, juristic activism, social activism.

A. ***Technical activism*** Judicial activism of this type consists of a declaration of freedom to have recourse to a wide range of techniques and choices. It is called 'technical activism' because it is concerned merely with keeping juristic techniques open ended. Justice Bhagwati explains his view point thus: "At one level, it may take the form of simply ensuring that judges have the necessary freedom of action—freedom to choose alternative courses of action. Let me take an example. In 1966, the House of Lords delivered a Practice Statement which enables it to depart from its earlier decisions 'when it appears right to do so…'. This was in one sense a declaration of freedom from certain constraints that the House of Lords had imposed upon itself in 1897. Perhaps in 1897 it would have been impolitic for the judges to declare for themselves the power to reverse their decisions whenever they wanted. On the other hand, in 1966 it would have been equally impolitic for a post-war judiciary to declare that it was inextricably bound to its previous decisions. The judges of 1966 could be regarded as activists, though they were simply reassessing their political situation and the form in which they would treat their earlier decisions. The Practice Statement did no more than merely declare a freedom. Subsequent decisions of the House of Lords show that the basic conservatism of that august body was not lost by this newly declared freedom. It reversed its earlier decisions only in very few cases. It will call this kind of judicial activism 'technical activism'. It consists of a declaration of freedom to have recourse to a wide range of techniques and choices. Such an activism is 'technique open ended'."

"In this day and age", continues Justice Bhagwati, "most judges would confine to technical activism. They would be embarrassed not to be called activist in this sense. Thus, most judges of the Supreme Court of India have been anxious to declare the breadth of their power. They have declared that they are free to depart from their previous decisions. They have refused to put constraints on the jurisdiction of the Supreme Court to hear appeals from any court or tribunal in the country. They have assumed the power to tear the veil of official secrecy. They are clearly activists in the technical sense, though they use their declared powers to substantive effect only in rare cases."

B. ***Juristic activism*** Juristic activism, according to Justice Bhagwati, is not concerned merely with the appropriation of increased power, but is concerned as well with the creation of new concepts, irrespective of the purposes which they serve. The common law, asserts the learned Judge, is itself an example of the development of juristic activism. Over the centuries, it has been fashioned and refashioned to deal with new claims and demands; it has developed new concepts and invented new principles. Many of these were created to serve the existing *status quo* rather than to change it. The doctrine of common employment enunciated in *Priestley* v *Fowler*[3] is as much an example of juristic activism as the concept of negligence created in *Donoghue* v *Stephenson*.[4] In this kind of juristic activism, the judge is not concerned with the social consequences generated by the creation of new concepts or principles, or with the question as to whom these new concepts and principles will serve.

These new concepts and principles, says Justice Bhagwati, may help to preserve the *status quo*. They may impede equitable distribution of the social or material resources of the community or even, as a consequence, tend to defeat realization of the community or constitutional objectives. Even so, there is no reason to deny the title of activism to this kind of creative juristic activity. Indeed, no legal system which denies to itself some scope for this kind of judicial activism can survive.

The Supreme Court of India also has been quite creative in this sense. It has invented an impressive range of concepts in both public and private law. For example, the Supreme Court has used the doctrine of statutory interpretation imaginatively and, in the area of public law, English administrative law techniques inherited from the British have been creatively refashioned by the Supreme Court to form the basis of judicial review. It is, however, necessary to go beyond technical and juristic activism to inquire about the purpose for which such activism is practiced.

Technical and juristic activism considered in isolation, says Justice Bhagwati, obscures our understanding of the purpose behind such activism. It is important to try to discover why a particular kind of judicial creativity has been adopted and to inquire into the purpose which it seeks to serve. It is the instrumental use of judicial activism that needs to be considered, for judicial activism cannot be divorced from the purpose it serves. It cannot be judged in the abstract; it can be

3 [1837]3 M&W 1.
4 [1932] AC 562.

evaluated only in terms of its social objective. Even where the judge adheres to formal notions of justice and claims not to be concerned with the social consequences of what he decides, it is often a thin disguise, for in many such cases his instrumental objective is to preserve the *status quo*.

C. ***Social activism*** Social activism is activism directed towards achievement of social justice. Justice Bhagwati says: "To my mind, social activism is a most complex and challenging task facing the modern judiciary today, particularly in the developing countries such as India. The modern judiciary cannot afford to hide behind notions of legal justice and plead incapacity when social justice issues are addressed to it. This challenge is an important one, not just because judges owe a duty to do justice with a view to creating and moulding a just society, but because a modern judiciary can no longer obtain social and political legitimacy without making a substantial contribution to issues of social justice."

This is precisely what happened in the United States when the Supreme Court was striking down social legislation pertaining to the working hours of men, women and children. Interestingly, those who were supporting such social legislation intended to bring about social justice criticised the justices, who nullified such liberal legislation for their judicial activism, pleading for judicial restraint. In course of time, however, it became impossible for the Supreme Court to maintain that it provided justice to the large bulk of the U.S. population if it could not sustain the validity of such liberal legislation.

The Supreme Court of India also faced with a similar legitimation crisis. In the words of Justice Bhagwati "The Supreme Court of India for too long remained 'an arena of legal quibbling for men with long purses' but now increasingly the Supreme Court is being identified by justices as well as by people as the 'last resort for the oppressed and the bewildered'. Through a variety of techniques of judicial activism, it has begun converting much of constitutional litigation into public interest litigation, calculated to bring social justice within the reach of the common man. The Court has expanded the frontiers of fundamental rights and of natural justice, and in the process has rewritten some parts of the Constitution. The right to life and personal liberty under procedure established by law in Article 21 of the Constitution has been converted *de facto* and *de jure* into a procedural due process clause, contrary to the intention of the makers of the Constitution. This expanding right has encompassed, through a process of judicial interpretation, the right to bail, the right to speedy trial, the right to dignified treatment in custodial institutions, the right to legal aid in criminal proceedings and, above all, the right to live with basic human dignity. The Supreme Court has developed a new normative regime of rights, insisting that the State cannot act arbitrarily but instead must act reasonably and in the public interest, on pain of its action being invalidated by judicial intervention. The transition from a traditional captive agency with a low social visibility into a liberated agency with high socio-political feasibility is an interesting development in the career of the Indian appellate judiciary."

4 Aspects of judicial activism There are three aspects of judicial activism. The first aspect, says Justice Bhagwati, is to ignore the laws which have become redundant on account of changed circumstances and instead fashion new principles to meet the needs of the changing time.

The second aspect of judicial activism, in the view of Justice Bhagwati, today concerns the judge's attitude to the interpretation of statutes. All judges start with the words used in the statute but some adhere strictly to the literal meaning and no more. The limitation of this method is that in some statutes it is not possible to discover the meaning, a literal approach sometimes leads to absurd result. To cope with the challenges, many judges now adopt the purposive approach to statutes. What was the purpose of the statute? Parliament requires the draftsman to cover all possibilities, but this does not happen in actual practice. There are bound to be situations which were never envisaged by the draftsman and those gaps call for filling up. Lord Denning, says Justice Bhagwati, urged judges to fill the gaps. This requires an activist approach on the part of a judge.

The third aspect of judicial activism is ensuring implementation of judicial orders. In performing its activist role, the judiciary must ensure that its orders are capable of implementation, for no amount of judicial activism is useful if its orders are not judicially manageable and capable of implementation.

5 Features of judicial activism The most prominent feature of judicial activism is judicial valour. To act as an activist judge, judicial valour is required. Judges act as a collegiate body and naturally like to keep in step with other brother judges. They may not be interested in the applause of the public and instead may take care about the opinion of their colleagues on the bench and the legal profession. But according to Justice Bhagwati, no judge should allow his judicial philosophy to be submerged by the opinion of his colleagues since it is a sacred function of a judge to be guided by his own judicial philosophy for dispensing justice and this should be the bounden obligation of every judge in the country.

Another feature of judicial activism, says Justice Bhagwati, is a desire to get to grip with the reality of the case, to go by the spirit rather than the letter of the law. When constructing a will, Lord Mansfield constantly harped on the intention of the testator. He searched for the mischief at which an Act of Parliament was aimed.

The desire to mould the law to meet the needs of times is yet another feature of judicial activism. Social ideas and habits are constantly changing and the law has to keep pace with such changes, says Justice Bhagwati.

6 Judicial activism and myth in Anglo-Saxon tradition There is a myth strongly nurtured by the Anglo-Saxon tradition and propagated by many jurists that judges do not make law, that they merely interpret law. The proclaimed theory of judicial function is that law is there, existing and immanent, and judges merely find it. The law making function does not belong to them—it belongs to the legislature—and judges merely reflect what the legislature has said. Justice Bhagwati, however, is of the view that this statement hides the real nature of the judicial process. It has been deliberately constructed in order to isolate judges against vulnerability to public criticism, and to preserve their image of neutrality, which is regarded as necessary for enhancing their credibility. It also helps judges to escape accountability for what they decide, because they can always plead helplessness (even if the law they declare is unjust) by saying that it is the law made by the legislature and that they have no choice but to give effect to it. It is only natural that judges should wish to exercise power but not be accountable to anyone for such exercise. It too is natural for them to indulge in the fiction that they are merely carrying out the intention of the legislature or discovering the immanent something called the law.

Thus, says Justice Bhagwati, the tradition of the law and the craft of jurisprudence offer such judges plenty of dignified exits from the agony of a self-conscious wielding of power. This stance suits equally the lawyers and the scholars who find it more convenient to deal with immediate issues of technique and substance rather than look back to more fundamental questions of the role of the judge in a traumatically changing society. This explains the persistent attempt on the part of some lawyers and judges to convince the people about the truth of the fallacy that judges do not make law.

7 The real position: The judge as a law maker—a dimension of the justicing process Lord Reid, one of the greatest English judges, had no illusions about the potential for creativity in the judicial role and had no doubt that judges do take part in the law making process. In his book *'The Judge as Law Maker'*, Lord Reid said (p. 22): "There was a time when it was thought almost indecent to suggest that Judges make law—they only declare it. Those with a taste for fairy tales deem to have thought that in some Aladdin's cave there is hidden the common law in all its splendour and that on a judge's appointment there descends on him knowledge of the magic words 'Open Sesame'. Bad decisions are given when the judge has muddled the password and the wrong door opens. But we do not believe in fairy tales any more."

Richard A. Posner said[5]: "if to resolve the dispute the court must create a new rule or modify an old one, that is law creation. Judges defending themselves from accusations of judicial activism sometimes say they do not make law, they only apply it. It is true that in our system judges are not supposed to and generally do not make law with the same freedom that legislatures can and do; they are, in Oliver Wendell Holmes's phrase, 'confined from molar to molecular motions'. The qualification is important, but the fact remains that judges make, and do not just find and apply, law."

Justice Brennan once commented:[6] "The great judge is a bold judge, not because he changes his arm, but because he so perceives the philosophy and the history of the law that he can sweep aside the incidental and reach for the essential, and fashion and refashion the basic principles so that they can serve the society of his time. Boldness is a function of both understanding and courage. It requires understanding of the deepest values of the society, and courage in rejecting the applications of principle which serve as an incompatible value. And so the significant contribution, which judges are able to make to the society of their time is not confined to the application of principles, but includes more importantly the modification of principles to suit the public good of that time."

The judiciary plays an important role in the evolution of the law. In a democracy, Justice Bhagwati says, the courts participate in the law

5 The Federal Courts: Crisis and Reform 3(1985).

6 *New Growth of the Law—The Judicial Contribution* 6 Monash ULR 8(1978).

making and law reforming process and in so doing have constantly to make, unmake and remake the law. It is an endless process. The courts undertake this crucial but delicate task for a number of good reasons. Human society being dynamic, law cannot remain static. Legislature's inability to legislate at the same pace at which the society changes compels the courts to fill the void. Law is uncertain, it does not cover all the situations. As new situations arise from time to time, Justice Bhagwati says, the courts adopt and extend the well-established principles of law to meet such situations. It bears mentioning that the law making function of the judges is not comparable to that of the legislature. A Judge is bound by the factual context in which he has to apply a legal principle and he develops the law only to the extent necessary for the purpose of resolving the dispute before him. The law creative role of a judge is a social necessity, views Justice Bhagwati. Law has constantly to respond to societal changes otherwise there may be statism in law and progress may be stalled. No legislature in the world, howsoever active it may be, asserts Justice Bhagwati, can cope with the total law making required by any dynamic society.

The human language being not so perfect, it becomes very difficult to encompass the complex realities within the clear framework of law and to apply law to the endless diversity of human situations. The great task before the judiciary, views Justice Bhagwati, is to discover what law is in a given situation and to apply it with a view to doing justice to the parties before it. Now in this process of discovering law and interpreting and applying it, the judge performs a highly creative function and in this way a judge really makes the law.

Justice Bhagwati says:[7] "It is now recognised on all hands that judges do not merely discover law, but they also make law. Law making is an inherent and inevitable part of the judicial process. Even when a judge is concerned with interpretation of a Bill of Rights or a statute, there is ample scope for him to develop and mould the law. It is he who infuses life and blood into the dry skeleton provided by the legislature and creates a living organism appropriate and adequate to meet the needs of the society and by thus making and moulding the law, he takes part in the work of creation and this is much more true in the case of interpretation of the Constitution ... . Greatness on the Bench lies in creativity and it is only through bold and imaginative interpretation that the law can be moulded and developed and human rights advanced."

7 Excerpts from the speech on '*Domestic Application of Human Rights Norms*' at Abuja in 1991.

In expressing the role of a judge,[7] Justice Bhagwati says: "A judge is not a mimic. He is not an imitator, and greatness of a judge lies in creativity. The process of judging is a phase of never ending movement and sometime more is expected of a judge than mere imitative reproduction, lifeless repetition of a mechanical routine. It is for this reason that when a law comes before a judge, he has to invest it with meaning and content and in this process of interpretation he makes law. It is, therefore, essential that a judge must be in tune with the social needs and requirements and he must be above all a judicial statesman. He does not operate in vacuum. Where the language of the law is clear, then, of course, the judge must give effect to it, but there are many cases where it is possible to decide either way. In the types of cases where a decision, one way or other, will count for the future, will advance or retard, sometimes much, sometimes little, the development of the law in the proper direction depends on the judge who has to leap in the heart of legal darkness. Where the lamps of precedent and common law principles flicker and fade, there the judge gets an opportunity to mould the law and give it a shape and direction. To meet the needs of the society, the judges do make law and it is now recognized everywhere that judges take part in this law making function and, therefore, the judges make law. They have always to keep in mind the requirement of social justice. When a judge is called upon to interpret the law, there are quite often competing values clamouring for acceptance by him and the choice of value is guided by the social philosophy of the judge".

We have to accept the fact that in a democratic society which has a Constitution with a Bill of Rights or which has subscribed to regional or international instruments on human rights and particularly in a developing country which is seeking to build a new socio-economic order founded on justice and equality, judicial activism on the part of the judiciary is an imperative, both for strengthing and realization of basic human rights by large number of people in the country. Justice Bhagwati holds the view that judicial activism has opened a new dimension of the justicing process and expanded the reach and content of the fundamental rights and also facilitated easy access to justice to the vast masses of people who were otherwise priced out of the legal system. To quote Justice Bhagwati, "We have made interesting and exciting efforts in this direction and tried to make innovative use of judicial power for making the judicial process an effective instrument for protecting the dignity of the individual, broadening access to justice and ensuring realization of human rights in the widest perspective."

8 Judicial activism in USA In USA, the judiciary has the power of judicial review over laws passed by the legislature and over executive action. Judicial activism, once called in USA judicial supremacy or government by the judiciary, began in 1890s and continued through 1935-36. That phase is described as "the classic age of rampant judicial activism". During this period "the Supreme Court maintained a virtually unblemished record throughout most of American history of defending the rich and the powerful".[8] Roosevelt's re-election in 1936 brought a major change and the 'nine old men' who took the pro-active role surrendered and the new doctrine that was devised was that of judicial restraint. This was followed by the Warren Court's judicial activism, 1962-1969, which is known for expanding the number of both fundamental rights and suspect classes. In its modern garb, judicial activism with which we are familiar today "casts the (Supreme) Court as the institutional defender of the politically disadvantaged".[8]

American Presidents Thomas Jefferson and Abraham Lincoln had to bear the brunt of proactive judges; Jefferson calling them "sappers and miners" undermining the foundations of the confederation. The US Supreme Court even struck down legislation to give shape to Franklin Roosevelt's New Deal, and he publicly said that it had been acting as a policy making, and not as a judicial body.

The US Supreme Court now has been rendering judgments in discharge of its proactive role which are in tune and temper with the changing social needs. A classic example is the role played by the apex court as an active judiciary in ending racial segregation in the U.S. In *Dred Scott* v *Sandford*,[9] the Court held that a 'Negro' was the property of his master and not a 'citizen' thereby legitimizing slavery' and discrimination on the grounds of "color and creed". This doctrine was cast away a century later by the same court in *Brown* v *Board of Education*[10] when it said that slavery is a "de-humanizing" despicable institution denying human dignity to such an extent that no court of law can uphold it; and later that Court gave it a decent burial in *Bakke's* case.[11] The Court realized that the values which guided the society when *Dred Ecott's* case came to be decided had undergone a sea change and could not stand the scrutiny of the age when the judgments in *Brown* case and *Bakkey's* were given.

8 "*Constitutional Interpretation*" by Craig R. Ducat and Harold W. Chase, 5th Ed., p. 93.
9 15 LEd 691 (1857): 19 Howard 393 (1856).
10 347 US 483: 98 LEd 873 (1954).
11 *University of California Regents* v *Bakke* 438 US 265: 57 L Ed 2d 750 (1978).

The proactive mood of the Supreme Court now-a-days was best expressed by Earl Warren, before he came to the highest office as the U.S. Chief Justice, thus: "Where there is injustice, we should correct it; where there is poverty, we should stamp it out: where there is violence, we should punish it; where there is neglect, we should provide care." As Chief Justice, Earl Warren once said: "Our judges are not monks or scientists, but participants in the living stream of our national life, steering the law between the dangers of rigidity on the one hand and formlessness on the other. Our system faces no theoretical dilemma but a single continuous problem, how to apply the never changing principles of freedom to ever changing conditions."

9 Judicial activism in UK The absence of judicial review of the constitutionality of legislation is a marked feature of the U.K. Constitution. In *Duport Steels Ltd.* v *Sirs,*[12] Lord Diplock observed that when "Parliament legislates to remedy what the majority of its members at the time perceive be a defect or a lacuna in the existing law (whether it be the written law enacted by existing statutes or the unwritten common law as it has been expounded by the judges in decided cases), the role of the judiciary is confined to ascertaining from the words that Parliament has approved as expressing its intention what that intention was, and to giving effect to it. Where the meaning of the statutory words is plain and unambiguous it is not for the judges to invent fancied ambiguities as an excuse for failing to give effect to its plain meaning because they themselves consider that the consequences of doing so would be inexpedient, or even unjust or immoral. In controversial matters such as are involved in industrial relations there is room for differences of opinion as to what is expedient, what is just and what is morally justifiable. Under our Constitution it is Parliament's opinion on these matters that is paramount".

"A statute", continued Lord Diplock in *Duport Steels*' case (supra), "passed to remedy what is perceived by Parliament to be a defect in the existing law may in actual operation turn out to have injurious consequences that Parliament did not anticipate at the time the statute was passed; if it had, it would have made some provision in the Act in order to prevent them". If this be the case, observed Lord Diplock in *Duport Steel's* case (supra), it is for Parliament, not for the judiciary, to decide whether any changes should be made to the law as stated in the Act. These are matters on which there is a wide legislative choice, the exercise of which is likely to be influenced by the political complexion

12 [1980]1 All ER 529 (QBD).

of the government and the state of public opinion at the time amending legislation is under consideration.

Lord Scarman in *Duport Steels Ltd.* v *Sirs* (supra) observed that "in the field of statute law the judge must be obedient to the will of Parliament as expressed in its enactments. In this field Parliament makes and unmakes the law, the judge's duty is to interpret and to apply the law, not to change it to meet the judge's idea of what justice requires. Interpretation does, of course, imply in the interpreter a power of choice where differing constructions are possible. But our law requires the judge to choose the construction which in his judgment best meets the legislative purpose of the enactment. If the result be unjust but ineviable, the judge may say so and invite Parliament to reconsider its provision. But he must not deny the statute. Unpalatable statute law may not be disregarded or rejected, merely because it is unpalatable. Only if a just result can be achieved without violating the legislative purpose of the statute may the judge select the construction which best suits his idea of what justice requires".

In UK, the court's power of judicial review is only confined to executive action. The judiciary can review and quash executive action if it is contrary to law made by the legislature. But even in that limited field, the court's proactive role has created a hue and cry. Lord Roskill in *CCSU* case[13] observed that "since about 1950 ..... there has been a dramatic and indeed a radical change in the scope of judicial review. This change has been described, by no means critically, as an upsurge of judicial activism." Judicial activism in Great Britain has gathered further impetus with the delivery in 1966 a Practice Statement by the House of Lords that they were not bound by their previous decisions and that they could deviate from the same when it appears right to do so. The role of the courts in reviewing administrative acts and decisions has now become far more active and creative.

Since 1967, there has been a striking increase both in the frequency with which judicial review has been invoked and in the readiness of the courts to intervene. The resurgence of judicial activism has involved a reassessment of the appropriate points at which to draw the line dividing matters of public administration and policy from issues that can properly concern the courts.

13 *Council of Civil Service Unions* v *Minister for the Civil Service* [1984]3 All ER 935, 953: [1984]3 WLR 1174 (HL): [1985] AC 374.

The nature of judicial activism in England in administrative field can best be explained by referring to a few cases.

- At common law, discovery of documents could not be ordered against the Crown in proceedings to which it was a party. This rule was abolished by Section 28 of the Crown Proceedings Act 1947, subject, however, to two important provisos: that its abolition was not to affect any rule of law which authorised the withholding of any document or the refusal to answer any question on the ground that a disclosure or answer would be injurious to the public interest; and that disclosure of the very existence of a document was not to be enforced if in the opinion of a Minister it would be injurious to disclose whether it existed.

The first proviso referred to a body of judge-made rules constituting the doctrine of "Crown privilege", as expounded by Viscount Simon L.C., speaking for a unanimous House of Lords, in *Duncan* v *Cammell, Laird & Co.*[14] According to this doctrine, no matter whether the Crown was or was not a party to the proceedings, documents otherwise relevant and liable to production must not be produced if the public interest requires that they should be withheld. This test may be found to be satisfied either (*a*) by having regard to the contents of the particular document, or (*b*) by the fact that the document belongs to a class which, on grounds of public interest, must as a class be withheld from production.

For this purpose, the sole arbiter of the public interest was to be a Minister of the Crown. If the objection to the production of a document were taken by a Minister after personal scrutiny (or, if he were unavailable, by the permanent head of the department) and in the proper manner and form, his affidavit or certificate that its production would be contrary to the public interest had to be accepted by the court as conclusive; a court was not entitled to inspect the document in order to determine whether there was any reasonable ground for the assertion that its production would be contrary to the public interest, or for any other purpose.

Examples of situations in which a Minister could reasonably object to disclosure were where disclosure would be injurious to national defence, or to good diplomatic relations, or where the practice of keeping a class of documents secret is necessary for the proper functioning of

14 [1942] AC 624, 636.

the public service.[15] A particular illustration of this last ground of objection was that the candour and completeness of communications with, or within, a public department might be prejudiced if they were ever liable to be disclosed in subsequent litigation.[16]

Some of the legal principles laid down in *Duncan's* case, and the administrative practices to which they gave their blessing, were open targets for criticism.

In 1968 the House of Lords, in *Conway* v *Rimmer*[17] took advantage of its newly assumed power to depart from its own precedents[18] and unanimously overruled the broader statements in *Duncan's* case. The claim for privilege was made on the "class" basis and the need to ensure candour of communication within the public service. The appellant, a former probationer constable, was suing the respondent, a former police superintendent, for malicious prosecution, and was seeking discovery of various reports in the hands of the police for which Crown privilege had been claimed on the ground either that they were confidential reports on suitability for employment or that they were reports to superior officers concerning investigation into the commission of crime. The claim to privilege was disallowed. The House of Lords decided to inspect the documents privately, and then ordered that they be disclosed to the appellant.

The decision was of first-rate importance, confirming the re-emergence of a judicial review as a significant factor in English administrative law. It marked the end of a long chapter and the beginning of a new one.

The House of Lords decided that when a claim to withhold evidence for reasons of public interest is duly made, a court must attempt to determine where, in the circumstances of a particular case, the balance should be struck between the possible prejudice to the interests of government and the administration of justice.

- The decision of the House of Lords in *Padfield* v *Minister of Agriculture, Fisheries and Food*[19] is an important landmark in the current era of judicial activism in the exercise of discretionary powers by an administrative authority. In the said case, the Minister had

15 *Ibid* at 642.
16 *Ibid* at 635.
17 [1968] AC 910.
18 Practice Statement [1966]1 WLR 1234.
19 [1968] AC 997.

refused to appoint a committee, as he was statutorily empowered to do when he thought fit, to investigate complaints made by members of the Milk Marketing Board that the majority of the Board had fixed milk prices in a way that was unduly unfavourable to the complainants. The House of Lords held that the Minister's discretion was not unfettered and that the reasons he had given for his refusal showed that he had acted *ultra vires* by taking into account factors that were legally irrelevant and by using his power in a way calculated to frustrate policy of the Act. The House of Lords further observed that even had the Minister given no reasons for his decision, the court would not have been powerless to intervene: for once a *prima facie* case of misuse of power had been established, it would have been open to the court to infer that the Minister had acted unlawfully if he had declined to supply any justification at all for his decision.

The *Padfield* case (supra) involved a procedural aspect of administrative decision-making. In subsequent cases,[20] the courts have not shrunk from invalidating the exercise of discretion in circumstances where it was impossible or difficult for the same substantive decision to be reached within the existing statutory framework. Another feature of the cases decided after the Padfield has been the willingness of the courts to assert their power to scrutinize the factual bases upon which discretionary powers have been exercised.

Judicial activism in U.K. assumed such aggressive stance that in some of the cases the House of Lords had to intervene to thwart a possible clash with the executive and the Parliament. Two of these cases relate to judicial activism of Lord Denning.

In Re. *a Company*,[21] the Court of Appeal presided over by Lord Denning M.R. entertained an appeal and reversed the trial judge in a case in which the statute provided for no appeal. In so doing, Lord Denning was of the view that the provision excluding an appeal "is not a bar to the appeal to this court. There are many cases now which show that if a judge misconstrues a statute by giving himself jurisdiction when he has none or by refusing jurisdiction when he has it, then he makes an error which goes to the jurisdiction: and there is an appeal to this court, no matter how wide the words which seem to exclude it ...."

20 *Congreve* v *Home Office* [1976] QB 629; *Laker Airways Ltd.* v *Department of Trade* [1977] QB 643; *R.* v *Home Secretary, ex p. Phansopkar* [1976] QB 606; *Daymond* v *Plymouth City Council* [1976] AC 609; *Secretary of State for Education and Science* v *Tameside M.B.C.* [1977] AC 1014.

21 [1980]1 All ER 284.

The Court of Appeal was, of course, reversed by the House of Lords in Re. *Racal Communications Ltd.*[22]

In *Duport Steels* v *Sirs*,[23] in reversing the Court of Appeal which did not follow a decision directly in point of the House of Lords, Lord Diplock said: "It endangers continued public confidence in the political impartiality of the judiciary, which is essential to the continuance of the rule of law, if judges, under the guise of interpretation, provide their own preferred amendments to statutes which experience of their operation has shown to have had consequences that members of the court before whom the matter comes consider to be injurious to the public interest."

And Lord Scarman in *Duport Steels* case (supra) started his discussion with the observation that the case raised "some profound questions as to the proper relationship in our society between the courts, the government and Parliament", and went on to say: "My basic criticism of ... judgments in the Court of Appeal is that in their desire to do justice the court failed to do justice according to law. When one is considering law in the hands of the judges, law means the body of rules and guidelines within which society requires its judges to administer justice. Legal systems differ in the width of the discretionary power granted to judges: but in developed societies limits are invariably set, beyond which the judges may not go. Justice in such societies is not left to the unguided, even if experienced, sage sitting under the spreading oak tree".

Lord Scarman in *Duport Steels* case (supra) further observed: "In our society the judges have in some aspects of their work a discretionary power to do justice so wide that they may be regarded as law makers. The common law and equity, both of them in essence systems of private law, are fields where, subject to the increasing intrusion of statute law, society has been content to allow the judges to formulate and develop the law. The judges, even in this, their very own field of creative endeavour, have accepted, in the interests of certainty, the self-denying ordinance of *stare decisis*, the doctrine of binding precedent; and no doubt this judicially imposed limitation on judicial law making has helped to maintain confidence in the certainty and even-handedness of the law."

22 [1980]2 All ER 634.
23 [1980]1 All ER 529.

"But in the field of statute law", continued Lord Scarman in *Duport Steels* case (supra), "the judge must be obedient to the will of Parliament as expressed in its enactments. In this field Parliament makes and unmakes the law, the judge's duty is to interpret and to apply the law, not to change it to meet the judge's idea of what justice requires. Interpretation does, of course, imply in the interpreter a power of choice where differing constructions are possible. But our law requires the judge to choose the construction which in his judgment best meets the legislative purpose of the enactment. If the result be unjust but inevitable, the judge may say so and invite Parliament to reconsider its provision. But he must not deny the statute. Unpalatable statute law may not be disregarded or rejected, merely because it is unpalatable. Only if a just result can be achieved without violating the legislative purpose of the statute may the judge select the construction which best suits his idea of what justice requires. Further, in our system the *stare decisis* rule applies as firmly to statute law as it does to the formulation of common law and equitable principles. And the keystone of *stare decisis* is loyalty throughout the system to the decisions of the Court of Appeal and this House. The Court of Appeal may not overrule a House of Lords decision; and only in the exceptional circumstances set out in the practice statement of 26th July 1966 will this House refuse to follow its own previous decisions."

"Within these limits," Lord Scarman observed in *Duport Steels* case (supra), "which cannot be said in a free society possessing elective legislative institutions to be narrow or constrained, judges, as the remarkable judicial career of Lord Denning MR himself shows, have a genuine creative role. Great judges are in their different ways judicial activists. But the Constitution's separation of powers, or more accurately functions, must be observed if judicial independence is not to be put at risk. For, if people and Parliament come to think that the judicial power is to be confined by nothing other than the judge's sense of what is right (or, as Selden put it, by the length of the Chancellor's foot), confidence in the judicial system will be replaced by fear of it becoming uncertain and arbitrary in its application. Society will then be ready for Parliament to cut the power of the judges. Their power to do justice will become more restricted by law than it need be, or is today."

10 Judicial activism in India The Indian judiciary is stronger than that of the US. It has the power of judicial review over constitutional amendments, which the American judiciary does not possess. The scope for judicial activism in India is much more, therefore, than that existing either in USA or UK.

India is a multi lingual and multi religious country. Between the society and the culture of the country on the one hand and the Constitution of India on the other, Justice Bhagwati asserts, a constant contradiction remains. One of the major contradictions is that when the caste issue dominates the Indian society with the people belonging to the lower caste deprived of opportunity, the Indian Constitution guarantees equal opportunities for all. Caught between their inherent contradictions, the apex court of the country, according to Justice Bhagwati, had to make intervention on many occasions when the problems arising out of the contradictions went out of control of the political power of the country. Judicial activism thus started to maintain balance. Justice Bhagwati in this context says that it is axiomatic that if a question brought before the court is purely a political question not involving determination of any legal or constitutional right or obligation, the court would not entertain it, since the court is concerned only with adjudication of legal rights and liabilities. But merely because a question has a political complexion, that by itself is not ground, warns Justice Bhagwati, why the court should shrink from performing its duty under the Constitution, if it raises an issue of Constitutional determination.

A few examples may focus on the trend, nature and extent of judicial activism and the judges role in law making in India.

- Soon after the Constitution of India came into force in 1950, the Supreme Court in *A.K. Gopalan's* case[1] placed a rather narrow and restrictive interpretation upon Article 21[2] of the Constitution. By a majority, it held in that case that "... 'the procedure established by law' means procedure established by a law made by the State" and the Court refused to infuse in that procedure the principles of natural justice. The judgment in *Gopalan's* case (supra) was mainly based on the literal interpretation of language of the Constitution and the facts of the particular case before the Court. The law has not, however, remained static on the issue. Twenty eight years after the judgment in *Gopalan's* case (supra), the Supreme Court acting through Justice Bhagwati in *Maneka Gandhi's* case[3] gave wider meanings of the words "life", "liberty" and "procedure" established by law" in Article 21 of the

1 *A.K. Gopalan* v *State of Madras* AIR 1950 SC 27: 1950 SCR 88.
2 Article 21 provides: "No person shall be deprived of his life or persons liberty except according to procedure established by law".
3 *Maneka Gandhi* v *Union of India* AIR 1978 SC 597: (1978)1 SCC 248.

Constitution. It was pronounced in *Maneka Gandhi's* case (supra) that the procedure contemplated by Article 21 must be 'right, just and fair' and not arbitrary; it must pass the test of reasonableness and the procedure should be in conformity with the principles of natural justice and unless it is so, it would be no procedure at all and the requirement of Article 21 would not be satisfied. It may be noted that the right to life and personal liberty under procedure established by law in Article 21 has been converted *de facto* and *de jure* into a procedural Due Process Clause by the decision in *Maneka Gandhi's* case contrary to the intention of the makers of the Constitution and ignoring the advice Mr. Justice Frankfurter of USA gave to the Constitutional Adviser Dr. B.N. Rao. Based on *Maneka Gandhi's* case (supra), a number of decisions[4] followed that created a new normative regime of rights insisting that the State cannot act arbitrarily but instead must act reasonably and in the public interest on pain of its action being invalidated by judicial intervention and led to the development of most spectacular evolution of the law on Article 21 of the Constitution. The Supreme Court thus through its proactive role widening the import of Article 21 expanded the ambit of constitutional provisions to enforce the human rights of the citizens and sought to bring the Indian law in conformity with the global trends in human rights jurisprudence. The case of *Maneka Gandhi* represented a high-water mark in judicial activism in the area of personal freedoms and Justice Bhagwati was held by civil liberatarians as a 'trailblazer'.

- In the post emergency period, the Supreme Court using its proactive role developed a new doctrine called the doctrine of arbitrariness to weed out substantive inequality. Here also Justice Bhagwati's activist approach played a dominant role in the interpretation of the equality clause (Article 14) in the Constitution. In *E.P. Royappa* v *State of Tamil Nadu*,[5] Justice Bhagwati speaking on behalf of himself, Justice Chandrachud, and Justice Krishna Iyer held that an action that was arbitrary was *per se* violative of equality. While explaining this new doctrine in *Ajay Hasia* v *Khalid Mujib*,[6] Justice Bhagwati said: "It was

4 *M.H. Hoskot* v *State of Maharashtra* AIR 1978 SC 1548: (1978)3 SCC 544: 1978 Cr LJ 1978: (1979)1 SCR 192; *Hussainara Khatoon* v *Home Secretary, State of Bihar* AIR 1979 SC 1960: AIR 1979 SC 1369: AIR 1979 SC 1377: AIR 1979 SC 1819; *Sunil Batra* v *Delhi Administration* (1978)4 SCC 494: AIR 1978 SC 1675: 1978 Cr LJ 1741: (1979)1 SCR 392; *Sunil Batra* v *Delhi Administration* 1980 Cr LJ 1099: (1980)2 SCR 557: AIR 1980 SC 1579; *Francis Coralie Mullin* v *Administrator, Union Territory of Delhi* AIR 1981 SC 746: 1981 Cr LJ 306: (1981)2 SCR 516: (1981)1 SCC 608.

5 AIR 1974 SC 555: (1974)2 SCR 348.

6 AIR 1981 SC 487.

for the first time in *E.P. Royappa* v *State of Tamil Nadu* that this Court (Supreme Court) laid bare a new dimension of Article 14 and pointed out that that article has highly activist magnitude and it embodies a guarantee against arbitrariness. Equality is a dynamic concept with many aspects and dimensions and it cannot be 'cribbed, cabined and confined' within traditional and *doctrinaire limits*. From a positivist point of view, equality is antithetic to arbitrariness. In fact, equality and arbitrariness are sworn enemies: one belongs to the rule of law in a republic, while the other, to the whim and caprive of an absolute monarch." The doctrine of arbitrariness expanded it wings in the field of natural justice also. In *Union of India* v *Tulsiram Patel*,[7] the Supreme Court observed that violation of a rule of natural justice results in arbitrariness which is the same as discrimination and where discrimination is the result of the State action, it is a violation of Article 14 of the Constitution.

- In 1978, Parliament by the Constitution (Forty-fourth Amendment) Act, 1978 amended the Constitution to delete the right to property and compensation from the chapter of fundamental rights and make it only a legal right which one could be deprived of by the authority of the law. The amended right was placed under Article 300A of the Constitution. It is important to note that Parliament could delete the right to property as a fundamental right by constitutional amendment in view of the unanimous finding of the Supreme Court in *Kesavananda Bharati* v *State of Kerala*[8] that right to property was not a basic feature of the Constitution. In that sense, the judiciary conceded that it was for Parliament to decide the extent of property rights in the Constitution and determine the economic policies of the nation without the judiciary sitting in judgment over them. The trend still continues. A case in point is *Balco Employees Union* v *Union of India*,[9] where the Supreme Court refused to interfere in the economic policies of the State. At the same time, however, the Court in *Kesavananda's* case (supra) seized and retained the commanding heights of judicial power by asserting the power of the judiciary to annul a constitutional law. Judicial review and the independence of the judiciary were pronounced to be the basic unalterable features of the Constitution. It was held in *Kesavananda's* case by the process of judicial interpretation that though in Article 368 of the Constitution there are no express words which limit the power of

7 AIR 1985 SC 1416: (1985)3 SCC 398.
8 AIR 1973 SC 1461: (1973)4 SCC 225.
9 (2002)2 SCC 33.

Parliament for amending the Constitution yet that power is not unlimited or unrestricted. The power of amendment of the Constitution, the Supreme Court observed, does not entitle Parliament to amend the Constitution in such way as to alter or affect the basic structure of the Constitution. All the constitutional amendments nullified after the *Kesavananda* doctrine are in essence those which denied judicial review or interfered with judicial process. Thus, in *Minerva Mills Ltd.* v *Union of India*[10] the Supreme Court observed that section 55 of the Constitution (Forty-second Amendment) Act 1976, which inserted sub-sections (4) and (5) in Article 368 is void since, in the views of Chandrachud, CJ, Gupta, Untwalia and Kailasam, JJ., it removed all limitations on the power of the Parliament to amend the Constitution and confered power upon it to amend the Constitution damaging or destroying its basic or essential features or structure and in the opinion of justice Bhagwati it damaged the basic structure of the Constitution and went beyond the amending power of Parliament.

• Public law jurisprudence necessitates the adoption of different approach by the judiciary while grappling with issues of public importance. An area of public importance where the judiciary made an innovative approach was standing for access to the court. The Supreme Court found that in a country which has vast differentials, it cannot turn away from the claims and demands of social justice and still honour its claim to be a court for all the citizens of the country. It found that the main obstacle which deprived the poor and the disadvantaged of effective access to justice was the traditional rule of standing which insists that only a person who has suffered a specific legal injury by reason of actual or threatened violation of his legal rights or legally protected interests can bring an action for judicial redress. It is only the holder of the right who can sue for actual or threatened violation of the right, and no other person can file an action to vindicate such a right. The rule effectively barred the doors of the court to large masses of people who on account of poverty and ignorance could not utilize the judicial process. It was felt that even if legal aid offices were established for them, it would be impossible for them to take advantage of the legal aid programme because most of them lack awareness of their constitutional and legal rights; and even if they were made aware of their rights, many of them would lack the capacity to assert them. In what is known as the Judges Appointments and Transfer case,[11] the Supreme Court acting through Justice Bhagwati departed from the

10 AIR 1980 SC 1789.
11 *S.P. Gupta* v *Union of India* 1981 Supp (1) SCC 574: AIR 1982 SC 149.

traditional rule of standing and broadened access to justice and also evolved, institutionalized and legitimized what has come to be known as "epistolary jurisdiction", where the Court can be moved by just addressing a letter on behalf of the disadvantaged class of persons. Epistolary jurisdiction was a major breakthrough achieved by the Supreme Court through its proactive role in bringing justice closer to the large masses of people.

As a result of the liberalization of the *locus standi* rule and legalization and institutionalization of the espistolary jurisdiction by Justice Bhagwati, the portals of the court were thrown open to the poor, the ignorant and the illiterate and their cases started coming before the court through public interest litigation, otherwise shortly known as "PIL". Through public interest litigation, the court has granted access to persons inspired by public interest to invite judicial intervention against abuse of power or misuse of power or inaction of the government. "PIL", Justice Bhagwati says, "represents a sustained effort on the part highest judiciary to provide access to justice for the deprived sections of Indian humanity. With a legal architecture designed for a colonial administration and a jurisprudence structured around a free-market economy, the Indian judiciary could not accomplish much in fulfilling the constitutional aspirations of the vast masses of underprivileged people during the first three decades of freedom". It is interesting to note that the initial justification for PIL was a limited one, namely, the amelioration of the plight of the poor and the disadvantaged and the enforcement of their human rights. The Supreme Court in the beginning started by dealing with cases involving prisoners and gross human rights abuses.

The first PIL case involved a *habeas corpus* petition by a Delhi-based lawyer, Kapila Hingorani, on behalf of 19 prisoners who had been held in custody for years on end pending trial in the State of Bihar. Mrs. Hingorani had filed her petition after reading in a newspaper article about such 'undertrials', many of whom had been detained for period longer than the maximum prison terms awardable for the offences with which they had been charged. The Supreme Court issued orders releasing such prisoners *en masse* on personal bonds. In the legal world, the case is known as *Husainara Khatoon* v *State of Bihar*.[12] Close on its heels, came another case *Khatri* v *State of Bihar*[13] in which

12 AIR 1979 SC 1360.
13 AIR 1981 SC 928.

several inmates of a jail, also in Bihar, had been willfully blinded by the police. Here, the Supreme Court apart from ordering rehabilitation of the inmates through vocational training in an institution for the blind awarded also monetary compensation to the victims. Soon the areas under PIL expanded to include bonded labour,[14] unorganized labour,[15] tribes affected by developmental projects,[16] environmental protection,[17] public health,[18] public sanitation,[19] management of state-run hospitals,[20] management of blood banks,[1] conservation of wildlife,[2] distribution of government largesse,[3] road traffic management,[4] maintenance of standards in public education,[5] to mention only a few.

In *Laxmi Kant Pandey's* case,[6] the Supreme Court speaking through Justice Bhagwati laid down guidelines for inter-country adoption.[7] Guidelines were also issued by the apex court against sexual harassment of working women at the workplace.[8] In yet another case, the Supreme Court framed schemes of admission in educational institutions throughout India, and made the right to education into a fundamental right from a Directive of State Policy.[9] In issuing such guidelines and/or schemes, the Supreme Court's action in the garb of judicial law-making amounted to legislating like a legislature. Critics often say that the making of an entirely new law which the Supreme Court did through directions in the above cases is not legitimate judicial function. But Justice Bhagwati says that the Supreme Court had to legislate through directions only because the State had failed to make any law to deal with the situations such as inter-country adoption and that its direction could be replaced by legislation of the legislature. The Supreme Court's decisions in various public interest litigation cases had so much

14 *Bandhua Mukti Morcha* v *Union of India* AIR 1984 SC 802.
15 *People's Union of Democratic Rights* v *Union of India* AIR 1982 SC 1473.
16 *Karjan Jalasay YASAS Samity* v *State of Gujarat* AIR 1987 SC 532.
17 *MC Mehta* v *Union of India* AIR 1998 SC 2340.
18 *Ashok* v *Union of India* (1997)5 SCC 10.
19 *Municipal Council, Ratlam* v *Vardichand* AIR 1980 SC 1622.
20 *S.R. Kapoor* v *Union of India* AIR 1990 SC 752.
1 *Common Cause* v *Union of India* (1996)1 SCC 753.
2 *M.C. Mehta* v *Union of India* (1997)3 SCC 715.
3 *Common Cause* v *Union of India* (1996)6 SCC 530.
4 *M.C. Mehta* v *Union of India* AIR 1998 SC 186.
5 *Meera Massy* v *S.R. Mehrotra* AIR 1998 SC 1153.
6 *Laxmi Kant Pandey* v *Union of India* AIR 1987 SC 232.
7 (AUTHORS' NOTE: For detailed guidelines *vide* Chapter 3.
8 *Visakha* v *State of Rajasthan* AIR 1997 SC 3011: (1997)6 SCC 241; *Apparel Export Promotion Council* v *A.K. Chopra* (1999)1 SCC 759.
9 *Unnikrishnan* v *A.P.* (1993)4 SCC 111.

social, political and economic ramifications that the apex court earned the epithet of 'the world's most powerful Court".

11 Judicial activism—under attack The legislators, politicians and the executives have often accused the judiciary of judicial overreach and taking over executive or legislative functions. On 7th December 2006, a bitterly divided Lok Sabha came together with remarkable alacrity to protect its turf against what is called "judicial overactivism". Though the debate admitted in Lok Sabha was to discuss only "judicial activism", the mood could barely conceal the political determination of the House to beat back an active judiciary. The protest against judicial overreach began in the form of a high concern by CPI leader Mr. Gurudas Dasgupta over the judiciary treading on the toes of the executive and legislature in complete disregard of the boundary laid down in the Constitution. Within no time, it had generated enough passion to lead Speaker Mr. Somnath Chatterjee to widen the ambit of the debate by converting what was supposed to be a discussions on Dasgupta's calling attention motion into a general discussion under Rule 193 of the Lok Sabha Rules. In essence, the discussion was held to set the stage for a collective demand for the judiciary to mind its own business.

Addressing a conference of Chief Ministers and Chief Justices on 8th April 2007, Dr. Manmohan Singh, the Prime Minister of India, zeroed in on PILs—the option often used by interest groups and individuals to challenge government policy—to argue that these should be subjected to filter. Though PILs have great utility for initiating corrective action, they should not become vehicles for settling political or other scores, observed the Prime Minister. "We need standards to screen PILs so that only PILs with a justifiable cause of action based on judicially manageable standards are taken up", he said, adding that the Supreme Court should frame rules in this regard. He reminded the judiciary that each organ of the state has "constitutionally assigned roles" and "each must respect the functions of the other" and further that the "dividing line between judicial activism and judicial overreach is a thin one". Citing an example, he said compelling action by authorities of state through the power of mandamus was an inherent power vested in the judiciary. But substituting *mandamus* with a takeover function of another institution may become a case of overreach. In other words, the Prime Minister had all but accused the judiciary of judicial overreach and taking over executive or legislative functions.

Delivering on 26th April 2007, the K.N. Katju Memorial Lecture on '*Separation of Powers under the Constitution and Judicial Activism*',

Lok Sabha Speaker Mr. Somnath Chatterjee warned: "The contention that the judiciary should take on itself the onerous responsibility of the governance of the country, in matters which the Constitution has imposed on either the executive or legislature, has serious implications". In a democracy, Chatterjee said, the executive authority 'must be and is accountable' to the people, and asked whether the judiciary was "accountable to anyone" if it "interfered" with the policy decisions of the executive and took decisions of a clearly administrative nature. The responsibility of managing public affairs should be left to those mandated by the Constitution because 'this accountability is what differentiates democracy from other systems of governance', he said. The lines separating the different organs of the state were getting blurred, Chatterjee said, as a 'a section of the judiciary seems to be of the view that it has authority by way of what is described as "judicial activism" to exercise powers which are earmarked by the Constitution for the legislature or the executive'.

In an article "Judicial 'overreach'? Overruled", published in the Guest Column of the Hindustan Times, Kolkata, on April 29, 2007, Fali S. Nariman, a leading constitutional expert and practicing lawyer wrote: "The 'Judicial overreach' the Prime Minister spoke about is the direct result of legislative and executive neglect or 'under-reach': poor performance in the making of laws and their execution. If the judges need to introspect, politicians also need to introspect and ask themselves whether they have fulfilled the aspirations of the people who put them at the wheel of governance. If judges are to get off the backs of parliamentarians, politicians and bureaucrats those who claim the right to govern must come up with a much better record of performance: only when they do, will the people of this great country give us back, majority governments both at the Centre and in the states".

The common man's view is that judiciary is not overstepping its limits in any way. All it is doing is ensuring that the law is enforced properly and the basic human rights embodied in the Constitution are made meaningful to the large masses of people in the country. If, as alleged by the politicians, the judiciary is encroaching on the turf of the executive and legislature, it is entirely due to the inaction on their part in performing and discharging their constitutional obligation. That obligation being sometimes a grey area, it has helped the court in expanding its area of influence. For instance, it cannot be said to be judicial adventurism when the Supreme Court rehabilated child worker, freed bonded labourers, got the load off scavengers, banned the felling of trees in the northeast or ordered the use of eco-friendly fuels in Delhi and Agra or the shifting of tanneries from Kolkata relying on Article 21 of the Constitution. It bears mentioning that protecting and improving the environment and public health are among the Directive Principles of State Policy and it is in the larger interests of society and citizens that the apex court had to intervene particularly when the legislature and the executive had failed to attend to these problems and carry out their constitutional obligations in this respect.

It is sometimes said that framing policy being the job of a government that is democratically elected and accountable, the courts should refrain from interfering in public matters. True it is, says Justice Bhagwati, that the courts cannot and should not interfere in policy matters but where the situation so demands the court within the parameters of the Constitution can certainly intervene in larger interest. It has to be noted in this context that instances are not rare when the government takes shelter behind the judiciary in cases it has to take unpopular actions like clearing slums and encroachment of public places. However, when enforcing orders leads to violent clashes as was seen in the recent sealing drive against unauthorized shops in Delhi, the government finds court orders unrealistic. That shows that the government adopts different yardsticks to suit its own convenience.

When the court is apprised of and is satisfied about gross violation of basic human rights, Justice Bhagwati views , it cannot fold its hands in despair and look the other way. It must respond to the cry of the oppressed and the down-trodden for justice by taking necessary action within the parameters of the Constitution and pass appropriate orders or directions in order to render full and effective relief.

The plea, often taken by those speaking against judicial activism, that the Constitution has not authorized the justices to sit in judgment on the wisdom of what the legislature and the executive branch do does not seem to be a sound one. The court always in exercise of its power of judicial review can void an executive action and even strike down a legislation found to be inconsistent with the Constitution. It does not matter that the legislation was passed unanimously or by majority decision by the Parliament. Those entrusted under the Constitution with the responsibility of managing public affairs, says Justice Bhagwati, should discharge it in a just, fair and reasonable manner. The requirement that every state action must satisfy the test of fairness and non-arbitrariness are judicially evolved principles which now form part of the constitutional law. Failure to do so and comply with the same only invite judicial intervention. It is to be noted that the function of the courts of law is to administer justice according to law and in doing so they need to respond to the hopes and aspirations of the people of the country.

It is essential in a country governed by the rule of law that every decision of the court of law must be made under the rule of law and not under the pressure of one group or another or under threat of adverse criticism by politicians. If a judge is to face personal criticism by political or pressure groups while deciding a case, it would most certainly undermine the independence of the judiciary. Unfortunately, this is what is happening now-a-days. The prevailing situation is explained by Justice Bhagwati thus: "There is a pernicious tendency on the part of some to attack judges if the decision does not go the way they want or if it is not in accordance with their views. Of course, there is nothing wrong in critically evaluating the judgment given by a judge because, as observed by Lord Atkin, justice is not a cloistered virtue and she must be allowed to suffer the criticism and respectful, though outspoken, comments of ordinary men and women. But improper and intemperate criticism of judges stemming from dissatisfaction with their decisions constitutes a serious inroad into the independence of the judiciary and, whatever may be the form or shape which such criticism takes, it has the effect of eroding the independence of the judiciary. Each attack on a judge for a decision given by him or her is an attack on the independence of the judiciary because it represents an attempt on the part of those who indulge in such criticism to coerce judicial conformity with their own preconceptions and, thereby, influence the decision making process".

Prof. H.P. Lee of Manash University, Australia, in one of his writings said that court should not be immune from criticism. "On the contrary, the judgment of the courts should be scrutinized and critically evaluated. But those who hold positions of power and influence in the country have a responsibility to ensure that the line between measured criticism of judgments and denigration of judges is not traversed".[10]

In Canada, it is said the journalists have declared open season on the judiciary. But often it is the politicians who are the worst offenders, as the experience of Australia and the United States show. In Australia,

10 H.P. Lee: "*Subverting Judicial Independence*", 1 CLPR (3)35 at 56 (1998).

Justice Michael Kirby says, the Wik decision[11] on native title fights brought on criticism in the most offensive language mostly from politicians. The justices were labeled as "bogus", "pusillanimous and evasive", "guilty of plunging Australia into an abyss, "a pathetic self-appointed group of Kings and Queens," etc. The matter went to such an extent that Chief Justice Brennan responded by way of an unprecedented letter to the Deputy Prime Minister on his Wik criticism. The experience of the United States was related by Justice Kirby thus: "The prize for the worst examples in a developed country in the genre

11 AUTHORS' NOTE: The issue in *Wik Peoples* v *Queensland* [(1996)187 CLR 1 was whether pastoral leases granted under colonial and State legislation necessarily extinguished native title over the same land. Although pastoral leases occupy two-fifths of Australian continent, the Native Title Act 1993 had not addressed the relationship between pastoral leases and native title in detail. Rather, relying on obiter comments in *Mabo* v *Queensland* (No. 2) [(1992)175 CLR 1, 68 (Brennan, J.), 110 (Deane and Gaudron, JJ.)], parliament had assumed that native title no longer existed on most pastoral land. In Wik, however, the High Court ruled by four to three that Parliament's assumption had been mistaken. Toohey, Gaudron, Gummow, and Kirby, JJ. formed the Wik majority. In their separate judgments they concluded that pastoral leases were statutory creations and, as such, did not necessarily grant lessees a right to exclusive possession at odds with native title. Instead, the rights attaching to the various forms of pastoral lease in Australia, and the impact of those rights on the common law entitlements of traditional owners, needed to be determined on a case-by-case basis. All four judges affirmed, however, that in the event of inconsistency between the rights of a pastoral lessee and those of native title holders, the pastoralists' entitlements took priority over those of traditional owners. By contrast, Brennan, CJ., with whom Dawson and McHugh, JJ. concurred, dissented. Consistently with parliament's understanding of the effect of Mabo, Brennan, CJ. found that the traditional form of pastoral lease in Australia operated to extinguish native title.

The finding of Wik—in effect that native title potentially covered far more of Australia than previously thought 'caused immediate political uproar'. The day after the judgment was handed down, the front page of the leading national daily newspaper seized on how the result in Wik had been 'unexpected' and 'rejects a key plank of the [recently elected] Howard Government's native title policy'. Over the weeks and months that followed, the High Court was subjected to a flood of criticism notably from the right of Australian politics, including from many senior political figures. Deputy Prime Minister Tim Fischer, in particular, directly reproached the Wik majority for 'judicial activism', describing the judgment of Kirby, J. as 'awful'. Other attacks on the Court by conservative politicians were even more strident. For instance, Queensland Premier Rob Borbidge was reported as describing the Court 'as an embarrassment which had to be brought under control'. It was engaged, he said, in a 'very deliberate strategy it seems .... to usurp the sovereignty of the parliaments of Australia'. Premier Borbidge argued for fundamental changes to the Court including the introduction of fixed-term judicial appointments and the creation of a body to oversee its work. One State Attorney General even argued for the election of judges.

of political attack on the judiciary must go to the United States of America. Of particular concern to outsiders (and possibly to citizens as well) has been the appearance of federal political leaders, looking around for themes for their electoral campaigns, selecting the easy targets of the judiciary as a means of promoting themselves as tough on law and order".[12] Indian politicians who have been ranting against judicial activism are no doubt in illustrious company of their brethren in Australia and United States.

12 Judicial activism—not an unguided missile Judicial activism, says Justice Bhagwati, casts a very delicate responsibility of judicial accountability which should pervade all through in the mind of the judiciary and it should neither give the impression of exceeding its jurisdiction or abdicating it. Judges in India are not in an unchartered sea in the decision making process. They have to justify their decision making within the framework of constitutional values. Shortly before his appointment to the High Court by the Howard Government in Australia in 2003, Justice Dyson Heydon delivered a speech entitled '*Judicial Activism and the Death of the Rule of Law*'[13] where Heydon said: "The more the courts freely change the law, the more the public will come to view their function as political; the more they would rightly be open to vigorous and direct pubic attack on political grounds; and the greater will be the demand for public hearings into the politics of judicial candidates before appointment and greater control over judicial behaviour after appointment ... All will multiply the threats to the rule of law which judicial activism has created."

Judicial activism, therefore, requires controlled exercise of judicial power. The decisions of courts must have jurisprudential base with clearly discernible principles. In a social environment where legislatures and bureaucrats have failed, judicial activism, views Justice Bhagwati, has to play within its constitutional obligations an important role in order to reach social justice to the suffering people.

Every organ of government, be it the executive or the legislature or the judiciary, derives its authority from the Constitution and it has to act within the limits of its authority and whether it has done so or not is for the court to decide. The court is the ultimate interpreter of the Constitution and when there is manifestly unauthorised exercise of

12 The Hon'ble Justice Michael Kirby: "*Attacks on Judges—A Universal Phenomenon*", 72 ALJ 599 at 601 (1998).

13 (2004)10 Otago LR 493.

power under the Constitution, it is the duty of the court to intervene. Let it not be forgotten, Justice Bhagwati asserts, the court's task is to identify the constitutional values in the constitutional plan and to work them into life in the cases that reach the court. Tact and restraint ought to temper any power but courage and the acceptance of responsibility have their place too. The court has sworn the oath of allegiance to the Constitution and is accountable to the people of the country. Whenever there is any violation of the Constitution, the court must intervene and set it right.

Principles to guide judicial activism Justice Bhagwati refers to a number of principles which a judge should remember in discharging his role as an activist judge in various fields of his activities and those are summarized as under:

(I) WHEN TWO LAWS CONFLICT WITH EACH OTHER. "It is emphatically the province and duty of the judicial department to say what the law is. Those who apply the rule to particular cases, must of necessity expound and interpret that rule. If two laws conflict with each other ,the courts must decide on the operation of each".[14]

"So if a law be in opposition to the constitution; if both the law and the constitution apply to a particular case, so that the court must either decide that case conformably to the law, disregarding the constitution; or conformably to the constitution, disregarding the law, the court must determine which of these conflicting rules governs the case. This is of the very essence of judicial duty.

"If, then, the courts are to regard the constitution, and the constitution is superior to any ordinary act of the legislature, the constitution, and no such ordinary act, must govern the case to which they both apply .... Why otherwise does it (the constitution) direct the judges to take an oath to support it?".[14]

(II) WHEN STATE POLICY IS INVOLVED. It is generally accepted that in matters of public policy courts will decline to exercise its power of judicial review unless the policy is either against the Constitution or some statute or is actuated by *mala fides*. Legality of the policy and not the wisdom or soundness thereof can be the subject of judicial review. Courts cannot act as appellate authorities examining the correctness, stability and appropriateness of a policy. The position of the law in U.K. and India on the issue may in this context be referred to.

14 *Marbury* v *Madison* [1803]5 US 137.

Lord Justice Lawton in *Laker Airways*[15] observed: "In the United Kingdom aviation policy is determined by ministers within the legal framework set out by Parliament. Judges have nothing to do with either policy making or the carrying out of policy. Their function is to decide whether a minister has acted within the powers given to him by statute or the common law. If he is declared by a court, after due process of law, to have acted outside his powers, he must stop doing what he has done until such time as Parliament gives him the powers he wants. In a case such as this I regard myself as a referee. I can blow my judicial whistle when the ball goes out of play; but when the game restarts I must neither take part in it nor tell the players how to play".

In so far as India is concerned, says Justice Bhagwati, the constitutionality of a policy may be liable to be tested under the judicial scanner.

(III) WHEN ADMINISTRATIVE DECISIONS ARE UNDER CHALLENGE.[16] When in arriving at a decision, the administrative authority takes into account factors that are irrelevant or uses its power *mala fide* or for collateral purpose or in a manner calculated to frustrate policy of any Act or gives no reason for its decision or a *prima facie* case of misuse of power is established, it would be open to the court to intervene. Courts will not be slow to exercise the powers of judicial review in order to strike down illegality or abuse or misabuse of power. It has to be noted that once a body is admitted to be a statutory body charged with the performance of a public duty or it is an authority charged with any executive or administrative functions, there is jurisdiction to grant an order of judicial review in a case when the statutory body or the executive or administrative authority fails to perform that public duty. A case in point is one relating to environment and forests. The State obligation for protection and improvement of environment and safeguarding of forests and wildlife is a principle fundamental in governance under Article 48A of the Constitution. This is also a fundamental duty of every citizen under Article 51A and it has been recognised by the Supreme Court as fundamental right included under Article 21 of the Constitution. A serious global threat to the environment and forests, coupled with the apathy and the inertia of the executive to take prompt action compelled judicial intervention which had the desired positive effect.[17]

15 [1977]2 WLR 234 at 267.

16 AUTHORS' NOTE: For detailed discussions on 'Administrative decisions and scope for judicial interference': Vide Chapter 10 on 'Judicial Review'.

17 *T.N. Godavarman Thirumulkpad* v *Union of India* AIR 1997 SC 1228.

(IV) WHEN LEGISLATIVE ACTIONS ARE QUESTIONED. The question as to whether the legislature applied its mind to the provisions of the statute before passing it and the motive of the legislature in passing a statute — both cannot be enquired into by the judiciary in exercise of its power of judicial review. A court can declare a statute unconstitutional only when it transgresses constitutional limitations. The interpretation of constitutional and legislative provisions change with the changing social environment Oliver Wendell Holmes said: "we do not realize how large a part of our law is open to reconsideration upon a slight change in the habit of the public mind".[18]

It bears mentioning here that it is not possible for any legislature within the time and resources at its disposal to anticipate all permutation and combination of circumstances which may arise in the future and the legislation which it, therefore, enacts cannot be adequate to deal with all such future situations and consequently there are bound to be gaps which the courts administering and applying the law have to fill in by constructive interpretation of the provisions of law having regard to its object and purpose. This is, Justice Bhagwati says, where the judiciary takes part in the law making process. It moulds the law, shapes the law by a process of creative interpretation and makes out of it a living organism suited to the needs of the changing society. "Our system of law permits", in the words of Mr. Justice Michael Kirby of Australia, "brilliant interaction between the stable, unelected, confirming elements of government (in the Court ....) and the democratic, creative but sometimes timorous and often unreliable elements of the temporary changing scene of political government (represented in Parliament and in the ministry)". "Out of the interaction", continues Justice Kirby, "between these branches of Government one hopes that a harmony will emerge. Ordinarily it does".

(V) WHEN POWER OF JUDICIAL REVIEW IS EXERCISED. Judicial statesmanship demands that a judge must assert the power of judicial review in such manner that the order made by the judge is capable of being implemented.

13 Conclusion There are a large number of people facing exploitation and injustice, and in this conflict, violence and stress of the people, Justice Bhagwati says, Indian Judiciary has an important role to play. The judiciary has to prevent and remedy abuse and misabuse of powers. Judges have to abandon their self-restraint and adopt activist

18 Holmes: *The Path of the Law* (1920).

role in order to bring social and distributive justice to these suffering people. The judges have to bring about innovations in the judicial process and procedure so as to meet the challenges and hurdles in ensuring social justice to these suffering groups.

We have to note, in the words of V.R. Krishna Iyer, that the "richest man in the world, with the most luxurious life ever, is in India now. The poorest pariah who prefers suicide to humiliating life, being landless, homeless and starving, is also in India. And yet in constitutional diction we are a socialist, secular, democratic Republic. 'The unkindest cut of all' is that Bharat boasts of a judicature which blinks at the commercialization of primary and higher education, dignity of life, and *fiat justicia* which, in reality, remains 'untouchable and unreachable'. Truly our justice system reminds us of Pontius Pilate who sent Jesus to crucifixion and robber Barabbas to enjoy free life's pleasures. We need a revolutionary transformation in society where social justice is the people's right and courts give priority to humanity over legality". A judge, says Justice Bhagwati, should do justice by interpreting and administering the law in such a manner so as to fulfil the hopes and aspirations of millions of people in the country and ensuring to them a life of dignity where they would be able to participate in the fruits of freedom and liberty on any equal basis.

"We, who have not experienced poverty and hunger, want and destitution, talk platitudinously of freedom and liberty but these words have no meaning for a person who has not even a square meal per day, hardly a roof over his head and scarcely one piece of cloth to cover his shame."

—P.N. BHAGWATI[1]

12

Bonded Labour

An Affront to Basic Human Values

SYNOPSIS

1 Connotation Strictly speaking, a bonded labourer means a labourer who incurs or has or is presumed to have incurred a bonded debt and a bonded debt means an advance obtained or presumed to have been obtained by a bonded labourer under or in pursuance of the bonded labour system, so says Justice Bhagwati in a leading case.[2] Whenever it is shown that a labourer is made to provide forced labour, the court, points out Justice Bhagwati, would raise a presumption that he is required to do so in consideration of an advance or other economic consideration received by him and he is, therefore, a bonded labourer. This presumption, Justice Bhagwati says, may be rebutted by the employer but unless and until satisfactory material is produced in rebutting this presumption, the court must proceed on the basis that the labourer is a bonded labourer.[2]

1 *Neeraja Chaudhary* v *State of UP* (1984)3 SCC 243, per Bhagwati, J.
2 *Bandhua Mukti Morcha* v *Union of India* (1984)3 SCC 161.

2 Historical past The system of bonded labour has been prevalent in various parts of the country since long prior to the attainment of political freedom and it constitutes an ugly and shameful feature of our national life. This system, based on exploitation by a few socially and economically powerful persons trading on the misery and sufferings of large numbers of men and holding them in bondage, is a relic of a feudal hierarchical society which hypocritically proclaims the divinity of man but treats large masses of people belonging to the lower rungs of the social ladder or economically impoverished segments of the society as dirt and chattels. It is now statistically established that most of bonded labourers are members of Scheduled Castes and Scheduled Tribes or other backward classes. This system under which one person can be bonded to provide labour to another for years and years until an alleged debt is supposed to be wiped out which never seems to happen during the lifetime of the bonded labourers is totally incompatible, says, Justice Bhagwati, with the new egalitarian socio-economic order which we have promised to build and it is not only an affront to basic human dignity but it also constitutes gross and revolting violation of constitutional values.

3 Constitutional and statutory inhibition The system of bonded labour stands prohibited by Article 23 of the Constitution which prohibits "traffic in human being and begar and other similar forms of forced labour" practised by any one. It, however, appears, highlights Justice Bhagwati, that though the Constitution was enacted as far back as 26th January 1950 and many years passed since then, no serious effort was made to give effect to Article 23 to stamp out the shocking practice of bonded labour. It was only in 1976 that Parliament enacted the Bonded Labour System (Abolition) Act 1976 providing for the abolition of bonded labour system with a view to preventing the economic and physical exploitation of the weaker sections of the people.

Justice Bhagwati laments that the pernicious practice of bonded labour has not yet been totally eradicated even after the enactment of the Bonded Labour System (Abolition) Act 1976 from the national scene and that it continues to disfigure the social and economic life of the country. In various parts of the country and significantly, as is pointed out in the report of the National Seminar on "Identification and Rehabilitation of Bonded Labour", a large number of them belongs to Scheduled Castes, and Scheduled Tribes account for the next largest number while the few who are not from Scheduled Castes or Scheduled Tribes are generally landless agricultural labourers. It is absolutely essential, says Justice Bhagwati, that we would unhesitatingly declare that it is a constitutional imperative that the bonded labourers must be identified and released from the shackles of bondage so that they can assimilate themselves in the mainstream of civilized human society and realize the dignity, beauty and worth of human existence. The process of identification and release of bonded labourers, opines Justice Bhagwati, is a process of discovery and transformation of non-beings into human-beings. This process of discovery and transformation poses a serious problem since the social and economic milieu in which it has to be accomplished is dominated by elements hostile to it. But this problem, says Justice Bhagwati, has to be solved if we want to emancipate those who are living in bondage and serfdom and make them equal participants in the fruits of freedom and liberty. It is a problem, says Justice Bhagwati, which needs urgent attention of the Government, both at the Centre and at the States and when the Directive Principles of State Policy have obligated the Central and the State Governments to take step and adopt measures for the purpose of ensuring social justice to the have-nots and the handicapped, it is not right on the part of the concerned Governments to shut their eyes to the inhuman exploitation to which the bonded labourers are subjected. It is not uncommon, laments Justice Bhagwati, to find that the administration in some States is not willing to admit the existence of bonded labour, even though it exists in their territories. The administration should not feel shy, says Justice Bhagwati, in admitting the existence of bonded labour because it is not the existence of bonded labour that is a slur on the administration but its failure to take note of it and to take all necessary steps for the purpose of putting an end to the bonded labour system by quickly identifying, releasing and permanently rehabilitating the bonded labourers. What is needed, says Justice Bhagwati, is determination, dynamism and a sense of social commitment on the part of the administration to free bonded labourers and rehabilitate them and wipe out this ugly inhuman practice which is a blot on our national life. If the political and administrative apparatus has a sense of commitment to the constitutional values and is determined to take action for identifying, releasing and rehabilitating bonded labourers, despite pressure and pulls from different quarters, much can be done for securing emancipation and rehabilitation of bonded labourers.

4 Suggestions to improve upon the functioning of the Bonded Labour System (Abolition) Act 1976 Justice Bhagwati offered a number of suggestions to improve upon the functioning of the Bonded Labour System (Abolition) Act 1976.

Vigilance committee has to be constituted—whether bonded labourers exist or not Section 13 of the Act 1976 provides for constitution of a vigilance committee in each district and each sub-division of a district. The function of the vigilance committee being to identify bonded labourers, if there are any, and to free and rehabilitate them, it would not be right for any State not to constitute vigilance committee on the assumption that there are no bonded labourers at all.[3]

District Magistrate to take up the work of identification of bonded labourers as a priority task The District Magistrates have a central role to play under the provisions of the Act and the State Governments would do well to instruct the district magistrates to take up the work of identification of bonded labour as one of their top priority tasks. There are certain areas of concentration of bonded labour which can be easily identified on the basis of various studies and reports made by the Government authorities, social action groups and social scientists from time to time. These areas of concentration on bonded labour are mostly to be found in stone quarries, brick kilns and amongst agricultural landless labourers and such areas must be mapped out by each State Government and task forces should be assigned for identification and release of bonded labour. Labour camps should be held periodically in these areas with a view to educating the labourers and for this purpose, the assistance of the National Labour Institute may be taken because the National Labour Institute has the requisite expertise and experience of holding such camps.[3]

Officers dealing with the problems of bonded labour be properly trained and sensitised It is necessary, observes Justice Bhagwati,[4] that officers who are posted at different levels to deal with the problems of bonded labour including their identification, release and rehabilitation should be properly trained and sensitised so that they may feel a sense of involvement with the misery and suffering of the poor and they may carry out their functions with total dedication to the cause of removal of poverty and in a manner which will inspire the confidence of the weaker sections of the community including the bonded labour.

3 *Bandhua Mukti Morcha* v *Union of India* (1984)3 SCC 161.
4 *Neeraja Chaudhary* v *State of UP* (1984)3 SCC 243.

Justice Bhagwati views that[5] every officer who is placed in charge of identification, release and rehabilitation of bonded labour should be made fully conscious of his great responsibility and he should be imbued with a sense of purpose and dedication.

It is also essential, says Justice Bhagwati,[5] that there should be constant check and supervision over the activities of the officers charged with the task of securing identification, release and rehabilitation of bonded labourers and the district and sub-divisional level vigilance committees should be reorganised and activated and their meetings should be more frequent.

Social action groups be involved in the task of identification and release of bonded labourers Non-political social action groups and voluntary agencies and particularly those with a record of honest and competent service for Scheduled Castes and Scheduled Tribes, agricultural labourers and other unorganized workmen should be involved by the vigilance committees and the district magistrates in the task of identification and release of bonded labourers, for it is primarily through such social action groups and voluntary agencies alone that it would be possible to eradicate bonded labour system because social action groups and voluntary agencies comprising men and women, dedicated to the cause of emancipation of bonded labour, will be able to penetrate through the secrecy under which very often bonded labourers are required to work and discover the existence of bonded labour and help to identify and release bonded labourers.[6] These social action groups may appear to be marked by a sense of militancy, but they alone will be able to deliver the goods, observed Justice Bhagwati.[7]

Rehabilitation of the released bonded labourers an important task Poverty and destitution are almost perennial features of Indian rural life for large numbers of unfortunate ill-starved humans in this country and it would be nothing short of cruelty and heartlessness to identify and release bonded labourers merely to throw them at the mercy of the existing social and economic system which denies to them even the basic necessities of life such as food, shelter and clothing, says Justice Bhagwati[7] The learned Judge asks:[7] what will be the use of 'identification' and 'release' of bonded labourers if after attaining their so-called freedom from bondage from a master they are consigned to a

5 *Neeraja Chaudhary* v *State of UP* (1984)3 SCC 243.
6 *Bandhua Mukti Morcha* v *Union of India* (1984)3 SCC 161.
7 *Ibid.*

life of another bondage, namely, bondage to hunger and starvation, where they have nothing to hope for—not even anything to die for—and they do not know whether they will be able to secure even a morsel of food to feed the hungry stomachs of their starving children? What would they prize more: freedom and liberty with hunger and destitution staring them in the face or some food to satisfy their hunger and the hunger of their near and dear ones, even at the cost of freedom and liberty? The answer is obvious. It is, therefore, imperative, says Justice Bhagwati[8] that neither the Government nor the court should be content with merely securing identification and release of bonded labourers but every effort must be made by them to see that the freed bonded labourers are properly and suitably rehabilitated after identification and release. Otherwise these unfortunate human beings for whom life is a long unceasing rigel with no resources except perhaps a forlorn hope, who cannot even cry for help because they know that it will be cry in the wilderness which no one will hear and who drag on their earthly existence in the hope that one day death will relieve them from their misery and suffering, would ask the Legislature, the Executive and the Judiciary, "what have you done for us; have we not a right to live with human dignity and share with all of you the fruits of freedom and development or are we consigned to a life of slavery and starvation where we see before our eyes the emaciated bodies of our children with hollow cheeks, sunken eyes and shrivelled bodies withering away and dying?" Justice Bhagwati reminds that it is the plainest requirement of Articles 21 and 23 of the Constitution that bonded labourers must be identified and released and on release, they must be suitably rehabilitated. The Bonded Labour System (Abolition) Act 1976 has been enacted pursuant to the Directive Principles of State Policy with a view to ensuring basic human dignity to the bonded labourers and any failure of action on the part of the State Government in implementing the provisions of this legislation would be the clearest violation of Article 21 apart from Article 23 of the Constitution.[8]

Justice Bhagwati highlighted the four main features of the concept of rehabilitation based on the findings of Ministry of Labour, Government of India and identified those areas as under:

(*a*) Psychological rehabilitation must go side by side with physical and economic rehabilitation.

8 *Bandhua Mukti Morcha* v *Union of India* (1984)3 SCC 161.

(*b*) the physical and economic rehabilitation has fifteen major components, namely;

(*i*) allotment of house-sites and agricultural land;

(*ii*) land development;

(*iii*) provision of low cost dwelling units;

(*iv*) agriculture;

(*v*) provision of credit;

(*vi*) horticulture;

(*vii*) animal husbandry;

(*viii*) training for acquiring new skills and developing existing skills;

(*ix*) promoting traditional arts and crafts;

(*x*) provision of wage employment and enforcement of minimum wages;

(*xi*) collection and processing of minor forest produce;

(*xii*) help;

(*xiii*) medical and sanitation;

(*xiv*) supply of essential commodities;

(*xv*) education of children of bonded labourers and protection of civil rights.

(*c*) There is scope for bringing about an integration among various central and centrally sponsored schemes and on-going schemes of the State Governments for a more qualitative rehabilitation. The essence of such integration is to avoid duplication, i.e., pooling resources from different sources for the same purpose. It should be ensured that while funds are not drawn from different sources for the same purpose, funds drawn from different sectors in different components of the rehabilitation schemes are integrated skillfully.

(*d*) While drawing up any scheme/programme of rehabilitation of freed bonded labour, the latter must necessarily be given the choice between the various alternatives for their rehabilitation and such programmes should be finally selected for execution as would meet the total requirement of the families of freed bonded labourers to enable them to cross the poverty line on the one hand and to prevent them from sliding back to debt bondage on the other.

Educating the workmen employed in stone quarries and stone crushers—a necessity It is found that workmen employed in stone quarries and stone crushers are, apart from poverty and helplessness, deprived of the right and benefits conferred upon them under various social welfare laws enacted for their benefits and are subjected to deception and exploitation because they are totally ignorant of their rights and entitlements. It is this ignorance which is to some extent responsible for the total denial of the rights and benefits conferred upon them. It is, therefore, necessary to educate the workmen employed in stone quarries and stone crushers so that they become aware as to what are the rights and benefits to which they are entitled under the various social welfare laws. The knowledge of their rights and entitlements will give them the strength to fight against their employers for securing their legitimate dues and it will go a long way towards reducing, if not eliminating, their exploitation.[9]

If the guidelines given by Justice Bhagwati would have been implemented in letter and spirit, the implementation of the Bonded Labour System (Abolition) Act would have been effective leading to elimination or control of the bonded labour system but unfortunately the suggestions have been ignored.

9 *Bandhua Mukti Morcha* v *Union of India* (1984)3 SCC 161.

"No one shall be subjected to torture or to cruel, inhuman or degrading treatment or punishment. In particular, no one shall be subjected without his free consent to medical or scientific experimentation."

—International Covenant on Civil and Political Rights, 1966 (Art. 7)

13

Human Rights in Modern Times

[An analysis from Indian perspective]

SYNOPSIS

1 Human rights and the charter of the United Nations The concept of human rights in modern times begins with the Charter of the United Nations which included, as one of its basic principles, promotion and encouragement of respect for human rights and fundamental freedoms. The United Nation's concern for human rights and fundamental freedoms was focused in the Universal Declaration of Human Rights adopted by the General Assembly on 10th December 1948. The Universal Declaration merely laid down certain general principles having moral force and set out certain standards for achievement of human rights. It did not have the force of law and was more in the nature of a binding moral commitment, a yardstick of international standards and a path-finding instrument. The Preamble of the Declaration recites that the member-States have pledged themselves to achieve, in co-operation with the United Nations, the promotion of universal respect for and observance of human rights and fundamental freedoms. The Declaration was proclaimed "as a common standard of achievement for all peoples and all nations, to the end that every individual and every organ of society, keeping this Declaration constantly in mind, shall strive by teaching and education to promote respect for these rights and freedoms and by progressive measures, national and international, to secure their universal and effective recognition and observance, both among the peoples of Member States themselves and among the peoples of the territories under their jurisdiction." The Declaration represented the first endeavour of the United Nations to elaborate the normative ramifications of the concept of human rights. Though in some of its articles it dealt with social and economic rights, its greater emphasis was on the civil and political rights. Of the thirty articles of the Declaration, only seven dealt with economic and social rights and curiously enough it made no reference to the right of self-determination, a principle which the developing countries consider crucial for realization of a range of other human rights. The reason, says Justice Bhagwati, obviously was that the Declaration was drafted at a time when the world was still haunted by the night-marish experiences of the horrible Nazi and Fascists regimes. It was also a world in which majority of developing countries of today were still under the colonial yoke and did not have the opportunity to participate in the framing of the Charter as also of the Declaration as they did in the framing of the two subsequent international instruments. But the fact remains that the Declaration has made a tremendous impact throughout the world inspiring national constitutions and laws as well as conventions on various specific rights and it has been invoked on numerous occasions by the United Nations in support of action on worldwide scale for the solution of human rights problem in specific fields as also in regard to concrete human rights situations.

The Declaration was the first of the series of documents intended to constitute an International Bill of Rights and it was followed by two important Covenants transforming the principles enunciated in the Declaration into treaty provisions entailing obligation on the part of each ratifying country. One was the International Covenant on Civil and Political Rights and its Optional Protocol and the other was the International Covenant on Economic, Social and Cultural Rights. These two International Covenants and the Optional Protocol were adopted by the General Assembly on 16th December 1966, and another decade passed before they were ratified by a sufficient number of countries to bring them into force. When the number of ratifying countries reached 35, the International Covenant on Economic, Social and Cultural Rights came into effect on 3rd January 1976, and the International Covenant on Civil and Political Rights entered into force on 23rd March 1976 together with its optional protocol. The extraordinary feature of these Covenants is that they are more than treaties between two States. They are also binding commitments made in the international arena by a State towards its own citizens and others.

2 Indian approach to human rights India has althrough adopted an elitist approach to civil and political rights, so said Justice Bhagwati at an interview. Ever since independence, protagonists of human rights, according to Justice Bhagwati, have generally devoted their energies to rights which are immediately meaningful only to the upper and middle classes. They remained preoccupied with superstructure of civil and political rights of urban and rural elite to the exclusion of other human rights. Even where civil and political rights have been enacted in the Constitution and made enforceable through the judicial process, it is largely the rich and the well-to-do who have taken advantage of the judicial process. Justice Bhagwati said in an interview "it is absolutely essential that we get out of the obsession with the grandiose concept of human rights and come to the grass root conception of the same". There are quite a few human rights embodied in the International Covenant on Civil and Political Rights which touch the people at the grass root level but which have unfortunately not received sufficient attention from human rights activists in developing countries. It is surprising that though Article 7 of the International Covenant on Civil and Political Rights prescribes that no one shall be subjected to torture or to cruel, inhuman or degrading treatment or punishment, India has not included this immunity as a basic fundamental right. It was left to the judiciary in India to spell out this vital protection from Article 21 of the Constitution. So also are placed Articles 8 to 10 and 14 of the International Covenant on Civil and Political Rights which prescribe important human rights concerning freedom from servitude, right to liberty and security of person, freedom from arbitrary arrest and detention, right to trial within a reasonable time and pre-trial release and freedom from discrimination in the administration of criminal justice. These rights hardly received any attention though these are the articles which confer protection on the poor and downtrodden sections of the community who constantly come into conflict with laws because laws are often used against them for repressive purposes for protection of the vested interests. The Supreme Court of India, however, did not allow the administration to ignore or violate these rights.

It was for the first time in *Maneka Gandhi's* case[1] that the Supreme Court acting through Justice Bhagwati laid down that under Article 21 of the Constitution, a procedure prescribed by law for depriving a person of his life or personal liberty should be "reasonable, fair and just" and if a law depriving any person of his life or personal liberty

1 *Maneka Gandhi* v *Union of India* AIR 1978 SC 578.

prescribes a procedure which is unreasonable, unfair or unjust, the law would be void.

It was relying on the interpretation of Article 21 as made in *Maneka Gandhi's* case (supra), that the Supreme Court held in *Hussainara Khatoon's* case[2] that the system of monetary bail was improper and laid down for the first time new and more liberal norms consistent with human rights on which the accused persons should be released on bail pending trial. The Supreme Court, acting through Justice Bhagwati, pointed out that a new insight should inform our approach in the matter of pre-trial release and if the court is satisfied after taking into account on the basis of information placed before it, that the accused has his roots in the community and is not likely to abscond, it need not insist on monetary bond with sureties and may safely release the accused on his personal bond. The Supreme Court thus helped to advance the principle as enshrined in Article 9 Clause (3) of the International Covenant on Civil and Political Rights which provides that a person awaiting trial should be released subject to guarantees to appear for trial and took a positive step in the direction of bringing about conformity with Article 28 of the Draft Principles on Equality in the Administration of Justice and Article 16 Clause (2) of the Draft Principles of Freedom from Arbitrary Arrest and Detention.

Justice Bhagwati in *Hussainara Khatoon's* case (supra) laid down that legal aid to an indigent accused in a criminal trial is implicit in the guarantee of the fundamental right enshrined in Article 21 because any procedure which does not provide for legal representation to a poor accused when he is in jeopardy of his life or personal liberty cannot be regarded as 'reasonable, fair or just' under an adversary system of administration of justice. So far the Supreme Court had interpreted the fundamental rights as merely imposing restrictions on the authority of the State but for the first time in *Hussainara Khatoon's* case (supra) the Supreme Court invested the fundamental right under Article 21 with a positive content requiring affirmative action on the part of the State.

Justice Bhagwati also held in *Hussainara Khatoon's* case (supra) that the right to a reasonably expeditious trial is an integral and essential part of the fundamental rights embodied in Article 21 and the State is under a constitutional mandate to do whatever is necessary to ensure expeditious investigation and speedy trial.

2 *Hussainara Khatoon* v *Home Secretary, State of Bihar* AIR 1979 SC 1360: AIR 1979 SC 1369: AIR 1979 SC 1377: AIR 1979 SC 1819.

The Supreme Court thus recognised the right to legal aid in a criminal trial and the right to speedy trial as basic human rights in the field of administration of criminal justice and gave them a constitutional significance. But that was not the end of the concern of the Supreme Court in the area of human rights. The Court has often quoted the following observation of Field, J., in *Munn* v *Illinois*:[3] "By the term "life" ... something more is meant than mere animal existence. The inhibition against its deprivation extends to all those limbs and faculties by which life is enjoyed. The provision equally prohibits the mutilation of the body by the amputation of an arm or leg ...". Bhagwati, J., in *Francis Coralie* v *Union Territory of Delhi*[4] observed: "We think that the right to life includes the right to live with human dignity and all that goes along with it, namely, the bare necessaries of life such as adequate nutrition, clothing and shelter over the head and facilities for reading, writing and expressing oneself in diverse forms, freely moving about and mixing and commingling with fellow human beings".

It bears mentioning here that though some of the most important civil and political rights are enacted as fundamental rights in Part III of the Constitution, they do not cover the entire range of human rights embodied in the two International Covenants. Human rights, Justice Bhagwati views, are derived from the inherent dignity of the human person and they cover every aspect of life and not just a small number of preferred freedoms against the State. The conferment of fundamental rights and the pride of place given to them in the Indian Constitution have been responsible to some extent in eclipsing the importance of a vast number of other human rights. It is sometimes forgotten that fundamental rights simply do not exist for large sections of the population in a developing country like India. Large numbers of men, women and children who constitute the vast majority of people are today living a sub-human existence in conditions of abject poverty. These poor and deprived sections of humanity are not in a position to enforce any fundamental right. The only solution for making fundamental rights meaningful to these large sections of the society would be to remake the material conditions and restructure the social and economic order so that they may be able to realize the economic, social and cultural rights. There is a close relationship between civil and political rights on the one hand and economic, social and cultural rights on the other, and this relationship is so obvious that the International Human Rights

3 [1877]94 US 113.
4 AIR 1981 SC 746, 752: (1981)1 SCC 608.

Conference in Tehran called by the General Assembly in 1968 declared in a final proclamation: "Since human rights and fundamental freedoms are indivisible, the full realization of civil and political rights without the enjoyment of economic, social and cultural rights is impossible." So also the General Assembly in Resolution A/32/130 passed on 16th December 1977 reiterated that "All human rights and fundamental freedoms are indivisible and interdependent and equal attention and urgent consideration should be given to the implementation, promotion and protection of both civil and political rights and economic, social and cultural rights", because the full realization of civil and political rights is impossible without the enjoyment of economic, social and cultural rights. This is the reason why in the developing countries there is now greater emphasis on realization of social, economic and cultural rights for the vast masses of people who are living in want and destitution. Two other recent developments also have contributed to emphasizing realization of social, economic and cultural rights. One is the decision of the Human Rights Commission that it will also examine violation of social, economic and cultural rights (as stated in the Bulletin of Human Rights, Vol. 19) and the other is the increasing recognition which has now been given to the right to development as a human right.

It is now realized that right to development is a basic human right without the realization of which it is not possible to enjoy any other human rights. It is not only social, economic and cultural rights which are geared to economic development prevailing in a country but even the protection of civil and political rights is, to some extent, linked with the stage of development in the country. There can be no meaningful exercise of many human rights in a country where economic resources are scarce and the bulk of the population lives below the poverty line or at best on marginal level of subsistence. The right to development is, therefore, one of the most important basic human rights, so says Justice Bhagwati. The right to development is now acknowledged both as an individual and a collective right and in fact several international bodies such as the International Commission of Jurists have started concentrating their efforts on developing and elaborating the various constituent elements of this right to development. It is utmost important to note, says Justice Bhagwati at an interview, "if the large masses of people who inhabit the developing countries of the Third World are to achieve full and equal realization of the right to development, it is necessary that they should have effective access to: (*a*) tangible resources to achieve their basic needs of productive and equitably paid work, sufficient nutrition, health care and hygiene, shelter, energy resources, clean water and air; (*b*) the necessary intangible resources, especially education and information, to enable them better to utilize resources, and to participate freely in the process of development; (*c*) structures of production and (*d*) facilities and services to organize themselves to participate, monitor, evaluate and review development programmes and processes and to hold accountable those responsible for their implementation".

It is not enough merely to make declaration and pass resolutions about human rights which are essential for full development of the human personality. Human rights must be effectively implemented and they must not be allowed to remain merely pious declarations. We have to fashion, says Justice Bhagwati, new tools and innovate new strategies for the purpose of actualizing the human rights and making them meaningful for the large masses of our people. We have to democratize our remedies for enforcement of these human rights so that they become available to every citizen in the country irrespective of his caste, community, religion or means. Until the Judges Appointment and Transfer case,[5] the doors of the courts, though theoretically open to one and all, were in reality slammed against the poor, for the poor just could not afford to approach the courts to enforce their human rights.

The enormous delay and expense of the legal system effectively barred the poor to have access to justice. The poor were priced out of the legal system; they were functional out-laws. They had, observed Justice Bhagwati, no choice but to suffer, in anguished silence and in the despair of helplessness and frustration, violations of their human rights by powerful sections of the community, ruthless exploiters and even insensate politicians and bureaucracy. They are often victims of governmental and police lawlessness and are totally without any remedy against this oppression and injustice. The courts, said Justice Bhagwati, were too remote for them and even if they could approach the courts, they did not have the social or material resources to fight. It is not that the situation has improved now. Even now in some parts of the country deprivation and exploitation continue unabated; the basic human rights of the poor are violated; they are denied the basic necessities of life; they do not enjoy the right to education and many of them are still illiterate. The benefits of social welfare laws and governmental schemes and measures, according to Justice Bhagwati, are not reaching them

5 *S.P. Gupta* v *Union of India* AIR 1982 SC 149.

and these benefits are either siphoned off by intermediaries or are directed into wrong pockets or are confined only to the upper crust. Law is being used against the poor for repressive purposes and, in some places, the machinery of police instead of aiding the vulnerable sections allows itself to be utilized for assisting and perpetuating their actions. The rich and the powerful rarely get caught even if they commit anti-social or economic offences and even if they are caught, they manage to escape from the long arms of the law, because they have large material resources. It is only the poor and the downtrodden, laments Justice Bhagwati, who get entangled in the web of the law, for the law seems to be meant only for them and not for the rich and affluent.

Access to justice was, therefore, felt very necessary for the poor and downtrodden for protection of their human rights. The Supreme Court took the lead in the matter and threw the doors of the courts open by broadening the doctrine of *locus standi* and made it possible for the problems of the poor to be brought before the courts. It was in the Judges Appointment and Transfer case[6] that the Supreme Court, acting through Justice Bhagwati, departed form the ordinary rule of Anglo-Saxon jurisprudence under which an action can be brought only by a person to whom legal injury is caused, and laid down that where by reason of poverty or disability or socially or economically disadvantaged position a person or class of persons cannot approach the courts for judicial redress, any member of the public or social action group acting *bona fide* can maintain an application in the High Court under Article 226 and in the Supreme Court under Article 32 seeking judicial redress for the legal injury caused to such persons or class of persons and in such a case, the courts will not insist on a regular writ petition to be filed by the public spirited individual or social action group espousing their cause and readily respond even to a letter addressed by such individual or social action group. Bhagwati J. in delivering the leading judgment came out with a precedent and quoted with approval the observation of Lord Diplock in *R.* v *I.R.C. Ex P. Fed of Self Employed*[7] to the effect: "It would be a great lacuna in our system of public law if a pressure group, like a federation, or even a single public spirited tax payer, were prevented by out-dated technical rules of *locus standi* from bringing the matter to the attention of the court to vindicate the rule of law and get the unlawful conduct stopped." Gupta, Desai, Pathak and Tulzapurkar, JJ., agreed with Bhagwati J. with the result that five out of the seven judges were

6 *S.P. Gupta* v *Union of India* AIR 1982 SC 149.
7 [1982] AC 617 at p. 644.

parties to the widening of the scope of the rule of *locus standi*. This widening of the rule of *locus standi* and creation of a new epistolary jurisdiction have introduced a new dimension in the legal and judicial process and opened up a new vista of a totally different kind of litigation for enforcing basic human rights of the poor and the deprived sections of the community and ensuring basic human dignity to them. The courts are now entertaining social action litigation initiated by means of writ petition or even letters addressed by social activists, lawyers, journalists, law academics and social action groups and using their constitutional power of intervention with a view to ameliorating the miseries of the people, "arising from repression, governmental lawlessness and administrative deviance". The people have now come to identify the courts as a last resort for the oppressed. The transition from a traditional captive agency with a low social visibility into a liberated agency with a high socio-political visibility, considers Justice Bhagwati, is a remarkable development in the career of our appellate judiciary. The courts are now through their liberated jurisdiction forcing the pace of socio-economic change and compelling the governments and the bureaucrats to perform their constitutional duty of protecting the poor against social and economic injustices and ensuring realization of basic human rights.

There are all sorts of cases now coming before the courts, presenting problems of the deprived and vulnerable sections of the community; there are cases of under-trial as well as convicted prisoners, women in protective custody, children in juvenile institutions, bonded and migrant workmen, unorganized labour, untouchables and scheduled tribes, landless agricultural labourers who fall prey to faulty mechanization, women who are bought and sold, slum and pavement dwellers and victims of extra-judicial executions, and many more. The courts are now through judicial creativity evolving for the poor and the downtrodden new rights which are part of basic human rights but which are today inchoate and struggling to be born and which before their births are sought to be stifled by the exploiting class. "We are aware", says Justice Bhagwati at an interview, "that the judiciary is often being criticised for its activist role in the matter but, that is natural to happen because whenever there is change, there is bound to be resistance and whenever there is forward movement, there is bound to be turbulence. We must not forget what George Barnard Shaw said: "All great truths begin as blasphemies". If through the process of democratization of remedies, courts are pressed by the people to activise human rights and extinguish and wipe out exploitative injustice and executive arbitrariness, that is bound to provoke opposition from those interested in maintaining the *status quo*. Despite vicious and motivated criticism by persons who have arrogated to themselves the position of saviours of democracy and human rights but who are nothing more than sanctimonious humbugs far removed from the realities of Indian life and totally oblivious of the miseries and sufferings of millions of our people, the courts have been battling for people's rights and with the sword of justice in their hands, the courts in India will continue to do so undeterred by these critics, for the courts owe an obligation to the people of this country and under the Constitution they are created as sentinels on the *qui vive* for protection of the rights not only of a fortunate few but of the large masses of people steeped in poverty and ignorance".

Justice Bhagwati, however, reminds that the judicial process cannot by itself bring about effective implementation of human rights. It is not possible in a large country like India with a vast population for the judicial process to solve the problems and remove all ills of everyone. Moreover, the orders made by the courts, reminds Justice Bhagwati, are not self-executing; they have to be observed and enforced by the instrumentalities of the State. The institutions of our political system which could ordinarily be relied upon for protecting the poor and the deprived against exploitation and ensuring to them their social entitlements and satisfaction of their minimum needs and providing them their just and legitimate share in the fruits of development, have also, to some extent, become dysfunctional, because each of them has developed a set of values which is not only self-serving but also hinders the process of social transformation without which basic human dignity cannot be ensured to everyone in the country. Justice Bhagwati says that there are a large number of human rights that actually exist as part of the fabric of the law but much of our social legislation conferring these rights has remained symbolic. It declares rights for the weaker sections of the community in the knowledge that these rights may never be actualized. The poor and the weak are bought off with symbolism of declared but unenforced rights. It is necessary that legislation of this nature should be de-symbolised. This can only happen if the people for whom these rights are intended can use them effectively and make, what are symbolic rights, a reality.

'Everyone has the right to life, liberty and security of person'

—Universal Declaration of Human Rights, 1948 (Art. 3)

14

Human Rights and Criminal Justice System

SYNOPSIS

1 Human rights in criminal jurisprudence and the provisions of the Constitution

Article 20

2 Protection against ex-post facto operation of criminal law and Article 20(1)

3 Constitutional protection against double jeopardy and Article 20(2)

4 Privilege against self-incrimination and Article 20(3)

5 Emergence of the principle of immunity from interrogation and the controversy surrounding it

6 Early judicial response tended to dilute the principle in India

7 Privilege against self-incrimination rediscovered and resurrected

8 Judgment made no appreciable dent in the exercise of investigatory power

9 Right to be informed of the grounds of arrest and produced before the Magistrate—a part of criminal jurisprudence

Article 21

10 Article for long remained a lifeless incantation of the right to life and personal liberty

11 Scenario changed with Maneka Gandhi's case

12 Article 21 in aid of under-trial prisoners

13 Right to free legal assistance implicit in Article 21

14 Bail rules liberalised

15 Speedy trial as a fundamental right implicit in Article 21

16 Immunity against degrading treatment elevated to the status of fundamental right under Article 21

17 Jail administration humanized in accordance with the principle of right to live with human dignity

18 A convict not denuded of all fundamental rights

19 Bar fetter to a prisoner violative of basic human dignity

20 Routine handcuffing prohibited

21 Solitary confinement of a prisoner under death sentence violative of fundamental rights

1 Human rights in criminal jurisprudence and the provisions of the Constitution In dealing with human rights in criminal jurisprudence, an attempt has been made to deal primarily with human rights conferred by the Constitution of India and contained in Articles 20, 21.

ARTICLE 20

2 Protection against ex-post facto operation of criminal law and Article 20(1) It is a basic principle of criminal law in every civilised society that no person can be convicted of an offence for an act which was not an offence under the law in force at the time when it was committed. No act can constitute an offence by enacting legislation with retrospective effect. So also no one can be subjected to a greater penalty than what was provided under the law in force when the offence was committed. The protection against *ex-post facto* operation of criminal law, says Justice Bhagwati, is enacted as a constitutional right under clause (1) of Article 20 of the Constitution.

3 Constitutional protection against double jeopardy and Article 20(2) Clause (2) of Article 20 enacts constitutional protection against double jeopardy. No person can be vexed twice for the same offence. Even before the Constitution was framed, Justice Bhagwati says, this principle was enacted in the Code of Criminal Procedure but the Constitution makers considered it to be such an important safeguard that instead of leaving it precariously dependent on the good sense of the legislature, they thought it fit to include it as a constitutional protection so that it could not be lightly interfered with by any legislature by just amending the Code of Criminal Procedure. These two non-controversial safeguards contained in Clauses (1) and (2) of Article 20 are to be found in the criminal jurisprudence of almost every matured democracy.

4 Privilege against self-incrimination and Article 20(3) Article 20(3) of the Constitution provides: "No person accused of any offence shall be compelled to be a witness against himself."

The expression "accused of any offence" used in Article 20(3) must mean formally accused in *praesenti not in futuro*—not even imminently.[1] For invoking the constitutional rights against testimonial compulsion guaranteed under Article 20(3), it must appear that a formal accusation has been made against the party pleading the guarantee and that it relates to the commission of an offence which in the normal course may

1 *Nandini Satpathy* v *P.L. Dani* AIR 1978 SC 1025: (1978)2 SCC 424.

result in prosecution.[2] Normally a person stands in the character of an accused when a First Information Report is lodged against him in respect of an offence before an officer competent to investigate it, or when a complaint is made of an offence before a Magistrate competent to try or sent to another Magistrate for trial of the offence.[3]

The expression "to be a witness against himself" in Article 20(3), says Justice Bhagwati, means more than the court process. Any giving of evidence, any furnishing of information, if likely to have an incriminating impact, answers the description of being witness against himself.[4] 'To be witness against oneself' is not confined to particular offence regarding which the questioning is made but extends to other offences about which the accused has reasonable apprehension of implication from his answer.

Article 20(3), asserts Justice Bhagwati, makes the denial of the right to question an accused person to compel him to be a witness against himself a part of the fundamental law of the land, so that the maxim '*nemo tenetur se ipsum tenetur*' which, literally translated means, a man cannot represent himself as guilty became clothed in this country with the impregnability of a constitutional enactment.

But the safeguard contained in Clause (3) of Article 20, namely, the privilege against self-incrimination, is not free from controversy. Since the adoption of this privilege in common law world as a principle of criminal jurisprudence, there has been a perennial controversy over it. There has always been considerable debate as to the utility of this principle of protection against self-incrimination and serious doubts have been expressed in various quarters to the effect that this principle has tended to defeat justice.

5 Emergence of the principle of immunity from interrogation and the controversy surrounding it The driving force behind the refusal to permit forced self-incrimination is the system of torture by investigators and courts from medieval times to modern days. Law is a response to life and the English rule of the accused's privilege of silence may easily be traced as a sharp reaction to the Court of Star Chamber where self-incrimination was not regarded as wrongful. Indeed the central feature of the criminal procedure at that time was the examination of the accused. The horror and terror that then prevailed gave rise, by way of

2 *Raja Narayanlal Bansilal* v *M.P. Mistri* AIR 1961 SC 29: (1961)1 SCR 417.
3 *R.C. Mehta* v *State of West Bengal* AIR 1970 SC 940: (1969)2 SCR 461.
4 *Nandini Satpathy* v *P.L. Dani* AIR 1978 SC 1025: (1978)2 SCC 424.

reaction, to reverential principle of immunity from interrogation for the accused. It bears mentioning here that we cannot afford to write off the fear of police torture leading to forced self-incrimination as a thing of the past. Indian history does not permit it, contemporary world history does not condone it. An article titled 'Minds Behind Bars', published in December, 1977 issue of the Listner, tells an awesome story: "The technology of torture all over the world is growing ever more sophisticated—new devises can destroy a prisoner's will in a matter of hours—but leave no visible marks or signs of brutality. And government-inflicted terror has evolved its own dark sub-culture. All over the world, torturers seem to feel a desire to appear respectable to their victims ... There is an endlessly inventive list of new methods of inflicting pain and suffering on fellow human beings that quickly cross continents and ideological barriers through some kind of international secret-police net work ...".

In support of this principle it is claimed that protection of the accused against self-incrimination promotes active investigation from external sources to find out the truth and proof of alleged or suspected crime instead of extortion of confessions or information on universal suspicion. The first obligation of the criminal justice system, it must not be forgotten says Justice Bhagwati, is to secure justice by seeking and substantiating truth through proof. That obligation of the criminal justice system will be the first casualty in the absence of protection against self-incrimination. The absence of protection against self-incrimination will make 'the police lazy and unenterprising', will brutalise the police, harden the prisoner against the society, and lower the esteem in which the administration of justice is held by the public.

On the other hand, opinion has been strongly held by some that this rule has an undesirable effect on social interest and that in the detection of crime the State is confronted with overwhelming difficulties as a result of this privilege. It is said this privilege has become a hiding place of crime and has outlived its usefulness and the rights of the accused are amply protected without this privilege and that no innocent person is in need of it. This controversy is a part of the larger controversy, namely, which of the two interests shall prevail,—the interest of the possibly innocent or the social interest in detecting the crime and punishing the guilty.

To strike the balance between the needs of law enforcement on the one hand and the protection of the citizen from oppression and injustice at the hands of the law-enforcement machinery on the other is a perennial problem of statecraft. The pendulum over the years has swung to the right. Even as long ago as the opening of the twentieth century, Justice Holmes (of USA) declared that 'at the present time in this country (USA) there is more danger that criminals will escape justice than that they will be subject to tyranny.' As the century unfolded, the danger increased. In the United States since the case of *Miranda* v *Arizona*[5] there has been retreat from stress on protection of the accused and gravitation towards society's interest in connecting law-breakers. Currently, the trend in the American jurisprudence, according to legal journals, is that respect for (constitutional) principles is eroded when they leap their proper bounds to interfere with the legitimate interests of society in enforcement of its law. The emphasis has shifted in balancing the interests. But even so, Justice Bhagwati views, the principle against self-incrimination remains an important safeguard and it has been accepted in Indian Constitution as part of the criminal jurisprudence of the country. It enacts a measure of protection against over-bearing and intimidatory tactics which are unfortunately still present.

6 Early judicial response tended to dilute the principle in India In the early years of judicial history subsequent to the enactment of the Constitution, the principle of protection against self-incrimination did not appear to be looked upon with favour by the courts. Judicial response to this protection tended to dilute it rather than strengthen it. The scope and application of this protection were narrowed down by the Supreme Court in a number of decisions. Thus, it was held that the protection did not apply to administrative investigations and inquiries and it applied to police investigations only when the person was formally accused of an offence. The protection did not apply to searches and seizures under a search warrant. The protection certainly comprehended oral testimony but it did not extend to documentary evidence unless the document was based on the personal knowledge of the accused or such physical examination of the accused as finger-prints, signatures or specimen writings. Even a narrow view was taken of compulsion. There was no presumption that a statement made by the accused while in police custody was involuntary. There was hardly a case where a statement other than a confession made by an accused during custodial interrogation was excluded on the basis of the privilege against self-incrimination.

5 [1966]384 US 436: 16 L Ed 2d 694.

7 Privilege against self-incrimination rediscovered and resurrected But the change came in 1978. In the year 1978, the privilege against self-incrimination was rediscovered and resurrected by the Supreme Court in *Nandini Satpathy* v *P.L. Dani*.[6] This decision dealt with the philosophy behind the privilege against self-incrimination and defined and delineated the contours of this privilege. It infused a new life into this privilege which had otherwise become merely a paper protection. The Court speaking through V.R. Krishna Iyer, J., laid down in this case a few propositions intended to act as concrete guidelines to provide protection to an accused person in police custody. The Court pointed out that the prohibitive sweep of the protection against self-incrimination goes back to the stage of police interrogation and is not confined only to court proceedings. The ban on self-accusation and right to silence, pointed out the Court, goes beyond the case in question and protects the accused in regard to other offences pending or imminent which may deter him from voluntary disclosure of incriminatory matter. The Court held that if there is any mode of pressure, subtle or crude, mental or physical, direct or indirect, but sufficiently substantial, applied by the policeman for obtaining information from an accused strongly suggestive of guilt, it becomes 'compelled testimony', violative of the privilege against self-incrimination enshrined in Article 20(3). The Court also held that compulsion may be presumed in case of custodial interrogation by the police unless certain safeguards erasing duress are adhered to. The Court agreeing with the view expressed in the American case *Miranda* v *Arizona*[7] observed that the police ought to permit a lawyer to assist the accused if he can afford one, but the police need not wait for more than reasonable time for the arrival of the lawyer. However, the Court in *Nandini Satpathy's* case was not willing to go with the Miranda view holding that the State should make a lawyer available to the accused if he is indigent. The Court disapproved of the warning contained in *Miranda* case (supra) that the financial ability of the individual has relation to the scope of the right involved here. The privilege against self-incrimination secured by the Constitution applies to all individuals observed the Court in *Nandini Satpathy's* case. The Court also in this case adopted the liberal view that the police must invariably warn the accused and record that fact about the right to silence against self-incrimination, and where the accused is literate take the written acknowledgment from him. But what warning will be

6 AIR 1978 SC 1025: (1978)2 SCC 424.
7 [1966]384 US 436: 16 L Ed 2d 694.

somewhat of a different kind than what is in the United States is that in the United States the accused has a right to complete silence but under the Court's ruling in *Nandini Satpathy's* case, the accused has the right to refuse to answer only the incriminating questions. In other words, the view taken by the Court was that non-incriminatory questions can be asked and the accused is bound to answer where there is no clean tendency to incriminate. The Court made a distinction between relevance and examination. The Court pointed out that the tendency to expose oneself to criminal charges is something more than relevance and less than confession. The Court observed:[8] "Irrelevance is impermissible but relevance is licit but when relevant questions are loaded with guilty inference in the event of an answer being supplied, the tendency to incriminate springs into existence. We hold further that the accused person cannot be forced to answer questions merely because the answers thereto are not implicative when viewed in isolation and confined to that particular case. He is entitled to keep his mouth shut if the answer sought has a reasonable prospect of exposing him to guilt in some other accusation actual or imminent, even though the investigation underway is not with reference to that. We have already explained that in determining the incriminatory character of an answer, the accused is entitled to consider—and the Court while adjudging will take note of—the setting, the totality of circumstances, the equation, personal and social, which have a bearing on making an answer substantially innocent but in effect guilty in import. However, fanciful claims, unreasonable apprehensions and vague possibilities cannot be the hiding ground for an accused person. He is bound to answer where there is no clear tendency to criminate."

8 Judgment made no appreciable dent in the exercise of investigatory power The above observation of the Court in *Nandini Satpathy's* case, according to Justice Bhagwati, is likely to create difficulty in practice because in most of the cases when an offence is being investigated, it would be difficult to make fine distinction between what is relevant and what is incriminatory. When a person is accused of an offence, all relevant facts will have to be viewed from the point of criminality and there will be hardly any fact without this element. "I believe", says Justice Bhagwati in one of his interviews, "the police has not been happy with this ruling of the Court in *Nandini Sathpathy's* case, as it has felt that it would hamper its investigatory powers. The judgment does not seem to have made any appreciable dent in the exercise of

8 *Nandini Satpathy* v *P.L. Dani* AIR 1978 SC 1025 at p. 1046 (para 55).

investigatory powers in actual practice. It is only if we have a highly sophisticated police force with special skills and techniques and modern scientific methods of investigation that it can investigate and detect offences without resorting to testimonial compulsion during custodial interrogation and comply in letter and in spirit with the holding of *Nandini Satpahty's* case." Justice Bhagwati further added that an accused while under investigation by the police would not ordinarily be able to decide whether he is entitled to claim the privilege of silence in respect of the particular questions asked in interrogation because he would not be in a position to meet a fine distinction as to whether the answers would have incriminating effect or not.

9 Right to be informed of the grounds of arrest and produced before the Magistrate—a part of criminal jurisprudence The right of a person arrested to be informed of the grounds of arrest and his right to be produced before the nearest Magistrate within 24 hours of such arrest as contained in Article 20 are rights, says Justice Bhagwati, which have always been part of criminal jurisprudence of the country. There has, however, been occasional violation of these rights. Cases are not unknown, points out Justice Bhagwati, where persons are arrested by the police but no entry of arrest is made in the register and it is only when the police decides to produce the person arrested before the Magistrate that they make an entry of arrest in the register, thus creating a record showing that they have complied with the requirement of production within 24 hours. But this violation goes unnoticed and un-redressed because quite often the person arrested does not know that the Constitution and the law give him protection against detention by the police by providing that he shall be produced before the nearest Magistrate within 24 hours and that is the reason why, when produced before the Magistrate, he is unable to point out to the Magistrate that this right of his has been violated. Moreover, the Magistrate before whom the person arrested is produced also does not care to enquire from the person arrested as to how long he has been kept in police custody. "This type of violation of constitutional and legal right", says Justice Bhagwati in an interview, "can easily be avoided if only there is greater awareness amongst the people about the rights conferred upon them by the Constitution and the police and the Magistracy become keenly sensitive to the rights of the people".

ARTICLE 21

10 Article for long remained a lifeless incantation of the right to life and personal liberty The human rights which invest criminal jurisprudence with a certain amount of humanism have been discussed above; but by far the most important human rights in criminal jurisprudence are enshrined in Article 21 of the Constitution. This article was for long a lifeless incantation of the right to life and personal liberty which had very little positive intent. After the enactment of the Constitution the Supreme Court had for almost 27 years taken the view that this article merely embodied the Diceyian concept of the rule of law that no one can be deprived of his life and personal liberty by executive action unsupported by law. It was a protection against executive action which had no authority of law. If there was a law which provided some sort of procedure, it was enough to deprive a person of his life and personal liberty. Justice S.R. Das in *A.K. Gopalan* v *State of Madras*[9] gave an illustration that if a law provided that the cook of the Bishop of Rochester be boiled in oil, it would be valid under Article 21.

11 Scenario changed with Maneka Gandhi's case *Maneka Gandhi's* case altered the scenario. In *Maneka Gandhi* v *Union of India*,[10] which according to many jurists marks a water-shed in the history of the constitutional law of the country, the Supreme Court acting through Justice Bhagwati for the first time took the view that Article 21 affords protection not only against executive action but also against legislation and no law can deprive a person of his life or personal liberty unless it prescribes a procedure which is reasonable, fair and just and it would be for the court to determine whether the procedure is reasonable, fair and just and if it is not, the court will strike down the law as unconstitutional. Thus, Article 21 introduced procedural due process in the constitutional law of India through creative interpretation inspired by judicial activism. Justice Bhagwati points out an interesting episode in this context. When the Constitution was in the process of being framed, Mr. B.N. Rao who was the constitutional adviser had gone to the United States in order to have discussions with leading jurists in that country. He was advised by Mr. Justice Frankfurter of the United States Supreme Court not to include the due process clause in the Indian Constitution. The Constitution of the United States contains the due process clause and it is by virtue of due process clause that the Supreme Court of the United States is empowered to question and adjudicate the procedural as well as substantive reasonableness of Congressional and State Legislation. The due process clause has vested the Supreme Court of the United States with a vast power of judicial

9 AIR 1950 SC 27: 1950 SCR 88.
10 AIR 1978 SC 597: (1978)1 SCC 248.

review and that is why it has come in for criticism at the hands of Judges and jurists who believe in judicial restraint as against judicial activism. The question of inclusion of the due process clause in Article 21 of the Constitution was discussed in the Constituent Assembly but it was ultimately decided not to include it and instead, the phrase used was "except according to procedure established by law". However, with a view to forging greater protection for the citizen in respect of his life and personal liberty, the Supreme Court introduced the requirement of reasonable, fair and just procedure and thus brought the concept of procedural due process. This new interpretation of Article 21, by Justice Bhagwati, apparently innocuous, became the harbinger of a most dramatic development of constitutional law, particularly in the filed of criminal jurisprudence. Quite a few of the human rights in the area of criminal jurisprudence owe their origin to Article 21 of the Constitution. This new interpretation of Article 21 brought about significant reform in the administration of criminal justice so far as undertrial prisoners are concerned.

12 Article 21 in aid of under-trial prisoners One pathetic aspect of criminal justice administration in India has been an unduly large number of under-trial prisoners languishing in jails. The statistics show that at any given point of time the percentage of under-trial prisoners has always exceeded that of convicts. A 1981 statistical data as relied upon by Justice Bhagwati in *Hussainara Khatoon* v *State of Bihar*[11] showed that out of total jail population of 1,41,767 as on 30th June 1981, there were as many as 87,144 under-trial prisoners representing 61.5% of the total jail population.

These under-trial prisoners consisted principally of two categories: one representing those who were denied bail by the courts on account of their involvement in serious offences and the other consisting of those who could not furnish bail for one reason or the other. These under-trial prisoners were herded together in jail where problem of over-crowding had reached unmanageable proportions and they were living in shockingly horrible conditions. The position indeed was so deplorable in the State of Bihar that many of these under-trial prisoners were languishing in jails for years without even their trial having commenced. The Law Commission of India studied this problem in its 78th Report on "Congestion of Under-trial Prisoners in Jails" (February, 1979). But the real break through came when a lady lawyer

11 *Hussainara Khatoon* v *State of Bihar* AIR 1979 SC 1360: AIR 1979 SC 1369: AIR 1979 SC 1377: AIR 1979 SC 1819.

practicing in the Supreme Court brought a public interest litigation in the Supreme Court based on a report appearing in the Indian Express. Justice Bhagwati while in the apex court examined the matter in great depth and gave various directions in a series of decisions which have come to be known as *Hussainara Khatoon* decisions.[12]

In *Hussainara Khatoon's* case, the Supreme Court acting through Justice Bhagwati found from the counter affidavit filed by the State of Bihar that there were quite a few women prisoners who were in jail without even been accused of any offence, merely because they happened to be victims of an offence or they were required for the purpose of giving evidence. They were, in the language used by the Bihar police, in 'protective custody'. The Supreme Court pointed out that the expression 'protective custody' is a euphemism calculated to disguise what is really and in truth nothing but imprisonment and the so called 'protective custody' is nothing short of a blatant violation of personal liberty guaranteed under Article 21, because there is no provision of law under which a woman can be kept in jail by way of 'protective custody' merely because she is required for the purpose of giving evidence. The Supreme Court, acting through Justice Bhagwati, immediately gave a direction that "all women and children who are in the jails in the State of Bihar under 'protective custody' or who are in jail because their presence is required for giving evidence or who are victims of offence should be released and taken forthwith to the welfare homes or rescue homes and should be kept there and properly looked after".

The Supreme Court also found that there were quite a few under-trial prisoners who had been in jail for periods longer than the maximum term for which they could have been sentenced, if convicted and yet their trials have not commenced. The Supreme Court reprimanded the administration as well as the judiciary in the State of Bihar for the shocking state of affairs which betrayed complete lack of concern for human values and directed that these under-trial prisoners "should be released forthwith as continuance of their detention is clearly illegal and in violation of their fundamental right under Article 21."

13 Right to free legal assistance implicit in Article 21 The Supreme Court also became concerned with the issue as to why was it that large numbers of under-trial prisoners were rotting in jails for years without their trial having been commenced? Why were they not on bail,

12 *Hussainara Khatoon* v *State of Bihar* AIR 1979 SC 1360: AIR 1979 SC 1369: AIR 1979 SC 1377: AIR 1979 SC 1819.

particularly those who were charged with offences which were bailable? The Court, acting through Justice Bhagwati, observed that these under-trial prisoners were in jail presumably because no application for bail had been made on their behalf either because they were not aware of their rights to obtain release on bail or on account of their poverty they were unable to engage a lawyer to apply for bail and in quite a few cases, being too poor, they were unable to furnish bail. The Supreme Court came to the conclusion that the unfortunate state of affairs cried aloud for introduction of a comprehensive and dynamic legal service programme. In the Indian Constitution there is no specifically enumerated constitutional right to legal aid for an accused person. Clause (1) of Article 22 provides that no person who is arrested shall be denied the right to consult and to be defended by a legal practitioner of his choice, but according to the interpretation placed on this provision by the Supreme Court in *Janardhan Reddy* v *State of Hyderabad*,[13] this provision does not carry with it the right to be provided the services of a legal practitioner at State cost. There is of course Article 39A introduced in the Constitution in 1976 but this Article merely contains a Directive Principle of State Policy. It enacts a mandate that the State shall provide free legal aid by suitable legislation or schemes or in any other way, to ensure that opportunities for justice are not denied to any citizen by reason of economic or other disabilities. There is thus an obligation laid on the State to provide free legal service but it is not an obligation enforceable in a court of law and does not confer a constitutional right on the accused to secure free legal assistance. The Supreme Court filled up this constitutional gap through creative judicial interpretation of Article 21 following upon *Maneka Gandhi's* case. The Supreme Court in *M.H. Hoskot* v *State of Maharashtra*[14] observed: "Judicial justice, with procedural intricacies, legal submissions and critical examination of evidence, leans upon professional expertise, and a failure of equal justice under the law is on the cards where such supportive skill is absent for one side. Our judicature, moulded by Anglo-American models and our judicial process, engineered by kindred legal technology, compel the collaboration of lawyer-power for steering the wheels of equal justice under the law." Black, J. in *Gideon* v *Wainwright*[15] observed that "in our adversary system of criminal justice, any person held into court, who is too poor to hire a lawyer cannot be

13 AIR 1951 SC 217: 1951 SCR 344.

14 AIR 1978 SC 1548: (1978)3 SCC 544: 1978 Cr LJ 1978: (1979)1 SCR 192, per Krishna Iyer, J.

15 [1963]372 US 335: 9 L Ed 2d 799.

assured a fair trial unless counsel is provided for him". "The more serious the likely consequences, the greater is the probability that a lawyer should be appointed", so observed Douglas, J., in *John Richard Argersinger* v *Raymond Hamlin*.[16]

In *M.H. Hoskot* v *State of Maharashtra*[17] and in *Hussainara Khatoon* v *Home Secretary, State of Bihar*,[18] the Supreme Court held that a procedure which does not make legal services available to an accused person who is too poor to afford a lawyer and who would, therefore, go through the trial without legal assistance cannot possibly be regarded as 'reasonable, fair and just'. It is an essential ingredient of reasonable, fair and just procedure to a prisoner who seeks his liberation through the courts process that he should have legal services made available to him. The right to free legal assistance is an essential element of any reasonable, fair and just procedure for a person accused of an offence and it must be taken as implicit in the provisions of Article 21. The Supreme Court thus spelt out that the State is under a mandate to provide a lawyer to an accused person if the circumstances of the case and the needs of justice so require, provided of course the accused person does not object to the provision of such lawyer. Justice Bhagwati lamented in *Hussainara Khatoon* v *Home Secretary, State of Bihar*[19] that "barring a few, many of the State Governments do not seem to be alive to their constitutional responsibility in the matter of provision of free legal services in the field of criminal justice." "Let it not be forgotten", cautions Justice Bhagwati, "that if law is to seek justice, legal aid is an absolute imperative". If free legal services are not provided to an accused, the trial itself may run the risk of being violated as contravening Article 21.

14 Bail rules liberalised The next question which arose in *Hussainara Khatoon's* case[20] was as to when and under what circumstances should bail be granted and what should be the nature of such bail. One reason, says Justice Bhagwati, why legal and judicial system continually deny justice to the poor by keeping them for long years in pre-trial detention is highly unsatisfactory bail system prevailing. It suffers from a property oriented approach which seems to proceed on the erroneous assumption that risk of monetary loss is the only deterrent against fleeing from

16 [1972]407 US 25: 32 L Ed 2d 530.
17 AIR 1978 SC 1548: (1978)3 SCC 544: 1978 Cr LJ 1978: (1979)1 SCR 192, per Krishna Iyer, J.
18 AIR 1979 SC 1369, per Bhagwati, J.
19 AIR 1979 SC 1377.
20 *Hussainara Khatoon* v *Home Secretary, State of Bihar* AIR 1979 SC 1360.

justice. The Code of Criminal Procedure, even after re-enactment, continues to adopt the same antiquated approach as the earlier code enacted towards the end of the last century and where an accused is to be released on his personal bond, it insists that the bond should contain a monetary obligation requiring the accused to pay a sum of money in case he fails to appear at the trial. Moreover, as if this were not sufficient deterrent to the poor the courts mechanically and as a matter of course insist that the accused should produce sureties who will stand bail for him and these sureties must again establish their solvency to be able to pay up the amount of the bail in case the accused fails to appear to answer the charge. This system of bail, observes Justice Bhagwati, operates very harshly against the poor and it is only the non-poor who are able to take advantage of it by getting themselves released on bail. The poor find it difficult to furnish bail even without sureties because very often the amount of the bail fixed by the courts is so unrealistically excessive that in a majority of cases the poor are unable to satisfy the police or the Magistrate about their solvency for the amount of the bail and where the bail is with sureties, as is usually the case, it becomes an almost impossible task for the poor to find persons sufficiently solvent to stand as sureties. The result is that either they are fleeced by the police and revenue officials or by touts and professional sureties and sometimes they have even to incur debts for securing their release or, being unable to obtain release, they have to remain in jail until such time as the court is able to take up their cases for trial, leading to grave consequences, namely (1) though presumed innocent, they are subjected to psychological and physical privations of jail life; (2) pre-trial detention disrupts their family life and in most cases becomes economically disastrous for the family; and (3) it prevents them from contributing to the preparation of their defense. It is here, says Justice Bhagwati, that the poor find our legal and judicial system oppressive and heavily weighted against them and they find themselves hopelessly in a position of inequality with the non-poor. The Legal Aid Committee appointed by the Government of Gujarat under the Chairmanship of Justice Bhagwati pointed out in its Report how the practice of fixing the amount of bail without taking into account relevant factors, such as the individual financial circumstances of the accused and probability of his fleeing before trial, is harsh and oppressive and discriminates against the poor. It is necessary to appreciate that the risk of monetary loss is not the only deterrent against fleeing from justice, but there are other factors which act as equal deterrents against fleeing. If the Court is satisfied, after taking into account, on the basis of information placed before it, that the accused has his roots in the community and is not likely to abscond, it can safely release the accused on his personal bond. To determine whether the accused has his roots in the community which would deter him from fleeing, the Court should, in regard to the accused, points out Justice Bhagwati, take into account: (*i*) the length of his residence in the community; (*ii*) his employment status, history and his financial condition; (*iii*) his family ties and relationships; (*iv*) his reputation, character and monetary condition; (*v*) his prior criminal record including any record of prior release on recognizance or on bail; (*vi*) the identity of responsible members of the community who would vouch for his reliability; (*vii*) the nature of the offence charged and the apparent probability of conviction and the likely sentence in so far as these factors are relevant to the risk of non-appearance; and (*viii*) any other factor indicating the ties of the accused to the community or bearing on the risk of willful failure to appear.

It bears mentioning, however, that if facts are brought to the notice of the court which would show that having regard to the condition and background of the accused, his previous record and the nature and circumstances of the offence there may be a danger of his tampering with the witnesses or there may be a substantial risk of his non-appearance through the trial, as for example, where the accused is a notorious bad character or a confirmed criminal or the offence is serious, the court may not release the accused on bail at all and even if the court is inclined to release him on bail, the court may insist on bail with sureties. The same view has been taken by the International Commission of Jurists, a leading human rights organization. According to the said organization, there are four grounds on which an accused may be kept in jail and may not be released on bail. And these four grounds are: (*i*) in case of a very grave offence; (*ii*) if the accused is likely to interfere with witnesses or impede the course of justice; (*iii*) if the accused is likely to commit the same or any other offence; (*iv*) if the accused may fail to appear for trial. It may be pointed out that even where an accused is released on his personal bond, it is necessary to caution the court that the amount of the bond which it fixes should not be based merely on the charge. The decision as regards the amount of the bond should be individualised decision depending upon the individual financial circumstances of the accused and the probability of its absconding.

The Supreme Court, says Justice Bhagwati, thus helped to advance the right enshrined in Clause (3) of Article 9 of the International Covenant on Civil and Political Rights which provides that persons awaiting trial should be released subject to guarantees to appear for trial and took a positive step in the direction by bringing about conformity with Article 28 of the Draft Principles on Equality in the Administration of Justice which lays down that "National laws concerning provisional release from custody pending or during trial shall be so framed as to eliminate any requirement of pecuniary guarantees" and Article 16 Clause (2) of the Draft Principles of Freedom from Arbitrary Arrest and Detention which provides that "to ensure that no person shall be denied the possibility of obtaining provisional release on account of lack of means, other forms of provisional release than upon financial security shall be provided." These other forms of provisional release, according to Justice Bhagwati, may include release into the custody of a responsible person or organization, release on promise not to leave a specified address or to reside in a specified place or to appear at regular intervals before a stated authority, release upon temporary surrender of identity papers or release upon an undertaking to appear before the authorities whenever legally summoned to do so. The view taken by Justice Bhagwati in *Hussainara Khatoon's* case met with favourable response of the Central Government. This became evident from the statement made by the then Minister of Home Affairs in the Rajya Sabha on 19th July 1982.

The Law Commission of India, says Justice Bhagwati, has also expressed itself in favour of liberalizing bail rules. It has favoured (*a*) offences punishable upto three years' imprisonment as bailable, unless the nature of offence is such that it requires a different approach; (*b*) giving discretion to the courts to release a person on bail or personal bond without sureties, whether the offence is bailable or non-bailable; (*c*) compulsorily releasing a person on personal bond in case of bailable offence, if within a month he is not able to produce sureties; and (*d*) not keeping the amount of bail at an excessive amount.

15 Speedy trial as a fundamental right implicit in Article 21 Speedy trial means reasonably expeditious trial. In the United States speedy trial is one of the constitutionally guaranteed rights The Sixth Amendment to the US Constitution provides: "In all criminal prosecution, the accused shall enjoy the right to a speedy and public trial." In the case of the Indian Constitution speedy trial is not specifically enumerated as a fundamental right. It was in the dawn of post-emergency era that judicial inovativeness delved deep into the fundamental rights philosophy and discovered the right of speedy trial implicit in the broad sweep and enforcement of Article 21 of the Constitution. It was with the decision of Justice Bhagwati in *Maneka Gandhi* v *Union of India*,[21]

21 AIR 1978 SC 597.

the most important single decision in the history of Indian judicial thought, that the whole concept of fundamental rights jurisprudence was revolutionized by declaring that "the principle of reasonableness, which legally as well as philosophically, is an essential element of equality or non-arbitrariness pervades Article 14 like a brooding omnipresence and the procedure contemplated by Article 21 must answer the test of reasonableness in order to be in conformity with Article 14". This is the basic principle which germinated into the right of speedy trial as fundamental right, and found expression in the decision of the Supreme Court in *Hussainara Khatoon* v *Home Secretary, State of Bihar*.[1] Following the dictum in *Maneka Gandhi's* case, the apex court acting through Justice Bhagwati for himself and A.D. Koshal, J. in *Hussainara Khatoon* v *Home Secretary, State of Bihar*,[2] observed that the procedure prescribed by law for depriving a person of his liberty cannot be 'reasonable, fair and just' unless that procedure ensures a speedy trial for determination of the guilt of such person. No procedure which does not ensure a reasonably quick trial can be regarded as 'reasonable, fair or just'. If a person is deprived of his liberty under a procedure which is not 'reasonable, fair or just', such deprivation would be violative of his fundamental right under Article 21 and he would be entitled to enforce such fundamental right and secure his release. There can, therefore, be no doubt, said Justice Bhagwati, that speedy trial, and by speedy trial he meant reasonably expeditious trial, is an integral and essential part of fundamental right to life and liberty enshrined in Article 21. Justice Bhagwati, in *Hussainara Khatoon* v *Home Secretary, State of Bihar*[3] pointed out that the State is under a constitutional obligation to take all steps necessary for ensuring speedy trial to the accused and the State cannot be permitted to deny this Constitutional right of speedy trial on the ground that the State has no adequate financial resource to incur the necessary expenditure needed for improving the administrative and judicial apparatus with a view to ensuring speedy trial. "The law", it was observed in *Rhem* v *Malclm*,[4] "does not permit any Government to deprive its citizens of constitutional rights on a plea of poverty". Judge Blackmum in *Jackson* v *Bishop*[5] observed: "Humane considerations and constitutional requirements are not, in this day, to be measured by dollar considerations ...". The

1 AIR 1979 SC 1360.
2 AIR l979 SC 1360.
3 AIR 1979 SC 1369.
4 377 F Supp 995.
5 404 F Supp 2d 571.

Supreme Court in its anxiety to protect and enforce the right of speedy trial did not remain content with mere formulation and recognition of the right but proceeded further to add that the Court as the guardian of the fundamental rights of the people, as the sentinel on the *qui vive*, is entitled to enforce this right by issuing necessary direction to the State which may include taking of positive action, such as, augmenting and strengthening the investigative machinery, setting up new courts, building new court houses, providing more staff and equipment to the courts, appointment of additional Judges and other measures calculated to ensure speedy trial. Justice Bhagwati adopted an activist approach and took positive steps in the direction of implementing Article 14 clause (3) of the International Covenant on Civil and Political Rights which lays down that everyone shall be entitled in the determination of any criminal charge against him "to be tried without undue delay" and Article 16 of the Draft Principles on Equality in the Administration of Justice which reiterates that everyone shall be guaranteed the right to prompt and speedy hearing. The beginning so made continued unabated in the judicial pronouncements made in the following years—vide: *State of Maharashtra* v *Champalal Punjajj Shah*,[6] *T.I. Vatheeswaran* v *Tamil Nadu*,[7] *Mithu* v *State of Punjab*.[8] In one of his interviews, Justice Bhagwati says that the constitutional right of an accused to a speedy and public trial in all criminal prosecutions flows from Article 21 of the Constitution by virtue of procedural mandate and is identical in content with the express constitutional guarantee inserted by the Sixth Amendment in the American Constitution. He further says that once the constitutional guarantee of a speedy trial and the right to a 'fair, just and reasonable procedure' under Article 21 have been violated, the accused is entitled to an unconditional release and the charges against him would fall on that ground. Justice Bhagwati reminded that many of the unfortunate men and women confined in jail do not remember when they entered the jail and for what offence. They have over the years cease to be human beings; they are mere ticket numbers. It is high time, appeals Justice Bhagwati, that "the public conscience is awakened and the Government as well as the judiciary begin to realize that in the dark cells of our prisons there are large number of men and women who are waiting patiently, impatiently perhaps, but in vain, for justice—a commodity which is tragically beyond their reach and grasp".

6 AIR 1981 SC 1675.
7 AIR 1983 SC 361.
8 AIR 1983 SC 473: (1983)2 SCC 277.

16 Immunity against degrading treatment elevated to the status of fundamental right under Article 21 The case of *Frances Coralie Mullin* v *Delhi Administration*[9] provided for advancing human rights in the field of criminal jurisprudence. The Court led by Justice Bhagwati held in this case that the right to life protected under Article 21 is not confined merely to the right to physical existence but it also includes within its broad matrix the right to the use of every faculty or limb through which life is enjoyed as also the right to live with basic human dignity. The Court in *Frances Coralie Mullin's* case (supra) pointed out that the right to live with basic human dignity is an integral part of reasonable, fair and just procedure. The State cannot, therefore, by law or otherwise deprive any person of the right to live with basic human dignity and hence torture or cruel, inhuman or degrading treatment or punishment which trenches upon human dignity would be impermissible under the Constitution. The Supreme Court thus elevated immunity against torture or cruel, inhuman or degrading treatment or punishment to the status of a fundamental right under Article 21, though it is not specifically enumerated as a fundamental right in the Constitution. The Court thus incorporated Article 7 of the International Covenant on Civil and Political Rights into the constitutional jurisprudence of the country.

17 Jail administration humanized in accordance with the principle of right to live with human dignity The case of *Sheela Barse* v *State of Maharashtra*[10] dealt with the confinement in a lock-up of an accused where he is temporarily confined before being produced before Magistrate or remanded to police custody. It is commonly known that conditions in police lock-ups are far from satisfactory. This is testified even by the Government appointed A.N. Mulla Committee on Jail Reforms which points out in paragraph 12.6 of its report: "Most of these lock-ups have insufficient accommodation and are without even such basic facilities, light, water and ventilation. Sanitary conditions in these lock-ups are also utterly unsatisfactory. There seem to be no rules or scales prescribed for the diet or bedding for those detained in police lock-ups. There are no Visiting Committees which could inspect or report about the conditions prevailing in these lock-ups. The essential requirements of law with regard to the time limit for keeping in custody a person arrested without warrant are often flouted. The very first

9 AIR 1981 SC 746: (1981)1 SCC 608.
10 AIR 1983 SC 378: (1983)2 SCC 96.

encounter of a person with the criminal justice system thus invokes in him reaction of abhorrence for and distrust in the criminal justice system. Conditions of police lock-ups need to be urgently improved." The Supreme Court led by Justice Bhagwati in the case of *Sheela Barse* (supra) gave detailed directions with a view to improving the conditions in the lock-ups and providing adequate protection to the arrested persons and particularly to women confined in the police lock-ups. These directions were, *inter alia*, to the following effect:

(*i*) Four or five police lock-ups should be selected in reasonably good localities where only female subjects should be kept and they should be guarded by female constables.[11] Female suspects should not be kept in the same police lock-up in which male suspects are detained. Interrogation of women should be carried out only in the presence of women police officers/constables.

(*ii*) Whenever a person is arrested by the police without warrant, he must be immediately informed of the grounds of his arrest and in case of every arrest, it must be immediately made known to the arrested person that he is entitled to apply for bail. The State Legal Aid Board should get a pamphlet prepared setting out the legal rights of an arrested person and printed copies of the pamphlet in Marathi, Hindi and English should be affixed in each cell in every police lock-up and should be read out to the arrested person in any one of the three languages which he understands as soon as he is brought to the police station.

(*iii*) Whenever a person is arrested and taken to the police lock-up, intimation of the fact of such arrest must immediately be given to the nearest Legal Aid Committee so that immediate steps can be taken for the purpose of providing legal assistance to the arrested person at State cost.

(*iv*) In the city of Bombay, a City Sessions Judge to be nominated by the Principal Judge of the City Court, preferably a lady judge who should make surprise visits to the police lock-ups periodically with a view to providing the arrested person an opportunity to air their grievances and should be spread over in every part of the country ascertaining what are the

11 AUTHORS' NOTE: Justice Bhagwati feels that what was meant for the City of Bombay should not be confined to that. This facility of all female police lock-up should be spread over in every part of the country.

conditions in the police lock-up and whether the requisite facilities of law are being carried out. The City Sessions Judge should draw the attention of the Police Commissioner or the Home Department to the lapses, if any, and if even this approach fails, the City Sessions Judge might further report to the Chief Justice of the State.[12] Immediately a person is taken to the police lock-up, the police must obtain from him the name of any relative or friend whom he would like to be informed about his arrest and the police should get in touch with such relative or friend and inform him about the arrest; and lastly.

(*v*) The Magistrate before whom the arrested person is produced should enquire from him whether he has any complaint of torture or maltreatment in police custody and inform him that he has a right under section 54 of the Code of Criminal Procedure to be medically examined.

Shockingly poor and miserable conditions prevailing in jails and the treatment meted out to prisoners have also attracted considerable attention in recent years. Notwithstanding these shocking conditions prevailing in the Indian jails, nothing much seems to have been done by the Central Government or the State Governments, says Justice Bhagwati, barring appointment from time to time of committees for suggesting reforms in prisons, the last of such committees being the A.N. Mulla Committee on Jail Reforms. Here also the Supreme Court had to take the initiative in order to humanize jail administration to some extent.

18 A convict not denuded of all fundamental rights The Supreme Court held in the two *Sunil Batra* cases,[13] that convicts are not merely by reason of conviction denuded of all the fundamental rights which they otherwise possess. The compulsion under the authority of law, following upon a conviction, to live in a prison house results in deprivation of only certain fundamental freedoms such as the right to move freely throughout the territory of India or the right to practice a profession. But the Constitution guarantees other freedoms of which deprivation is not necessitated by the fact of incarceration. All other freedoms belong to the convict—"to read and write, to exercise and recreation, to

12 AUTHORS' NOTE: Justice Bhagwati views that the direction as made applicable to City of Bombay should squarely apply to other metropolitan cities too.

13 *Sunil Batra* v *Delhi Administration* AIR 1978 SC 1675: AIR 1980 SC 1579.

meditation and chant, to protection from heat and cold, freedom from indignities like compulsory nudity, forced sodomy and other unbearable vulgarity, to movement within the prison campus subject to requirements of discipline and security, to the minimal joys of self-expression, to acquire skills and techniques and all other fundamental rights tailored to the limitation of imprisonment," subject of course to reasonable restrictions in public interest. Jawaharlal Nehru in his Autobiography asked: "If a court of law sentences a person to imprisonment, does it follow that not only his body but also his mind should be incarcerated? Why should not the minds of prisoners be free even though their bodies are not?" Nehru himself in his Autobiography replied the question thus: "Those in charge of the prison administration in India be horrified at such a question, for their capacity for new ideas and sustained thought is usually limited".[14] The Court should stand, says Justice Bhagwati, four square between a prisoner and the methodology of destroying completely the spirit and undermining the sanity of the prisoner in jail. Within the cell, fundamental concepts of decency should prevail as otherwise barbaric conditions and degrading circumstances shall do violence to civilised standards of human decency.

19 Bar fetter to a prisoner violative of basic human dignity The Supreme Court speaking through Justice Bhagwati in the first *Sunil Batra* case[15] held that bar fetters which curtail to a very considerable extent locomotion which is one of the facets of personal liberty cannot be put on a prisoner unless it is absolutely necessary to do so, having regard to the dangerous character and propensity of the prisoner. The Supreme Court observed that subjecting a prisoner to bar fetter for an unusually long period without due regard to the safety of the prisoner and the security of the prison would be violative of basic human dignity and hence impermissible under the Constitution. Bar fetters could not be put to the prisoner by the jail authorities, says Justice Bhagwati, unless accompanied by certain important procedural safeguards, which include inter alia that: (*a*) it must be absolutely necessary to put fetters; (*b*) the reasons for doing so must be recorded; (*c*) the basic condition of dangerousness must be well-grounded; (*d*) natural justice must be observed; (*e*) the fetters must be removed at the earliest opportunity; (*f*) there should be a daily review of the absolute need for bar fetters; and finally, (*g*) if it is found that the fetters must continue

14 An Autobiography by Jawaharlal Nehru, Chapter XLIV—Prison Humours, p. 346 at p. 350.

15 *Sunil Batra* v *Delhi Administration* AIR 1978 SC 1675.

beyond a day, it would be illegal unless an outside agency like the District Magistrate or Sessions Judge directs its continuance.

20 Routine handcuffing prohibited Having outlawed bar fetters except under special circumstances and with adequate safeguards, the Supreme Court proceeded to condemn the handcuffs and chaining prisoners in *Prem Shankar Shukla* v *Delhi Administration.*[16] The Supreme Court, acting through V.R. Krishna Iyer, J., held in this case that no prisoner shall be handcuffed or fettered routinely or merely for the convenience of the custodian or escort. Justice Bhagwati, concurred with the view expressed by V.R. Krishna Iyer, J. in *Prem Shankar's* case that the compulsion of security must be so pressing that no alternative will meet except handcuffs. There must be material sufficiently stringent to satisfy a reasonable mind that there is clear and present danger of escape of the prisoner who is being transported by breaking out of the police cordon and further that by adding to the escort party or other strategy, he cannot be kept under control. Even where, in extreme circumstances, handcuffs becomes necessary, the escorting officer must record the reasons for doing so and further the escorting officer must show the reasons so recorded to the Presiding Judge and get his approval. The judicial officer before whom the prisoner is produced must also interrogate the prisoner for finding out whether he has been subjected to handcuffs and if he has been, the escorting officer must be asked to explain his action. The Supreme Court struck down as arbitrary and irrational the classification of prisoners for the purpose of handcuffs into 'better class' and 'ordinary' and laid down that the same condition must apply in all cases whether a prisoner should be handcuffed or not.

21 Solitary confinement of a prisoner under death sentence violative of fundamental rights The Supreme Court, it may be pointed out, also expressed itself emphatically in the first *Sunil Batra* case[17] against solitary confinement and pointed out that solitary confinement has degrading and dehumanizing effect on the prisoner. Jawhar Lal Nehru in his Autobiography said: "Solitary confinement, even for a short period, is a most painful affair; for it to be prolonged for years is a terrible thing. It means the slow and continuous deterioration of the mind, till it begins to border on insanity; and the appearance of a look of vacancy, or a frightened animal type of expression. It is the killing of

16 AIR 1980 SC 1535: (1980)3 SCC 526: 1980 Cr LJ 930.
17 *Sunil Batra* v *Delhi Administration* AIR 1978 SC 1675.

the spirit by degrees, the slow vivisection of the soul. Even if a man survives it, he becomes abnormal and an absolute misfit in the world".[18] The apex court in first *Sunil Batra's* case[19] pointed out that it would be violative of the fundamental rights to impose solitary confinement on a prisoner under death sentence, not as a consequence of violation of prison discipline, but on the sole ground that he is a prisoner under sentence of death. It is only where the sentence of death becomes finally executable that a prisoner would be liable to be dealt with under section 30(2) of the Prison Act and then also he cannot be treated differently from other prisoners except in two respects, namely, that during confinement he must be kept in a cell apart from other prisoners but he must be within the sight and sound of other prisoners and shall be subject to a day and night watch by guard. Save and except for these two restrictions, he is not to be denied any of the amenities like games, newspapers, books and meeting prisoners and visitors subject, of course, to reasonable regulation of prison management. The two *Sunil Batra* cases and *Prem Shankar's* case have sought to humanize jail administration and to convert jails into correctional institutions. But even so, points out Justice Bhagwati, the problem of humanization of jail administration remains, because there are hardly any jails in the country where the directions given by the Supreme Court are being scrupulously observed. It is high time, says Justice Bhagwati, that every State Government sets up a high-powered committee presided over by a sitting High Court Judge which should periodically inspect the jails within the State for the purpose of securing compliance with the law laid down by the Supreme Court in the *Sunil Batra* cases and *Prem Shankar's* case.

One can notice that most of the human rights discussed above have been evolved by the judiciary through a process of creative interpretation. This entire human rights jurisprudence with reference to criminal justice system has been the result of a startling and remarkable development of the law following the land mark decision of Justice Bhagwati in *Maneka Gandhi's* case. This new jurisprudence which has been largely developed by Justice Bhagwati as a result of a case-to-case development is a most fascinating one and has set the path for future development of the law on human rights.

18 Jawaharlal Nehru—An Autobiography, Chapter XXX In Naini Prison, p. 217 at p. 222.

19 *Sunil Batra* v *Delhi Administration* AIR 1978 SC 1675.

Every saint has a past and every sinner a future.
— An Indian conviction based on faith and experience.

15

Death Penalty
An Affront to Human Rights

SYNOPSIS

1 Introduction Death Penalty is a controversial topic. There are a few who favour its retention while the others, forming the majority view by now, demand its abolition. Justice Bhagwati regards men as an embodiment of divinity and he, therefore, stands morally against death penalty. According to Justice Bhagwati, death penalty does neither serve any social purpose nor advance any constitutional value and is totally arbitrary and unreasonable so as to be violative of Articles 14, 19 and 21 of the Constitution. The learned Judge agrees with Bernard Shaw when he said "Criminals do not die by the hands of the law. They die by the hands of other men. Assassination on the scaffold is the worst form of assassination because there it is invested with the approval of the society ...... Murder and capital punishment are not opposites that cancel one another but similars that breed their kind". Justice Bhagwati pointed out that it was Mahatma Gandhi, the Father of the Nation, who said years ago, reaffirming what Prince Satyavan said on capital punishment in Shanti Parva of Mahabharata that "Destruction of individuals can never be a virtuous act." The Father of the Nation wrote long ago in The Harijan: "God alone can take life because he alone gives it." This sentiment, says Justice Bhagwati, has been echoed by many eminent men like Leonardo da Vinci, John Bright, Victor Hugo and Berdyaev.

If we are convinced that torture and inhuman punishment is absolutely prohibited then the ultimate irrevocable punishment of execution should also be prohibited. V.R. Krishna Iyer, J., in an essay *"Death Penalty: An Unmitigated Evil?"* contained in his book *Perspectives in Criminology Law and Social Change* wrote: "Capital punishment is a cruelly callous investment by unsure and unkempt society in punitive dehumanization and cowardly strategy based on horrendous superstition that cold-blooded human sacrifice by professional hangmen engaged by the State will propitiate the goddess of Justice to bless Mother Earth with a crimeless community. The authentic voice of the divinity and dignity of humanity, echoed in many national constitutions and now underscored in the Universal Declaration, has been that of the Buddha and Gandhi and not of Manu and Hammurabi, Beccaria and Bentham, not Bradley and Bosanquet, are the torch-bearers in this area".

This chapter deals with Justice Bhagwati's view on the subject primarily relying on his dissenting opinion as expressed in *Bachan Singh* v *State of Punjab*.[1]

2 Death penalty—worldwide status from retentionist view point Despite the international outcry against the continuation of the death penalty, it has retained its traditional position, says Justice Bhagwati, in many Asian, African as well as North American criminal codes, authorised by the respective country's constitution. Some 84 countries, according to

1 (1982)3 SCC 24.

the Amnesty International survey, retained and enforced death penalty at the end of 2001. In 2005, 94 per cent of all known executions took place in China, Iran, Saudi Arabia and the USA. Based on public reports available, Amnesty International estimated that at least 1,770 people were executed in China during the year, although the true figures were believed to be much higher. A Chinese legal expert was quoted as stating the figure for executions as approximately 8,000 based on information from local officials and judges, but official national statistics on the application of the death penalty remained classified as a state secret. Iran executed at least 94 people and Saudi Arabia at least 86, but the totals may have been much higher. 60 people were executed in USA.

Since 2000, executions have been carried out thus: Beheading (in Saudi Arabia and Iraq); Electrocution (in USA) ; Hanging (in Egypt, Iran, India, Japan, Jordan, Pakistan, Singapore and other countries); Lethal injection (in China, Guatemala, Philippines, Thailand, USA); Shooting (in Belarus, China, Somalia, Taiwan, Uzbekistan, Viet Nam and other countries); Stoning (in Afghanistan, Iran).

The countries where executions have been carried out in 2005 are: Bangladesh, Belarus, China, Indonesia, Iran, Iraq, Japan, Jordan, Korea (North), Kuwait, Libya, Mongolia, Pakistan, Palestinian Authority, Saudi Arabia, Singapore, Somalia, Taiwan, USA, Uzbekistan, Viet Nam, Yemen.

The countries where death sentences have been imposed in 2005 are: Afghanistan, Algeria, Bahamas, Bahrain, Bangladesh, Belize, Barbados, Burkina Faso, Burundi, China, Congo (Democratic Republic), Egypt, Ethiopia, Ghana, Guinea, India, Indonesia, Iran, Iraq, Jamaica, Japan, Jordan, Kazakhstan, Korea (North), Korea (South), Kuwait, Laos, Lebanon, Libya, Malawi, Malaysia, Mali, Mongolia, Morocco, Nigeria, Oman, Pakistan, Philippines, Qatar, Saudi Arabia, Singapore, Somalia, Sri Lanka, Sudan, Syria, Taiwan, Tanzania, Trinidad And Tobago, United States of America, Uzbekistan, Viet Nam, Yemen, Zimbabwe.

Taking into consideration the size of the population living under retentionist criminal law regimes, approximately 70% of the world population still lives under the rule of the death penalty.

The scope of the death penalty covers, besides murder, various other offences. Besides murder, death penalty can be imposed for serious cases of rape, property offences, drug offences, e.g., for trafficking of heroin of more than 50 grams, as well as for a range of other criminal offences displaying not too serious criminal behaviour—at least from an international perspective—for which perpetrators can be put to death. Drug trafficking offences in particular, inclusive of soft drugs, such as, cannabis, have been put under the threat of the death penalty in many Asian countries. It is also armed robbery or even moral offences which can attract death sentences in various Arab countries.

3 Eminent persons view in support of retention of death penalty Utilitarian considerations, moral aspects and social attitudes are highlighted by retentionists in justifying retention of death penalty. There is a mix of preventive and moral arguments in support of the death penalty pointing towards the goals of general deterrence, positive general prevention as well as reducing the risk of victims taking the law into their own hands.

It is said by the retentionists: "Who so sheddeth man's blood, by man shall his blood be shed".[2] There is an ancient tradition, going back to biblical times, but endorsed by the mainstream philosophers, from Plato to Thomas Aquinas, from Thomas Hobbes to Immanuel Kant, Thomas Jefferson, John Stuart Mill, and C.S. Lewis, that a fitting punishment for murder is the execution of the murderer. One prong of this tradition epitomized in the thinking of Aquinas and Kant holds that because human beings, as rational agents, have dignity, one who with malice aforethought kills a human being forfeits his right to life and deserves to die. The other class of thinkers exemplified by Jeremy Bentham, Mill, and Ernest van den Haag, holds that punishment ought to serve as a deterrent and that capital punishment is an adequate deterrent to prospective murders.

4 Death penalty not prohibited under the Constitution of India Our Constitution, says Justice Bhagwati, does not in so many terms prohibit capital punishment. In fact, it recognises death sentence as one of the penalties which may be imposed by law. Article 21 provides *inter alia* that no one shall be deprived of his life except according to procedure established by law. This clearly postulates that a person may be deprived of his life in accordance with the procedure prescribed by law or in other words, law may provide a procedure which according to the decision of the Supreme Court in *Maneka Gandhi* v *Union of India*[3] must be

2 Genesis 9:6.
3 AIR 1978 SC 597: (1978)1 SCC 248.

reasonable, fair and just procedure, for inflicting death penalty on a person. Article 72(1)(*c*) recognises the possibility of a sentence of death being imposed on a person convicted of an offence inasmuch as it provides that the President shall have the power to suspend, remit or commute the sentence of any person who is convicted of an offence and sentenced to death. It is, therefore, not possible to contend that the imposition of death sentence for conviction of an offence is in all cases forbidden by the Constitution.

In India, the statute permits imposition of death penalty. The judicial stand is that the death sentence is to be awarded in the "rarest of rare cases". If the court is not in a position to come to the conclusion that a case is not the "rarest of rare cases", the judges may feel that the appropriate sentence to be awarded is the life sentence. It is a judicial discretion circumscribed by parameters set out by the Supreme Court. In many cases, where the period between the sentencing and the execution has been particularly long, the Supreme Court has commuted a death sentence to life sentence. Indian courts have developed an aversion to capital punishment. Courts in Tamil Nadu, Uttar Pradesh and Delhi awarded over 60 life imprisonments on a single day in October 2007.

In army, a soldier was sentenced to death by a court martial in Jammu and Kashmir in early 2007. Sources in the army could not recall the last time a court martial gave such a sentence. The order was issued by a Summary General Court Martial. It is rare for an army court martial to issue such a sentence even if army law is more rigid than civilian law. In army, death sentence may be awarded not only for willful murder but also for treason leading to murder. Under the Army Act, death sentence may be given for mutiny and cowardice in the face of the enemy. But while awarding death sentence, the army is guided by the Supreme Court directive that it should give such a sentence only in the "rarest of the rare" cases. A soldier has the right to appeal against the sentence to both superior authorities in the army and to a civil court. If the sentence is confirmed, it is executed by civilian authorities. The soldier does not face a firing squad.

India where over 280 death row convicts are at present waiting for execution and where death sentence is executed by hanging is searching for a more 'humane' form of execution. Lethal injection had been recommended by the Law Commission. The proposal was, however, opposed by the members of the medical fraternity citing reasons of personal ethics.

5 Abolition of death penalty—worldwide trend There are quite a large number of countries, points out Justice Bhagwati, which have abolished death penalty *de jure* or in any event, *de facto*. Statistics show that death penalty has been abolished in nearly two-thirds of the world. The addendum to the Report of the Amnesty International on "The Death Penalty" points out that as of 30th May 1979, the countries which have abolished death penalty for all offences include Australia, Brazil, Colombia, Costa Rica, Denmark, Dominican Republic, Ecuador, Fiji, Finland, Federal Republic of Germany, Honduras, Iceland, Luxembourg, Norway, Portugal, Sweden, Uruguay and Venezuela, and according to this Report, Canada, Italy, Malta, Netherlands, Panama, Peru, Spain and Switzerland have abolished death penalty in time of peace, but retained it for specific offences committed in time of war. The Report also states that Algeria, Belgium, Greece, Guyana, Ivory Coast, Seychelles and Upper Volta have retained the death penalty on their statute-books but they did not conduct any executions for the period from 1973 to 30th May 1979. South Africa abolished the death penalty as a result of its Constitutional Court's determination in 1995 that the death penalty violated the constitutional prohibition on cruel, inhuman, or degrading treatment. Death penalty has been abolished, either formally or in practice, in several other countries such as Argentina, Bolivia, most of the Federal States of Mexico, Nicaragua, Israel and Turkey. Russia has called a moratorium on death sentence. Nearer home, in Nepal there is no death sentence.

Position in China In September 2007, China has issued an order urging judges to avoid executing criminals in all but the most extreme circumstances. The order follows reports of widespread wrongful convictions and criticism that lower courts arbitrarily impose the death penalty. It is the latest effort by Beijing to reform capital punishment in China. Judges have been ordered to use the death penalty more sparingly by showing leniency for murderers who cooperate with authorities and to non-violent "white-collar" criminals. "Capital punishment" should only be given to an extremely smaller number of serious offenders, the Supreme Court of China said.

Position in United Kingdom In the United Kingdom death penalty stands abolished from the year 1965 save and except for offences of treason and certain forms of piracy and offences committed by members of the armed forces during war time. It deserves mentioning here that the Evans case in England in which an innocent man was hanged in 1949 played a large role in the abolition of capital punishment in that country. It may be pointed out that an attempt was made in the United Kingdom in December 1975 to reintroduce death penalty for terrorist offences involving murder but it was defeated in the House of Commons and once again a similar motion moved by a conservative Member of Parliament that "the sentence of capital punishment should again be available to the courts" was defeated in the House of Commons in a free vote on 19th July 1979.

Position in USA The US Supreme Court held in 2002 that imposition of the death penalty on the 'mentally retarded' is prohibited as violating the constitutional prohibition on 'cruel and unusual punishments'. It is now the law of the land. In 2005, the US Supreme Court held that it was unconstitutional for the death penalty to be imposed on those who were minors at the time of the offence. International norms, it requires mentioning, prohibit the execution of juvenile offenders, the insane, and pregnant women.

The death penalty is under an unprecedented review in the US, mostly involving questions about lethal injection, by far the most common method of execution. About one-third of the 38 states that allow capital punishment have halted or delayed executions while legal and ethical challenges are resolved. The latest was Tennessee where the governor called for a comprehensive review of current execution procedures and future protocols. Governor Phil Bredesen said he supports capital punishment, but the state in preparing to address a legal challenge to lethal injection had found "deficiencies with our written procedures that raise concerns that they are not adequate to preclude mistakes in the future." One issue in Tennessee involves vagueness on how much of the deadly drugs need to be administered. Nationwide, some state lawmakers are debating whether the condemned unduly suffer during execution. In 2006, Florida halted executions after a convicted killer took 34 minutes to die when needles carrying the drugs were improperly inserted. It took almost 90 minutes to carry out the execution of Joseph Clark in May, 2006 at the Ohio prison of USA. The execution amounted to punishment that was cruel and unusual. The Ohio prison authorities struggled to inject the condemned prisoner with lethal drugs that failed to work.

Justice Potter Stewart of U.S. Supreme Court once said that the imposition of death penalty on defendants in USA is as freakish and arbitrary as who gets hit by a bolt of lightning.

In 1994, near the end of his distinguished career of the Supreme Court of the United States, Justice Harry Blackmun wrote an influential dissent in the body of law on capital punishment. Twenty years earlier he was part of the Court that issued the landmark Furman decision.[4] The Court decided that the death penalty statutes in use throughout the country were fraught with severe flaws that rendered them unconstitutional. To many, it looked like the Furman decision meant the end of the death penalty in the United States. But this was not the case. Many states responded to Furman by developing and enacting new and improved death penalty statutes. In 1976, four years after it had decided Furman, Justice Blackmun joined the majority of the United States Supreme Court in deciding to give the states a chance with these new and improved death penalty statutes. But twenty years later, after affirming hundreds of death penalty decisions, Justice Blackmun came to the realization, in the twilight of his distinguished career that the death penalty remains fraught with arbitrariness, discrimination, caprice and mistake. He expressed frustration with a 20-year struggle to develop procedural and substantive safeguards. In a now famous dissent he wrote in 1994: "From this day forward, I no longer shall tinker with the machinery of death".[5]

In making a blanket commutation of all death row inmates, Illinois Governor George Ryan said: "Our capital system is haunted by the demon of error, error in determining who among the guilty deserves to die."

Hugo Bedan in his book 'The Death Penalty in America' has individually documented seventy-four cases since 1893 in which it has been responsibly charged and in most of them proved beyond doubt, that persons were wrongly convicted of criminal homicide in America. Eight out of these seventy-four, though innocent, were executed. Redin, Gardener, Frank and others have specifically identified many more additional cases. These are cases in which it has been possible to show from discovery of subsequent facts that the convictions were erroneous and innocent persons were put to death, but there may be many more cases where by reason of the difficulty of uncovering the facts after

4 *Furman* v *Georgia* 408 US 238.

5 Vide: Prepared text of Governor George Ryan's speech delivered at Northwestern University College of Law on January 11, 2003, announcing his commutation of all of Illinois's death sentences, published in the book 'Debating the Death Penalty' edited by Hugo Bedeau and Paul Cassell, published by Oxford University Press.

conviction, let alone after execution, it may not be possible to establish that there was miscarriage of justice. The jurist Olivecroix, applying a calculus of probabilities to the chance of judicial error, concluded as far back as in 1860 that approximately one innocent man was condemned out of every 257 cases. The proportion may sound low in relation to moderate punishment but in relation to capital punishment, the proportion is infinitively high. When Hugo wrote that he preferred to call the guillotine Lesurques (the name of an innocent man guillotined in the Carrier de Lyon case), he did not mean that every man who was decapitated was a Lesurques but that one Lesurques was enough to wipe out the value of capital punishment for ever. It is interesting to note that where cases of wrongful execution have come to public attention, they have been a major force to call for abolition of death penalty.

The concern over the possibility of miscarriage of justice prompted reformer Edward Livingston as early as in 1820s and such critics as Charles C. Burleigh, Horace Greeley, William Howells, and Sing-Sing Warden Lewis Lawes throughout the nineteenth and twentieth centuries as well as the American League to fight for abolition of capital punishment. In 1987, Hugo Adam Bedau and Michael Radelef published a law review article that made a strong case that the danger of total miscarriages was real. In 1993, three erroneously sentenced inmates were released from death row. Of the three, Federico Macias was convicted in 1984 in Texas; Walter McMillan was convicted in Alabama in 1988; and Gregory Wilhoit was convicted in 1987 in Oklahoma. Naturally, abolitionists have sought to capitalize on the issue of erroneous death sentence. They have tried to draw the nation's attention to the issue through press releases, reports and speeches, and they have rallied around particular convicts as exemplars of what is wrong with the death penalty as a whole.

The survey above shows that there is a definite trend throughout the world towards abolition of death penalty.

6 Role of United Nations towards abolition of death penalty It is significant to note that the United Nations has also taken great interest in the abolition of capital punishment. In the Charter of the United Nations signed in 1945, the founding States emphasized the value of individual's life, stating their will to "achieve international cooperation .... in promoting and encouraging respect for human rights and for fundamental freedoms for all without distinction as to race, sex, language or religion". Though the San Francisco Conference did not address itself to the issue of death penalty specifically, the provisions of the Charter paved the way for further action by United Nations bodies in the field of human rights, by establishing a Commission on Human Rights and, in effect, charged that body with formulating an International Bill of Human Rights. Meanwhile, the Universal Declaration of Human Rights was adopted by the General Assembly in its Resolution 217-A (III) of December 10, 1948. Article 3 of the Declaration provided: "Everyone has the right to life, liberty and security of person". Article 5 thereof laid down: "No one shall be subjected to torture or to cruel, inhuman or degrading treatment or punishment".

The United Nations position on the question of death penalty was expected to be stated more specifically in the International Covenant on Civil and Political Rights, the drafting of which had been under way since the first session of the Commission on Human Rights in 1947. But during the 11 year-period of drafting of the relevant provision of the Covenant, two main approaches to the issue of capital punishment became evident: one stressed the need for barring the death penalty and the second placed emphasis on restricting its application to certain cases. The proponents of the first position suggested either the total abolition of the death penalty or its abolition in time of peace or for political offences. This approach was, however, regarded as unfeasible, since many countries, including abolitionist ones, felt that the provision for an outright ban on the death penalty would prevent some states from ratifying the Covenant, but at the same time, it was insisted by many countries that the Covenant should not create the impression of supporting or perpetuating death penalty and hence a provision to this effect should be included. The result was that the second approach stressing everyone's right to life and emphasizing the need for restricting the application of capital punishment with a view to eventual abolition of the death penalty, won greater support and Article 6 of the Covenant as finally adopted by the General Assembly in its Resolution 2200(XXI) of 16th December 1966 provided as follows:

> (1) Every human being has the inherent right to life. This right shall be protected by law. No one shall be arbitrarily deprived of his life.
>
> (2) In countries which have not abolished the death penalty, sentence of death may be imposed only for the most serious crimes in accordance with the law in force at the time of the commission of the crime and not contrary to the provisions of the present Covenant and to the Convention on the

Prevention and Punishment of the Crime of Genocide. This penalty can only be carried out pursuant to a final judgment rendered by a competent court.

(3) When deprivation of life constitutes the Crime of Genocide, it is understood that nothing in this Article shall authorize any State Party to the present Covenant to derogate in any way from any obligation assumed under the provisions of the Convention on the Prevention and Punishment of the Crime of Genocide.

(4) Anyone sentenced to death shall have the right to seek pardon or commutation of the sentence. Amnesty, pardon or commutation of the sentence of death may be granted in all cases.

(5) Sentence of death shall not be imposed for crimes committed by persons below eighteen years of age and shall not be carried out on pregnant women.

(6) Nothing in this Article shall be invoked to delay or prevent the abolition of capital punishment by any State Party to the present Covenant.

Article 7 of the Covenant corresponding to Article 5 of the Universal Declaration of Human Rights reaffirmed that no one shall be subjected to torture or to cruel, inhuman or degrading treatment or punishment.

So deep and profound was the United Nations' concern, says Justice Bhagwati, with the issue of death penalty that the General Assembly in its Resolution 1396 (XIV) of 20th November 1959 invited the Economic and Social Council to initiate study of the question of capital punishment, of the laws and practices relating thereto, and of the effects of capital punishment and the abolition thereof on the rate of criminality. Pursuant to this Resolution, the Economic and Social Council activised itself on this issue and at its instance a substantive report was prepared by the noted French Jurist Marc Ancel. The report entitled "Capital Punishment" was the first major survey of the problem from an international standpoint on the deterrent aspect of the death penalty and in its third chapter, it contained a cautious statement "that the deterrent effect of the death penalty is, to say the least, not demonstrated". This view had been expressed not only by abolitionist countries in their replies to the questionnaires but also by some retentionist countries. The Ancel Report along with the Report of the ad hoc Advisory Committee of Experts on the Prevention of Crime and the Treatment of Offenders which examined it in January 1963 was presented to the Economic and Social Council at its 35th Session when its Resolution 934(XXXV) of 9th April 1963 was adopted. By this Resolution, the Economic and Social Council urged member governments inter alia to keep under review the efficacy of capital punishment as a deterrent to crime in their countries and to conduct research into the subject and to remove this punishment from the criminal law concerning any crime to which it is, in fact, not applied or to which there is no intention to apply it. This Resolution clearly shows that there was no evidence supporting the supposed deterrent effect of the death penalty and that is why the Economic and Social Council suggested further research on the topic. Moreover, the urging of the de facto abolitionist countries by this Resolution to translate the position into de jure terms constituted an implicit acceptance of the principle of abolition. The same year, by Resolution 1918 (XVIII) of 5th December 1963, the General Assembly endorsed this action of the Economic and Social Council and requested the Economic and Social Council to invite the Commission on Human Rights to study and make recommendations on the Ancel Report and the comments of the ad hoc Advisory Committee of Experts. The General Assembly also requested the Secretary-General to present a report on new developments through the Economic and Social Council. Norval Morris, an American Professor of criminal law and criminology, accordingly prepared a Report entitled "Capital Punishment: Developments 1961-1965" and amongst other things, this Report pointed out that there was a steady movement towards legislative abolition of capital punishment and observed with regard to the deterrent effect of death penalty that: "With respect to the influence of the abolition of capital punishment upon the incidence of murder, all of the available data suggest that where the murder rate is increasing, abolition does not appear to hasten the increase; where the rate is decreasing abolition does not appear to interrupt the decrease; where the rate is stable, the presence or absence of capital punishment does not appear to affect it".

The Commission on Human Rights considered this Report and adopted a draft General Assembly Resolution which was submitted by the Economic and Social Council to the General Assembly and on 26th November 1968, the General Assembly adopted this draft with certain modifications as its Resolution 2393 (XXIII) inviting member governments to take various measures and requesting the Secretary-General to invite member governments "to inform him of their present attitude to possible further restricting the use of the death penalty or to its total abolition" and to submit a report to the Economic and Social

Council. The Secretary-General accordingly submitted his Report to the Economic and Social Council at its 50th Session in 1971. This Report contained a finding that "most countries are gradually restricting the number of offences for which the death penalty is to be applied and a few have totally abolished capital offences even in wartimes". The discussion in the Economic and Social Council led to the adoption of Resolution 1574(L) of 20th May 1971 which was reaffirmed by General Assembly Resolution 2857 (XXVI) of 20th December 1971. This latter Resolution clearly affirmed that: "In order to guarantee fully the right to life, provided for in Article 3 of the Universal Declaration of Human Rights, the main objective to be pursued is that of progressively restricting the number of offences for which capital punishment may be imposed, *with a view to the desirability of abolishing this punishment in all countries*."

In 1973 the Secretary-General submitted to the Economic and Social Council at its 54th Session his third Report on capital punishment as requested by the Council and at this session, the Council adopted Resolution 1745(LIV) in which, *inter alia*, it invited the Secretary-General to submit to it periodic updated reports on capital punishment at five-year intervals starting from 1975. A fourth Report on capital punishment was accordingly submitted in 1975 and a fifth one in 1980. Meanwhile, the General Assembly at its 32nd Session adopted Resolution 32/61 on 8th December 1977 and this Resolution reaffirmed 'the desirability of abolishing this', that is, capital 'punishment' in all countries.

More recently, a General Assembly committee of the United Nations passed on 15th November 2007 a draft resolution calling for an end to the death penalty, an effort critics complained marked an attempt to interfere with the sovereignty of UN member states. The 99-52 vote on 15th November 2007 in favour of the resolution in the assembly's human rights committee capped two days of often heated debate that saw the United States taking the unusual step of siding with countries such as Iran and Syria on an issue that has so far failed to win approval in the world body. A total of 33 countries abstained. Over a dozen amendments –including the right to life of unborn children were introduced and soundly defeated. "I strongly hope that in approving this resolution we will be starting a process in which we will be all .... walking together along the same path", said Italy's UN ambassador Marcello Spatafora, one of the draft resolution's sponsors. The draft resolution, co-sponsored by European Union states and 60 other countries, must still be submitted to the entire 192-member General

Assembly for a vote. If approved, it would be non-binding, but would carry moral weight. It calls on those countries that still allow capital punishment to respect international standards that safeguard the rights of condemned inmates. It also calls on capital punishment countries to "establish a moratorium on executions with a view to abolishing the death penalty," and calls upon those who have abolished the punishment not to reintroduce it. Over the two days of debate, countries opposed to the resolution, including Antigua and Barbados and Syria, argued that it smacked of moral righteousness on the part of proponents and that it touched on issues of national sovereignty. But Spatafora said the resolution's backing was broad. "It is not only European and that's why it is successful," Spatafora told reporters. "That is the difference to understand from previous attempts" to pass a moratorium resolution.[6]

It will thus be seen, says Justice Bhagwati, that the United Nations has gradually shifted from the position of a neutral observer concerned about but not committed on the question of death penalty, to a position favouring the eventual abolition of the death penalty. The objective of the United Nations, according to Justice Bhagwati, has been and that is the standard set by the world body that capital punishment should ultimately be abolished in all countries.

7 View of a few eminent persons on abolition of death penalty Jai Prakash Narayan, the great humanist, while speaking on abolition of death penalty, said: "To my mind, it is ultimately a question of respect for life and human approach to those who commit grievous hurts to others. Death sentence is no remedy for such crimes. A more humane and constructive remedy is to remove the culprit concerned from the normal milieu and treat him as a mental case. I am sure a large proportion of the murderers could be weaned away from their path and their mental condition be sufficiently improved to become useful citizens. In a minority of cases, this may not be possible. They may be kept in prison houses till they die a natural death. This may cast a heavier economic burden on society than hanging. *But I have no doubt that a humane treatment even of a murderer will enhance man's dignity and make society more human*".

Andrei Sakharov in a message to the Stockholm Conference on Abolition of Death Penalty organised by Amnesty International in 1978 expressed himself firmly against death penalty thus: "I regard the death penalty as a savage and immoral institution which undermines

6 *Times of India*, Kolkata (17.11.2007).

the moral and legal foundations of a society. A State, in the person of its functionaries, who like all people are inclined to making superficial conclusions, who like all people are subject to influence, connections, prejudices and egocentric motivations for their behaviour, takes upon itself the right to the most terrible and irreversible act—the deprivation of life. Such a State cannot expect an improvement of the moral atmosphere in its country. *I reject the notion that the death penalty has any essential deterrent effect on potential offenders. I am convinced that the contrary is true—that savagery begets only savagery*... .I am convinced that society as a whole and each of its members individually, not just the person who comes before the courts, bears a responsibility for the occurrence of a crime .... I believe that the death penalty has no moral or practical justification and represents a survival of barbaric customs of revenge. Bloodthirsty and calculated revenge with no temporary insanity on the part of the judges, and therefore, shameful and disgusting."

Tolstoy also protested against death sentence in an article "I Cannot be Silent" and said: "Twelve of those by whose labour we live, the very men whom we have depraved and are still depraving by every means in our power—from the poison of vodka to the terrible falsehood of a creed we impose on them with all our might, but do not ourselves believe in—twelve of those men strangled with cords by those whom they feed and clothe and house, and who have depraved and still continue to deprave them—twelve husbands, fathers, and sons, from among those upon whose kindness, industry, and simplicity alone rests the whole of Russian life, are seized, imprisoned, and shackled. Then their hands are tied behind their backs lest they should seize the ropes by which they are to be hung, and they are led to the gallows".

Victor Hugo in the spirit of the Bishop created by him in his Les Miserables said on abolition of death penalty: "We shall look upon crime as a disease. Evil will be treated in charity instead of anger. The change will be simple and sublime. The cross shall displace the scaffold, reason is on our side, feeling is on our side, and experience is on our side".

Mahatma Gandhi also wrote to the same effect in his simple but inimitable style: "Destruction of individuals can never be a virtuous act. The evildoers cannot be done to death. Today there is a movement afoot for the abolition of capital punishment and attempts are being made to convert prisons into hospitals as if they are persons suffering from a disease".

8 Infliction of death penalty—not blessed by the Indian Constitution The existence of the provisions for death penalty in the Indian Constitution as said earlier does not, however, mean that the infliction of death penalty is blessed by the Constitution or that it has the imprimatur or seal of approval of the Constitution. The question, says Justice Bhagwati, still remains open as to whether the prescription of death penalty by any particular law is violative of any provision of the Constitution and more particularly Articles 14 and 21 thereof, and, therefore, rendered unconstitutional. This question has to be answered in the context of section 302 of the Indian Penal Code read with section 354(3) of the Criminal Procedure Code taking into consideration (*i*) the true nature of death penalty and its involvement in terms of human anguish and suffering; and (*ii*) the test of proportionality of the sentence to the offence.

9 Legislative development shifting the punitive centre of gravity from life-taking to life sentence If we look at the legislative history of the relevant provisions of the Indian Penal Code and the Code of Criminal Procedure, we find that in our country there has been a gradual shift against the imposition of death penalty. "The legislative development, through several successive amendments, has shifted the punitive centre of gravity from life-taking to life-sentence", said Justice Bhagwati. Sub-section (5) of section 367 of the Code of Criminal Procedure 1898 as it stood prior to its amendment by Act 26 of 1955 provided: "If the accused is convicted of an offence punishable with death, and the court sentences to any punishment other than death, the court shall in its judgment state the reasons why sentence of death was not passed".

This provision laid down that if an accused was convicted of an offence punishable with death, the imposition of death sentence was the rule and the awarding of a lesser sentence was an exception and the court had to state the reasons for not passing the sentence of death. In other words, the discretion was directed positively towards death penalty.

But, by the Amending Act 26 of 1955 which came into force with effect from 1st January 1956, this provision was deleted with the result that from and after that date, it was left to the discretion of the court on the facts of each case to pass a sentence of death or to award a lesser sentence. Where the court found in a given case that, on the facts and circumstances of the case, the death sentence was not called for or there were extenuating circumstances to justify the passing of the lesser sentence, the court would award the lesser sentence and not impose the death penalty. Neither death penalty nor life sentence was the rule under the law as it stood after the abolition of sub-section (5) of section 367 by the Amending Act 26 of 1955 and the court was left "equally free to award either sentence".

But then again, there was a further shift against death penalty by reason of the abolitionist pressure and when the new Code of Criminal Procedure, 1973 was enacted, section 354, sub-section (3) provided:

> "When the conviction is for an offence punishable with death or, in the alternative, with imprisonment for life or imprisonment for a term of years, the judgment shall state the reasons for the sentence awarded, and, in the case of sentence of death, the special reasons for such sentence."

The Court is now, therefore, required under the provisions of section 354(3) to state the reasons for the sentence awarded and in case of sentence of death, special reasons are required to be stated. It will thus be seen that life sentence is now the rule and it is only in exceptional cases, for special reasons, that death sentence can be imposed. The legislature has, however, not indicated what are the special reasons for which departure can be made from the normal rule and death penalty may be inflicted. The legislature has not given any guidance as to what are those exceptional cases in which, deviating from the normal rule, death sentence may be imposed. This is left entirely to the unguided discretion of the court, a feature, which, in Justice Bhagwati's opinion, has lethal consequences so far as the constitutionality of death penalty is concerned. But one thing is clear, says Justice Bhagwati, that through these legislative changes "the disturbed conscience of the State on the question of legal threat to life by way of death sentence has sought to express itself legislatively", the stream of tendency being towards cautions abolition.

It is also interesting to note that a further legislative attempt towards restricting and rationalizing death penalty was made in the late seventies. A Bill called Indian Penal Code (Amendment) Bill 1972 for amending Section 302 was passed by the Rajya Sabha in 1978 and it was pending in the Lok Sabha at the time when *Rajendra Prasad* case[7] was decided and though it ultimately lapsed with the dissolution of the Lok Sabha, it shows how strongly were the minds of the elected representatives of the people agitated against "homicidal exercise of

7 *Rajendra Prasad* v *State of U.P.* (1979)3 SCC 646: AIR 1979 SC 916: 1979 Cr LJ 792.

discretion" which is often an "obsession with retributive justice in disguise". This Bill sought to narrow drastically the judicial discretion to impose death penalty and tried to formulate the guidelines which should control the exercise of judicial exercise in this punitive area. But unfortunately the Bill though passed by the Rajya Sabha could not see its way through the Lok Sabha and was not enacted into law. Otherwise perhaps the charge against the present section 302 of the Indian Penal Code read with section 354, sub-section (3) of the Code of Criminal Procedure that it does not indicate any policy or principle to guide the exercise of judicial discretion in awarding death penalty, would have been considerably diluted, though even then, to quote Justice Bhagwati, "I doubt very much whether that section could have survived the attack against its constitutionality on the ground that it still leaves the door open for arbitrary exercise of discretion in imposing death penalty".

10 True nature of death penalty and its involvement in terms of human anguish and suffering The problem of constitutional validity of death penalty cannot be appreciated in its proper perspective, says Justice Bhagwati, without an adequate understanding of the true nature of death penalty and what it involves in terms of human anguish and suffering.

A. ***Death penalty irrevocable*** In the first place, Justice Bhagwati asserts, death penalty is irrevocable; it cannot be recalled. It extinguishes the flame of life for ever and is plainly destructive of the right to life, the most precious right of all, a right without which enjoyment of no other rights is possible. It silences for ever a living being and despatches him to that "undiscovered country from whose bourn no traveller returns" nor, once executed, "can storied urn or animated bust back to its mansion call the fleeting breath". It is by reason of its cold and cruel finality that death penalty is qualitatively different from all other forms of punishment. If a person is sentenced to imprisonment, even if it be for life, and subsequently it is found that he was innocent and was wrongly convicted, he can be set free. Of course, the imprisonment that he has suffered till then cannot be undone and the time he has spent in the prison cannot be given back to him in specie but he can come back and be restored to normal life with his honour vindicated, if he is found innocent. But that is not possible where a person has been wrongly convicted and sentenced to death and put out of existence in pursuance of the sentence of death. In his case, even if any mistake is subsequently discovered, it will be too late; in every way and for every purpose it will be too late, for he cannot be brought back to life. The execution of the sentence of death in such a case makes miscarriage of justice irrevocable. Justice Bhagwati asks : "On whose conscience will this death of an innocent man lie?" The State through its judicial instrumentality would have killed an innocent man. How is it different from a private murder? Questions Justice Bhagwati. That is why Lafayatte said: "I shall ask for the abolition of the penalty of death until I have the infallibility of human judgment demonstrated (to) me".

It is argued on behalf of the retentionists that having regard to the elaborate procedural safeguards enacted by the law in cases involving capital punishment, the possibility of mistake is more imaginary than real and these procedural safeguards virtually make conviction of an innocent person impossible. But Justice Bhagwati says: 'I do not think this argument is well founded. It is not supported by factual data. Hugo Bedau in his well known book. "The Death Penalty in America" has individually documented seventy- four cases since 1893 in which it has been responsibly charged and in most of them proved beyond doubt, that persons were wrongly convicted of criminal homicide in America. Eight out of these seventy-four, though innocent, were executed. Redin, Gardener, Frank and others have specifically identified many more additional cases. R.T. Paget and S.S. Silverman in their book *"Hanged and Innocent*" unearthed a number of cases in Britain where death penalty was inflicted on persons who were later found innocent. The authors narrate eye-opening incidents of several cases where truth came out after the execution. These are cases in which it has been possible to show from discovery of subsequent facts that the convictions were erroneous and innocent persons were put to death, but there may be many more cases where by reason of the difficulty of uncovering the facts after conviction, let alone after execution, it may not be possible to establish that there was miscarriage of justice. The jurist Olivecroix, applying a calculus of probabilities to the chance of judicial error, concluded as far back as in 1860 that approximately one innocent man was condemned out of every 257 cases. The proportion seems low but only in relation to moderate punishment. In relation to capital punishment, the proportion is infinitively high. When Hugo wrote that he preferred to call the guillotine Lesurques (the name of an innocent man guillotined in the Carrier de Lyon case), he did not mean that every man who was decapitated was a Lesurques, but that one Lesurques was enough to wipe out the value of capital punishment for ever. It is interesting to note that where cases of wrongful execution have come to public attention, they have been a major force responsible for bringing about abolition of death penalty. The Evans case in England in which an innocent man was hanged in 1949 played a large role in the abolition of capital punishment in that country. Belgium also abjured capital punishment on account of one such judicial error and so did Wisconsin, Rhode Island and Maine in the United States of America'.

'Howsoever careful may be the procedural safeguards erected by the law before death penalty can be imposed', says Justice Bhagwati, 'it is impossible to eliminate the chance of judicial error. No possible judicial safeguards can prevent conviction of the innocent. Students of the criminal process have identified several reasons why innocent men may be convicted of crime. In the first place, our methods of investigation are crude and archaic. We are, by and large, ignorant of modern methods of investigation based on scientific and technological advances. Our convictions are based largely on oral evidence of witnesses. Often, witnesses perjure themselves as they are motivated by caste, communal and factional considerations. Some time they are even got up by the police to prove what the police believes to be a true case. Sometimes there is also mistaken eye witness identification and this evidence is almost always difficult to shake in cross-examination. Then there is also the possibility of a frame up of innocent men by their enemies. There are also cases where an over zealous prosecutor may fail to disclose evidence of innocence known to him but not known to the defence. The possibility of error in judgment cannot, therefore, be ruled out on any theoretical considerations. It is indeed a very live possibility and it is not at all unlikely that so long as death penalty remains a constitutionally valid alternative, the court or the State acting through the instrumentality of the court may have on its conscience the blood of an innocent man.'

The possibility of a frame up of innocent men by their enemies and the possibility of judicial error resulting there from as said earlier are not figment of imagination. The story of Suzanne and Daniel as described in the Bible is a living instance of that. The story goes like this:

Babylon was ruled by a Council of Elders. Suzanne was a married woman of breathtaking beauty and these old men were no different from the old men of today. Each is supposed to have cast a lecherous glance at her. Each tried to fornicate with her. But the virtue of the woman was stronger than the persistence of these old men. She resisted and four old men contrived to bring against her a false charge of adultery with a young man, unknown. Since the judiciary had not been separated from the executive, the prosecutor, the witness and the judge were all rolled into one. The judicial process ended in a verdict of guilty and a sentence of death was pronounced. The Bible records that a crowd had collected to witness the blood of this young woman flow. But from the crowd arose the first lawyer of history. A young man said, "I don't believe that this woman is guilty". He asked for the right to cross-examine the old men. A young inexperienced lawyer displayed the first attempt at cross-examination. The bravado of the young man impressed the crowd who conceded that he should be allowed to ask questions. By a very rudimentary cross-examination, he landed the four old men in what is called in modern court parlance glaring contradictions. One said that this adultery had taken place under the open skies; another said it had taken place under the banyan tree and so on. By the time Daniel finished his cross-examination, the crowd was howling for the blood of these old men. False charges which end in sentences of death being pronounced is a matter of ancient history, but young Daniels are not to be found everywhere.

It is sometimes argued that, on the reasoning cited above, every criminal trial must necessarily raise the possibility of wrongful conviction and if that be so, are we going to invalidate every form of punishment? But, Justice Bhagwati says: 'this argument, I am afraid, is an argument of despair. There is a qualitative difference between death penalty and other forms of punishment. I have already pointed out that the former extinguishes the flame of life altogether and is irrevocable and beyond recall while the latter can, at least to some extent be set right, if found mistaken. This vital difference between death penalty and imprisonment was emphasized by Mahatma Gandhi when he said in reply to a German writer: "I would draw distinction between killing and detention and even corporal punishment. I think there is a difference not merely in quantity but also in quality. I can recall the punishment of detention. I can make reparation to the man upon whom I inflict corporal punishment. But once a man is killed, the punishment is beyond recall or reparation."

The same point was made by the distinguished criminologist Leon Radzinowicz when he said: "The likelihood of error in a capital sentence case stands on a different footing altogether." Judicial error in imposition of death penalty would indeed be crime beyond punishment. This is the drastic nature of death penalty, terrifying in its consequences, which has to be taken into account in determining in constitutional validity.

B. ***Death penalty barbaric and inhuman in its effect*** Death penalty, says Justice Bhagwati, is barbaric and inhuman in its effect—mental and physical – upon the condemned man and is positively cruel.

PSYCHOLOGICAL EFFECT OF DEATH PENALTY ON PRISONER. This aspect is narrated by Justice Bhagwati thus: 'Psychological effect on the prisoner in the death row is disastrous. One psychiatrist has described death row as a "grisly laboratory" "the ultimate experimental stress in which the condemned prisoner's personality is incredibly brutalised". He points out that the strain of existence on death row is very likely to produce acute psychotic breaks. Some inmates are driven to ravings or delusions but the majority sink into a sort of catatonic numbness under the overwhelming stress. Intense mental suffering is inevitably associated with confinement under sentence of death. Anticipation of approaching death can and does produce stark terror. Justice Brennan in his opinion in *Furman* v *Georgia*[8] as a reason for holding the capital punishment to be unconstitutional observed that "mental pain is an inseparable part of our practice of punishing criminals by death, for the prospect of pending execution exacts a frightful toll during the inevitable long wait between the imposition of sentence and the actual infliction of death". Krishna Iyer, J. also pointed out in *Rajendra Prasad's* case[9] that "the excruciation of long pendency of the death sentence with the prisoner languishing near-solitary suffering all the time, may make the death sentence unconstitutionally cruel and agonising". The California Supreme Court, also in finding the death penalty per se unconstitutional remarked with a sense of poignancy: "The cruelty of capital punishment lies not only in the execution itself and the pain incident thereto, but also in the dehumanising effects of the lengthy imprisonment prior to execution during which the judicial and administrative procedures essential to due process of law are carried out. Penologists and medical experts agree that the process of carrying out a verdict of death is often so degrading and brutalizing to the human spirit as to constitute psychological torture"'.

Justice Bhagwati further pointed out: 'In Re *Kemmler*[10] the Supreme Court of the United States accepted that "punishments are cruel when they involve a lingering death, something more than the mere extinguishment of life." Now a death would be as lingering if a man spends several years in a death cell awaiting execution as it would be if the method of execution takes an unacceptably long time to kill the victim. The pain of mental lingering can be as intense as the agony of

8 408 US 238.

9 *Rajendra Prasad* v *State of U.P.* (1979)3 SCC 646: AIR 1979 SC 916: 1979 Cr LJ 792.

10 136 US 436.

physical lingering. Justice Miller also pointed out in Re *Medley*[11] that "when a prisoner sentenced by a court to death is confined to the penitentiary awaiting the execution of the sentence, one of the most horrible feelings to which he can be subjected during that time is the uncertainty during the whole of it...as to the precise time when his execution shall take place". He acknowledged that such uncertainty is inevitably "accompanied by an immense mental anxiety amounting to a great increase of the offender's punishment.'"

But quite apart from this excruciating mental anguish and severe psychological strain which the condemned prisoner has to undergo on account of the long wait from the date when the sentence of death is initially passed by the sessions court until it is confirmed by the High Court and then the appeal against the death sentence is disposed of by the Supreme Court and if the appeal is dismissed, then until the clemency petition is considered by the President and if it is turned down, then until the time appointed for actual execution of the sentence of death arrives, the worst time for most of the condemned prisoners, says Justice Bhagwati, would be the last few hours when all certainty is gone and the moment of death is known. Dostoyevsky who actually faced a firing squad only to be reprieved at the last instant, described this experience thus: "...the chief and the worst pain is perhaps not inflicted by wounds, but by your certain knowledge that in an hour, in ten minutes, in half a minute, now this moment your soul will fly out of your body, and that you will be a human being no longer, and that that's certain the main thing is that it is certain... Take a soldier and put him in front of a cannon in battle and fire at him and he will still hope, but read the same soldier his death sentence for certain, and he will go mad or burst out crying. Who says that human nature is capable of bearing this without madness? Why this cruel, hideous, unnecessary and useless mockery? Possibly there are men who have sentences of death read out to them and have been given time to go through this torture, and have then been told, you can go now, you've been reprieved. Such men could perhaps tell us. It was of agony like this and of such horror that Christ spoke. No you can't treat a man like that!"

We have also accounts of execution of several prisoners in the United States which show how in these last moment condemned prisoners often simply disintegrate. Canns has in frank and brutal language bared the terrible psychological cruelty of capital punishment:

11 134 US 160.

"Execution is not simply death. It is just as different in essence, from the privation of life as a concentration camp is from prison ... .It adds to death a rule, a public premeditation known to the future victim, an organisation, in short, which is in itself a source of moral sufferings more terrible than death... For there to be equivalence, the death penalty would have to punish a criminal who had warned his victim of the date at which he would inflict a horrible death on him and who, from that moment, onward, had confined him at his mercy for months. Such a monster is not encountered in private life". There can be no stronger words to describe the utter depravity and inhumanity of death sentence.

PHYSICAL PAIN AND SUFFERING INVOLVED IN DEATH PENALTY. The physical pain and suffering which the execution of the sentence of death involves is also no less cruel and inhuman. In India, the method of execution followed is hanging by the rope. Electrocution or application of lethal gas has not yet taken its place as in some of the western countries. "It is, therefore, with reference to execution by hanging", said Justice Bhagwati, "that I must consider whether the sentence of death is barbaric and inhuman as entailing physical pain and agony". Although the Royal Commission on Capital Punishment 1949-53 found that amongst all the methods of execution hanging is the most humane method of execution and so also in *Ichikawa* v *Japan*,[12] the Japanese Supreme Court held that execution by hanging does not correspond to 'cruel punishment' inhibited by Article 36 of the Japanese Constitution, yet one thing is clear that hanging is undoubtedly accompanied by intense physical torture and pain.

Justice Bhagwati referred to Warden Duffy of San Quentin, a high security prison in the United States of America, who described the hanging process with brutal frankness in lucid details thus: "The day before an execution the prisoner goes through a harrowing experience of being weighed, measured for length of drop to assure breaking of the neck, the size of the neck, body measurement et cetera. When the trap springs he dangles at the end of the rope. There are times when the neck has not been broken and the prisoner strangles to death. His eyes pop almost out of his head, his tongue swells and protrudes from his mouth, his neck may be broken, and the rope many times takes large portions of skin and flesh from the side of the face that the noose is on. He urinates, he defecates, and droppings fall to the floor while witnesses look on, and at almost all executions one or more faint or have to be

12 Vide: David Pannick on "*Judicial Review of Death Penalty*", page 73.

helped out of the witness-room. The prisoner remains dangling from the end of the rope for 8 to 14 minutes before the doctor, who has climbed up a small ladder and listens to his heartbeat with a stethoscope, pronounces him dead. A prison guard stands at the feet of the hanged person and holds the body steady, because during the first few minutes there is usually considerable struggling in an effort to breathe".

If the drop is too short, points out Justice Bhagwati, there will be a slow and agonising death by strangulation. On the other hand, if the drop is too long, the head will be torn off. In England centuries of practice have produced a detailed chart relating a man's weight and physical condition to the proper length of drop, but even there mistakes have been made. In 1927, a surgeon who witnessed a double execution wrote: "The bodies were cut down after fifteen minutes and placed in an antechamber, when I was horrified to hear one of the supposed corpses give a gasp and find him making respiratory efforts, evidently a prelude to revival. The two bodies were quickly suspended again for a quarter of an hour longer...Dislocation of the neck is the ideal aimed at, but, out of all my post-mortem findings, that has proved rather an exception, in the majority of instances the cause of death was strangulation and asphyxia".

These passages clearly establish beyond doubt that the execution of sentence of death by hanging does involve intense physical pain and suffering, though it may be regarded by some as more humane than electrocution or application of lethal gas.

If this be the true mental and physical effect of death sentence on the condemned prisoner and if it causes such mental anguish, psychological strain and physical agony and suffering, Justice Bhagwati says, it is difficult to see how it can be regarded as anything but cruel and inhuman. The only answer which can be given for justifying this infliction of mental and physical pain and suffering is that the condemned prisoner having killed a human being does not merit any sympathy and must suffer this punishment because he deserves it. No mercy can be shown to one who did not show any mercy to others. But, this justificatory reason cannot commend itself to any civilised society because it is based on the theory of retribution or retaliation and at the bottom of it lies the desire of the society to avenge itself against the wrong doer. That is not a permissible penological goal, points out Justice Bhagwati.

11 Sentence to be proportionate to the offence It is an essential element of the rule of law, views Justice Bhagwati, that the sentence imposed must be proportionate to the offence. The utilitarian value of the punishment has nothing to do with the proportionality to the offence.

Position in Canada In Canada, in the case of *Rex* v *Miller and Cockriell*[13] the principle of proportionality has been recognised by Laskin, CJ. speaking on behalf of Canadian Supreme Court as "one of the constitutional criteria of 'cruel and unusual treatment or punishment' prohibited under the Canadian Bill of Rights. Laskin, CJ., pointed out in that case: "It would be patent to me, for example, that death as a mandatory penalty today for theft would be offensive to section 2(*b*). That is because there are social and moral considerations that enter into the scope and application of section 2(*b*). Harshness of punishment and its severity in consequences are relative to the offence involved but, that being said, there may still be a question (to which history too may be called in aid of its resolution) whether the punishment prescribed is so excessive as to outrage standards of decency. That is not a precise formula for section 2(*b*) but I doubt whether a more precise one can be found."

Position in India In India, Justice Bhagwati says, the principle of proportionality flows directly as a necessary element from Articles 14, 19 and 21 of the Constitution of India. If a law provides for imposition of a sentence which is disproportionate to the offence, it would be arbitrary and irrational, for it would not pass the test of reason and would be contrary to the rule of law and void under Articles 14, 19 and 21 of the Constitution. If, for example, death penalty is prescribed for the simple offence of theft–as indeed it was at one time in the seventeenth century England–it would be clearly excessive and wholly disproportionate to the offence and hence arbitrary and irrational by any standards of human decency and it would be impossible to sustain against the challenge of the above mentioned articles of the Constitution. It must, therefore, be taken to be clear beyond doubt that the proportionality principle constitutes an important constitutional criterion in India for adjudging the validity of a sentence imposed by law.

Position in USA The Courts in the United States have recognised the validity of the proportionality principle. In *Gregg* v *Goergia*,[14] Stewart, J.,

13 70 DLR (3d) 324.
14 428 US 153: 49 L.Ed 2d 859 (1976).

speaking for the plurality of the American Supreme Court said that "to satisfy constitutional requirements, the punishment must not be excessive...the punishment must not be out of proportion to the severity of the crime". This constitutional criterion was also applied in *Coker* v *Georgia*[15] to invalidate the death penalty for rape of an adult woman. While, J., with whom Stewarts and Blackmun, JJ., agreed, said, with regard to the offence of rape committed against an adult woman: "a sentence of death is grossly disproportionate and excessive punishment for the crime of rape and is therefore forbidden by the Eighth Amendment as cruel and unusual punishment". Likewise, in *Lockette* v *Ohio*[16] where the defendant sat outside the scene of robbery waiting to drive her accomplices away and contrary to plan, the robbers murdered three victims in the course of their robbery and she was convicted and sentenced to death by resort to the doctrine of vicarious liability, the Supreme Court of the United States applying the same principle of proportionality held the death sentence unconstitutional. Marshall, J., pointed out that because the appellant was convicted under a theory of vicarious liability, the death penalty imposed on her "violates the principle of proportionality embodied in the Eighth Amendment's prohibition" and White, J., also subscribed to the same reasoning when he said, "the infliction of death upon those who had no intent to bring about the death of the victim is...grossly out of proportion to the severity of the crime". The Supreme Court of the United States in holding such view relied upon the Eighth Amendment which prohibits cruel and unusual treatment or punishment.

Position under international charters Mr. David Pannick in his book Judicial Review of the Death Penalty pointed out that international charters of rights express or imply the principle of proportionality. Article 7 of the International Covenant on Civil and Political Rights forbids torture and cruel, in human or degrading treatment or punishment and so does Article 3 of the European Convention on Human Rights. It has been suggested by Francis Jacobs, a factor to be considered in deciding whether the death penalty, in particular circumstances, was contrary to Article 3 would be whether it was disproportionate to the offence.

A. UTILITARIAN VALUE OF PUNISHMENT HAS NOTHING TO DO WITH THE PROPORTIONALITY TO THE OFFENCE. In considering the question of

15 433 US 584: 53 L.Ed 2d 982 (1977).
16 438 US 586: 57 L.Ed 973 (1978).

proportionality *vis-a-vis* the constitutionality, the existence of rational legislative purpose becomes a necessary condition but not a sufficient one. For example, the death penalty for theft would deter most potential thieves and may have a unique deterrent effect in preventing the commission of the offence and may thus serve the legislative purpose of controlling the crime; still it would be wholly disproportionate and excessive, for the social effect of the penalty is not decisive of the proportionality to the offence.

The European Court of Human Rights observed in *Tyrer* v *U.K.*[17] that "a punishment does not lose its degrading character as deterrent or aid to crime control. Above all, as the court must emphasise, it is never permissible to have recourse to punishments which are contrary to Article 3, whatever their deterrent effect may be". Article 3 of the European Convention on Human Rights, it may be noted, forbids torture and cruel, inhuman and degrading treatment and punishment.

B. SENTENCE OF DEATH FOR MURDER—WHETHER SATISFIES THE TEST OF PROPORTIONALITY. The proportionality between the offence and death penalty, views Justice Bhagwati, has to be judged by reference to various objective factors, such as, international standards or norms or the climate of international opinion, modern penological theories and evolving standards of human decency.

(I) *INTERNATIONAL STANDARDS & INTERNATIONAL OPINIONS—NOT SATISFYING THE TEST OF PROPORTIONALITY BETWEEN THE OFFENCE AND DEATH PENALTY.* Justice Bhagwati points out that the international standard or norm which is being evolved by the United Nations is against death penalty and so also is the climate of opinion in most of the civilized countries.

(II) *PENOLOGICAL GOALS NOT SATISFYING THE TEST OF PROPORTIONALITY BETWEEN THE OFFENCE AND DEATH PENALTY.* There are three justifications, according to Justice Bhagwati, traditionally advanced in support of punishment in general, namely, reformation, denunciation by the community, or retribution, and deterrence. These are the three ends of punishment, its three penological goals, with reference to which any punishment prescribed by law must be justified. If it cannot be justified with reference to one or the other of these three penological purposes, it would have to be condemned as arbitrary and irrational, for in a

17 2 EHRRI (1978).

civilized society governed by the rule of law, no punishment could be inflicted on an individual unless it serves some social purpose.

(*a*) *Constitutionality of death penalty with reference to the reformatory end of punishment as one of the penological goals.* The civilised goal of criminal justice, in the view of Justice Bhagwati, is the reformation of the criminal and death penalty means abandonment of this goal for those who suffer it. Obviously death penalty cannot serve the reformatory goal because it extinguishes life and puts an end to any possibility of reformation. In fact, it defeats the reformatory end of punishment. Protagonists of death penalty say that though there may be a few murderers whom it may be possible to reform and rehabilitate, what about those killers who cannot be reformed and rehabilitated? Why should the death penalty be not awarded to them? In the words of Justice Bhagwati, the above argument advanced by the protagonists cannot be sustained. There is no way of accurately predicting or knowing with any degree of moral certainty that a murderer will not be reformed or is incapable of reformation. All we know is that there have been many many successes even with the most vicious of cases. Was Jean Valjean of Les Miserbles not reformed by the kindness and magnanimity of the Bishop? Was Valmiki a sinner not reformed and did he not become the author of one of the world's greatest epics? Was Chandashoka, the sinner, not reformed and did he not become the Dharmashoka? Were the dacoits of Chambal not transformed by the saintliness of Achariya Vinoba Bhave and Jai Prakash Narain? We have also the examples of Nathan Leopold, Paul Crump and Edger Smith who were guilty of the most terrible and gruesome murders but who, having escaped the gallows, became decent and productive human beings. These and many other examples clearly show that it is not possible to know beforehand with any degree of certainty that a murderer is beyond reformation. Then, asked Justice Bhagwati, would it be right to extinguish the life of a human being merely on the basis of speculation—and it can only be speculation and not any definitive certainty–that he cannot be reformed. There is divinity in every man and to Justice Bhagwati's mind no one is beyond redemption. It was Ramakrishna Paramhansa, one of the greatest saints of the 19th century, who said, “Each soul is potentially divine”. There is Brahma in every living being as the Upanishad says and to the same effect we find a remarkable utterance in the Brahmasukta of Atharvaveda where a sage exclaims: “Indeed these killers are Brahma; these servants (or slaves) are Brahma; these cheats and rogues are also manifestation of one and the same Brahma itself.” Therefore, once the dross of Tamas is removed and Satva is brought forth by methods of rehabilitation such as community service, yoga, meditation and satsang or holy influence, a change definitely takes place and the man is reformed. This is not just a fancy or idealised view taken by Indian philosophical thought, but it also finds support from the report of the Royal Commission on Capital Punishment set up in the United Kingdom where it has been said: "Not that murderers in general are incapable of reformation, the evidence plainly shows the contrary". "Indeed", continued the report of the Royal Commission, "the experience of countries without capital punishment indicates that the prospects of reformation are at least as favourable with murderers as with those who have committed other kinds of serious crimes." The hope of reforming even the worst killer is based on experience as well as faith and to legitimate the death penalty even in the so called exceptional cases where a killer is said to be beyond reformation, would be to destroy this hope by sacrificing it at the altar of superstition and irrationality. "I would not, therefore, speaking for myself", said Justice Bhagwati, "be inclined to recognise any exception, though Justice Krishna Iyer has done so in *Rajendra Prasad's* case,[18] that death penalty may be legally permissible where it is found that a killer is such a monster or beast that he can never be reformed". Moreover, it may be noted, as pointed out by Albert Camus, that in resorting to this philosophy of elimination of social monsters, we would be approaching some of the worst ideas of totalitarianism or the selective racism which the Hitler regime propounded. Sir Ernest Gowers, Chairman of the Royal Commission on Capital Punishment, also emphasized the disturbing implications of this argument favouring elimination of a killer who is a social monster and warned thus: "If it is right to eliminate useless and dangerous members of the community, why should the accident of having committed a capital offence determine who should be selected. These are only a tiny proportion and not necessarily the most dangerous....It can lead to Nazism". The theory that a killer who is believed to be a social monster or beast should be eliminated in defence of the society cannot, therefore, be accepted and it cannot provide a justification for imposition of death penalty even in this narrow class of cases, pointed out Justice Bhagwati.

(*b*) *Constitutionality of death penalty with reference to the denunciation by the community or retribution as one of the penological goals.* The argument which is sometimes advanced in support of the death penalty

18 *Rajendra Prasad* v *State of U.P.* (1979)3 SCC 646: AIR 1979 SC 916: 1979 Cr LJ 792.

is that every punishment is to some extent intended to express the revulsion felt by the society against the wrong doer and the punishment must, therefore, be commensurate with the crime and since murder is one of the gravest crimes against society, death penalty is the only punishment which fits such crime and hence, it must be held to be reasonable. This argument, says Justice Bhagwati, is founded on the denunciatory theory of punishment which apparently claiming to justify punishment as the expression of the moral indignation of the society against the wrong doer, represents in truth and reality an attempt to legitimise the feeling of revenge entertained by the society against him.

The denunciatory theory was put forward as an argument in favour of death penalty by Lord Denning before the Royal Commission on Capital Punishment thus: "The punishment inflicted for grave crimes should adequately reflect the revulsion felt by the great majority of citizens for them. It is a mistake to consider the objects of punishment as being deterrent or reformative or preventive and nothing else. The ultimate justification of any punishment is not that it is a deterrent but that it is the emphatic denunciation by the community of a crime, and from this point of view there are some murders which in the present state of opinion demand the most emphatic denunciation of all, namely, the death penalty...".

The Royal Commission on Capital Punishment seemed to agree with Lord Denning's view about this justification for the death penalty and observed "...the law cannot ignore the public demand for retribution which heinous crimes undoubtedly provoke; it would be generally agreed that, though reform of the criminal law ought, sometimes, to give a lead to public opinion, it is dangerous to move too far in advance of it."

Though garbed in highly euphemistic language by labelling the sentiment underlying the above observation as reprobation and not revenge, its implication can hardly be disguised that the death penalty is considered necessary not because the preservation of the society demands it, but because the society wishes to avenge itself for the wrong done to it. Despite its high moral tone and phrase, the denunciatory theory is nothing but an echo of what Stephen said in rather strong language: "The criminal law stands to the passion of revenge in much the same relation as marriage to the sexual appetite."

The denunciatory theory, views Justice Bhagwati, is a remnant of a primitive society which has no respect for the dignity of man and the worth of the human person and seeks to assuage its injured conscience by taking revenge on the wrong doer. Revenge is an elementary passion of a brute and betrays lack of culture and refinement. The manner in which a society treats crime and criminals affords the surest index of its cultural growth and development. Long ago, mentions Justice Bhagwati, in the year 1910 Sir Winston Churchill gave expression to this social truth when he said in his inimitable language: "The mood and temper of the public with regard to the treatment of crime and the criminals is one of the most unfailing tests of civilization of any country. A calm dispassionate recognition of the right of accused, and even of the convicted, criminal against the State, a constant heart-searching by all charged with the duty of punishment...tireless efforts towards the discovery of curative and regenerative processes, unfailing faith that there is a treasure if you can only find it in the heart of every man—these are the symbols, which, in treatment of crime and the criminals, mark and measure the stored-up strength of a nation and are sign and proof of the living virtue in it".

A society which is truly cultured, a society which is reared on a spiritual foundation like the Indian society-can never harbour a feeling of revenge against a wrong doer, says Justice Bhagwati. On the contrary, it would try to reclaim the wrong doer and find the treasure that lies in his heart. The wrong doer is as much as part of the society as anyone else and by exterminating him, Justice Bhagwati asks: would the society not injure itself? If a limb of the human body becomes diseased, should we not try to cure it instead of amputating it? Would the human body not be partially disabled? Would it not be rendered imperfect by the amputation? Would the amputation not leave a scar on the human body? Would the human body not cease to be what it was intended by its maker? But if the diseased limb can be cured, would it not be so much better that the human body remains intact in all its perfection. Similarly the society also would benefit if one of its members who has gone astray and done some wrong can be reformed and regenerated. It will strengthen the fabric of the society and increase its inner strength and vitality. Let it not be forgotten, says Justice Bhagwati, that no human being is beyond redemption. There is divinity in every human being, if only we can create conditions in which it can blossom forth in its full glory and effulgence. It can dissolve the dross of criminality and make God out of man. "Each soul", said Shri Ramakrishna Paramhansa as referred to earlier, "is potentially divine" and it should be the endeavour of the society to reclaim the wrong doer and bring out the divinity in him and not to destroy him in a fit of anger or revenge. Retaliation can have no place in a civilised society and particularly in the land of Buddha and Gandhi, cautions Justice Bhagwati. The law of Jesus must prevail over the lex talionis of Moses: "Thou shalt not kill" must penologically overpower "Eye for an eye and tooth for a tooth."

The society has made tremendous advance in the last few decades and today the concept of human rights has taken firm root in our soil and there is a tremendous wave of consciousness in regard to the dignity and divinity of man. To take human life even with the sanction of the law and under the cover of judicial authority, says Justice Bhagwati, is retributive barbarity and violent futility, travesty of dignity and violation of the divinity of man. So long as the offender can be reformed through the rehabilitatory therapy which may be administered to him in the prison or other correctional institute and he can be reclaimed as a useful citizen and made conscious of the divinity within him by techniques such as meditation, how can there be any moral justification for liquidating him out of existence? In such a case, asserts Justice Bhagwati, it would be most unreasonable and arbitrary to extinguish the flame of life within him, for no social purpose would be served and no constitutional value advanced by doing so.

Justice Bhagwati pointed out that most philosophers have rejected retribution as a proper goal of punishment. Plato wrote: "He who desires to inflict rational punishment does not retaliate man who is punished, and he who sees him punished, may be deterred from doing wrong again. He punishes for the sake of prevention...."

Even in contemporary America, says Justice Bhagwati, it is firmly settled that retribution has no proper place in its criminal justice system. The New York Court of Appeals pointed out in a leading judgment in *People* v *Oliver*:[19] "The punishment or treatment of offenders is directed toward one or more of three ends: (1) to discourage and act as a deterrent upon future criminal activity; (2) to confine the offender so that he may not harm society; and (3) to correct and rehabilitate the offender. There is no place in the scheme for punishment for its own sake, the product simply of vengeance or retribution."

Similarly, the California Supreme Court has held that "to conclude that the Legislature was motivated by a desire for vengeance" would be "a conclusion not permitted in view of modern theories of penology."

The same view has been adopted in official studies of capital punishment. The British Royal Commission on Capital Punishment

19 1 NY 2d 152.

concluded that "modern penological thought discounts retribution in the sense of vengeance". The Florida Special Commission on Capital Punishment, which recommended retention of the death penalty on other grounds, rejected "vengeance or retaliation" as "justification for the official taking of life."

The reason for the general rejection of retribution as a purpose of the criminal justice system has been stated concisely by Professors Michael and Wechsler thus: "Since punishment consists in the infliction of pain, it is, apart from its consequence, an evil: consequently it is good and therefore just only if and to the degree that it serves the common good by advancing the welfare of the person punished or of the rest of the population ...... Retribution is itself unjust since it requires some human beings to inflict pain upon others, regardless of its effect upon them or upon the social welfare".

The Prime Minister of Canada Mr. Pierre Trudeaux, addressing the Canadian Parliament, pleading for abolition of death penalty, posed a question in the same strain: "Are we as a society so lacking in respect for ourselves, so lacking in hope for human betterment, so socially bankrupt that we are ready to accept state vengeance as our penal philosophy?"

It is difficult to appreciate, says Justice Bhagwati, how a feeling of vengeance whether on the part of the individual wronged or the society can ever be regarded as a healthy sentiment which the State should foster. It is true that when a heinous offence is committed, not only the individual who suffers as a result of the crime but also the entire society is oppressed with a feeling of revulsion, but as Arthur Koestler has put it in his inimitable style in his "Reflections on Hanging": "Though easy to dismiss in reasoned argument on both moral and logical grounds, the desire for vengeance has deep, unconscious roots and is roused when we feel strong indignation or revulsion—whether the reasoning mind approves or not. This psychological fact is largely ignored in abolitionist propaganda—yet it has to be accepted as a fact. The admission that even confirmed abolitionists are not proof against occasional vindictive impulses does not mean that such impulses should be legally sanctioned by society, any more than we sanction some other unpalatable instincts of our biological inheritance. Deep inside every civilized being there lurks a tiny Stone Age man, dangling a club to rob and rape, and screaming an eye for an eye. But we would rather not have that little fur-clad figure dictate the law of the land."

"I have no doubt in my mind", says Justice Bhagwati, "that if the only justification for the death penalty is to be found in revenge and retaliation, it would be clearly arbitrary and unreasonable punishment falling foul of Articles 14 and 21".

(c) *Constitutionality of death penalty with reference to the deterrent effect as one of the penological goals.* Protagonists argue that capital punishment acts as a deterrent against potential murderers. "This is", says Justice Bhagwati, "to my mind, a myth, which has been carefully nurtured by a society which is actuated not so much by logic or reason as by a sense of retribution". It is really the belief, according to Justice Bhagwati, in retributive justice that makes the death penalty attractive. The question whether the death penalty has really and truly a deterrent effect is an important issue which has received careful attention over the last 66 years in several countries including the United States of America. Probably no single subject in criminology has been studied more. Obviously, no penalty will deter all murders and probably any severe penalty will deter many. The key question, therefore, is not whether death penalty has a deterrent effect but whether death penalty has a greater deterrent effect than life sentence. Justice Bhagwati asks: Does death penalty deter potential murderers better than life imprisonment? The burden rests on the State to establish by producing material before the Court or otherwise, that death penalty has greater deterrent effect than life sentence in order to justify its imposition under the law. If the State fails to discharge this burden which rests upon it, the Court would have to hold that death penalty has not been shown to have greater deterrent effect and it does not, therefore, serve a rational legislative purpose.

The historical course through which death penalty has passed in the last 175 years or so shows that the theory that death penalty acts as a greater deterrent than life imprisonment is wholly unfounded. Not more than a century and seventy five years ago, in a civilised country like England, death penalty was awardable even for offences like shoplifting, cattle stealing and cutting down of trees. It is interesting to note that when Sir Samuel Romully brought proposal for abolition of death penalty for such offences, there was a hue and cry from lawyers, judges, parliamentarians and other so called protectors of social order and they opposed the proposal on the ground that death penalty acted as a deterrent against commission of such offences and if this deterrent was removed, the consequences would be disastrous. The then Chief Justice said while opposing abolition of capital punishment for shop-lifting: "Where terror of death which now, as the law stood, threatened the depredator to be removed, it was his opinion the consequence would be that shops would be liable to unavoidable losses from depredations and, in many instances, bankruptcy and ruin must become the lot of honest and laborious tradesmen. After all that had been said in favour of this speculative humanity, they must all agree that the prevention of crime should be the chief object of the law; and terror alone would prevent the commission of that crime under their consideration".

On a similar Bill, the Lord Chancellor remarked: "So long as human nature remained what it was, the apprehension of death would have the most powerful cooperation in deterring from the commission of crimes; and he thought it unwise to withdraw the salutary influence of that terror."

The Bill for abolition of death penalty for cutting down a tree was opposed by the Lord Chancellor in these terms: "It did undoubtedly seem a hardship that so heavy a punishment as that of death should be affixed to the cutting down of a single tree, or the killing or wounding of a cow. But if the Bill passed in its present state a person might root up or cut down whole acres of plantations or destroy the whole of the stock of cattle of a farmer without being subject to capital punishment."

Six times the House of Commons passed the Bill to abolish capital punishment for shop- lifting, six times the House of Lords threw out the Bill, the majority of one occasion including all the judicial members, one Arch Bishop and six Bishops. It was firmly believed by these opponents of abolition that death penalty acted as a deterrent and if it was abolished, offences of shop-lifting etc. would increase. But it is a matter of common knowledge that this belief was wholly unjustified and the abolition of death penalty did not have any adverse effect on the incidence of such offences. So also it is with death penalty for the offence of murder.

It is an irrational belief unsubstantiated by any factual data or empirical research that death penalty acts as a greater deterrent than life sentence and equally unfounded is the impression that the removal of death penalty will result in increase of homicide. The argument that the rate of homicide will increase if death penalty is removed from the statute book has always been advanced by the established order out of fear psychosis, because the established order has always been apprehensive that if there is any change and death penalty is abolished, its existence would be imperilled. This argument has, in the opinion of

Justice Bhagwati, no validity because, beyond a superstitious belief, for which there is no foundation in fact and which is based solely on unreason and fear, there is nothing at all to show that death penalty has any additionally deterrent effect not possessed by life sentence. Arthur Koestler tells us an interesting story that in the period when pick-pockets were punished by hanging in England, other thieves exercised their talents in the crowds surrounding the scaffold where the convicted pickpocket was being hanged. Statistics compiled in England show that out of 250 men hanged, 170 had previously attended one or even two public executions and yet they were not deterred from committing the offence of murder which ultimately led to their conviction and hanging. It is a myth nurtured by superstition and fear that death penalty has some special terror for the criminal which acts as a deterrent against the commission of the crime. Even an eminent Judge like Justice Frankfurter of the Supreme Court of the United States expressed the same opinion when he said in the course of his examination before the Royal Commission on Capital Punishment: "I think scientifically the claim of deterrence is not worth much".

The Royal Commission on Capital Punishment, says Justice Bhagwati, after four years of investigation which took it throughout the continent and even to the United States, also came to the same conclusion: "Whether the death penalty is used or not and whether executions are frequent or not, both death penalty states and abolition states show rates which suggests that these rates are conditioned by other factors than the death penalty". And then again, it observed in support of this conclusion: "The general conclusion which we have reached is that there is no clear evidence in any of the figures we have examined that the abolition of capital punishment has led to an increasing homicide rate or that its introduction has led to a fall."

Several studies have been carried out in the United States of America for the purpose of exploring the deterrent effect of death penalty and two different methods have been adopted. The first and by far the more important method seeks to prove the case of the abolitionists by showing that the abolition of capital punishment in other countries has not led to an increase in the incidence of homicide. This is attempted to be shown either by comparing the homicide statistics of countries where capital punishment has been abolished with the statistics for the same period of countries where it has been retained or by comparing statistics of a single country in which capital punishment has been abolished, for periods before and after abolition or where capital punishment has been reintroduced, then for the period before and after its reintroduction.

The second method relates to comparison of the number of executions in a country in particular years with the homicide rate in the years succeeding. Now, so far as the comparison of homicide statistics of countries which have abolished capital punishment with the statistics of countries which have retained it is concerned, it may not yield any definitive inference, because in most cases abolition or retention of death penalty may not be the only differentiating factor but there may be other divergent social, cultural or economic factors which may affect the homicide rates. It is only if all other factors are equal and the only variable is the existence or non-existence of death penalty that a proper comparison can be made for the purpose of determining whether death penalty has an additional deterrent effect which life sentence does not possess, but that would be an almost impossible controlled experiment. It may, however, be possible to find for comparison a small group of countries or states, preferably contiguous and closely similar in composition of population and social and economic conditions generally, in some of which capital punishment has been abolished and in others not. Comparison of homicide rates in these countries or states may afford a fairly reliable indication whether death penalty has a unique deterrent effect greater than that of life sentence. Such groups of states have been identified by Professor Sellin in the United States of America and similar conditions perhaps exist also in Newzealand and the Australian States. The figures of homicide rate in these states do not show any higher incidence of homicide in states which have abolished death penalty than in those which have not. Professor Sellin points out that the only conclusion which can be drawn from these figures is that there is no clear evidence of any influence of death penalty on the homicide rates of these states. In one of the best known studies conducted by him, Professor Sellin compared homicide rates between 1920 and 1963 in abolition states with the rates in neighbouring and similar retention States. He found that on the basis of the rates alone, it was impossible to identify the abolition states within each group. A similar study comparing homicide rates in states recently abolishing the death penalty and neighbouring retention states during the 1960's reached the same results. Michigan was the first State in the United States to abolish capital punishment and comparisons between Michigan and the bordering retention states of Ohio and Indiana states with comparable demographic characteristics did not show any significant differences in homicide rates. Professor Sellin therefore concluded: "You cannot tell from ...the homicide rates alone, in contiguous, which are abolition and which are retention states; this indicates that capital crimes are dependent upon factors other than the mode of punishment."

Students of capital punishment, says Justice Bhagwati, have also studied the effect of abolition and introduction of death penalty upon the homicide rate in a single state. If death penalty has a significant deterrent effect, abolition should produce a rise in homicides apart from the general trend and reintroduction should produce a decline. After examining statistics from 11 states, Professor Sellin concluded that "there is no evidence that the abolition of capital punishment generally causes an increase in criminal homicides, or that its reintroduction is followed by a decline. The explanation of changes in homicide rates must be sought elsewhere."

Some criminologists, points out Justice Bhagwati, have also examined the short term deterrent effects of capital punishment. One study compared the number of homicides during short periods before and after several well-publicized executions during the twenties and thirties in Philadelphia. It was found that there were significantly more homicides in the period after the executions than before—the opposite of what the deterrence theory would suggest. Other studies have also shown that in those localities where capital punishment is carried out, the incidence of homicide does not show any decline in the period immediately following well-publicized executions when, if death penalty had any special deterrent effect, such effect would be greatest. Sometimes, as Bowers points out in his book on "Executions in America", the incidence of homicide is higher. In short, there is no correlation between the ups and downs of the homicide rate on the one hand and the presence or absence of the death penalty on the other.

Numerous other studies were also made by jurists and sociologists in regard to the deterrent effect of death penalty. The studies are almost unanimous that death penalty has no greater deterrent effect than life imprisonment. Dogan D. Akman, a Canadian criminologist, in a study made by him on the basis of data obtained from the records of all Canadian penitentiaries for the years 1964 and 1965 observed that the threat of capital punishment has little influence on potential assaulters. So also on the basis of comparison of homicide and execution rates between Queensland and other Australian States for the period 1860-1920, Barber and Wilson concluded that the suspension of capital punishment from 1915 and its abolition from 1922 in Qneensland did not have any significant effect on the murder rate. Chambliss, another criminologist, also reached the same conclusion in his article on "Types of Deviance and the Effectiveness of Legal Sanctions"[20] namely, that "given the preponderance of evidence, it seems safe to conclude that capital punishment does not act as an effective deterrent to murder". Then, says Justice Bhagwati, we have the opinion of Fred, J. Cook who says in his article on "Capital Punishment: Does it Prevent Crime?" that "abolition of the death penalty may actually reduce rather than encourage murder." The European Committee on Crime Problems of the Council of Europe gave its opinion on the basis of data obtained from various countries who are Members of the Council of Europe that these data did not give any "positive indication regarding the value of capital punishment as a deterrent". It is not desirable to burden this chapter with reference to all the studies which have been conducted at different times in different parts of the world but Justice Bhagwati referred to a few of them, namely "Capital Punishment as a Deterrent to Crime in Georgia" by Frank Gibson, "The Death Penalty in Washington State" by Hayner and Crannor, Report of the Massachusett Special Commission Relative to the Abolition of the Death Penalty in Capital Cases, "The use of the Death Penalty-Factual Statement" by Walter C Reckless, "Why was Capital Punishment resorted in Delaware" by Glenn W. Samuelson, "A Study in Capital Punishment" by Leonard O. Savitz, "The Deterrent Influence of the Death Penalty" by Karl F. Schuessler, "Murder and the Death Penalty" by E.H. Sutherland, "Capital Punishment: A case for Abolition" by Tidmarsh, Halloran and Connolly, "Can the Death Penalty Prevent Crime" by George B. Vold and "Findings on Deterrence with Regard to Homicide" by Wilkens and Feyerherm. Those studies, one and all, have taken the view that "statistical findings and case studies converge to disprove the claim that the death penalty has any special deterrent value" and that death penalty "fails as a deterrent measure". Arthur Koestler also observes in his book on "Reflections on Hanging" that the figures obtained by him from various jurisdictions which have abolished capital punishment showed a decline in the homicide rate following abolition. The Report made by the Department of Economic and Social Affairs of the United Nations also reaches the conclusion that "the information assembled confirms the now generally held opinion that the abolition or...suspension of the death penalty does not have the immediate effect of appreciably increasing the incidence of crime." These various studies to which reference has been made clearly establish beyond doubt that death penalty does not have any special deterrent effect which life sentence

20 (1967) Wisconsin Law Review 703.

does not posses and that in any event there is no evidence at all to suggest that death penalty has any such special deterrent effect.

There is unfortunately, points out Justice Bhagwati, no empirical study made in India to assess, howsoever imperfectly, the deterrent effect of death penalty. But we have the statistics of the crime of murder in the former States of Travancore and Cochin during the period when the capital punishment was on the statute book as also during the period when it was kept in abeyance.

Statistics of murder cases during the period when capital punishment was kept in abeyance.[1]

Year	Travancore	Cochin	Total for Travancore & Cochin
1945	111 cases	22	133
1946	135 cases	13	148
1947	148 cases	26	174
1948	160 cases	43	203
1949	114 cases	26	140
1950	125 cases	39	164
Total	793	169	962

Statistics of murder cases during the period when capital punishment was in vogue.[1]

Year	Travancore	Cochin	Total for Travancore & Cochin
1951	141 cases	47	188
1952	133 cases	32	165
1953	146 cases	54	200
1954	114 cases	57	171
1955	99 cases	30	129
1956	97 cases	17	114
Total	730	237	967

These figures show that the incidence of the crime of murder did not increase at all during the period of six years when the capital punishment was in abeyance. This is, it may be noted, in line with the experience of other countries where death penalty has been abolished.

1 Vide: Introduction of Shri Mohan Kumar Mangalam to the book titled *'Can the State Kill its Citizen'* by Shri Subramaniam.

Justice Bhagwati points out that it is not a rational conviction but merely an unreasoned belief which is entertained by some people including a few penologists, judges, jurists and legislators that death penalty has a uniquely deterrent effect. When you ask these persons as to what is the reason why they entertain this belief, they will not be able to give any convincing answer beyond stating that basically every human being dreads death and ,therefore, death would naturally act as a greater deterrent than life imprisonment. The same argument was advanced by Sir James Fitz James Stephen, the draftsman of the Indian Penal Code in support of the deterrent effect of capital punishment. That great judge and author said in his "Essay on Capital Punishment": "No other punishment deters men so effectually from committing crimes as the punishment of death. This is one of those propositions which it is difficult to prove simply because they are in themselves more obvious than any proof can make them. It is possible to display ingenuity in arguing against it, but that is all. The whole experience of mankind is in the other direction. The threat of instant death is the one to which resort has always been made when there was an absolute necessity of producing some results.... No one goes to certain inevitable death except by compulsion. Put the matter the other way, was there ever yet a criminal who when sentenced to death and brought out to die would refuse the offer of a commutation of a sentence for a severest secondary punishment? Surely not. Why is this ? It can only be because 'all that a man has will be given for his life'. In any secondary punishment, however terrible, there is hope; but death is death; its terrors cannot be described more forcibly."

The Law Commission in its Thirty-fifth Report also relied largely on this argument for taking the view that "capital punishment does act as a deterrent." It set out the main points that weighed with it in arriving at this conclusion and the first and foremost amongst them was that: "Basically every human being dreads death", suggesting that death penalty has, therefore, a greater deterrent effect than any other punishment. But this argument is not valid and a little scrutiny will reveal that it is wholly unfounded, asserts Justice Bhagwati. In the first place, even Sir James Fitz James Stephen concedes that the proposition that death penalty has a uniquely deterrent effect not possessed by any other punishment, is one which is difficult to prove, though according to him it is self-evident. Secondly, there is a great fallacy underlying the argument of Sir James Fitz James Stephen and the Law Commission. This argument makes no distinction between a threat of certain and imminent punishment which faces the convicted murderer and the threat of a different problematic punishment which may or may not influence a potential murderer. Murder may be unpremeditated under the stress of some sudden outburst of emotion or it may be premeditated after planning and deliberation. Where the murder is unpremeditated, as for example, where it is the outcome of a sudden argument or quarrel or provocation leading to uncontrollable anger or temporary imbalance of the mind—and most murders fall within this category—any thought of possibility of punishment is obliterated by deep emotional disturbance and the penalty of death can no more deter than any other penalty. Where murder is premeditated it may either be the result of lust, passion, jealousy, hatred, frenzy or frustration or it may be a cold calculated murder for monetary or other consideration. The former category of murder would rule out any possibility of deliberation or a weighing of consequences; the thought of the likelihood of execution after capture, trial and sentence would hardly enter the mind of the killer. So far as the latter category of murder is concerned, several considerations make it unlikely that the death penalty would play any significant part in his thought. Since both the penalties for murder, death as well as life sentence, are so severe as to destroy the future of any one subjected to them, the crime would not be committed by a rational man unless he thinks that there is little chance of detection. What would weigh with him in such a case is the uncertainty of detection and consequent punishment rather than the nature of punishment. It is not the harshness or severity of death penalty which acts as a deterrent. A life sentence of twenty years would act as an equally strong deterrent against crime as death penalty, provided the killer feels that the crime would not go unpunished. More than the severity of the sentence, it is the certainty of detection and punishment that acts as a deterrent. The Advisory Council on the Treatment of Offenders appointed by the Government of Great Britain stated in its Report in 1960: "We were impressed by the argument that the greatest deterrent to crime is not the fear of punishment but the certainty of detection." Professor Hart emphasized the same point, refuting the argument of Sir James Fitz James Stephen in these words: "This (Stephen's) estimate of the paramount place in human motivation of the fear of death reads impressively but surely contains a *suggestio falsi* and once this is detected its cogency as an argument in favour of the death penalty for murder vanishes for there is really no parallel between the situation of a convicted murderer over the alternative of life imprisonment in the shadow of the gallows and the situation of the murderer contemplating his crime. The certainty of death is one thing, perhaps for normal people nothing can be compared with it. But the existence of the death penalty does not mean for the murderer certainty of death now. It means not very high probability of death in the future. And, futurity and uncertainty, the hope of an escape, rational or irrational, vastly diminishes the difference between death and imprisonment as deterrent and may diminish to vanishing point...The way in which the convicted murderer may view the immediate prospect of the gallows after he has been caught must be a poor guide to the effect of this prospect upon him when he is contemplating committing his crime".

It is also a circumstance of no less significance bearing on the question of deterrent effect of death penalty, that, even after detection and arrest, the likelihood of execution for the murderer is almost nil. In the first place, the machinery of investigation of offences being what it is and the criminal law of our country having a tilt in favour of the accused, the killer can look forward to a chance of acquittal at the trial. Secondly, even if the trial results in a conviction, it would not, in all probability, be followed by a sentence of death. Whatever may have been the position prior to the enactment of the Code of Criminal Procedure, 1973, it is now clear, says Justice Bhagwati, that under section 354 sub-section (3), life sentence is the rule and it is only in exceptional cases for special reasons that death sentence may be awarded. The entire drift of the legislation is against infliction of death penalty and the courts are most reluctant to impose it save in the rarest of ~~rare~~ cases. It is interesting to note that there have been numerous cases where even after special leave petitions against sentence of death were dismissed, review petitions have been entertained and death sentence commuted by the Supreme Court. Then there is also the clemency power of the President under Article 72 and of the Governor under Article 161 of the Constitution and in exercise of this power, death sentence has been commuted by the President or the Governor, as the case may be, in a number of cases. The chances of imposition of death sentence following upon a conviction for the offence of murder are, therefore, extremely slender. This is also evident from the Government of India's figure for the years 1974 to 1978. The statistical information made available from the Government of India shows the total number of offences of murder committed inter alia during the years 1974-77. These figures showed that on an average about 17,000 offences of murder were committed in India every year during the period 1974 to 1977, and if we calculate on the basis of this average, the total number of offences of murder during the period of five years from 1974 to 1978 would come to about 85,000. Now, according to the statistical information made available from the Government of India, out of these approximately 85,000 case of murder, there were only 288 in which death sentence was imposed by the sessions court and confirmed by the High Courts and out of them, in 12 cases death sentence was commuted by the President and in 40 cases, by the Governors and death sentence was executed in only 29 cases. It will thus be seen that during the period of five years from 1974 to 1978, there was an infinitesingly small number of cases, only 29 out of an aggregate number of approximately 85,000 cases of murder, in which death sentence was executed. Of course, the figure of the Government of India did not include the figures from the States of Bihar, Jammu and Kashmir, West Bengal and Delhi Administration but the figures from these three States and from the Union Territory of Delhi would not make any appreciable difference. It is obvious, therefore, that even after conviction in a trial, there is high degree of probability that death sentence may not be imposed by the sessions court and even if death sentence is imposed by the sessions court, it may not be confirmed by the High Court and even after confirmation by the High Court, it may not be affirmed by this Court and lastly, even if affirmed by the Supreme Court, it may be commuted by the President of India under Article 72 or by the Governor under Article 161 of the Constitution in exercise of the power of clemency. The possibility of execution pursuant to a sentence of death is ,therefore, almost negligible, particularly after the enactment of section 354 sub-section (3) of the Code of Criminal Procedure 1973 and it is difficult to see how in these circumstances death penalty can ever act as a deterrent. The knowledge that death penalty is rarely imposed and almost certainly, it will not be imposed takes away whatever deterrent value death penalty might otherwise have. The expectation, bordering almost on certainty, that death sentence is extremely unlikely to be imposed is a factor that would condition the behaviour of the offender and death penalty cannot in such a situation have any deterrent effect. The risk of death penalty being remote and improvable, it cannot operate as a greater deterrent than the threat of life imprisonment. Justice Brennan and Justice White have also expressed the same view in *Furman* v *Georgia*,[2] namely, that, when infrequently and arbitrarily imposed, death penalty is not a greater deterrent to murder than is life imprisonment.

2 408 US 238.

12 Constitutional vires of death penalty vis-a-vis the provisions of the Indian Penal Code read with the provisions of the Criminal Procedure Code

Death penalty, according to Justice Bhagwati, destroys the most fundamental right of all, namely, the right to life which is the foundation of all other fundamental rights. The right to life, says the learned judge, stands on a higher footing than even personal liberty, because personal liberty too postulates a sentient human being who can enjoy it. Where, therefore, a law authorizes deprivation of life, the reasonableness, fairness and justness of the procedure prescribed by it on such deprivation must be established by the State.

Death penalty as provided under Section 302 of the Indian Penal Code read with section 354, sub-section (3) of the code of Criminal Procedure 1973, does not for reasons already discussed, subserve any legitimate end of punishment, since by killing the murderer it totally rejects the reformative purpose and it has no additional deterrent effect which life sentence does not possess and it is, therefore, not justified by the deterrence theory of punishment. It can, therefore, be said, asserts Justice Bhagwati, that death penalty has no rational nexus with any legitimate penological goal or any rational penological purpose and it is arbitrary and irrational and hence violative of Articles 14 and 21 of the Constitution.

Again, arbitrariness and irrationality in the provisions of section 354(3) of the Code of Criminal Procedure prescribing death penalty can be established in other way also. Section 354(3) provides that in case of offence of murder, life sentences shall be the rule and it is only in exceptional cases for special reasons that death penalty may be awarded. But what are the special reasons for which the Court may award death penalty is a matter on which section 354, sub-section (3) is silent. There is not even any guidance in that behalf provided by any other provision of law. It is left to the judge to grope in the dark for himself and in the exercise of his unguided and unfettered discretion, he decides what reasons may be considered as 'special reasons' justifying award of death penalty and whether in a given case any such special reasons exist which should persuade the court to depart from the normal rule and inflict death penalty on the accused. The critical choice between physical liquidation and lifelong incarceration is thus left to the discretion of the court and no legislative light is shed as to how this deadly discretion is to be exercised. The court is left free to navigate in an uncharted sea without any compass or directional guidance.

There being no legislative policy or principle to guide, court in exercising its discretion in this delicate and sensitive area of life and death, the exercise of discretion of the Court is bound to vary from judge to judge. What may appear as special reasons to one judge may not so appear to another and the decision in a given case whether to impose the death sentence or to let off the offender only with life imprisonment would, to a large extent, depend upon who is the judge called upon to make the decision. The reasons for this uncertainty in the sentencing process is two-fold. Firstly, the nature of the sentencing process is such that it involves a highly delicate task calling for skills and talents very much different from those ordinarily expected of lawyers. This was pointed out clearly and emphatically by Mr. Justice Frankfurther in the course of the evidence he gave before the Royal Commission on Capital Punishment thus: "I myself think that the bench—we lawyers who become Judges—are not very competent, are not qualified by experience, to impose sentence where any discretion is to be exercised. I do not think it is in the domain of the training of lawyers to know what to do with a fellow after you find out he is a thief. I do not think legal training has given you any special competence. I, myself, hope that one of these days, and before long, we will divide the functions of criminal justice. I think the lawyers are people who are competent to ascertain whether or not a crime has been committed. The whole scheme of common law judicial machinery-the rule of evidence, the ascertainment of what is relevant and what is irrelevant and what is fair, the whole question of whether you can introduce prior crimes in order to prove intent-I think lawyers are peculiarly fitted for that task. But all the questions that follow upon ascertainment of guilt, I think require very different and much more diversified talents than the lawyers and judges are normally likely to possess".

Even if considerations relevant to capital sentencing were provided by the legislature, it would be a difficult exercise for the judges to decide whether to impose the death penalty or to award the life sentence. But without any such guidelines given by the legislature, the task of the judges becomes much more arbitrary and the sentencing decision is bound to vary with each judge. Secondly, when unguided discretion is conferred upon the court to choose between life and death, by providing a totally vague and indefinite criterion of 'special reasons' without laying down any principles or guidelines for determining what should be considered to be 'special reasons', the choice is bound to be influenced by the subjective philosophy of the judge called upon to pass the sentence and on his value system and social philosophy will depend whether the accused shall live or die. No doubt the judge will have to give 'special reasons' if he opts in favour of inflicting the death penalty, but that does not eliminate arbitrariness and caprice, firstly because there being no guidelines provided by the legislature, the reasons which may appeal to one judge as 'special reasons' may not appeal to another, and secondly, because reasons can always be found for a conclusion that the judge instinctively wishes to reach and the judge can *bona fide* and conscientiously find such reason to be 'special reasons'.'

It is now recognised on all hands, says Justice Bhagwati, that judicial conscience is not a fixed conscience; it varies from judge to judge depending upon his attitudes and approaches, his predilections and prejudices, his habits of mind and thought and in short all that goes with the expression "social philosophy". We lawyers and judges like to cling to the myth that every decision which we make in the exercise of our judicial discretion is guided exclusively by legal principles and we refuse to admit the subjective element in judicial decision making. But that myth, says Justice Bhagwati, now stands exploded and it is acknowledged by jurists that the social philosophy of the judge plays a not inconsiderable part in moulding his judicial decision and particularly the exercise of judicial discretion. There is nothing like complete objectivity in the decision making process and especially so, when this process involves making of decision in the exercise of judicial discretion. Every judgment, views Justice Bhagwati, necessarily bears the impact of the attitude and approach of the judge and his social value system. The learned judge in this context, quoted Justice Cardozo's analysis of the mind of a Judge in his famous lectures on "Nature of Judicial Process":

> "We are reminded by William James in a telling page of his lectures on Pragmatism that every one of us has in truth an underlying philosophy of life, even those of us to whom the names and the notions of philosophy are unknown or anathema. There is in each of us a stream of tendency, whether you choose to call it philosophy or not, which gives coherence and direction to thought and action. Judges cannot escape that current any more than other mortals. All their lives, forces which they do not recognize and cannot name, have been tugging at them- inherited instincts, traditional beliefs, acquired convictions; and the resultant is an outlook on life, a conception of social needs, a sense in James' phrase of 'the total push and pressure of the cosmos,' which when reasons are nicely balanced, must determine where choice shall fall. In this mental background every

problem finds its setting. We may try to see things as objectively as we please. Nonetheless, we can never see them with any eyes except our own".

It may be noted that the human mind, even at infancy, is no blank sheet of paper. In the words of Justice Bhagwati: "We are born with predisposition and the process of education, formal and informal, and, our own subjective experiences create attitudes which affect us in judging situations and coming to decisions". Jerome Frank says in his book "Law and the Modern Mind", in an observation with which Justice Bhagwati finds himself in entire agreement: "Without acquired 'slants' preconceptions, life could not go on. Every habit constitutes a pre-judgment; were those pre-judgments which we call habits absent in any person, were he obliged to treat every event as an unprecedented crisis presenting a wholly new problem, he would go mad. Interests, points of view, references, are the essence of living. Only death yields complete dispassionateness, for such dispassionateness signifies utter indifference....An 'open mind' in the sense of a mind containing no preconceptions whatever, would be a mind incapable of learning anything, would be that of an utterly emotionless human being".

'It must be remembered', cautions Justice Bhagwati, 'that "a Judge does not shed the attributes of common humanity when he assumes the ermine." The ordinary human mind is a mass of preconceptions inherited and acquired, often unrecognised by their possessor. "Few minds are as neutral as a sheet of plain glass and indeed a mind of that quality may actually fail in judicial efficiency, for the warmer tints of imagination and sympathy are needed to temper the cold light of reason, if human justice is to be done." It is, therefore, obvious that when a judge is called upon to exercise his discretion as to whether the accused shall be killed or shall be permitted to live, his conclusion would depend to a large extent on his approach and attitude, his predilections and preconceptions, his value system and social philosophy and his response to the evolving norms of decency and newly developing concepts and ideas in penological jurisprudence. One Judge may have faith in the Upanishad doctrine that every human being is an embodiment of the divine and he may believe with Mahatma Gandhi that every offender can be reclaimed and transformed by love and it is immoral and unethical to kill him, while another Judge may believe that it is necessary for social defence that the offender should be put out of way and that no mercy should be shown to him who did not show mercy to another. One Judge may feel that the Naxalites, though guilty of murders, are dedicated souls totally different from ordinary criminals as they are motivated not by any self-interest but by a burning desire to bring about a revolution by eliminating vested interests and should not therefore be put out of corporeal existence while another Judge may take the view that the Naxalities being guilty of cold premeditated murders are a menace to the society and to innocent men and women and therefore deserve to be liquidated. The views of Judges as to what may be regarded as "special reasons" are bound to differ from judge to judge depending upon his value system and social philosophy with the result that whether a person shall live or die depends very much upon the composition of the Bench which tries his case and this renders the imposition of death penalty arbitrary and capricious and hence violative of Articles 14 and 21 of the Constitution'.

The above conclusion reached by Justice Bhagwati is not based merely on theoretical or a prior considerations. If an analysis is made of decisions given over a period of years, it will be found that in fact there is no uniform pattern of judicial behaviour in the imposition of death penalty and the judicial practice does not disclose any coherent guidelines for the award of capital punishment. The judges have been awarding death penalty or refusing to award it according to their own scale of values and social philosophy and it is not possible to discern any consistent approach to the problem in the judicial decisions. It is apparent from a study of the judicial decisions that some Judges are readily and regularly inclined to sustain death sentences, others are similarly disinclined and the remaining waver from case to case. Even in the Supreme Court, there are divergent attitudes and opinions in regard to the imposition of capital punishment. If a case comes before one Bench consisting of judges who believe in the social efficacy of capital punishment, the death sentence would in all probability be confirmed but if the same case comes before another Bench consisting of judges who are morally and ethically against the death penalty, the death sentence would most likely be commuted to life imprisonment. The former would find and Justice Bhagwati says this not in any derogatory or disparaging sense, but as a consequence of psychological and attitudinal factors operating on the minds of the judges constituting the Bench—'special reasons' in the case to justify award of death penalty while the latter would reject any such reasons as special reasons. It is also quite possible that one Bench may, having regard to its perceptions, think that there are special reasons in the case for which death penalty should be awarded while another Bench may *bona fide* and conscientiously take a different view and hold that there are no special reasons and that only life sentence should be imposed and it may not be possible to assert objectively and logically as to who is right and who is wrong, because the exercise of discretion in a case of this kind, where no broad standards or guidelines are supplied by the legislature, is bound to be influenced by the subjective attitude and approach of the judges constituting the Bench, their value system, individual tone of their mind, the colour of their experience and the character and variety of their interests and their predispositions. This arbitrariness in the imposition of death penalty is considerably accentuated, says Justice Bhagwati, by the fragmented Bench structure of our courts where Benches are inevitably formed with different permutations and combinations from time to time and cases relating to the offence of murder come up for hearing sometimes before one Bench, sometimes before another, some times before a third and so on. Prof. Blackshield has in his article on 'Capital Punishment in India' published in Volume 21 of the Journal of the Indian Law Institute[3] pointed out how the practice of Bench formation contributes to arbitrariness in the imposition of death penalty. It is well-known that so far as the Supreme Court is concerned, while the number of judges has increased over the years, the number of judges on Benches which hear capital punishment cases has actually decreased. Most cases are now heard by two–Judge Benches. Prof. Blackshield has abstracted 70 cases in which the Supreme Court had to choose between life and death while sentencing an accused for the offence of murder and analysing these 70 cases he has pointed out that during the period 28th April 1972 to 8th March 1976, only eleven judges of the Supreme Court participated in 10% or more of the cases. He has listed these eleven Judges in an ascending order of leniency based on the proportion for each judge of plus votes (i.e. votes for the death sentence) to total votes and pointed out that these statistics show how the judicial response to the question of life and death varies for judge to judge. It is significant to note that out of 70 cases analysed by Prof. Blackshield, 37 related to the period subsequent to the coming into force of section 354 sub-section (3) of the Code of Criminal Procedure 1973. If a similar exercise is performed with reference to cases decided by the Supreme Court after 8th March 1976, that being the date upto which the survey carried out by Prof. Blackshield was limited, the analysis will reveal the same pattern of incoherence and arbitrariness, the decision to kill or not to kill being guided to a large extent by the composition of the

3 Pages 137-226, April-June issue, 1979.

Bench. Justice Bhagwati for example, referred to *Rajendra Prasad's* case[4] decided on 9th February 1979. In this case, the death sentence imposed on Rajendra Prasad was commuted to life imprisonment by a majority consisting of Krishna Iyer and J., Desai, J., A.P. Sen, J. dissented and was of the view that the death sentence should be confirmed. Similarly in one of the cases, namely, *Bachan Singh* v *State of Punjab*[5] when it was first heard by a Bench consisting of Kailasam and Sarkaria, JJ., Kailasam, J. was definitely of the view that the majority decision in *Rajendra Prasad's* case[6] was wrong and that is why he referred that case to the Constitution Bench. So also in *Dalbir Singh* v *State of Punjab*,[7] the majority consisting of Krishna Iyer, J. and Desai, J. took the view that the death sentence imposed on Dalbir Singh should be commuted to life imprisonment while A.P. Sen, J. struck to the original view taken by him in *Rajendra Prasad's* case and was inclined to confirm the death sentence. It will, thus, be seen that the exercise of discretion whether to inflict death penalty or not depends to a considerable extent on the value system and social philosophy of the judges constituting the Bench.

The most striking example of freakishness in imposition of death penalty is provided by *Harbans Singh's* case[8] which involved three accused, namely, Jeeta Singh, Kashmira Singh and Harbans Singh. These three persons were sentenced to death by the Allahabad High Court by a judgment and order dated 20th October 1975 for playing an equal part in jointly murdering a family of four persons. Each of these three persons preferred a separate petition in the Supreme Court for special leave to appeal against the common judgment sentencing them all to death penalty. The special leave petition of Jeeta Singh came up for hearing before a Bench consisting of Chandrachud, J. (as he then was), Krishna Iyer, J. and N.L. Untwalia, J. and it was dismissed on 15th April 1976. Then came the special leave petition preferred by Kashmira Singh from jail and this petition was placed for hearing before another Bench consisting of Fazal Ali, J. and Bhagwati, J. who granted leave to Kashmira Singh limited to the question of sentence and by an order dated 10th April 1977 the learned judges allowed his

4 *Rajendra Prasad* v *State of U.P.* AIR 1979 SC 916: (1979)3 SCC 646: 1979 Cr LJ 792.

5 (1979)3 SCC 727: 1979 SCC (Cri) 830: (1979)3 SCR 1193.

6 AIR 1979 SC 916: (1979)3 SCC 646: 1979 Cr LJ 792.

7 (1979)3 SCR 1059: (1979)3 SCC 745: 1979 SCC (Cri) 848: AIR 1979 SC 1384: 1979 Cr LJ 1058.

8 *Harbans Singh* v *State of U.P.* (1982)2 SCC 101: 1982 SCC (Cri) 361.

appeal and commuted his sentence of death into one of imprisonment for life. The result was that while Kashmira Singh's death sentence was commuted to life imprisonment by one Bench, the death sentence imposed on Jeeta Singh was confirmed by another Bench and he was executed on 6th October 1981, though both had played equal part in the murder of the family and there was nothing to distinguish the case of one from that of the other. The special leave petition of Harbans Singh then came up for hearing and this time, it was still another Bench which heard his special leave petition. The Bench consisted of Sarkaria and Singhal, JJ. and they rejected the special leave petition of Harbans Singh on 16th October, 1978. Harbans Singh applied for review of this decision, but the review petition was dismissed by Sarkaria, J. and A.P. Sen, J. on 9th May 1980. It appears that though the registry of the Supreme Court had mentioned in its office report that *Kashmira Singh's* death sentence was already commuted, that fact was not brought to the notice of the Court specifically when the special leave petition of Harbans Singh and his review petition were dismissed. Now since his special leave petition as also his review petition were dismissed by the Supreme Court, Harbans Singh would have been executed on 6th October 1981 along with Jeeta Singh, but fortunately for him he filed a writ petition in the Supreme Court and on that writ petition, the Court passed an order staying the execution of his death sentence. When this writ petition came up for hearing before a still another Bench consisting of Chandrachud, CJ., D.A. Desai and A.N. Sen, JJ., it was pointed out to the Court that the death sentence imposed on Kashmira Singh had been commuted by a Bench consisting of Fazal Ali, J. and Justice Bhagwati and when this fact was pointed out, the Bench directed that the case be sent back to the President for reconsideration of the clemency petition filed by Harbans Singh. This is a classic case, says Justice Bhagwati, which illustrates the judicial vagaries in the imposition of death penalty and demonstrates vividly, in all its cruel and stark reality, how the infliction of death penalty is influenced by the composition of the Bench, even in cases governed by section 354 sub-section (3) of the Code of Criminal Procedure 1973. The question may well be asked by the accused: Am I to live or die depending upon the way in which the Benches are constituted from time to time? Is that not clearly violative of the fundamental guarantees enshrined in Articles 14 and 21?

If we study the judicial decisions given by the courts over a number of years, points out Justice Bhagwati, we find judges resorting to a wide variety of factors in justification of confirmation or commutation of death sentence and these factors when analysed fail to reveal any coherent pattern. This is the inevitable consequence of the failure of the legislature to supply broad standards or guidelines which would structure and channelise the discretion of the court in the matter of imposition of death penalty. Of course, Justice Bhagwati makes it clear that when he said this, he does not wish to suggest that if broad standards or guidelines are supplied by the legislature, they would necessarily cure death penalty of the vice of arbitrariness or freakishness. Mr. Justice Harlan pointed out in *McGautha* v *California*[9] the difficulty of formulating standards or guidelines for channelising or regulating the discretion of the court in these words: "Those who have come to grips with the hard task of actually attempting to draft means of channeling capital sentencing discretion have confirmed the lesson taught by... history...To identify before the fact those characteristics of criminal homicides and their perpetrators which call for the death penalty, and to express these characteristics in language which can be fairly understood and applied by the sentencing authority, appear to be tasks which are beyond present human ability".

But whether adequate standards or guidelines can be formulated or not which would cure the aspects of arbitrariness and capriciousness, the fact remains that no such standards or guidelines have yet been provided by the legislature with the result that the court has till date unguided and untrammelled discretion in choosing between death and life imprisonment as penalty for the crime of murder and this leads to considerable arbitrariness and uncertainty. This is evident from a study of the decided cases which clearly shows that the reasons for confirmation or commutation of death sentence relied upon by the court in different cases defy coherent analysis.

Dr. Raizada has, in his monumental doctoral study entitled "Trends in sentencing; a Study of the Important Penal Statutes and Judicial Pronouncements of the High Courts and the Supreme Court" identified a large number of decisions of the Supreme Court where inconsistent awards of punishment have been made and the judges have frequently articulated their inability to prescribe or follow consistently any standards or guidelines. He has classified cases upto 1976 in terms of the reasons given by the Court for awarding or refusing to award death sentence. The analysis made by him is quite rewarding and illuminating.

9 402 US 183.

(*i*) One of the reasons given by the Courts in a number of cases for imposing death penalty is that the murder is 'brutal', 'cold blooded', 'deliberate', 'unprovoked', 'fatal', 'gruesome', 'wicked', 'callous', 'heinous' or 'violent'. But the use of these labels for describing the nature of the murder is indicative only of the degree of the Court's aversion for the nature or the manner of commission of the crime and it is possible that different judges may react differently to these situations and moreover, some judges may not regard this factor as having any relevance to the imposition of death penalty and may therefore decline to accord to it the status of "special reasons". In fact, there are numerous cases, where despite the murder being one falling within these categories, the Court has refused to award death sentence. For example, Janardharan whose appeal was decided along with the appeal of Rajendra Prasad had killed his innocent wife and children in the secrecy of night and the murder was deliberate and cold blooded, attended as it was with considerable brutality, and yet the majority consisting of Krishna Iyer, J. and D.A. Desai, J. commuted his death sentence to life imprisonment. So also Dube had committed triple murder and still his death sentence was commuted to life imprisonment by the same two learned Judges, namely, Krishna Iyer, J. and D.A. Desai, J. It is therefore clear that the epithets mentioned above do not indicate any clearcut well defined categories but are merely expressive of the intensity of judicial reaction to the murder, which may not be uniform in all judges and even if the murder falls within one of these categories, that factor has been regarded by some judges as relevant and by others, as irrelevant and it has not been uniformly applied as a salient factor in determining whether or not death penalty should be imposed.

(*ii*) There have been cases where death sentence has been awarded on the basis of constructive or joint liability arising under sections 34 and 149. (vide: *Babu* v *State of U.P.*[10] *Mukhtiar Singh* v *State of Punjab*.[11] *Masalti* v *State of U.P.*[12] and *Gurcharan Singh* v *State of Punjab*.[13]) But, there are equally a large number of cases where death sentence has not been awarded because the criminal liability of the accused was only under section 34 or section 149. There are no established criteria for awarding or refusing to award death sentence to an accused who himself did not give the fatal blow but was

10 (1965)2 Cr LJ 539: (1965)2 SCR 771: AIR 1965 SC 1467: (1966)1 SCJ 287.

11 1971 Cr LJ 1298: (1972)4 SCC 843: AIR 1971 SC 1864.

12 (1965)1 Cr LJ 226: (1964)8 SCR 133: AIR 1965 SC 202: (1965)1 SCJ 605.

13 (1963)1 Cr LJ 323: (1963)3 SCR 585: AIR 1963 SC 340.

involved in the commission of murder along with other assailants under section 34 or section 149.

(*iii*) The position as regards mitigating factors also shows the same incoherence. One mitigating factor which has often been relied upon for the purpose of commuting the death sentence to life imprisonment is the youth of the offender. But this too has been quite arbitrarily applied by the Supreme Court. There are cases such as *State of U.P.* v *Summan Dass*,[14] *Raghubir Singh* v *State of Haryana*[15] and *Gurudas Singh* v *State of Rajasthan*[16] where the Supreme Court took into account the young age of the appellant and refused to award death sentence to him. Equally there are cases such as *Bhagwan Swarup* v *State of U.P.*[17] and *Ragho Mani* v *State of U.P.*[18] where the Supreme Court took the view that youth is no ground for extenuation of sentence. Moreover there is also divergence of opinion as to what should be the age at which an offender may be regarded as a young man deserving of commutation. The result is that as pointed out by Dr. Raizada, in some situations young offenders who have committed multiple murders get reduction in life sentence whereas in others, "where neither the loss of as many human lives nor of higher valued properly" is involved, the accused are awarded death sentence.

(*iv*) One other mitigating factor which is often taken into account is delay in final sentencing. This factor of delay after sentence received great emphasis in *Ediga Anamma* v *State of A.P.*,[19] *Chawla* v *State of Haryana*,[20] *Raghubir Singh* v *State of Haryana*,[1] *Bhoor Singh* v *State of Punjab*,[2] *State of Punjab* v *Hari Singh*[3] and *Gurudas Singh* v *State of Rajasthan*[4] and in these cases delay was taken into account for the purpose of awarding the lesser punishment of life imprisonment. In fact, in *Raghubir Singh* v *State of Haryana*[5] the fact that for 20 months the specter of death penalty must have been tormenting his soul was

14 1972 Cr LJ 487: (1972)3 SCC 201: 1972 SCC (Cri) 275.
15 AIR 1974 SC 677: (1975)3 SCC 37: 1974 SCC (Cri) 733: 1974 Cr LJ 603.
16 AIR 1975 SC 1411: (1975)4 SCC 490: 1975 SCC (Cri) 556: 1975 Cr LJ 1218.
17 1971 Cr LJ 413: (1971)3 SCC 759: 1972 SCC (Cri) 71: AIR 1971 SC 429.
18 AIR 1977 SC 703: (1976)4 SCC 297: 1976 SCC (Cri) 616: 1977 Cr LJ 345.
19 AIR 1974 SC 799: (1974)4 SCC 443: 1974 SCC (Cri) 479: 1974 Cr LJ 683.
20 AIR 1974 SC 1039: (1974)4 SCC 579: 1974 SCC (Cri) 615: 1974 Cr LJ 791.
1 AIR 1974 SC 677: (1975)3 SCC 37: 1974 SCC (Cri) 733: 1974 Cr LJ 603.
2 AIR 1974 SC 1256: (1974)4 SCC 754: 1974 SCC (Cri) 664: 1974 Cr LJ 929.
3 AIR 1974 SC 1168: (1974)4 SCC 552: 1974 SCC (Cri) 588: 1974 Cr LJ 822.
4 AIR 1975 SC 1411: (1975)4 SCC 490: 1975 SCC (Cri) 556: 1975 Cr LJ 1218.
5 AIR 1974 SC 677: (1975)3 SCC 37: 1974 SCC (Cri) 733: 1974 Cr LJ 603.

held sufficient to entitle the accused to reduction in sentence. But equally there are a large number of cases where death sentences have been confirmed, even when two or more years were taken in finally disposing of the appeal (vide: *Rishideo Pande* v *State of U.P.*,[6] *Bharwad Mepa* v *State of Bombay*.[7]) These decided cases show that there is no way of predicting the exact period of prolonged proceeding which may favour an accused. Whether any importance should be given to the factor of delay and if so to what extent are matters entirely within the discretion of the Court and it is not possible to assert with any definitiveness that a particular period of delay after sentencing will earn for the accused immunity from death penalty. It follows as a necessary corollary from these vagaries in sentencing arising from the factor of delay, that the imposition of capital punishment becomes more or less a kind of cruel judicial lottery. If the case of the accused is handled expeditiously by the prosecution, defence lawyer, sessions court, High Court and the Supreme, Court, then this mitigating factor of delay is not available to him for reduction to life sentence. If, on the other, hand, there has been lack of despatch, engineered or natural, then the accused may escape the gallows, subject of course to the judicial vagaries arising from other causes. In other words, the more efficient the proceeding, the more certain the death sentence and *vice-versa*.

(*v*) The embroilment of the accused in an immoral relationship has been condoned and in effect, treated as an extenuating factor in *Raghubir Singh* v *State of Haryana*[8] and *Vasant Laxman More* v *State of Maharashtra*[9] while in *Lajar Masih* v *State of U.P.*,[10] it has been condemned and in effect treated as an aggravating factor. There is thus no uniformity of approach even so far as this factor is concerned.

All these factors singly and cumulatively indicate not merely that there is an enormous potential of arbitrariness in the award of death penalty by the High Courts and the Supreme Court but that, in fact, death sentences have been awarded arbitrarily and freakishly.

Professor Blackshield has also in his article on "Capital Punishment in India" commented on the arbitrary and capricious nature of imposition of death penalty and demonstrated forcibly and almost conclusively

6 1955 Cr LJ 873: AIR 1955 SC 331.
7 (1960)2 SCR 172: AIR 1960 SC 289: 1960 SCJ 478.
8 AIR 1974 SC 799: (1974)4 SCC 443: 1974 SCC (Cri) 479: 1974 Cr LJ 683.
9 AIR 1974 SC 1697: (1974)4 SCC 778: 1974 SCC (Cri) 688: 1974 Cr LJ 1166.
10 AIR 1976 SC 653: (1976)1 SCC 806: 1976 SCC (Cri) 195: 1976 Cr LJ 580.

that arbitrariness and uneven incidence are inherent and inevitable in a system of capital punishment. He has taken the decision of the Supreme Court in *Ediga Anamma* v *State of Andhra Pradesh*[11] as the dividing line and examined the judicial decisions given by the Supreme Court subsequent to the decision in *Ediga Anamma's* case, where apex court had to choose between life and death under Section 302 of the Indian Penal Code. The cases subsequent to the decision in *Ediga Anamma's* case (supra) have been chosen for study and analysis presumably because that was the decision in which the Supreme Court for the first time set down some working formula whereby a synthesis could be reached between death sentence and life imprisonment and Krishna, Iyer, J. speaking on behalf of the Court, formulated various grounds which, in his opinion, might warrant death sentence as an exceptional measure. But, despite this attempt made in *Ediga Anamma's* case (supra) to evolve some broad standards or guidelines for imposition of death penalty, the subsequent decisions, as pointed out by Professor Blackshield, display the same pattern of confusion, contradictions and aberrations as the decisions before that case. The learned author has taken 45 reported decisions given after *Ediga Anamma's* case (supra) and shown that it is not possible to discern any coherent pattern in these decisions and they reveal contradictions and inconsistencies in the matter of imposition of death penalty. This is how the learned author has summed up his conclusion after an examination of these judicial decisions: "But where life and death are at stake, inconsistencies which are understandable may not be acceptable. The hard evidence of the accompanying "kit of cases" compels the conclusion that, at least in contemporary India, Mr. Justice Douglas' argument in *Furman* v *Georgia*[12] is correct: that arbitrariness and uneven incidence are inherent and inevitable in a system of capital punishment; and that therefore—in Indian constitutional terms, and in spite of *Jagmohan Singh*[13]—the retention of such a system necessarily violates Article 14's guarantee of 'equality before the law'."

It is clear from a study of the decisions of the higher courts on the life-or-death choice that judicial adhocism or judicial impressionism, dominates the sentencing exercise and the infliction of death penalty suffers from the vice of arbitrariness and caprice.

11 AIR 1974 SC 799: (1974)4 SCC 443: 1974 SCC (Cri) 479: 1974 Cr LJ 683.
12 408 US 238.
13 *Jagmohan Singh* v *State of U.P.* AIR 1973 SC 947: (1973)1 SCC 20: 1973 SCC (Cri) 169: 1973 Cr LJ 370.

'I may point out', said Justice Bhagwati, 'that Krishna Iyer, J. has also come to the same conclusion on the basis of his long experience of the sentencing process. He has analysed the different factors which have prevailed with the judges from time to time in awarding or refusing to award death penalty and shown how some factors have weighed with one judge, some with another, some with a third and so on, resulting in chaotic arbitrariness in the imposition of death penalty. I can do no better than quote his own words in *Rajendra Prasad's* case: "Law must be honest to itself. Is it not true that some judges count the number of fatal wounds, some the nature of the weapon used, others count the corpses or the degree of horror and yet others look into the age or sex of the offender and even the lapse of time between the trial Court's award of death sentence and the final disposal of the appeal? With some judges, motives, provocations, primary or constructive guilt, mental disturbance and old feuds, the savagery of the murderous moment or the plan which has preceded the killing, the social milieu, the sublimated class complex and other odd factors enter the sentencing calculas. Stranger still, a good sentence of death by the trial Court is sometimes upset by the Supreme Court because of law's delays. Courts have been directed execution of murderers who are mental cases, who do not fall within the McNaghten rules, because of the insane fury of the slaughter. A big margin of subjectivism, a preference for old English precedents, theories of modern penology, behavioural emphasis or social antecedents, judicial hubris or human rights perspectives, criminological literacy or fanatical reverence for outworn social philosophers buried in the debris of time except as part of history—this plurality of forces plays a part in swinging the pendulum of sentencing justice erratically."

This passage from the judgment of the learned judge exposes, in language remarkable for its succinctness as well as eloquence, the vagarious nature of the imposition of death penalty and highlights a few of the causes responsible for its erratic operation. I find totally in agreement with these observations of the learned judge'.

It is sometimes argued that having regard to the nature of the sentencing process, it is impossible to lay down any standards or guidelines which will provide for the endless and often unforeseeable variations in fact situations and sentencing discretion has necessarily to be left to the court and the vesting of such discretion in the court, even if no standards or guidelines are provided by the legislature for structuring or channeling such discretion, cannot be regarded as arbitrary or unreasonable. 'This argument', observed Justice Bhagwati, 'plausible though it may seem, is in my opinion not well founded and must be rejected. It is true that criminal cases do not fall into set behaviouristic patterns and it is almost impossible to find two cases which are exactly identical. There are, as pointed out by Sarkaria, J. in the majority judgment in *Bachan Singh* v *State of Punjab*[14] "countless permutations and combinations which are beyond the anticipatory capacity of the human calculus". Each case presents its own distinctive features, its peculiar combinations of events and its unique configuration of facts. That is why, in the interest of individualised justice, it is necessary to vest sentencing discretion in the court so that appropriate sentence may be imposed by the court in the exercise of its judicial discretion, having regard to the peculiar facts and circumstances of a given case, or else the sentencing process would cease to be just and rational and justice would be sacrificed at the altar of blind uniformity. But at the same time, the sentencing discretion conferred upon the court cannot be altogether uncontrolled or unfettered. The stratagem which is therefore followed by the legislatures while creating and defining offences is to prescribe the maximum punishment and in some cases, even the minimum and leave it to the discretion of the court to decide upon the actual term of imprisonment. This cannot be regarded as arbitrary or unreasonable since the discretion that is left to the court is to choose an appropriate term of punishment between the limits laid down by the legislature, having regard to the distinctive features and the peculiar facts and circumstances of the case. The conferment of such sentencing discretion is plainly and indubitably essential for rendering individualised justice. But where the discretion granted to the court is to choose between life and death without any standards or guidelines provided by the legislature, the death penalty does become arbitrary and unreasonable. The death penalty is qualitatively different from a sentence of imprisonment. Whether a sentence of imprisonment is for two years or five years or for life, it is qualitatively the same, namely, a sentence of imprisonment, but the death penalty is totally different. It is irreversible; it is beyond recall or reparation; it extinguishes life. It is the choice between life and death which the court is required to make and this is left to its sole discretion unaided and unguided by any legislative yardstick to determine the choice. The only yardstick which may be said to have been provided by the legislature is that life sentence shall be the rule and it is only in exceptional cases for special reasons that death penalty may be awarded, but it is

14 (1980)2 SCC 684; 1980 SCC (Cri) 580.

nowhere indicated by the legislature as to what should be regarded as 'special reasons' justifying imposition of death penalty. The awesome and fearful discretion whether to kill a man or to let him live is vested in the court and the court is called upon to exercise this discretion guided only by its own perception of what may be regarded as 'special reasons' without any light shed by the legislature. It is difficult to appreciate how a law which confers such unguided discretion on the court without any standards or guidelines on so vital an issue as the choice between life and death can be regarded as constitutionally valid. If, I may quote the words of Harlan, J.: "Our scheme of ordered liberty is based, like the common law, on enlightened and uniformly applied legal principles, not on ad hoc notions of what is right or wrong in a particular case".'

Justice Bhagwati views: 'There must be standards or principles to guide the court in making the choice between life and death and it cannot be left to the court to decide upon the choice on an ad hoc notion of what it conceives to be "special reasons" in a particular case. That is exactly what we mean when we say that the Government should be of laws and not of men and it makes no difference in the application of this principle, whether men belong to the administration or to the judiciary. It is a basic requirement of the equality clause contained in Article 14 that the exercise of discretion must always be guided by standards or norms so that it does not degenerate into arbitrariness and operate unequally on persons similarly situate. Where unguided and unfettered discretion is conferred on any authority, whether it be the executive or the judiciary, it can be exercised arbitrarily or capriciously by such authority, because there would be no standards or principles provided by the legislature with reference to which the exercise of the discretion can be tested. Every form of arbitrariness, whether it be executive waywardness or judicial adhocism is anathema in our constitutional scheme. There can be no equal protection without equal principles in exercise of discretion. Therefore the equality clause of the Constitution obligates that whenever death sentence is imposed, it must be a principled sentence, a sentence based on some standard or principle and not arbitrary or indignant capital punishment. It has been said that "a Judge untethered by a text is a dangerous instrument" and I may well add that judge power, uncanalised by clear principles, may be equally dangerous when the consequence of the exercise of discretion may result in the hanging of a human being. It is obvious that if judicial discretion is not guided by any standard or norms, it would degenerate into judicial caprice, which, as is evident from the foregoing discussion, has in fact happened and in such a situation, unregulated and unprincipled sentencing discretion in a highly sensitive area involving a question of life and death would clearly be arbitrary and hence violative of the equal protection clause contained in Article 14. It would also militate against Article 21 as interpreted in *Maneka Gandhi's* case[15] because no procedure for depriving a person of his life can be regarded as reasonable, fair and just, if it vests uncontrolled and unregulated discretion in the court whether to award death sentence or to inflict only the punishment of life imprisonment. The need for well recognised principles to govern the deadly discretion is so interlaced with fair procedure that unregulated power not structured or guided by any standards or principles would fall foul of Article 21'.

It was contended on behalf of the respondents in *Bachan Singh's* case that the absence of any standards or guidelines in the legislation did not affect the constitutional validity of the death penalty, since the sentencing discretion being vested in the court, standards or principles for regulating the exercise of such discretion could always be evolved by the court and the court could by a judicial fiat lay down standards or norms which would guide the judge in exercising his discretion to award the death penalty. Justice Bhagwati negatived this contention in his dissenting opinion in *Bachan Singh's* case[16] thus: 'Now it is true that there are cases where the court lays down principles and standards for guidance in the exercise of the discretion conferred upon it by a statute, but that is done by the court only in those cases where the principles or standards are gatherable from the provisions of the statute. Where a statute confers discretion upon a court, the statute may lay down the broad standards or principles which should guide the court in the exercise of such discretion or such standards or principles may be discovered from the object and purpose of the statute, its underlying policy and the scheme of its provisions and sometimes, even from the surrounding circumstances. When the court lays down standards or principles which should guide it in the exercise of its discretion, the court does not evolve any new standards or principles of its own but merely discovers them from the statute. The standards or principles laid down by the court in such a case are not standards or principles created or evolved by the court but they are standards or principles enunciated by the legislature in the statute and are merely discovered by the court as a matter of statutory interpretation. It is not legitimate

15 *Maneka Gandhi* v *Union of India* AIR 1978 SC 597: (1978)2 SCR 62: (1978)1 SCC 248.

16 *Bachan Singh* v *State of Punjab* (1982)3 SCC 24, 119 (para 77).

for the court to create or evolve any standards or principles which are not found in the statute, because enunciation of such standards or principles is a legislative function which belongs to the legislative and not to the judicial department. Moreover, it is difficult to see how any standards or principles which would adequately guide the exercise of discretion in the matter of imposition of death penalty can be evolved by the court. Sarkaria, J. himself has lamented the impossibility of formulating standards or guidelines in this highly sensitive area and pointed out in the majority judgment in *Bachan Singh's* case[17] ".. "there is little agreement among penologists and jurists as to what information about the crime and criminal is relevant and what is not relevant for fixing the dose of punishment for a person convicted of a particular offence. According to Cessare Beccaria, who is supposed to be the intellectual progenitor of today's fixed sentencing movement, 'crime are only to be measured by the injury done to society'. But the 20th Century sociologists do not wholly agree with this view. In the opinion of Von Hirsch, the 'seriousness of a crime depends both on the harm done (or risked) by the act and degree of actor's culpability'. But how is the degree of that culpability to be measured? Can any thermometer be devised to measure its degree?"

The above passage from the majority judgment, asserts Justice Bhagwati, provides a most complete and conclusive answer to the contention that the court may evolve its own standards or principles for guiding the exercise of its discretion. This is not a function which can be satisfactorily and adequately performed by the court more particularly when the judicial perception of what may be regarded as proper and relevant standards or guidelines is bound to vary from judge to judge having regard to his attitude and approach, his predilections and prejudices and his scale of values and social philosophy.

Justice Bhagwati further observed: 'I am fortified in this view by the decision of the Supreme Court of the United States in *Furman* v *Georgia*.[18] The question which was brought before the Court for consideration in that case was whether the imposition and execution of death penalty constituted "cruel and unusual punishment" within the meaning of the Eighth Amendment as applied to the States by the Fourteenth Amendment. The Court, by a majority of five against four, held that the death penalty as then administered in the United States was unconstitutional, because it was being used in an arbitrary manner

17 *Bachan Singh* v *State of Punjab* (1980)2 SCC 684 at p. 741 (para 171).
18 408 US 238.

and such arbitrariness in capital punishment was a violation of the Eighth Amendment prohibition against "cruel and unusual punishment" which was made applicable to the States by the Fourteenth Amendment. The view taken by the majority decision in this case was that a law which gives uncontrolled and unguided discretion to the Judge (or the jury) to choose arbitrarily between death sentence and life imprisonment for a capital offence violates the Eighth Amendment which inhibits cruel and unusual punishment. Brennan J. and Marshall, J. took the view that the death penalty was per se unconstitutional as violative of the prohibition of the Eighth Amendment. Brennan, J. held that the death penalty constituted cruel and unusual punishment as it did not comport with human dignity and it was a denial of human dignity for a State arbitrarily to subject a person to an unusually severe punishment which society indicated that it did not regard as acceptable and which could not be shown to serve any penal purpose more effectively than a significantly less drastic punishment. Marshall, J. stated that the death penalty violated the Eighth Amendment because it was an excessive and unnecessary punishment and also because it was morally unacceptable to the people of the United States. The other three learned Judges namely, Douglas, J., Stewart, J. and White, J. did not subscribe to the view that the death penalty was per se unconstitutional in all circumstances but rested their judgment on the limited ground that the death penalty as applied in the United States was unconstitutional. Douglas, J. argued that "we deal with a system of law and of justice that leaves to the uncontrolled discretion of judges or juries the determination whether defendants committing these crimes should die or be imprisoned. Under these laws no standards govern the selection of the penalty. People live or die dependent on the whim of one man or of twelve." Stewart, J. also voiced his concern about the unguided and unregulated discretion in the sentencing process and observed: "...the Eighth and Fourteenth Amendments cannot tolerate the infliction of a sentence of death under legal systems that permit this unique penalty to be so wantonly and so freakishly imposed." The remaining four Judges, namely, Burger, C.J. Blackmun, J. Powell, J. and Rehnquist, J. took the opposite view and upheld the constitutional validity of the death penalty in its entirety'.

Sarkaria, J. speaking on behalf of the majority in *Bachan Singh* v *State of Punjab*[19] has brushed aside the decision in *Furman* v *Georgia*[20]

19 (1980)2 SCC 684 at p. 737 (para 160).
20 408 US 238.

as inapplicable in India on the ground that we "do not have in our Constitution any provision like the Eighth Amendment nor are we at liberty to apply the test of reasonableness with the freedom with which the Judges of the Supreme Court of America are accustomed to apply the 'due process' clause."

Justice Bhagwati in his dissenting opinion in *Bachan Singh* v *State of Punjab*,[1] however, disagreed with this reasoning put forward in the majority judgment. The learned Judge said: 'though there is no explicit provision in our Constitution prohibiting cruel and unusual punishment, this Court (Supreme Court) has in *Francis Mullin's* case[2] held that immunity against torture or cruel and unusual punishment or treatment is implicit in Article 21 and therefore, if any punishment is cruel and unusual, it would be violative of basic human dignity which is guaranteed under Article 21. Moreover, in *Maneka Gandhi's* case[3] the Supreme Court has by a process of judicial interpretation brought in the procedural due process clause of the American Constitution by reading in Article 21 the requirement that the procedure by which a person may be deprived of his life or personal liberty must be reasonable, fair and just. Douglas, J. has also pointed out in *Furman's* case[4] that "there is increasing recognition of the fact that the basic theme of equal protection is implicit in 'cruel and unusual' punishment. A penalty...should be considered 'unusually' imposed, if it is administered arbitrarily or discriminatorily" and thus brought in the equal protection clause for invalidating the death penalty. It is also significant to note that despite the absence of provisions like the American due process clause and the Eighth Amendment, this Court (Supreme Court) speaking through Desai, J. said in *Sunil Batra (I)* v *Delhi Administration*[5] "..... treatment of a human being which offends human dignity, imposes avoidable torture and reduces the man to the level of a beast would certainly be arbitrary and can be questioned under Article 14..."

Krishna Iyer, J. was more emphatic and he observed in the same case.[6] "True, our Constitution has no 'due process' clause or the VIII

1 (1982)3 SCC 24 at p. 121.
2 *Francis Coralie Mullin* v *Administrator, Union Territory of Delhi* (1981)2 SCR 516: (1981) 1 SCC 608: 1981 SCC (Cri) 212: 1981 Cr LJ 306.
3 *Maneka Gandhi* v *Union of India* AIR 1978 SC 597: (1978)1 SCC 248: (1978)2 SCR 621.
4 *Furman* v *Georgia* 408 US 238.
5 (1978)4 SCC 494 at p. 579 (para 241): AIR 1978 SC 1675: 1979 SCC (Cri) 155: 1978 Cr LJ 1741.
6 (1978)4 SCC 494 at p. 518 (para 52).

Amendment; but, in this branch of law, after *Cooper*[7] and *Maneka Gandhi*[8] the consequence is the same. For what is punitively outrageous, scandalizingly unusual or cruel or rehabilitatively counter-productive is unarguably unreasonable and arbitrary and is shot down by Article 14 and 19".'

It should be clear from these observations in *Sunil Batra's* case[9] to which Chandrachud, C.J. was also a party, that Sarkaria, J. speaking on behalf of the majority Judges in *Bachan Singh* v *State of Punjab*[10] was in error in relying on the absence of the American due process clause and the Eighth Amendment for distinguishing the decision in *Furman's* case[11] and upholding death penalty. The decision in *Furman's* case (supra) cannot, therefore, be rejected as inapplicable in India, says Justice Bhagwati. This decision clearly supports the view that where uncontrolled and unregulated discretion is conferred on the court without any standards or guidelines provided by the legislature, so as to permit arbitrary and uneven imposition of death penalty, it would be violative of both Articles 14 and 21.

It may be pointed out that subsequent to the decision in *Furman's* case (supra) and as a reaction to it, the legislatures of several States in the United States passed statutes limiting or controlling the exercise of discretion by means of explicit standards to be followed in the sentencing process. These 'guided discretion' statutes provided standards typically in the form of specific aggravating and mitigating circumstances that must be taken into account before death sentence can be handed down. They also provided for separate phases of the trial to determine guilt and punishment and for automatic appellate review of death sentences. The constitutional validity of some of these 'guided discretion' statutes was challenged in *Gregg* v *Georgia*[12] and companion cases and the Supreme Court of the United States upheld these statutes on the ground that providing specific sentencing guidelines to be followed in a separate post conviction phase of the trial would free the sentencing decision of arbitrariness and discrimination. There is considerable

7 *R.C. Cooper* v *Union of India* (1970)1 SCC 248: (1970) 3 SCR 530: AIR 1970 SC 564.

8 *Maneka Gandhi* v *Union of India* AIR 1978 SC 597: (1978) 1 SCC 248: (1978)2 SCR 621.

9 (1978)4 SCC 494 at p. 579 (para 241): AIR 1978 SC 1675: 1979 SCC (Cri) 155: 1978 Cr LJ 1741.

10 (1980)2 SCC 684.

11 *Furman* v *Georgia* 408 US 238.

12 428 US 153: 49 L Ed. 2d 859 (1976).

doubt expressed by leading jurists in the United States in regard to correctness of this decision because in their view the guidelines provided by these statutes in the form of specific aggravating and/or mitigating circumstances are too broad and too vague to serve as an effective guide to discretion. In fact, while dealing with the challenge to the constitutional validity of a 'guided discretion' statute enacted by the Legislature of Massachusettes, the Supreme Court of Massachusettes by a majority held in District Attorney for the *Suffolk District* v *Watson*[13] that the statute providing for imposition of death penalty was unconstitutional on the ground that it was violative of Article 26 of the Declaration of Rights of the Massachusettes Constitution which prohibits infliction of cruel or unusual punishment. Henneseey, CJ. pointed out that in enacting the impugned statute the Legislature of Massachusettes had clearly attempted to follow the mandate of the *Furman* opinion[14] and its progeny by promulgating a law of guided and channelled jury discretion, but even so it transgressed the prohibition of Article 26 of the Declaration of Rights of the State Constitution. The learned Chief Justice observed: "... it follows that we accept the wisdom of *Furman*,[14] that arbitrary and capricious infliction of death penalty is unconstitutional. However, we add that such arbitrariness and discrimination, which inevitably persists even under a statute which meets the demands of *Furman*,[14] offends Article 26 of the Massachusettes Declaration of Rights." "But", Justice Bhagwati says, "we are not concerned here with the question as to whether the decision in *Gregg's* case[15] represents the correct law or the decision of the Massachusettes Supreme Court in *Watson's* case.[16] That controversy does not arise in India because neither the Indian Penal Code nor any other provision of law sets out any aggravating or mitigating circumstance or any other considerations which must be taken into account in determining whether death sentence should be awarded or not. Here the sentencing discretion conferred upon the court is totally uncontrolled and unregulated or if I may borrow an expression from Furman's decision, it is 'standardless' and 'unprincipled'."

Justice Bhagwati pointed out that there are certain safeguards provided in the Code of Criminal Procedure, 1973 which are designed to obviate errors in the exercise of judicial discretion in the matter of

13 Mass Adv. Sh (1980).
14 *Furman* v *Georgia* 408 US 238.
15 428 US 153: 49 L Ed 2d 859 (1976).
16 Mass Adv. Sh (1980).

imposition of death penalty. Section 235 sub-section (2) bifurcates the trial by providing two hearings—one at the pre-conviction stage and another at the pre-sentence stage so that at the second stage following upon conviction, the court can gather relevant information bearing on the question of punishment and decide, on the basis of such information, what would be the appropriate punishment to be imposed on the offender. Section 366 sub-section (1) requires the court passing a sentence of death to submit the proceedings to the High Court and when such reference is made to the High Court for confirmation of the death sentence, the High Court may under section 367 direct further inquiry to be made or additional evidence to be taken and under section 368, confirm the sentence of death or pass any other sentence warranted by law or annul or alter the conviction or order a new trial or acquit the accused. Section 369 enjoins that in every reference so made, the confirmation of the sentence or any new sentence or order passed by the High Court, shall, when such court consists of two or more judges, be made, passed and signed by at least two of them. Then, there is also a proviso in section 379 which says that when the High Court on appeal reverses an order of acquittal and convicts the accused and sentences him to death, the accused shall have a right to appeal to the Supreme Court. Lastly there is an over-riding power conferred on the Supreme Court under Article 136 to grant, in its discretion, special leave to appeal to an accused who has been sentenced to death. These are undoubtedly some safeguards provided by the legislature, but in the absence of any standards or principles provided by the legislature to guide the exercise of the sentencing discretion and in view of the fragmented bench structure of the High Courts and the Supreme Court, these safeguards cannot be of any help in eliminating arbitrariness and freakishness in imposition of death penalty. Judicial ad hocism or waywardliness would continue to characterise the exercise of sentencing discretion whether the Bench be of two judges of the High Court or of two or three judges of the Supreme Court and arbitrary and uneven incidence of death penalty would continue to afflict the sentencing process despite these procedural safeguards. The reason is that these safeguards are merely peripheral and do not attack the main problem which stems from lack of standards or principles to guide the exercise of the sentencing discretion. Stewart, J. pointed out in *Gregg* case[17], "...the concerns expressed in *Furman*[18] that the penalty of death

17 *Gregg* v *Georgia* 428 US 153: 49 L Ed 2d 859 (1976).
18 *Furman* v *Georgia* 408 US 238.

not be imposed in an arbitrary or capricious manner can be met by a carefully drafted statute that ensures that the sentencing authority is given adequate information and guidance. As a general proposition these concerns are best met by a system that provides for a bifurcated proceeding at which the sentencing authority is apprised of the information relevant to the imposition of sentence and provided with standards to guide its use of the information." The first requirement that there should be a bifurcated proceeding at which the sentencing authority is apprised of the information relevant to the imposition of sentence is met by the enactment of section 235 sub-section (2), but the second requirement that the sentencing authority should be provided with standards to guide its use of the information is not satisfied and the imposition of death penalty under Section 302 of the Indian Penal Code read with Section 354 sub-section (3) of the Code of Criminal Procedure, 1973 must, therefore, be held to be arbitrary and capricious and hence violative of Articles 14 and 21 of the Constitution of India.

There is also one other characteristic of death penalty, says Justice Bhagwati, that is revealed by a study of the decided cases and it is that death sentence has a certain class complexion or class bias in as much as it is largely the poor and the down-trodden who are the victims of this extreme penalty. We would hardly find a rich or affluent person going to the gallows. Capital punishment, as pointed out by Warden Duffy is "a privilege of the poor." Justice Douglas also observed in a famous death penalty case "Former Attorney Pamsey Clark has said: 'it is the poor, the sick, the ignorant, the powerless and the hated who are executed'." So also Governor Disalle of Ohio State speaking from his personal experience with the death penalty said: "During my experience as Governor of Ohio, I found the men in death row had one thing in common; they were penniless. There were other common denominators, low mental capacity, little or no education, few friends, broken homes—but the fact that they had no money was a principal factor in their being condemned to death...."

The same point was stressed by Krishna Iyer, J. in *Rajendra Prasad's* case[19] with his usual punch and vigour and in hard hitting language distinctive of his inimitable style: "Who, by and large, are the men whom the gallows swallow? The white-collar criminals and the corporate criminals whose wilful economic and environmental crimes inflict mass deaths or who hire assassins and murder by remote control? Rarely.

19 *Rajendra Prasad* v *State of U.P.* (1979)3 SCC 646 at p. 674-75 (para 72).

With a few exceptions, they hardly fear the halter. The feuding villager, heady with country liquor, the striking workers desperate with defeat, the political dissenter and sacrificing liberator intent on changing the social order from satanic misrule, the waifs and strays whom society has hardened by neglect into street toughs, or the poor householder—husband or wife—driven by dire necessity or burst of tantrums—it is this person who is the morning meal of the macabre executioner." Justice Krishna Iyer continued in *Rajendra Prasad* case[20] "Historically speaking, capital sentence perhaps has a class bias and colour bar, even as criminal law barks at both but bites the proletariat to defend the proprietariat a reason which, incidentally, explains why corporate criminals including top executives who, by subtle processes, account for slow or sudden killing of large members by adulteration, smuggling, cornering, pollution and other invisible operations, are not on the wanted list and their offending operations which directly derive profit from mafia and white-collar- crimes are not visited with death penalty, while relatively lesser delinquencies have, in statutory and forensic rhetoric, deserved the extreme penalty".

There can be no doubt, asserts Justice Bhagwati, that death penalty in its actual operation is discriminatory, for it strikes mostly against the poor and deprived sections of the community and the rich and the affluent usually escape from its clutches. This circumstance also adds to the arbitrary and capricious nature of the death penalty and renders it unconstitutional as being violative of Articles 14 and 21.

The former President A.P.J. Abdul Kalam had reservations about death penalty and in one of his deliberations during his tenure as revealed on 26th October 2005, he said that the Centre should consider granting life terms to 20 convicts who were on death row. Kalam who studied each of the 20 cases concluded that only "poorest of the poor" are sentenced to death. The question is: Do the better off get away with heinous crime? Kalam wanted the Union Ministries of Home and Law to consider, besides the normal yardsticks like the heinous nature of the crime, aspects such as the advanced age of the convict, health, particularly mental condition, the family ties and the conduct in prison. Kalam's sympathy for the death row convicts was not sentimental mush. He sought a comprehensive policy on death penalty and mercy petitions after all aspects were discussed in Parliament.

20 *Rajendra Prasad* v *State of U.P.* (1979)3 SCC 646 at p. 675 (para 75).

13 Vice of arbitrariness in the imposition of death penalty—way of removal The only way in which the vice of arbitrariness in the imposition of death penalty can be removed, suggests Justice Bhagwati, is by the law providing that in every case where the death sentence is confirmed by the High Court there shall be an automatic review of the death sentence by the Supreme Court sitting as a whole and the death sentence shall not be affirmed or imposed by the Supreme Court unless it is approved unanimously by the entire Court sitting en banc and the only exceptional cases in which death sentence may be affirmed or imposed should be legislatively limited to those where the offender is found to be so depraved that it is not possible to reform him by any curative or rehabilitative therapy and even after his release he would be a serious menace to the society and, therefore, in the interest of the society he is required to be eliminated. Of course, for reasons already discussed such exceptional cases would be practically nil because it is almost impossible to predicate of any person that he is beyond reformation or redemption and, therefore, from a practical point of view death penalty would be almost non-existent. But theoretically it may be possible to say that if the State is in a position to establish positively that the offender is such a social monster that even after suffering life imprisonment and undergoing reformative and rehabilitative therapy, he can never be reclaimed for the society, then he may be awarded death penalty. If this test is legislatively adopted and applied by following the procedure mentioned above, the imposition of death penalty may be rescued from the vice of arbitrariness and caprice. But that is not so under the law as it stands today.

14 Alternative to death penalty If not death penalty, then what? The question of how society is to respond to aggravated murder if not by executions, is perhaps the oldest of all the issues raised by the two-century struggle in Western civilization to end the death penalty. The credibility of the anti-death penalty movement hinges on its ability to provide a convincing answer. Until very recently, death penalty supporters and opponents alike assumed that the alternative to executing killers was to put them behind bars for the rest of their lives. "Perpetual servitude", in fact, was advocated vigorously by one of the seminal figures in abolitionism the utilitarian philosopher Cesare Beccaria. Opinion surveys have consistently revealed that many Americans who otherwise support the death penalty are satisfied when persons convicted of aggravated murder are imprisoned for the rest of their lives rather than executed. Even more appealing is the idea of convict restitution arrangements, in which life-sentenced offenders compensate crime victims with money earned from their prison labour.

15 Conclusion A life sentence, says Justice Bhagwati is not only a just alternative to death penalty that it is also a human alternative. It is a just alternative because of the possibility of judicial error in arriving at the verdict of guilty, as has happened in many cases referred to earlier and it is an error which extinguishes life and even subsequent realization of the error cannot restore it back. It is a finality which cannot be corrected. The dead cannot be brought back to life. The death penalty lacks humane element because of the agony to which a condemned prisoner is subjected awaiting his execution. It is, therefore, high time that a civilized society seriously considers the abolition of the death penalty.

"I cannot persuade myself to pass an order......without a reasoned judgment, since the question is one of grave and momentous consequence involving, as it does, the validity of a constitutional amendment."

— P.N. BHAGWATI[1]

16

The Judgment that Created Fissure

The judgment that created fissure was the decision in *Minerva Mills Ltd.* v *Union of India*[1] touching upon the question of validity of the Constitution (Forty-second Amendment) Act 1976 and more particularly Section 4 of the Constitution (Forty-second Amendment) Act 1976 which amended Article 31C of the Constitution and Section 55 of the Constitution (Forty-second Amendment) Act 1976 which inserted Sub-clauses (4) and (5) in Article 368 of the Constitution.

Section 4 of the Constitution (Forty-second Amendment) Act 1976, which came into force with effect from 3rd January 1977 amended Article 31C of the Constitution by substituting the words and figures "all or any of the principles laid down in Part IV" for the words and figures "the principles specified in clause (*b*) or clause (*c*) of Article 39. Article 31C as amended, runs as under:

> "31C. *Saving of laws giving effect to certain directive principles.* Notwithstanding anything contained in Article 13, no law giving effect to the policy of the State towards securing all or any of the principles laid down in Part IV shall be deemed to be void on the ground that it is inconsistent with, or takes away or abridges any of the rights conferred by Article 14, Article 19 or Article 31, and no law containing a declaration that it is for giving effect to such policy shall be called in question in any court on the ground that it does not give effect to such policy:

1 AIR 1980 SC 1789: (1980)3 SCC 619.

Provided that where such law is made by the Legislature of a State, the provisions of this article shall not apply thereto unless such law, having been reserved for the consideration of the President, has received his assent."

Section 55 of the Constitution (Forty-second Amendment) Act 1976 which came into force with effect from 3rd January 1977, inserted Sub-clauses (4) and (5) in Article 368 and the said clauses read thus:

"(4) No amendment of this Constitution (including the provisions of Part III) made or purporting to have been made under this article (whether before or after the commencement of section 55 of the Constitution (Forty-second Amendment) Act 1976 shall be called in question in any court on any ground.

(5) For the removal of doubts, it is hereby declared that there shall be no limitation whatever on the constituent power of Parliament to amend by way of addition, variation or repeal the provisions of this Constitution under this article."

The case was heard by a five Judges' Bench composed of Y.V. Chandrachud, CJ., P.N. Bhagwati, A.C. Gupta, N.L. Untwalia and P.S. Kailasam, JJ. The hearing of the arguments commenced on 22nd October 1979 and ended on 16th November 1979.

The order to the case was passed on 9th May 1980 by Y.V. Chandrachud, CJ. and Gupta, Untwalia, and Kailasam, JJ. declaring:

(1) Section 4 of the Constitution 42nd Amendment Act is beyond the amending power of the Parliament and is void since it damages the basic or essential features of the Constitution and destroys its basic structure by a total exclusion of challenge to any law on the ground that it is inconsistent with, or takes away or abridges any of the rights conferred by Article 14 or Article 19 of the Constitution, if the law is for giving effect to the policy of the State towards securing all or any of the principles laid down in Part IV of the Constitution.

(2) Section 55 of the Constitution 42nd Amendment Act is beyond the amending power of the Parliament and is void since it removes all limitations on the power of the Parliament to amend the Constitution and confers power upon it to amend the Constitution so as to damage or destroy its basic or essential features or its basic structure.

The reasoned judgment to the case was delivered on 31st July 1980 by Chandrachud, CJ. on behalf of himself and Gupta, Untwalia and Kailasam, JJ.

Justice Bhagwati declined to pass an order on 9th May 1980 pronouncing upon the questions without a reasoned judgment since the questions were of grave and momentous consequence involving, as it did, the validity of constitutional amendments. He, therefore, preferred to pass a final order in this case along with his reasoned judgment which he did on 31st July 1980. In delivering his judgment, Justice Bhagwati openly conveyed his feeling that he did not subscribe to the practice of passing order and delivering reasoned judgment on different dates excepting in exceptional cases and expressed his displeasure against discarding the practice of having judicial conference or discussion amongst the judges after the completion of hearing but before delivering of the judgment. This is how Justice Bhagwati expressed his feeling on the issue:

> 'The hearing of the arguments commenced on 22nd October 1979 and it ended on 16th November 1979. I hoped that after the completion of the arguments on questions of such momentous significance, there would be a 'free and frank exchange of thoughts' in a judicial conference either before or after the draft judgment was circulated by my Lord the Chief Justice and I would either be able to share the views of my colleagues or if that was not possible, at least try to persuade them to agree with my point of view. But, I find myself in the same predicament in which the learned Chief Justice found himself in *Kesavanand Bharati* v *State of Kerala* 1973 (Supp) SCR 1: AIR 1973 SC 1461. The learned Chief Justice started his judgment in that case by observing:
>
> "I wanted to avoid writing a separate judgment of my own but such a choice seems to longer open. We sat in full strength of 13 to hear the case and I hoped that after a free and frank exchange of thoughts, I would be able to share the views of some one or the other of my esteemed brothers, but we were over-taken by adventitious circumstances", namely, so much time was taken up by counsel to explain their respective points of view that very little time was left to the Judges "after the conclusion of the arguments, for exchange of draft judgments".

Here also, I am compelled by similar circumstances, though not adventitious, to hand down a separate opinion without having had an opportunity to discuss with my colleagues the reasons which weighed with them in striking down the impugned constitutional amendments. Somehow or other, perhaps owing to extraordinary pressure of work with which this Court is overburdened, no judicial conference or discussion was held nor was any draft judgment circulated which could form the basis of discussion, though, as pointed out above, the hearing of the arguments concluded as far back as 16th November, 1979. It was only on 7th May, 1980, just two days before the closing of the Court for summer vacation, that I was informed by the learned Chief Justice that he and the other three learned Judges, who had heard this case along with me, had decided, to pass an Order declaring the impugned constitutional amendments *ultra vires* and void on the ground that they violated the basic features of the Constitution and that the reasons for this Order would be given by them later. I found it difficult to persuade myself to adopt this procedure, because there had been no judicial conference or discussion amongst the Judges where there could be free and frank exchange of views nor was any draft judgment circulated and hence I did not have the benefit of knowing the reasons why the learned Chief Justice and the other three learned judges were inclined to strike down the constitutional amendments. If there had been a judicial conference or discussion or the draft judgment setting out the reasons for holding the impugned constitutional amendments *ultra vires* and void had been circulated, it would have been possible for me as a result of full and frank discussion or after considering the reasons given in the draft judgment, either to agree with the view taken by my Lord the Chief Justice and the other three learned judges or if I was not inclined so to agree, then persuade them to change their view and agree with mine. That is the essence of judicial collectivism. It is, to my mind, essential that a judgment of a Court should be the result of collective deliberation of the judges composing the Court and it would, in my humble opinion, not be in consonance with collective decision making, if one or more of the judges constituting the Bench proceed to say that they will express their individual opinion, ignoring their colleagues and without discussing the reasons with them and even without circulating their draft judgment so that the colleagues have no opportunity of participating in the collective decision making process. This would introduce a chaotic situation in the judicial process and it would be an unhealthy precedent which this Court as the highest Court in the land—as a model judicial institution which is expected to set the tone for the entire judiciary in the country—should not encourage. Moreover, I felt that it was not right to pronounce an Order striking down a constitutional amendment without giving a reasoned judgment. Ordinarily, a case can be disposed of only by a reasoned judgment and the Order must follow upon the judgment. It is true that sometimes where the case involves the liberty of the citizen or the execution of a death sentence or where the time taken in preparing a reasoned judgment might prejudicially affect the winning party, this Court, does, in the larger interests of justice pronounce an order and give reasons later, but these are exceptional cases where the requirements of justice induce the Court to depart from the legally sanctioned course. But, there (sic-here ?) the court had in fact waited for about $5^1/_2$ months after the conclusion of the arguments and there was clearly no urgency which required that an order should be made though reasons were not ready; the delay of about $2^1/_2$ months in making the order was not going to injure the interests of any party, since the order was not going to dispose of the writ petition and many issues would still remain to be decided which could be dealt only after the summer vacation. Thus there would have been no prejudice to the interests of justice if the order had been made on the re-opening of the Court after the summer vacation supported by a reasoned judgment. These were the reasons which compelled me to make my Order dated 9th May, 1980 declining to pass an unreasoned order pronouncing on the validity of the impugned constitutional amendments and stating that I would "prefer to pass a final order in this case when I deliver my reasoned judgment". This order unfortunately led to considerable misunderstanding of my position and that is the reason why I have thought it necessary to explain briefly why I acted in the manner I did.'

In his reasoned judgment Justice Bhagwati declared Section 55 of the Constitution 42nd Amendment Act 1976, which inserted sub-clauses (4) and (5) in Article 368 as unconstitutional and void on the ground that it damages the basic structure of the Constitution and goes beyond the amending power of Parliament. Justice Bhagwati thus on the issue of the validity of section 55 of the Constitution 42nd Amendment Act agreed with the view expressed by Chandrachud, CJ. for himself and Gupta, Unwalia and Kailasam, JJ. But in so far as Article 4 of the Constitution 42nd Amendment Act is concerned, Justice Bhagwati did not subscribe to the view as expressed by Chandrachud, CJ. and others and held that on the interpretation placed on the amended Article 31C by him, it does not damage or destroy the basic structure of the Constitution and is within the amending power of Parliament and he, therefore, declared the amended Article 31C to be constitutional and valid.

Index